LATIN
AMERICA
IN THE
MIDDLE
PERIOD

LATIN AMERICA IN THE MIDDLE PERIOD

1750~1929

STUART F. VOSS

A Scholarly Resources Inc. Imprint
Wilmington, Delaware

Scholarly Resources Inc.
104 Greenhill Avenue
Wilmington, DE 19805-1897
www.scholarly.com

Library of Congress Cataloging-in-Publication Data

Voss, Stuart F.
   Latin America in the middle period, 1750–1929 / Stuart F. Voss.
      p. cm. — (Latin American silhouettes)
   Includes bibliographical references and index.
   ISBN 0-8420-5024-8 (alk. paper) — ISBN 0-8420-5025-6 (pbk. : alk. paper)
   1. Latin America—History. I. Title. II. Series.

F1412 .V79 2001
980—dc21   2001031144

To my wife,

Linda

About the Author

STUART F. VOSS received his doctorate in Latin American history from Harvard University in 1972. Since that time he has been teaching at Plattsburgh State University of New York, in the History Department and with the Latin American Studies Program, attaining the rank of Distinguished Service Professor. For nearly a decade he served as the coordinator of the Latin American Studies Program, initiating and then supervising its participation in the University Model of the Organization of American States. He has also created a regional high-school Model Organization of American States (OAS) for northern New York and western Vermont, the first of its kind in the Americas.

Voss's work includes a regional study of northwestern Mexico (*On the Periphery of Nineteenth Century Mexico, 1810–1877* [1982]); a coauthored synthesis of the role of prominent families in the Middle Period (*Notable Family Networks in Latin America* [1984]); and a broad-ranging essay on the Mexican Revolution of 1910, "Nationalizing the Revolution: Culmination and Circumstance," in *Provinces of the Revolution* (1990), edited by Thomas Benjamin and Mark Wasserman. He has also published articles in *The Americas* and the *Latin American Research Review*.

Contents

Acknowledgments

This synthesis of a Middle Period in the historical evolution of Latin America has been a work in progress for more than a decade. The patience, creative input, and support of many along the way have been vital to its completion.

At Plattsburgh State University (of New York) the administration was most generous in providing a year-long sabbatical at full pay in the early stages of the project for an initial broad reading of secondary materials. The library staff was most helpful in securing those books and journal articles. Though short on staff, the History Department absorbed the loss of course offerings during that year. Special thanks go to a department colleague, Dr. Vincent Carey, whose comments in reading portions of the manuscript and whose wise counsel through its publication stages have been most appreciated. I am also indebted to all the students in my Latin American history classes who over the years have served as a laboratory in which to test and revise the varied pieces of the synthesis puzzle as it became filled in. Their responses in discussion and role playing to unfamiliar concepts and perspectives challenged me to reword and rethink many of the main tenets of the manuscript.

A book proposal regarding the re-periodization of the conventional demarcation of Latin American history was not something that publishers quickly snapped up, especially with classroom use in mind. I am grateful to David Perry, whose initial support and encouragement for the idea provided an important base upon which to begin and solidify the project. At a critical stage, William Beezley gave prescient advice on possible avenues for securing publication. Above all, it has been Richard Hopper's editorial flexibility and judgment to see this project through that has brought it to fruition. In the publication process, Carolyn Travers and other members of his staff have been most helpful, attentive, and accommodating.

This synthesis of a Middle Period would not have been possible without the creative work of a generation of Latin American historians, who over the past three decades have produced a growing body of local and regional studies touching upon an array of topics. It is they to whom I am most indebted, and not simply for their published works. At conferences, their willingness to stretch beyond the comfortable confines of their immediate research to fit into the broad themes of panels I organized, their kind invitations for dinner with colleagues of their regional specialties, their sharing of conference papers, and their taking time to listen to my ideas and then offer new insights proved vital as a supplementary source, a sounding board, and a periodic infusion of encouragement.

Finally, I would like to thank my family for the sacrifices that they made at a most hectic and complicated time in our lives, patiently giving me space and time in which to work at the expense of their own needs and concerns. Above all, it has been my wife—throughout this period and throughout my entire professional career—who has made room and time in her life for my work, who has offered continuing encouragement, and who at key junctures has provided wise counsel as to how to balance this project (and earlier ones) with the rest of my life.

S.F.V.

Preface

The customary bipartite division of Latin American history into colonial and modern (or national) has recently come under increased questioning. At the centennial meeting of the American Historical Association in 1984, scholars familiar with the emerging historiography suggested an additional, interposed era identified as "the Middle Period." Analogous to the efforts of Europeans to define that which separated the ancient world from their own, some Latin American historians have begun to envision a transition period between what was colonial and what is modern in Latin America. Such a period spanned the independence war years and extended into the early twentieth century. Then it soon ebbed to the point of transformation into a contemporary, consistently modern Latin America. In this Middle Period certain colonial developments came to completion, principally the maturation of largely autonomous regional societies. At the same time, the possibilities for the formation of national, modernizing societies were created, though they would not fully come of age for more than a century. In the interim, some patterns that came to characterize the period—at once postcolonial, but not yet fully modern—emerged and then eventually waned.

Central to the historical construction of this Middle Period is a spatial perspective. Organizationally, it is a history of what happened to regional societies. Formed in the colonial period, they resisted full subordination by imperial powers, sought to reach their zenith in the relative political vacuum that arose in the wake of independence, but then were eventually subordinated to a national ordering of life. In large part this process is what makes this era distinctive. Methodologically, this spatial perspective arises from the regional focus of historiographical inquiry since 1970. The generalizations, the common currents to be synthesized for this Middle Period, emerge primarily from the regional society experiences that have been studied. They provide the bulk of examples and illustrations, though the differences and similarities in national histories are examined from time to time.

A number of important variables are closely tied to this spatially oriented framework: modernization (commercialization, industrialization, and secularization being its key facets), technological change, urbanization, and a social stratification that was no longer based on racial estates but was not yet based on class. Initially, these variables worked to intensify the regional organization of life. But by the late nineteenth century this spatial pattern had given way to an often bitter and irreconcilable struggle between regional and national interests and structures. Modern currents, technological change, and urbanization penetrated the regional societies in varying patterns of intensity and degrees of dispersion. Yet it was not until national elements and structures achieved dominance in the wake of the Great Depression that such modernizing currents became sufficiently uniform to set Latin America firmly in a new direction. Some regional interests bent; others broke. But almost everywhere regional patterns, if not destroyed, lost their self-determining prerogatives.

Social relations also underwent a fundamental transition. The informal, personal relations that had been the primary bonding force among people became increasingly formal and impersonal. By the early twentieth century, kinship and clientele ties were becoming superseded by voluntary interest-group association. The rise of new modernizing institutions fostered this supplantation. In the formal, public realm they filled the vacuum left by the demise of most colonial institutions from the late eighteenth to mid–nineteenth centuries. The social repercussions of technological innovation from the late nineteenth century onward also fostered this transformation of social relations.

Modernization and technological change also brought with them altered patterns of economic organization. From the late eighteenth century, entrepreneurial merchant capitalism had steadily replaced the medieval corporatist entities that had dominated colonial society. The spread of commercialization eroded longstanding modes and priorities of economic activity—whether they were highly controlled, protected, flexibly mixed (between self-sufficiency and market production), or even autonomously self-sufficient. Penetration of the fluctuating, increasingly specialized, dependent and interdependent forces of the international (and in time national) marketplace crossed another threshold in the late nineteenth century. Merchant capitalism yielded to industrial capitalism. Merchant-familial capital generation and management gave way to modern corporate capital formation and organization.

Culturally, modern currents moved more slowly. Family, parish, and community had remained the foundation of life as colonial society had been replaced by a new Middle Period society. The sacred, tradition-bound, statically oriented character of lifestyle was more firmly embedded as one moved down the social ladder. By contrast, as one moved up the social ladder, secularization and the modernizing assumption of the progressive evolution of thought and custom steadily made inroads, though this cultural transformation was notably uneven in pace and composition. By the early twentieth century, economic and technological change had reached such a scale and intensity that even most of those who might have preferred otherwise were finding that adaptation had become a necessity. Voluntary association and a national (and often cosmopolitan) orientation were supplanting parish and community as the pillars upon which rested the security and shared meaning of people's lives. Family, to a lesser extent, was being reduced to a subordinate role.

These primary transitions—geopolitical, social, economic, and cultural—were to a great extent complementary. Nevertheless, their degree of mutual reinforcement varied considerably after the mid–nineteenth century. In the early twentieth century their interconnection solidified. The circumstances and forces brought on by the Great Depression then served as a metamorphosis that completed the societal transformation. Latin America's Middle Period gave way to its Modern Era.

Prologue

The colonial world of the Americas was the product of many interacting factors. Two worlds met after having been separated for thousands of years. The Old engaged spatial settings that were both novel and familiar. The New encountered biological elements unprecedented in its long evolutionary experience. Both worlds confronted societies that were at varied stages of human development.

The resulting conquest of the New by the Old created new historical forces and possibilities for both worlds, but especially for the Americas. The New World became a colonial world, subjugated to outsiders' use. It became colonial quickly for most of its indigenous inhabitants, for those forcibly brought to it from Africa, and for those who were the biological byproduct of its conquest. It remained new for those in Europe, who continued to make discoveries about it and who profited from its subjugation. But for those Europeans whose families took root in the Americas, the New World in time would become for them, as well, a colonial world.

The Europeans, who became the protagonists of that world, originated from regional cultures that had been developing for hundreds of years. Distinct from one another in language and custom, they had been united under multiethnic empires or emerging national monarchies. In varying degrees these regional societies were in transition from a late medieval ordering of life to one governed by the new currents of pre-industrial capitalism, scientific learning, class stratification, and individual opportunity—one commonly termed "early modern."

As a consequence, Europeans brought with them different kinds of institutions, expectations, and understandings of both themselves and the new world they were encountering. The Iberians, with their long experience of the reconquest of the peninsula from the Muslims, carried with them the settlement institutions of encomienda (grant in tribute and labor of subject peoples) and the *municipio* (municipality). The first provided for the lordship over subject tributaries. The second encompassed local governance and resource distribution for colonists and in time for indigenous subjects of the crown. The English and Dutch transplanted the medieval practice of settlement through proprietary grants to the nobility but also employed charters to the new joint-stock trading companies to establish colonies. The French and Iberians relied on the medieval tradition of rural evangelism by missionaries from the regular orders. Iberians imported the classical institution of slavery that had been in continuance in the peninsula since ancient Rome. Northern Europeans brought less restrictive forms of servitude but soon borrowed the classical form of enslavement and transformed it into racial, chattel slavery.

Amerindians, likewise, had lived in assorted regional societies. At the time of the Conquest, two large empires existed (those of the Aztecs and the Inca), along with several smaller chiefdoms that held suzerainty over one or more of their neighbors. Yet Amerindians generally were in the midst of a period of warring city-states and tribes in much of the Americas. Moreover, even in the larger state societies the tribal basis of sociopolitical organization and cultural identity had endured. Paradoxically, in more difficult environmental settings than Europeans had known, Amerindians were at once more societally complex and organized (as in the Andes and from central Mexico to northern Guatemala) but also less culturally developed (as in the numerous marginal and simple farming peoples scattered throughout the Western Hemisphere). There was communication among these regional societies, but it was not nearly so extensive in frequency or in distance as that among Europeans.

The physical geography that hindered extensive interchange among most Amerindian regional societies tended to keep Europeans concentrated in the coastal areas of the Americas or in mountain valleys not too distant from the ocean. The interior of New Spain (Mexico) was the most notable exception to this pattern. The vast interior plains of both North and South America were walled by rugged, high mountains in the west and lower mountains in the east and were inhabited by scattered but mobile and fiercely resistant Amerindian tribes. There was little in the way of indigenous people to colonize yet considerable difficulty in colonizing these interior regions, given existing technology. The Caribbean Basin served the colonial world of the Americas in much the same way as the Mediterranean served the ancient world of Europe, the Middle East, and Africa. It provided connections east and west. The narrow isthmus at its western end facilitated communication north and south on the western side of the hemisphere until improved technology permitted regular circumnavigation between the Atlantic and Pacific. On the eastern side there was direct access to Europe and Africa, but the Caribbean also provided an important nexus for north-south interchange.

European governments had intentions of molding and regulating the newly conquered territories to become integral parts of their empires or nation-states. However, they encountered a number of obstacles. Instabilities at home and wars on the continent diverted resources and attention. Physical geography often made arduous communications with and among their diverse American possessions. The various regions frequently did not yield the valuable commodities that warranted the administrative expense and assiduity of the metropolitan centers. Also, European colonists were inclined toward private initiative and local prerogative.

Only the Spanish crown succeeded in establishing a significant level of centralized direction. It had the greatest incentive because the areas it explored had precious metals and dense, organized indigenous societies soon brought under exploitation. Spain also had the most experience, stemming from the long process of reconquering the peninsula from the Muslims. Yet its centralized control endured for little more than a century. By 1600, Spain's military power was in marked decline, especially at sea, and its economy was also waning, beset with inflation and insufficient capital investment in new enterprise. The crown continued its endeavor to devise legislation. Still, local and regional conditions and concerns largely determined the practice of such royal supervision.

The greatest impact of European metropolitan centers on colonial society in the Americas was in trade: the control of commodities crossing the Atlantic and Pacific Oceans and, to a lesser extent, those traversing the American regions. That colonial trade was a vital component of a capitalist international market system then in formation, whose expansion was driven by the needs of western Europe's imperial and national state societies. Those American regions with commodities in greatest demand by this emerging world market system and situated nearest to the principal lines of its trade were those most influenced. Pursuing profit maximization, the mercantile and bureaucratic agents of the metropolitan centers also sought to ensure labor supplies and to foster social control.

Nevertheless, the economic patterns and social relations that emerged in the colonial world of the Americas were not solely the product of those European-driven strategies, even when they coincided with the interests of the regions' notables. And they did not always do so. The great masses of colonial subjects ("popular classes" or "plebe") were also active participants in the determination of those patterns. The popular classes had their own strategies, centered around the goals of survival and resistance to subjugation.[1]

Disparate Regional Societies

New World patterns, then, took on a life of their own, not easily molded by either mercantile agents of Europe's world market system or bureaucrats of its imperial and national states. The colonial world of the Americas was fundamentally a collection of regional societies. Each was born of the particularities of physical geography; of the mix of European, Amerindian, and African racial and cultural traditions (and differences within each); and of the degree of its viability in terms of the European-driven world market system. They continued to evolve in the particular configurations that resulted from the linkage of several local variables: demographic trends, the relative value of exploited natural resources, the sociocultural adaptability and solidarity of the various population groups, and the networks of economic exchange.

Historical timing greatly affected the development of these regional colonial societies. All shared the common historical process of conquest, devastating indigenous population losses, and supplementation or virtual replacement by European settlers, African slaves, and those of mixed blood. This process came late for some regions, especially in the southern and western parts of North America, on the savanna peripheries of the Amazon Basin, and on the plains of South America. For other regions, individual stages or the whole process itself were foreshortened or extended. Depopulation of the Caribbean Basin's coastal areas was rapid, but their repopulation by Europeans and Africans went slowly for more than a century and then greatly accelerated in some islands. It must be remembered, too, that vast areas of the Americas (those with sparse populations) remained outside the colonial world— affected by it and influencing it in return but not subjugated by it.

The consequences of this variable process of colonialism for specific societal patterns can be seen clearly in labor systems. In some regions (principally the core areas of central Mexico and the central Andes), Indian slavery and encomienda (tribute) labor gave way to repartimiento (publicly recruited, paid, rotational) labor and then to wage labor, in an evolutionary process with some overlap (principally in the retention of repartimiento for mine labor in the Andes). Elsewhere, encomienda and repartimiento lingered for varying lengths of time (in Paraguay and northern New Spain, respectively, for example), and the enslavement of Indians continued through the middle of the eighteenth century where colonial and noncolonial regions bordered one another (most notably in the interior of Brazil). The importance of African slavery—and both the historical timing and rapidity of its introduction—also varied widely among colonial regions throughout the Americas.

Christianization offers another societal pattern revealing extensive regional variation. Indigenous populations of Amerindian state societies generally were Christianized by missionaries, and the missionaries were replaced with secular clergy within a few decades. Yet in highland Guatemala, priests from the orders remained until the beginning of the eighteenth century. In some districts of southern Mexico, conversion itself was not solidified until the first half of that century, and then by secular clergy. On the Chaco frontier in South America, missions were initiated by the previously unpacified Indians, necessitated by an alteration in survival strategies in the middle of the eighteenth century.[2]

Medieval Legacies

The diverse regional societies comprising the colonial world of the Americas were separated linguistically, administratively, and to a lesser degree commercially. However, there were affinities in other societal patterns that breached these imperial and cultural barriers. In some regions, European settlers were predominant, with more widespread landownership and distribution of wealth. In others, estate agriculture employing African slave labor predominated. In still others, a minority of Europeans held sway over indigenous populations through a number of economic and sociopolitical relationships. But by the early eighteenth century the most important affinity among the colonial regions of the New World was the extent to which their development paralleled (or in some cases even exceeded) the reordering of life in Europe along "early modern" lines.

Where European settlers were overwhelmingly predominant in the demographic mix, where maintenance of a European lifestyle required economic diversification, and where the imported European traditions were on the cutting edge of the transition to an early modern, pre-industrial, capitalist society—there a permutation occurred in the colonial world of the Americas. In the middle and northern colonies of English North America, a society emerged that was more fluid, more commercialized and entrepreneurial, more egalitarian in opportunity.[3] In the southern colonies of English North America and on the non-Iberian islands in the Caribbean, early modern institutions and pre-industrial capitalist structures were limited or compromised by medieval traditions of rigid hierarchy, legal distinctions, and corporatism. This situation resulted in the creation of a quasi-feudal landed society, dominated by an estate of white planters with wide prerogative and some legal privilege who presided over a servile labor force.

Throughout the colonial regions of Ibero-America, there was a rebirth of precapitalist (or noncapitalist) modes of production, including tribute, communal subsistence, slavery and less restrictive forms of servile labor, and peonage. Andean and central Mexican traditions of communal and public labor service were retained and adapted to provide labor for private enterprises as well. The medieval European system of rural evangelism also reinforced a number of ancient Amerindian patterns. Continued monastic tutelage depended on the retention of indigenous language and racial homogeneity, and the missionaries' material well-being came to hinge on traditional Amerindian forms of payment generated by the local subsistence economy. In the Yucatán, Mayan life was little disturbed. In the core Indian regions of the viceroyalty of Peru, traditional Andean society persisted under a partial overlay of and intermingling with Hispanic society.[4]

The Iberians not only reinforced noncapitalist, nonmodern societal patterns among the conquered Indians but they also replaced or grafted onto them European medieval patterns of thought and organization, in particular corporatism. In most regions, the kin-based communal system of land tenure and sociopolitical organization was supplanted by the ejido (communal landholdings based in individual families) and the cabildo (an elected yet hierarchical system of local government). The mission added another corporativist institution, the *cofradía*, whose introduction among both Indians and African slaves served several Iberian purposes. Above all, these replicas of the lay brotherhoods of medieval Iberia provided the organizational mechanism necessary to accommodate pagan religious practice and thought to a Christian ritual framework. The *cofradías* also functioned as socioreligious reinforcements of legally distinct groups based on race or occupation and to the political subdivisions of barrio (neighborhood) and pueblo (village).[5]

Such corporativist medieval structures as the *cofradía* were renewed in the New World among the Iberians themselves. In addition to their social and legal functions for all segments of the population, lay brotherhoods provided newcomers with social assistance, political and economic contacts, and a cultural anchor in a strange land. Guilds offered artisans protection against competition from non-European craftspeople initially and later from imported manufactures. For important merchants, guilds were a way to dominate the lines of trade.[6]

Rural landholding among the Iberians retained medieval impediments and overtones even as opportunities for capitalist enterprise expanded. Though the initial efforts by the conquistadors to found feudal estates failed, Spanish encomenderos (holders of an encomienda) employed tribute labor for commercial agricultural activities. They were succeeded by hacendados (owner of a hacienda, a large landed estate), who used publicly recruited labor and then debt peonage and land-use privileges to tie labor to their estates. Portuguese recipients of large grants of land employed first Indian slaves and then African slaves in the creation of their *fazendas* (Brazilian equivalent of the Spanish hacienda). Even the smallholders, whose numbers grew large in many regions, were compromised in their individual endeavors by the retention of the *ejido* and of control over access to other basic natural resources by the community. Many also became dependents of the large estate owners, exchanging personal and labor services for access to land.

Differences among the colonial regions of the Americas—in the extent to which their development had paralleled the reordering of life in western Europe along early modern lines—would prove crucial by the mid–eighteenth century. Then, the cumulative changes within the regional societies themselves began to combine with attempts by the European metropolitan centers to exert effective direct control over these colonial societies. This conjuncture of historical circumstances would usher in a new era of historical possibilities in the New World: creation of national societies; conquest and settlement of vast areas that had remained outside the colonial world; accelerated commercialization of the economy and the introduction of industrialization; full modernization of social organization and culture; democratization and liberalization of public life.

Although Anglo North America would move rapidly forward into that "newer" modern world of the Americas, what was to become Latin America would follow the earlier pattern of part of English North America during its colonial experience. Latin America would enter a Middle Period that provided it with a transition to the modern world. At the same time, this Middle Period of Latin America (as did Europe's Middle Ages) would lay important foundations and create unique characteristics for the modern society that would succeed it.

North America's transition from medieval to early modern had been completed in a colonial setting, which was predominantly regional in its ordering of life and in its societal experimentation.

Along with western Europe, it would be pioneering the modern industrial age. By contrast, Latin America's initial transformation would be from a post-Conquest, predominantly medieval society to one in which pre-industrial capitalism and the tenets of early modern thought, social relations, and political structure predominated. At the same time, Latin America would be called to move further, into a modern industrial age. Yet it would do so in relation to a modernizing, industrializing North Atlantic sphere already in the midst of development and expanding beyond its frontier, seeking to incorporate Latin America as a historical subsidiary. These new temporal and spatial realities would make Latin America's Middle Period a unique era, a unique world—one no longer colonial, but not yet fully modern.

Notes

1. Steve J. Stern, "Feudalism, Capitalism, and the World System in the Perspective of Latin America and the Caribbean," *American Historical Review* 93 (October 1988): 829–32, 848–72.

2. Adriaan C. Van Oss, *Catholic Colonialism: A Parish History of Guatemala, 1524–1821* (New York: Cambridge University Press, 1986); John K. Chance, *Conquest of the Sierra: Spaniards and Indians in Colonial Oaxaca* (Norman: University of Oklahoma Press, 1989), 150–75; James S. Saeger, "Another View of the Mission as a Frontier Institution: The Guaycuruan Reductions of Santa Fe, 1743–1810," *Hispanic American Historical Review* [hereafter, *HAHR*] 65 (August 1985): 495–502.

3. James A. Henretta and Gregory H. Nobles, *Evolution and Revolution: American Society, 1620–1820* (Lexington, MA: D. C. Heath, 1987); Bernard Bailyn, *The Origins of American Politics* (New York: Knopf, 1968).

4. Stern, "Feudalism, Capitalism, and the World System," 832–47; Nancy M. Farriss, "Remembering the Future, Anticipating the Past: History, Time, and Cosmology among the Maya of Yucatán," *Comparative Studies of Society and History* [hereafter, *CSSH*] 29:3 (1987): 579–83; Ward Stavig, "Ethnic Conflict, Moral Economy, and Population in Rural Cuzco on the Eve of the Thupa Amaro II Rebellion," *HAHR* 68 (November 1988): 741–44.

5. Detailed examples of the importation of corporatism for highland Guatemala can be found in Van Oss, *Catholic Colonialism*, 89–91, 109–15.

6. A. J. R. Russell-Wood, "Prestige, Power, and Piety in Colonial Brazil: The Third Orders of Salvador," *HAHR* 69 (February 1989): 60–69.

PART I ~ THE EMERGENCE OF A NEW SOCIETY, 1750–1820

1

Changes from Within and Without

Customarily in Latin American historiography, the turning point in the transformation of the colonial order has been identified with the period of the wars for independence from 1808 to 1826. Yet the resulting periodization scheme has left nagging questions. If the independence wars constituted the decisive break with the colonial order, why then did Latin American societies seem to retain so many unmodern patterns throughout the course of the nineteenth century? Why did these societies take so long to congeal into complex, comprehensive nation-states?

One response is to conclude that the colonial order continued well into the nineteenth century or perhaps beyond. Certainly, most islands in the Caribbean and some regions along its mainland shores were formally controlled by Europe through this period. In terms of economic structures, too, there is often clear evidence of pervasive colonial relationships in the rest of Latin America.

However, if the factor of the imperial relationship between metropolitan society and its subordinate colony is separated from the societal transformation process, then another, quite different perspective emerges. The imperial relationship did provide an important context for the ordering of society after the European conquest of the Americas. But as noted previously, the decisive context for the regional societies that emerged was the competing mix of medieval, pre-Columbian, and early modern patterns of life. In much of English North America, the transformation of society from medieval to early modern had already taken place by the middle of the eighteenth century, before the imperial relationship was rent.[1] By contrast, in most areas of Ibero-America—where the medieval had remained largely predominant over the early modern in the social order born of the European conquest— this transformation was only then beginning. The severing of the imperial relationship in the early nineteenth century accelerated and consummated a transformation of Ibero-American society already under way.

By the mid–eighteenth century in most regions of Ibero-America, demographic changes, along with new and expanded patterns of economic activity, were challenging the constraints inherent in the society born of the European conquest. After 1750 these cumulative forces were joined by a changing set of external circumstances. Imperial reform intruded with ever-greater intensity. The penetration of the world market system quickened, in part because of the imperial reforms and in part because of a generation of almost continuous, escalating imperial warfare that began in the early 1790s. In addition, that penetration was intensified by the initial outgrowth of industrial capitalism then arising in parts of western Europe. This conjuncture of internal and external forces engendered novel social configurations and political and cultural visions, which reinforced and guided the new directions that the colonial regional societies were beginning to follow. Succeeding external events triggered the independence movements in Ibero-America that accelerated the breakdown of the colonial order.

By the 1820s the regional societies that comprised the colonial world of Ibero-America had been transformed. Elements of the post-Conquest order remained, but they constituted either increasingly extraneous appendages to the new social order or foundational material that could be reconstructed and incorporated by it. The corner had been turned. On one side, elements of the predominantly precapitalist, pre–early modern ordering of life that had constituted colonial society in Spanish and Portuguese America could still be observed. But on the other, a new society had emerged, and the course of Latin America's history was squarely headed in that direction.

Demographic Change

The regional societies of Ibero-America had shared a common demographic experience until the mid–eighteenth century in terms of process but not outcome. Indigenous populations had declined precipitously (though at different rates and degrees of population loss), replaced by Europeans and Africans and those of mixed blood who were the products of the intermingling of the three races. Depending upon the region, the replacement was either partial, substantial, or almost (if not wholly) complete. Moreover, the numbers and proportions of these population groups varied widely among the colonial regions. In what is today Costa Rica the Amerindian population was largely replaced by those of European descent, but in northeastern Brazil those of African origins predominated, with a minority of whites and mixed bloods. In the Andes and southern Mexico, Amerindians continued to constitute the large majority of the population.

From the late seventeenth century into the mid–eighteenth century, the regional societies of what would become Latin America had been in varying stages of demographic recovery, stagnation, or decline. In general, the numbers of Creoles (those of European ancestry born in America) and *castas* (those of mixed blood) had been consistently expanding, though periodic epidemics had caused short-term losses. The decisive demographic variables had been the Indian and African segments of the colonial population. The aggregate and proportion of African slaves had increased dramatically in numerous regions, most notably in Brazil, in northern Venezuela, and on many Caribbean islands. Indian communities in many regions had recovered a portion of their former populations. In others the population appears to have stagnated during this period or even declined.[2] After midcentury, the recovery of the Indian population and the increase in slaves of African descent (despite their often high death rate) became more generalized. In addition, there was a considerable rise in the number of *peninsulares* immigrating to the New World, while the expansion of the *castas* quickened. This general demographic increase across Ibero-America resulted from a series of factors: new economic opportunities, epidemics, agricultural shortages and famines, and the depredations of unpacified Indians and runaway slave communities. Together, they determined a given region's aggregate population, as well as its complexity, distribution, and composition.

Migration (which increased after midcentury) was not only an important response to these demographic changes but also a principal mechanism in bringing about these changes in localities, districts, or entire regions. New settlements established effective Iberian control over frontier areas or filled in existing settled regions. Settlement hierarchies became more defined, including the emergence of many new provincial urban centers as foci of emerging regional identities and networks of economic and social interaction.[3]

The demographic changes that began after 1750 had varying effects on colonial society, depending upon a region's prior density and complexity of settlement. In the long-established core regions, which had relatively European-centered societies supported by a sedentary Indian and/or African base, there was an intensified conflict over resources in the countryside. In New Spain, many Indian communities found that their rising populations made subsistence impossible for growing numbers of households, especially with the quickening

penetration of village lands by non-Indians. Dependence on the haciendas—whether in the form of wages or labor in return for access to
land—became the means of subsistence for growing numbers of Indian communities. Migration to urban centers was the other alternative for those who lost out in the competition for rural resources. By
increasing the markets for commercial agricultural production, however, that migration only intensified the competition. In the Peruvian
sierra, migration's impact was less in terms of urban growth than in
altering the balance among distinct groups of Andean commoners. In
many highland districts the *mitayos* (those having kinship rights to village lands and obligations of public labor) were losing (to outsiders)
control over the multiple ecological zones that had been the basis for
their subsistence. They were even losing direction over the communities themselves.[4]

By the mid–eighteenth century, former frontier regions were of the
greatest importance territorially in the Spanish and Portuguese empires. They had been in varying degrees of transition toward the full,
elaborate, European-style society that had taken root in the core areas
from which they radiated. Intensifying demographic change thereafter o6˜ only accelerated that transition but also transformed its character. Indeed, the new society that would replace the colonial order would
emerge most readily in these older peripheral regions. Demographic
infilling produced complex, integrated networks of settlement. The
range of rural settlement types expanded and was more interwoven:
mission communities, multifamily hamlets, single-family ranchos, hacienda communities, and villages (either Indian, white-*casta*, or in combination). Migration and natural increase enlarged some settlements
into secondary urban centers and transformed some large towns into
regional urban centers. Migration fields began to define and intercon-
nect these levels of settlement and spatial identities.[5]

The principal urban centers of both these older peripheral regions
and of the core areas underwent marked modifications in their demographic character. Above all, the scale of population rose dramatically.
The population of Saltillo, which became the regional trade center for
northeastern New Spain, doubled from 1750 to 1793 and then doubled
again by 1813.[6] Such growth brought an enlargement of urban jurisdiction as outlying neighborhoods were incorporated and new ones
developed. It also resulted in higher population densities in many
neighborhoods of the city, affecting the type of dwellings of urban residents, the composition of their households, and their functions within
city life. The spatial mobility of these city dwellers also increased, es-

pecially for those who had come from the expanding migration field beyond the urban center. Within the city's swelling boundaries the possibilities for residency, occupational location, and recreational activity were augmented.

In new and existing frontier regions, settlement and pacification strategies, along with new economic opportunities, largely shaped demographic changes. All but a few experienced significant alterations in their population size and composition. Given that during this period (1750–1820) the indigenous population was limited in most of these frontier regions, the most important demographic change—second to aggregate growth—was increased racial intermixing. In many, those of mixed blood became the largest population segment. Imperial confrontation led to the encouragement of Spanish and Portuguese immigration and the introduction of African slaves in southern Brazil and in the Banda Oriental. In the latter by 1800 blacks constituted one-third of the population (26 percent slave and 6 percent free), and over the next three decades their numbers kept pace with the sizable immigration of whites from Europe and neighboring regions. In the interior plains of Venezuela, thousands of fugitive slaves and smaller numbers of former mission Indians lived either beyond the reach of the colonial establishment or provided a mobile, unsubmissive labor force for the spectacular rise of ranching introduced by Creoles and *peninsulares*.[7]

Economic Resurgence

The quickening pace of economic activity after midcentury was to a significant degree a function of the changes in the colonial population. Aggregate growth in population provided an expanding potential supply of workers. Increasing mobility facilitated the matching of that labor supply to employer demand. The new workers, in addition, enlarged the markets of producers of basic necessities and suppliers of inexpensive services. The profits from these economic activities in turn augmented markets for nonessentials. In a given region, expanding production was also a function of new or additional demand in other regions, often neighboring but sometimes at a considerable distance. Oftentimes, the source of this multiplier effect was production for the European market, which enlarged or created secondary internal markets. For two centuries, precious metals and sugar had constituted the great bulk of the export-driven stimulus for internal markets. But by the 1750s a wider range of exports served as motors for regional economies, notably cacao, hides, and dyes.

Expansion of Economic Activity

In some regions, economic expansion based upon intra- and interregional markets had begun in the late seventeeth and early eighteenth centuries. The revival of Mexican silver production not only affected secondary markets supplying the mines but also helped finance the second cacao boom in northern Venezuela and the growth of Caracas as that region's trade center. In central Brazil, the discovery of gold in Minas Gerais in the 1690s created local and regional markets for *fazendas* and farms, as well as for food and craft goods produced in the numerous towns established there. In southern New Spain, the expanding trade in textiles and cochineal dye forced upon the Indians through the *repartimiento de mercancias* (forced sale of goods) had fostered a growing internal market among the Indians by the beginning of the eighteenth century.[8]

After midcentury, the resurgence of economic activity became generalized, though some regions remained relatively stagnant or even declined. In many, the resurgence was based upon the expansion of existing sectors of production and services. Around growing urban centers and mining districts, the demand for necessities rose, attracting new suppliers and requiring greater commercialization of agriculture in the surrounding and neighboring agricultural districts.

Owners of large estates in the Guadalajara region of New Spain employed a number of strategies to exploit the burgeoning internal market. They converted lands previously used for raising livestock production to the intensive production of grain. Realizing that direct production was now more profitable than rent, they replaced tenants and sharecroppers with wage laborers from the growing pool of rural workers. Hacendados also put their own unused lands into production and disputed land rights on their borders. This led to conflicts with Indian villages, whose population growth was necessitating access to more land. Wealthy merchants and enterprising master artisans, presented with an abundant labor pool (resulting from migration, including Indians without adequate land on which to subsist), incorporated nonguild journeymen and increasingly dependent cottage craftspeople.[9]

Buenos Aires provides an example of expansion driven by the increase of both external and internal markets in a single economic sector. Hide exports from the region rose dramatically after 1750, and new lands to the south were converted into large livestock ranches. But the expansion also derived from the more intensive use of existing estancias (large landed estates in southern South America), much of whose production went to supply the growing market of the port of Buenos Aires. Its population of around 12,000 in 1744 had jumped to nearly 40,000 by 1810. A number of these estancias concentrated on a more intensive production of beef cattle for this burgeoning urban market. In south-central Brazil, specialization in sugar production in the wake of the Haitian Revolution of 1791, plus the expanding population of the port of Rio de Janeiro, created growing markets for nearby small producers of foodstuffs and livestock raisers in Rio Grande do Sul, Minas Gerais, and São Paulo.[10]

The opening of new sectors of production and services provided the prime stimulus for growth in many regions, especially in frontier areas, both older ones with minimal prior implantation of Iberian society and those brought initially under the control of the Portuguese and Spanish empires after 1750. In the grasslands of northern and southern South America, where transportation costs to more settled regions were not prohibitive, raising livestock became the motor for economic growth. In what is today the northeast "finger" of Argentina (the Corrientes–Entre Rios area), a cattle industry emerged to supply the neighboring Paraguayan market following the demise of the Jesuit missions and then by 1800 had found a place in the growing export market of hides through Buenos Aires. To the northeast across the Uruguay River, Portuguese military veterans of the border wars with Spain in the La Plata estuary began settling the Rio Grande frontier of southern Brazil after 1790. Sole beneficiaries of the land distribution, they established large estancias with a mixed system of African slaves and mixed-blood *agregados* (those who exchanged their labor for subsistence privileges). The ranchers found expanding markets in the regions to the north, initially reaching them through long cattle drives. All across the northern borderlands of New Spain from Texas to California, following closely on the heels of missionaries, Hispanic settlers (many of them immigrants from the Iberian peninsula) established haciendas and ranchos. They found commercial opportunities in varying degrees as older frontier regions to the south took on more and more of the economic attributes of the densely settled core regions.[11]

Though commercial crop production appeared in many new frontier areas, transportation costs—combined with distance from large population centers—severely limited its economic role, with a few exceptions. One of these was the Banda Oriental. The nearby Atlantic coast and the La Plata estuary made the region's rising port of Montevideo, the swelling population of Buenos Aires, and the more distant Brazilian coastal cities viable markets for grain. Estancias and farms mixed agriculture and stockraising.[12]

In older, core regions the stimulus from new economic activities came principally in the commercial and manufacturing sectors. Querétaro was one of five cities in New Spain in which the Spanish crown established factories after it instituted a monopoly on the processing of tobacco in 1767. The industry there employed 3,000 workers. Located in the Bajío region, in between the central core region east and west of Mexico City and the northern frontier, Querétaro was also well-positioned to respond to new opportunities in the textile industry. With greater proximity to the consuming mining districts in the Bajío and to the north, and to the wool-producing regions in the northern frontier, the city replaced Puebla as the leading textile center of the viceroyalty.[13]

Alterations in Economic Structures

The addition of new sectors moved many regional economies beyond the simple expansion of existing activities toward what economists define as economic growth. Whether such growth—as versus expansion—also resulted from structural changes in production and distribution is less certain.

The long-standing sources of working capital—church loans and chains of credit—expanded with the amplification of economic activity. In important commercialized regional centers, loans from varied ecclesiastical organizations expanded the financing of haciendas and ranchos. They lent funds to commercial firms as well. Lines of credit joining wholesaler to retailer and merchant to producer were extended. But it appears that other forms of investment were beginning to assume importance. In Michoacán and Guadalajara at the end of the eighteenth century, private lending was increasing faster than church loans. Wholesale merchants in New Spain's capital were making loans as well as credit extensions to retailers. They were investing directly in mining operations, primarily to gain access to silver to pay for imports at a time when there was a severe shortage of a circulating currency. They were also acquiring rural estates, not only for returns from agricultural activities but also for collateral to secure capital for other enterprises. Moreover, the merchants were themselves recipients of investment capital. Lawyers, bureaucrats, owners of rural estates and urban properties (including a significant number of women), and even some artisans made direct loans to merchants. More profitably, they established formal companies with merchants, especially retailers.[14]

Diversification became an increasingly important economic strategy after midcentury. It reduced risk at a time when the colonial economy generally was in greater flux. For families of considerable means, diversification provided a mix of activities that yielded a modest but guaranteed yield and speculative enterprises that held out the prospect of substantial profits if successful. It also enhanced the prospects for ensuring sources of supply and securing markets through vertical integration and complementarity. Thus, stock raisers acquired slaughterhouses, tanneries, and *obrajes* (textile sweatshops); international wholesale merchants established branches in other districts and regions; and grain producers owned mills and bakeries.[15]

In Cochabamba, where producers were increasingly deprived of distant markets for grain, hacendados diversified to maintain their dominant position in the economy. They expanded ownership of mills to compensate for low production returns and to facilitate storage of the grain sold by small producers so that in seasons of poor harvests hacendados could market it at higher prices. Tax farming (or contracting the collection) of the tithe (a royal tax on all agricultural production) allowed them to corner additional grain for storage and speculation. They expanded ownership of pack mules to secure less costly transportation for themselves and turn a profit on charges to others. The hacendados' large landholdings became increasingly valued as collateral to secure capital to finance these new investments. Other elements of the regional societies pursued these strategies where resources and opportunity permitted. Cochabamba's Indians diversified their economic activities and directed them toward local fairs, nearby towns, and even distant markets. Working as integrated family units, they cultivated crops, raised livestock, engaged in petty trade, and turned out petty manufactures. Around Guadalajara, as pressure over land use intensified, villagers turned to wood cutting, pottery making, charcoal burning, and stone quarrying to supplement their traditional reliance on subsistence farming. The transient rural population in the Banda Oriental combined subsistent farming and stock raising with seasonal labor on the wheat and livestock estancias when they needed silver money for necessities such as tobacco, yerba maté (Paraguayan herbal tea), or a poncho.[16]

As capital sources and economic strategies became more broadly diversified in most regional economies, labor systems began to simplify around private contractual labor and the use of enslaved Africans. This change resulted partly from royal intervention (as detailed later in the chapter). But to a large extent it stemmed from the demographic changes and process of economic resurgence then under way.

From the mid–seventeenth century, the forced labor systems involving Indians had begun to give way to privately contracted labor relations. The shift had originated in areas where Indian communities and slave plantations did not predominate—first in the central core of New Spain and then in other regions. Encomienda, repartimiento labor, and even some Indian slavery endured where royal authority was weak or where revenue-producing activities (especially mining) had few readily viable alternatives. After 1750, as the population grew significantly in most regions, a sufficient pool of wage labor was created where it had not previously existed. Noncoerced workers, those of mixed blood (and those Indians whose absorption of Iberian culture led them to be considered as such), formed the core of privately contracted wage labor. In addition, expanded economic opportunity made employers more willing—whether from greater feasibility or out of necessity—to negotiate wage labor.[17]

The retention or expansion of African slavery also hinged on the above considerations. Population growth in New Spain made slaves increasingly less valued through the course of the eighteenth century. However, in the older transition areas and new frontier zones of the Caribbean and eastern South America, economic expansion dictated otherwise. The pre-Conquest Indian population had generally been much less numerous or had virtually been annihilated after the Conquest. Whites and *castas* had little, if any, intention of submitting to the harsh work regimen and social controls that were customary in gang labor and domestic service, especially where access to land or more remunerative urban labor employment was still readily available. Thus, calculating labor costs and control over supply, employers in many of these eastern regions turned increasingly to African slavery as the most profitable means to expand and initiate their enterprises. In other eastern regions, they employed them as vital fixed long-term labor inputs, in combination with seasonal laborers. African slaves in the Banda Oriental, in addition to their initial use as domestics and artisanal laborers in the city center of Montevideo, were increasingly purchased for work as farmhands and ranch hands in the countryside and then as manufacturing workers in suburbs developing around the capital.[18]

Leverage was critical in determining the precise character of the expanding private contractual relations in the regions where African slavery was not predominant. Because the balance of leverage between employee and laborer varied considerably, the terms and compensation of employment took on a multiplicity of forms, and often two or more of them were combined in a mixed arrangement. The employers were weighing cost and availability. The laborers were seeking to maximize security and autonomy, though usually they had to sacrifice part of one to obtain more of the other.

In the eastern llanos (plains) of New Granada in northern South America, whites and some mestizos (mixed bloods) worked at designated tasks (manager, foreman, cowboy) for six months or a year at a pre-arranged salary. A growing, floating segment of the non-Indian population worked only as seasonal supplements on the livestock estates. Tributary Indians, a declining majority of the population, received much less but had their tribute obligations covered by their employers. The textile and tobacco industries in Querétaro, New Spain, also interwove multiple arrangements. Alongside the forced Indian laborers and a few mulatto slaves in the *obrajes* were free Indian workers, many of them coming to the city to work during the rainy summer months. There was also a growing cottage component organized by merchants and master artisans that competed with the traditional artisanal setup of masters, journeymen, and apprentices. In the new royal tobacco industry, Creoles dominated the supervisory level and, along with male *castas*, were the skilled wage workers. Women and Indians worked by the piece. Contracted mineworkers in Peru had considerably more leverage. To supplement their wages, they sought and obtained first a share of the ore they mined (usually an amount over a set quota) and then the right to mine independently on weekends. They could increase their income considerably by trading the ore independently or by refining it themselves in crude smelting ovens. By 1759, the Indians' share of refined ore had reached 38.1 percent.[19]

Running through the structural and quantitative changes in the regional economies after 1750 is the apparent growing prominence of women. Additional monographic studies may uncover a more extensive role of women in nonsubsistence, nondomestic activities in the economy through the course of the whole colonial period. From the late sixteenth century in Peruvian mining districts, women smelted or marketed the ore shares acquired by the male members of the family along with their wages from mine work. And in Oaxaca, it was mainly women who wove the cloth required of the Indian communities in exchange for the forced *repartimiento de mercancias* (forced sale of goods). That production expanded from the late seventeenth century, especially after 1750.[20]

Yet the limited evidence available suggests that women's role in the market economy expanded notably after the mid–eighteenth century. In Cochabamba, common women dominated all phases of the production of cotton cloth except weaving and served as the principal distributors for these textiles in the local markets. Jesuits relied on women for the production of textiles in the missions they established in the Chaco region of the La Plata. In a large urban center such as Querétaro, women were employed in large numbers in the textile industry, principally as cottage yarn spinners. They also made up two-thirds of the workforce in the royal tobacco factory. It appears "respectable" women of modest to precarious means handled most sales of the tobacco, usually working on commission.[21]

Bourbon reformers eagerly and intentionally sought such an increased role of women in the economy—more specifically, common women. These bureaucrats believed the colonial economy could be made more productive through women's participation in the workforce. They were thought to be more apt in the more "sedentary trades," thus freeing men for more complicated and arduous activities. In addition, employed women would enhance their families' income. Finally, and certainly not least, female labor was simply much cheaper than that of men, lowering costs to the consumers and raising the profit margins of producers.[22] To what extent the apparently greater participation of women in the market economy was owing to royal policy is not yet clear. Most likely, this change lay in the decisions of countless individual women themselves, as the demographic and economic changes beginning in the mid–eighteenth century led them into the workforce out of necessity or through enhanced opportunity.

A Conjuncture of Two Historical Currents

The temporal ordering of external factors in the transformation of colonial society in Ibero-America paralleled the changes from within. There was a cumulative character to certain external forces. Their influence on colonial society had been building well before the turn of the eighteenth century. Yet beginning in the 1750s, changes from without took on a markedly different and steadily increasing role in that societal transformation, and external and internal changes became increasingly intertwined. Delineating the boundaries between them becomes more complicated.

The internal-external historical equation has been a principal tool for historians examining the "late colonial period." However, that equation has been focused almost wholly on its impact on the imperial relationship between metropolitan society and subordinate colony to explain the initiation and consummation of the independence movements in the various Ibero-American regions. The assumption has been that the severance of that relationship was the starting point for the disintegration of the colonial order. But if that societal transformation was well under way before—and not as a result of—independence, then the central historiographical questions become: To what extent did changes from without interface with the changes within to transform colonial society? Would the transformation of the colonial order by internal changes alone have necessarily resulted in independence?

An American Perspective

From an internal New World vista, until the mid–eighteenth century, colonial society had become increasingly shaped by internal forces. The Iberian colonial world had not been the offspring of a common purpose. Neither Iberian conquerors, nor Amerindian survivors, nor the enslaved African immigrants were of one mind or purpose. The colonial world was far more a collection of sociocultural groups divided by geography, caste, and lifestyle, each seeking to assert its interests and shape the surrounding colonial world as much as possible.

In the wake of the Conquest the Spanish Hapsburgs (1516–1700) had tried and failed to cast a unified colonial society through a legal, absolutist mold. The Portuguese crown had only intervened to ensure permanent colonization. Both monarchies did, however, succeed in erecting patrimonial frameworks in which the colonial world could function. Their New World possessions were kingdoms, united through their person with their other kingdoms in Europe, Africa, and Asia. The wealth of those American kingdoms, from the monarchs' patrimonial viewpoint, belonged above all to themselves and to those individuals and groups of subjects upon whom the crowns conferred special, often exclusive, privileges. Aside from the church and the Roman Catholic religion it espoused—both of which had acquired a considerable degree of variation—respect for and loyalty to the crown provided the only common thread linking the disparate, contentious elements of colonial society. Their common bond was a willingness to abide by the crown's decision, the final arbiter when conflicts reached back to the peninsula.

Moreover, the distance between crown and colony had steadily widened. For as the international power of the Iberian monarchies declined precipitously through the course of the seventeenth century, effective authority had devolved to societies that had crystallized at the regional level, with integrated economic structures and economic linkages to neighboring regions. Within these regional societies, considerable economic power and political influence had come to reside in certain families (generally creole), often linked by marriage with one another and with *peninsulares*. With increasing frequency, the latter were royal officials. The sale of offices, begun in the late sixteenth century, had converted posts of duty into positions for profit. The interests of prominent families and royal officials at the district and regional levels had become more and more intertwined and the distinct line between local interests and royal ones increasingly blurred. For although peninsular officials were becoming mediators for interlaced wealthy families, the latter's members were occupying royal posts themselves in ever larger numbers after 1700. Privilege and prerogative were concentrating more and more in their hands and were less and less the result of imperial largesse.[23]

The growing autonomy of these prominent New World families and of the regions they had come to dominate was also the product of the steady erosion through the seventeenth century of the imperial boundaries separating regional societies throughout the New World. The British, French, and Dutch had employed buccaneers, privateering, and at times outright invasion to break down Iberian borders. Smuggling had become the most effective way to penetrate the Iberian realms. Yet in time, smuggling came to favor the needs and interests of the regional societies of the New World, whatever their European origins, more than the metropolitan centers to which they gave their largely titular allegiance.

The regional societies of the colonial New World had acquired a de facto autonomy by the mid–eighteenth century. Periodic and narrow efforts by the European powers to reverse this growing reality had largely failed. From an American perspective, the colonial world was one increasingly being determined by New World people themselves. Underlying their growing sense of historical responsibility were the series of accumulating internal changes that were beginning to alter the foundations of their colonial world.

A European Perspective

From an external, European vantage point, the consequences of the growing autonomy of their American possessions were quite different. They were primarily understood in terms of their impact on the colonial wealth being tapped by the metropolitan centers and the resulting impact this was having on the balance of power among them. The Dutch had been reduced to a minuscule role territorially and a minor role in illegal trade. Spain, still on the defensive, was preoccupied with reversing the decline in its share of New World wealth channeled back to the peninsula. Portugal, bolstered by an alliance with the

English (the Methuen Treaty of 1703), sought to extend its control over the vast Amazon interior and to best Spain in effectively settling the borderlands north of the La Plata estuary. England and France were the most expansionary, building upon their seventeenth-century inroads into the Caribbean and their push into the North American continent.

The imperial wars among these European powers—which escalated in frequency, duration, and scope through the course of the eighteenth century—were about access to and protection of the exploitable wealth (real and potential) of the regional societies of the New World. Control of trade and acquisition of territory were the objectives of these armed struggles. Internal changes within western Europe (especially in the north) intensified the conflict and raised the stakes with each successive round in this imperial chess game. The ideas of the Enlightenment and the administrative models of the Orient led to an enlarging bureaucratic vision of the potential for imperial control and initiative in the Americas. Improved technology in navigation and shipping provided greater regularity and flexibility in communications and transport, especially in removing the obstacles that had restricted navigation between oceans around Cape Horn. The acceleration of population growth fostered not only increased emigration to the New World but also a steady rise in the demand for American products. Finally, the emergence of industrialization expanded European markets for those products by turning them into consumer goods in greater quantities and at lower prices.

The value of their New World possessions to Europeans rose steadily through the eighteenth century. As individuals, families, and businesses, the Europeans were offered great opportunities by the Americas, whether through direct exploitation as colonists or indirectly through absentee ownership, marketing, or manufacturing. To monarchs and bureaucrats, the New World presented the prospect of greatly enhancing their nation's capabilities in the imperial struggle among the European powers. The result was an unmitigated resurgence of European involvement in the New World, which after midcentury steadily intensified. For some historians it constituted a "second Conquest," a "new imperialism," a "rediscovery."

Accelerating European penetration had profound consequences for the future direction of the history of the Americas. Into the 1750s, imperial bureaucracies instituted varied and uneven measures to enhance access to or control over trade. Spain sought to contain and reduce contraband by granting limited legal access to trade with its possessions. Other countries' unwillingness to comply with these restrictions led to wars with England (1739–1742, 1748–1750) and growing conflict with Portugal, though expansion of the colonies' illegal trade with France was tolerated as the price for a necessary alliance.

The Seven Years' War (1756–1763), however, provoked a sudden jump in the stakes of the European imperial rivalry and a resultant acceleration in European involvement in the colonial world. Major transfers of colonial territory markedly altered the balance of imperial power in the New World and in Europe itself. Ongoing debates and tentative commitments to reform were made in the years preceding that war. However, it was not until its outcome that England, Spain, and Portugal introduced consistent, coordinated policies intended to bring major structural changes in colonial government, economy, and society. From the Europeans' perspective, the necessity of preparing for the imperial wars that would follow to consolidate or redress the altered power relationships in Europe became intertwined with the growing determination to reverse the virtual autonomy of the regional societies of the New World.

The intersection of what had become incompatible intentions—European and American—on the necessary course in the development of the New World's regional societies became the fundamental context for the profound change in the colonial world of the Americas. It was a conjuncture not only of intentions but also of changing realities. A series of internal changes in both Europe and the Americas were propelling those intentions faster and further along a course that had been emerging among the regional societies of the New World for the better part of a century and among the European powers for several decades.

Dimensions of Imperial Reform

For the new Bourbon monarchy and Spanish bureaucrats, the principal lesson from the War of the Spanish Succession (1700–1713) was that only the rivalry among the other European powers had enabled the Spanish realms of Castile and Aragon to remain an important force in Europe. If the united kingdoms were to remain so and their possessions in the Indies were to be retained, there would have to be radical changes in both the peninsula and the New World. Focusing their efforts on the peninsula until 1750, the Bourbons transformed the two kingdoms into a nation-state politically, economically, and socially. Their New World territories thereafter were to be transformed as well, from being kingdoms coequal with the peninsula under the monarchy to colonies integrated into the metropolitan economy and body politic of the new Spanish nation-state. The long-standing economy based on privilege and a multitude of restrictions would be redirected toward greater diversity and productivity. Peripheral areas in the New World would have to be settled and administrated effectively. Direct, encompassing, centralized direction of colonial society would be required.

The Portuguese crown's motivation for imperial reform, by contrast, differed in timing and origin. Long a national monarchy, its relationship with Brazil had resembled more that of England with its North American possessions: private colonizing ventures gradually but increasingly coming under royal supervision and administration. But discovery of mineral wealth in the central interior (principally in Minas Gerais beginning in the 1690s) set off a great territorial and demographic expansion, a marked shift in the centers of wealth and importance, and a greatly enhanced potential for royal revenues leading to a stepped-up royal presence in Brazil. Jurisdictions were subdivided and added, a new judicial structure was instituted, and new treasury offices were created. However, after midcentury the gold-and-diamond-led economy began a steady decline, making new sources of revenue imperative. Even more, the nation's fortunes and future had by then come to rest on the wealth of Brazil, which now overshadowed that of Portugal's colonies in Africa and Asia.[24]

The mid–eighteenth century, then, was a critical turning point for both Iberian crowns. Portugal's drive toward effective, centralized control of its American colony had been more evident in the preceding half-century. Spain's implementation of such a colonial policy would not begin to become generalized until the mid-1760s. Yet for both the commitment to institute a new, fully hegemonic relationship with their possessions in the New World was finalized at midcentury.

The Means: More Direct Administrative Control

The initial laboratory for Bourbon imperial reform was Caracas in the wake of the rebellion of 1749. Responding to the revolt, royal policymakers under Ferdinand VI (1746–1759)—who exhibited a renewed Bourbon interest in Spain's American possessions—set forth a series of policies that foreshadowed the more comprehensive reforms instituted under Charles III (1759–1788) and his ministers. The goal of rebellion had been to end the commercial monopoly of the Caracas Company. Restoring its authority, the crown reformed the Caracas Company to assuage most of the grievances of the *caraquenos* (residents of Caracas). However, the crown also expanded its presence and control to the point that the era of Hapsburgian regional autonomy had ended.

Royal bureaucrats determinedly set about securing their control over Caracas's public life. The number of Creoles in colonial administration was restricted. In addition, the governor effectively subordinated the cabildo, even as it was expanded in personnel and responsibility. There was a corollary effort to manage the general populace. Candles in windows and a lamp outside the door of all residences were to be in place by 9 P.M. All males between the ages of 12 and 60 without employment deemed satisfactory were classified as vagabonds and given ten days to find work. Women without work were to be placed in "virtuous houses" to learn "good customs." Orphans were to be assigned to masters to learn trades. More telling were two important symbols of the new royal intention. A contingent of regular troops used to suppress the rebellion was permanently stationed in the greater Caracas area. The city's central plaza, formerly an open quadrangle functioning as the main town market, was refashioned into a controlled emporium, enclosed on three sides, to facilitate regulation and efficient taxation of retail trade. The sale of all such goods inside the city had to be conducted there.[25]

The policies implemented in response to the Caracas rebellion served as a precursor for a body of imperial reforms by the Spanish Bourbons that became imperative in the wake of the Seven Years' War. Thereafter, reforms were elaborated with ever greater comprehensiveness into the 1790s, when the start of almost continuous imperial warfare led to more pragmatic and short-term policies. As in Caracas, the primary means of establishing imperial reform was far greater direct administrative control.

The crown needed officials who were dependent and steadfast in carrying out the royal will, which meant the existing personnel had to be replaced. The cumulative effect of the sale of offices and patrimonial grants had produced a royal bureaucracy that by 1750 was staffed, below the viceroyal level, largely by Creoles, along with *peninsulares* who had become rooted in local society. Wealth, favoritism, and the networked interests of local prominent families were the nexus for their securing and conducting their offices. Consequently, revenues were lost through corruption and negligence, and royal decrees were not infrequently set aside. The most dangerous effect, however, was starkly revealed in the urban insurrection in Quito in 1765. In what constitutes the first of the major insurrections provoked in response to the reforms instituted under Charles III, the creole-dominated *audiencia* (a court of appeals that in some areas had executive functions) opposed the reforms that led to the revolt and then appeased the movement. The creole-dominated cabildo served as the chief organ of local opposition on behalf of the well-to-do of the city. *Peninsulares* formed the only constituency in support of fully complying with the dictates of higher royal authorities. After a decent interval, the members of the *audiencia* were replaced.[26]

After midcentury, the Spanish crown began phasing out the sale of offices, beginning with the *audiencia* posts. Primarily through a policy of attrition, a new group of bureaucrats steadily took hold of colonial administration. Appointed on the basis of merit (their abilities and prior service to the crown), they far more frequently placed royal interests above personal gain, and they were almost exclusively *peninsulares*. The Bourbons also sought the latter's support at the municipal level. The growing influx of immigrants, especially to the regional urban centers, offered a potential for greater compliance and loyalty at the lowest levels of colonial administration, which the crown increasingly tapped.[27] *Peninsulares*, in general, formed an increasingly important constituency that usually benefited from imperial reforms. And even when they did not, they were usually quick to uphold the principle of the supremacy of royal authority in the face of American questioning and defiance.

The de-Americanization of the colonial bureaucracy was also accomplished through the expansion of offices both spatially and functionally. Bureaucratic posts were augmented as the crown sought to establish direct administration over economic and fiscal activities previously contracted out to private individuals. Direct collection replaced tax farming. Direct administration was assumed over monopolies such as salt and playing cards and especially tobacco. The boldest, most innovative expansion of the bureaucracy came in the Bourbons' effort to bridge a critical gap in colonial administration, that between viceroyal authorities and district officials. The intendancy system in France and Spain had established effective royal control at the regional (often synonymous with provincial) level. The intendants in Spanish America were given direct supervision over the *subdelegados* (who replaced the *alcaldes mayores* and corregidores as royal district magistrates) and over the provincial capitals, which they administered directly. Moreover, they were given all of the essential powers of government, including the right of royal patronage over ecclesiastical institutions.[28]

The intendants were the showcase of the new breed of Bourbon bureaucrats: powerful, well-paid, professional (from the military, law, or the treasury), and almost exclusively peninsular. Nevertheless, both the Bourbon bureaucracy's professionalization and its service to the crown were uneven. In urban centers, especially where viceroys and *audiencias* resided, the imperial bureaucratic system achieved a considerable degree of effectiveness. For most imperial bureaucrats, security and prestige were the trade-off for the prohibition against owning real estate and from engaging in commercial ventures. Only a minority of royal officials—through wealth, family connections, or personal favoritism—were able to get around the constriction of the pursuit of personal opportunity. In provincial capitals, intendants were able in varying degrees to convert municipal government into an instrument of royal policy. Enlarging the cabildo and often recruiting *peninsulares* to municipal office, they were able to direct local government into new areas of activity that directly or indirectly established a greater royal intervention in people's lives.[29]

In the diverse communities of the countryside, however, the bureaucracy's professionalization and its fulfillment of royal intention remained limited. The flaw in the system was at the district level. The intendancies had stripped the *subdelegados* of their predecessors' considerable autonomy but had failed to provide a new basis for the effective exercise of authority. With inadequate remuneration and prior wealth and connections, the alliances they needed to gain leverage over competing groups in their districts resulted in dependency vis-à-vis local Creoles or, worse, in isolation from local society. Within a decade, many *subdelegados* began reinstituting the forced purchase of goods by Indian communities, especially in New Spain and highland Peru.[30]

The difference in the success of administrative reforms between the more Hispanic, urban population centers and those more rural and Indian-based appears to have also been a function of statistical capability. The Bourbons understood that an improved capacity for measuring the composition, location, and activity of the colonial population was essential for greater administrative control. The expanded number of more capable, subordinate officials made this goal attainable. Governments under the Enlightenment's influence, as Iberian monarchies were, had a strong predilection (for some, even an obsession) for census taking and informational surveys. Periodic censuses provided systematic aggregated population counts, as well as the specific distribution and composition of the colonial population. Royal officials also prepared inventories of capital, real estate, livestock holdings, and weapons. They compiled special reports on workers' wages, the number and worth of stores selling food and alcoholic beverages, and the production and consumption of various types of commodities. They organized special expeditions to gather scientific data that yielded detailed physical and cultural descriptions of diverse regions of the empire.[31]

With this enhanced statistical capability, the Spanish royal bureaucracy was more effectively able to formulate, implement, and coordinate a broad range of policies that it initiated in the New World. It organized a militia system for defense of the empire and instituted a program for the propagation and distribution of smallpox vaccine. Tax collection was reorganized and tax levies adjusted (usually upward). Educational institutions were expanded and a broad range of public improvements carried out in the localities.

In Portuguese America, the Marquis of Pombal, the powerful royal minister who effectively governed the realm from 1750 to 1777, also strove to enlarge and centralize royal authority. Under the strong influence of Enlightenment ideas he and other bureaucrats and intellectuals perceived the altered conditions facing the empire after 1750 and determined that more direct administrative control was imperative. The remaining private captaincies were abolished, with royal officials assuming governance. A whole new series of accounting offices were erected at the captaincy (provincial/regional) level. Boards of inspection were established in the four main ports to control the quality and price of sugar and tobacco, the principal colonial agricultural commodities. The tax collection system in the mining zone was augmented, and the militia was reformed and expanded.

Yet Pombal and his successors did not attempt to extend royal administrative presence in colonial society to the same extent as their Spanish counterparts. Many taxes continued to be farmed out to private individuals. Though Pombal sought restrictions on municipal autonomy, it appears that the *senados da camara* (municipal councils) retained a considerable degree of autonomy in comparison to the Spanish cabildos. Most important, Pombal did not disturb the control of prominent families at the district level. Indeed, their members shared in the new opportunities created by the expansion of royal offices. At the level of provincial governor, however, Pombal did try to appoint those infused with Enlightenment ideas and committed to his new state activism. However, in this he did not feel compelled to exclude *mazombos* (Creoles).[32]

The Burden: Paying More Taxes

Imperial reform in Ibero-America, indeed, in all the New World came with a price. The metropolitan centers were convinced that the colonies should assume a greater burden for their defense and reorganization. Whether by calculated manipulation, rationalization, or well-meaning mercantilist belief, royal policymakers blurred the distinction between American interests and European-driven concerns. As the price of imperial competition (and the cost of administrative reform to engage in it) rose after the mid–eighteenth century, regional societies felt the growing burden of empire being placed upon them.

One cost was political. Americans found their customary prerogatives, their de facto autonomy, being circumscribed as royal bureaucrats extended administrative control. Another cost was social and cultural. As colonial policymakers sought to attend to and reconcile the interests of the varied peoples in their New World possessions, social relationships were disrupted and cultural patterns challenged. Nevertheless, the cost most immediately and comprehensively felt was economic. The rising expense of imperial competition and warfare brought growing metropolitan control over revenue sources, constricting illegal activities through which revenues were lost and assuming direct operation of economic and fiscal activities to obtain greater proceeds. For some families and social groups this change meant interference in or loss of their economic interests. For almost all, it meant paying more taxes.

Unlike in English America, where the conquest of New France brought a sudden and sharp increase in the burden of empire for colonial subjects, in Ibero-America the mercantile and particularly the constitutional dimensions of imperial reform were slower to manifest themselves and to become entwined with the tax issue. Trade had been far more restricted in Ibero-America, and imperial reforms in general progressively liberalized commercial exchange (which did, however, adversely affect some regions and groups). Because Ibero-America had never had self-rule beyond the local level, taxes had always been levied directly by royal administration, so the tax issue did not acquire a constitutional character. Finally, having been multicultural realms from their very beginning, the Iberian empires were accustomed to royal arbitration among different sociocultural groups. What came into question in the wake of the imperial reforms were the particular social relationships altered in a given regional setting and, in time, the long-term impartiality of the crown.

Prior to 1750 the fiscal bureaucracy had remained small while forming an integral part of imperial governance. Under the late Bourbons, fiscal bureaucrats became much more numerous, and they had primary responsibility for generating ever greater revenues by expanding sources and improving collection. The very expansion of the fiscal bureaucracy itself was symptomatic of one dimension of the increasingly heavier tax burden on New World subjects: there were more and more officials and soldiers in royal service to pay for. Throughout the empire, regular army contingents were dispatched, and militia units were formed. The intendancy system and the expanded role of the fiscal branch enlarged the number of royal officials at the local and regional levels. The new viceroyalty of the La Plata (1776) and the Provincias Internas (a semi-autonomous, supraregional governance unit designed to unite and defend the northern frontier of New Spain) added still more bureaucrats and soldiers.[33]

Even as almost all felt the burden of more and higher tax levies, some experienced a loss of economic opportunity as well. The conversion from tax farming to direct royal collection of numerous revenue sources eliminated a lucrative activity for not a few colonial subjects. So, too, did the assumption of direct management over existing royal monopolies and the imposition of new ones. Those who opposed, and sometimes resisted these fiscal innovations that threatened their enterprises were joined by the secular (and often ecclesiastical) leaders of localities generally. They understood all too well the consequences of these fiscal reforms for their varied interests, which had long been sheltered from efficient taxation. In royal terms that translated into tax evasion. No matter how strenuously prominent Creoles might try to rationalize it, they had been quick to take whatever the crown had forfeited through its officials' neglect or venality.

The more efficient collection of taxes noticeably increased the burden of imperial reform on the well-to-do. Yet it was the countless common subjects of the realm who bore the far heavier burden. For those struggling to survive, margins were very small. Instrumental to the fiscal bureaucrats' greater efficiency and greater penetration into the flow and workings of life in urban barrios and rural villages was their growing statistical capability. Inventories of capital and property revealed the holdings of the well-to-do and modest of means more readily. But comprehensive censuses and regularization of the tribute lists left the poor with less and less anonymity to shield them from fiscal exactions levied on them for whom they were, along with their economic activities.

In the Andes, Indian commoners faced increasing fiscal pressure. The tribute obligation was extended to mestizos and to Indians formerly exempted: village officials, those in service to the church or the military, and even those of noble lineage. In the district of Cochabamba, intervention in village affairs, direct collection of taxes, the imposition of new taxes and much higher rates on the *alcabalas* (sales tax), and the establishment of customs stations and a provincial treasury resulted in a dramatic increase in royal revenues. Communal villagers were left

more impoverished than ever. The emerging group of peasant producers saw their meager yields on subsistence and market production eroding. Indian villagers in the Ecuadorian highlands north of Quito
dreadfully and defiantly anticipated the Bourbon fiscal reforms. Ru-
mors of a census and the restructuring of tribute collection left them so
fearful that they came to believe in an imaginary fiscal system: tribute
was paid to Spanish officials in the form of young village men who
would be branded and sold into slavery.[34]

Brazil appears not to have experienced such a heavy fiscal burden.
Administrative reforms were not as sweeping. There was less of an
enlargement of the bureaucracy to support and far less intervention at
the local and district level. Control there by prominent families was
left undisturbed. Specific groups might object to particular fiscal measures, but there was not the overall tenor of the metropolitan center's
gain at the Creoles' considerable expense, as in Spanish America.

Nevertheless, there were other, nonfiscal burdens felt heavily by
some Brazilians. The expulsion of the Jesuits in 1759—the most extreme of Pombal's policies to bring the Catholic Church fully under
state control—stripped the Indians of the Amazon region of their political, economic, and cultural protection. Moreover, under the guise of
ending legal discrimination, Pombal instituted a policy of forced acculturation that left them even more vulnerable. Interracial marriage
was to be encouraged; the use of indigenous languages was prohibited. Indians were required to work for wages, and schools were to be
established for their children. Direction and control over the villages
was transferred to non-Indians (until 1799). The burden of administrative reform that these Indians carried was displacement, destruction
of their way of life, and depopulation. Fewer than 20,000 remained by
the end of the century.[35]

The expulsion of the Jesuits had more varied repercussions in Spanish America than in Brazil. Many Indians experienced social, economic,
and cultural dislocations similar to those in Brazil. Some Creoles profited from the elimination of economic competition and from acquisition of assets and labor, especially in the frontier and peripheral areas.
But others felt the burden of exiled family members and friends, as
well as the immediate loss of the empire's most prominent educators,
who had staffed an extensive network of secondary schools in the important urban centers.[36]

Royal bureaucratic efforts at social control also burdened American subjects in diverse ways. The association of criminality and disso-
lute behavior with *pulquerias* made them the target of reform for a small
group of royal officials in New Spain between 1780 and 1800. To

strengthen social control, they tried either to limit consumption of pulque or curtail the clientele's option to linger. The reform failed, however, because drinkers were thereby encouraged to frequent clandestine spots, which only succeeded in reducing royal revenues. Social engineering was also applied to marriages in the military. The crown, having long sought their regulation (above all, to avoid families becoming a financial burden either on it or its officers), finally found an effective solution: the wife's social status was required to be at least equal to that of her officer-husband.[37]

The Benefits: Promoting the Economy

The logic of Iberian imperial reform was constructed on more than the simple premises of greater administrative control and of ensuring that New World subjects paid a greater share of the costs of the empire (or even sent a surplus to the peninsula). In addition, it assumed several benefits of imperial reform: the stimulation of economic activity, along with what the crown deemed improvements in its American subjects' social and cultural well-being. Yet these benefits were markedly skewed as to economic activity, social rank, and region. Royal intentions were unevenly pursued. More important, the benefits of imperial reform to New World subjects were compromised by an underlying and overriding presupposition: that the ultimate benefactors were to be the crown and the national (as versus imperial) subjects that it governed in the peninsula.

The introduction of free trade within the Spanish empire beginning in 1778 (completed with its extension to New Spain and Venezuela in 1789) brought widespread benefits to the New World spatially and to the peninsula. The increase in the value of this trade between 1782 and 1796 has been calculated at 400 percent over the base year of 1778. Free trade succeeded in promoting the exploitation of a range of agricultural products that formerly had been constricted or neglected: tobacco, cacao, sugar, cochineal and indigo dyes, hides, and so on. The La Plata, Venezuela, and the Caribbean islands joined New Spain and Peru as important centers of exports to the peninsula. This American trade not only covered the previous deficit in commercial exchange with Europe but even provided an overall surplus. Crown revenues rose markedly. The Spanish product share of the trade going to its New World empire increased from 38 percent to 52 percent between 1782 and 1796.[38]

It can be argued that the primary beneficiaries of widened commercial opportunities were immigrants from the peninsula. In such diverse trade centers as Saltillo in northern New Spain, the port of Veracruz on New Spain's east coast, and Asunción, Paraguay, immigrant merchants came to dominate the colonial trade. Still, mining remained a major focus in Bourbon efforts to expand New World trade and production. In New Spain, mine owners received support in rolling back the customary share rights of their workers. However, more important, the crown decided to cede some benefits from and control over the silver mining sector. In the following years it granted tax exemptions for renovations of old, waterlogged mines and for *alcabalas* on raw materials and supplies while lowering prices and increasing supplies of mercury and gunpowder. It also organized the miners into a guild, established a bank to help finance the industry, and founded a mining school to improve and diffuse mining technology. The more flexible, farsighted royal policy significantly contributed to the spurt in silver production after 1770. Almost immediately, tax yields and monopoly profits rose (principally in minting and the supply of mercury and gunpowder).[39]

Free trade within the Spanish empire expanded American agricultural exports until they comprised 44 percent of total imports to the peninsula by the 1790s. Labor and markets were principal determinants in Bourbon efforts to expand agricultural production, especially in the former peripheral regions. In the case of Venezuela, compensation for the heavy burden of imperial reform following the 1749 rebellion was largely confined to the prominent families of Caracas. Vagrancy laws gave them more leverage over workers, and the suppression of tobacco cultivation (freeing up more labor) and crown-induced expansion of slave importation added to the ranks of their cacao workers. Caracas's well-to-do also benefited from the Bourbon decision to permit the legal export of hides and live animals to the Caribbean islands. Joined to the growing market in the highland valleys and on the coast, it fostered a spectacular growth in stock raising. Crown policy was less successful in ensuring a disciplined labor force for their recently established ranches in the llanos. Town residency requirements, prohibitions against cattle slaughtering and transfers, and crown-supported raids against autonomous *llanero* settlements met with only limited success.[40]

The Bourbons were unwilling to make such a major commitment to spur economic activity for the Colombian interior plains further to the west, which lacked accessibility to the coast by land. The Orinoco River (flowing north and east into the Caribbean) offered a way out of the Colombian llanos' stagnant isolation. Yet each time the viceroy of New Granada submitted a plan to promote an eastern trade route, the crown yielded to the lobbying of the Cartagena and Santa Marta merchants on the north coast to block such competition. Even when the British seized Trinidad, located near the mouth of the Orinoco River (1797), the crown continued to see the Colombian llanos as a closed door to the highlands rather than a defensible, developable portal to the Caribbean. Not until 1804 did the crown budge. The eastern trade route was opened to two commodities (flour and cotton), but only in exchange for money in the Venezuelan port of La Guaira.[41]

Such inconsistencies in the benefits of imperial reform were the result of a web of factors that worked both in tandem and at cross-purposes. Short-term expediency vied with long-term planning. In interpreting the royal will the perspectives of policymaking bureaucrats differed in the scale of their responsibilities and in the extent and character of reform they envisioned. Perhaps, most important, American regional interests were juxtaposed with the national interests of the peninsula. The eastern slope of the Andes in Bolivia and northwestern New Spain illustrate the often markedly different outcomes in the efforts to reform whole regions.

By the 1780s, Cochabamba's notable-dominated commercial economy was in trouble. Highland mining-town markets for the region's grain production were eroding. Autonomous peasant-directed economic activities aimed at subsistence, with any surplus for largely intraregional markets, were claiming growing control over the factors of production. Cochabamba's first intendant, Francisco de Viedma, worked out an ambitious blueprint to rejuvenate market production in the region and revive its export capacity. The plan's core was the economic coupling of Cochabamba with the tropical and semi-tropical lowlands to the east, which had been administratively joined in 1784. The termination of the missions' wardship that followed Jesuit expulsion would foster industrious villages growing tropical crops for sierra markets. Indian and mestizo colonists from the densely populated Cochabamba valleys would join them, working on plantations and farms established by the latter's enterprising prominent families, who would also function as mercantile intermediaries.

Political will, more than market incentives, determined the fate of Viedma's blueprint for the region's economic transformation. When the highland centers of La Paz and especially Chuquisaca, which possessed the sole road to the lowlands, opposed the building of a royally funded road from Cochabamba to that area, the crown chose not to overrule them. And when the region's entrepreneurs sought guarantees of success—the provision of cheap labor, secure property rights, removal of protective barriers, and construction of roads—the crown was unwilling to exercise such economic intervention. Indeed, Bourbon preoccupations centered on resurrecting the disintegrating colonial economic order in the Andean highlands: extracting greater surplus through increased tribute and taxes on economic activity, which would harness Indian community labor once more to the Potosí mines. [42]

The contrast with northwestern New Spain is striking. With growing fears of foreign aggrandizement on the far northern frontier and with the existing framework of mission pacification and limited settlement no longer functioning even passably, the Bourbons intervened decisively in the region. They determined that only comprehensive policies, backed by a firm and continuing royal presence, could construct a stable frontier society that could serve as a base for extension of Spanish control many hundreds of miles to the north and west.

The crown curtailed frontier insecurities by expanding and improving the presidial garrisons to subjugate the rebellious Indian tribes within and pacify the marauding Apaches without. It strengthened civil and ecclesiastical administration while letting the missions fend for themselves under the disintegrating pressures of settler penetration. Royal treasury offices were established, which, along with the general mining reforms (which reduced the prices of salt and mercury), greatly stimulated mineral production. The crown encouraged the formation of towns through a settlement law (1791) which provided for generous amounts of land around the presidios to be granted to permanent settlers. A large number of enterprising *peninsulares* responded to the new climate of security and opportunity resulting from the crown's forceful intervention.[43]

The reforming imperial vision for Brazil was in many ways similar to that of the Bourbons for northwestern New Spain in particular and the peripheral regions in general. Forcefully focused by Pombal, the major emphasis was on the formerly neglected fringes: the Amazon basin and the southern plains. The crown made a firm commitment to settlement. The missions were dismantled, military detachments stationed where needed, and generous grants of land awarded. The benefits of imperial reform were widely spread; only a few regions appear to have declined or stagnated (Pará being the most notable case). Favorable international events, along with the largely complementary stimulus of economic expansion in the Amazon and southern regions, converted the potential of the Pombaline reforms in administration and economic policy into a rising and more general prosperity after 1780. The carioca region centered around Rio de Janeiro appears to have derived the most benefits from imperial reform in the long run. Designated as the colonial capital in 1763, marketing outlet for a growing agricultural hinterland, and hub of an intracoastal trade network (in turn linked to the Portuguese worldwide colonial market system), Rio's position had risen to one of dominance by 1800. Expanded economic and bureaucratic opportunities seemed not to have noticeably favored immigrants from the peninsula at the expense of native Brazilians.[44]

New External Realities

Each round of imperial warfare in the New World since the 1750s caused increasing dislocations: in trade, in transfers of colonial dominion, from imperial reforms. Most regions had been able to turn these dislocations to their advantage. Their combined effect had been generally to expand opportunities, even though (and often because) imperial controls were being strengthened. But the preeminence of Bourbon self-interest—the crown and its peninsular subjects as imperial reform's ultimate beneficiaries—had become ever more tightly intertwined with far-reaching alterations in European politics and society and in the Atlantic market, especially after 1790. This shift meant that the benefits of imperial reform for Americans were not only qualified and compromised but also would be often short-lived.

The French Revolution of 1789 triggered a quarter century of almost continuous instability and war. Europe itself was beset with fluctuation and upheaval. Imperial controls weakened. In Haiti, this led to the initiation of a slave revolt and the consolidation of an independent black republic. In Spanish America, the new external realities proved a double-edged sword. The Bourbons' growing debilitation undermined the supports for economic activity that imperial reforms had brought to many regions. At the same time, it led the crown to raise the tax burden to try to reverse the hemorrhaging of imperial power. The benefits of imperial reform for Americans began eroding. In some regions, the Bourbons' decline was felt more in terms of the weakening of restrictions than of support. There, new economic opportunities suddenly emerged. Yet, too often the externally induced fluctuations of this period could almost as quickly undermine them.

External realities were becoming fickle. Enterprising merchants and ship captains in the districts bordering the La Plata estuary responded to the opportunities presented by the growing breakdown of imperial mercantile controls. Naval warfare had steadily curtailed Spain's Atlantic shipping, and the British navy disrupted direct delivery to European markets. Platine merchants and shippers creatively reacted to the shifting fortunes of war and peace, linking three principal new trade routes into a triangle trade: Africa, Brazil, and the North Atlantic. Platine ships also went to Cuba and up the Pacific coast. Cattle products and Peruvian silver were exchanged for European manufactures and slaves. Buenos Aires's merchants' guild supported this trade by establishing a nautical school and maritime insurance. This promising beginning proved short-lived, however. Altered wartime conditions after 1803 brought first decline and then demise. Renewed war led to a more aggressive British naval force and then invasion (1806–07), with ships seized, scattered, and sold or turned to the quick profits of piracy. The crown closed the nautical school on the grounds that the *consulado* (merchants' guild) had overstepped its bounds. Then, when Britain became an ally (1808), its merchants flooded the La Plata markets, eliminated trade intermediaries, and disrupted the native credit network.[45]

The demise of the textile industry in Cochabamba was more precipitous, its origins less transient. When the war with Britain broke out in 1796, prior constraints on European competition were lifted. The region's textiles, which had emerged after 1750 as a peasant initiative to diversify their subsistence security, quickly reached markets all over the viceroyalty of the La Plata. Merchants with capital to control the mule trade and to market in large volume were pivotal to this sudden expansion. They also appear to have fostered a putting-out system, supplying and financing urban artisan clients. Yet these prominent merchants also understood the long-term implications of the crown's firm resistance to the eastern colonization scheme, which foreclosed that enhancement of the industry's competitive advantage (through the potential for increased supply and lowered cost of cotton). They invested only in distribution, ready to concentrate again on European imports when the shifting winds of the colonial market again changed direction, as they did after 1802 when the wartime barriers to European manufactures came down. The merchants' urban artisan clients were not so fortunate. Unable to make such adjustments, in debt and more dependent, they (along with rural cottage weavers) were left to fend for themselves as the textile industry collapsed around them.[46]

By contrast, the positive impact of the new external realities on most of Brazil's regional economies proved not to be ephemeral. The revolutions in North America, France, and Haiti—along with the growth of the cotton textile industry during the initial stage of France's and especially Britain's industrial revolution—altered the patterns of supply and demand of many Brazilian agricultural commodities. Export prices generally rose, and markets expanded from 1780 to 1800, especially for sugar and cotton. Moreover, this prosperity was not cut short by the changing wartime conditions in the early nineteenth century. Portugal's alliance with England protected and sustained markets for the region's varied primary exports.[47]

Such Ibero-American regions—where the onset of an era of war brought new economic opportunities, even if only a few years for most—were the exception. Elsewhere, the economic expansion driven by internal factors (and often by imperial reforms) was increasingly undermined by wartime dislocations and the escalating tax burden. The emerging peripheral regions—most notably Cuba, Venezuela, and the La Plata—especially felt the pressures induced by wartime interruptions of the lines of commerce. Their agricultural and pastoral exports were perishable within established time limits. Permission to trade with neutral countries eased this commercial pressure, but it was withdrawn for several years (1799–1801, 1802–1804). Even when reinstated, it suffered from obstructions and irregularities.[48] Meanwhile, Spain's almost continuous involvement in war (1793–1808) steadily boosted expenditures while curtailing trade and regular remittances of precious metals. The royal government became increasingly entrapped in short-term fiscal expediencies. The extended, comprehensive, integrative perspective of imperial reform gave way to an almost exclusive preoccupation with extracting as much revenue as possible from New World subjects.

The grandest scheme devised by the Bourbons for covering the ascending royal debt was the *consolidación de vales reales*. The massive issues of these essentially unbacked paper bills led to their great depreciation in value. The professed intention was to use the money from the sale of a variety of publicly and religiously held property in Spain (beginning in 1798), to redeem the *vales* (minus the annual 3 percent of the proceeds paid to the seller). But the *consolidación* soon became a cover for raising funds directly to meet current expenses. Renewed war with Britain in 1804 led the crown to extend this new form of tax levy to the New World. However, there most of the wealth of religious institutions was not in the form of property but already in paper form, as church loans, liens, and mortgages to laypeople engaged in a wide range of economic activities. In the short run, the well-to-do (those left holding the bag in the sudden demand for the redemption of church loans) were threatened with loss of property or bankruptcy. From a longer perspective, they were threatened with the ruin of virtually the only long-term credit system in the colonial economy, of which they had been the chief beneficiaries. All told, more than 15 million pesos were collected by the crown, two-thirds of which came from New Spain.[49]

The reaction to the law of consolidation was perhaps the clearest and most general expression of the growing doubts within the Spanish empire about whether the burdens of empire could any longer be justified by its benefits to New World subjects. Not only was the resentment against escalating taxes coming to a head, but there was also a cumulative alarm and anger at the seemingly never-ending intrusion of royal control of their lives.

In this, Spanish Americans were part of a larger hemispheric reality then emerging. The European colonial system, which had bound together the New World's regional societies in various imperial configurations, was breaking down under the weight of warfare and rising American discontent. Perhaps in time, the accumulating changes within the regional societies that began in the mid–eighteenth century alone would have ushered in this new historical context for the hemisphere. Nevertheless, first the commitment to ever-greater imperial control and then the upheavals and war within Europe itself thrust it upon them. In growing numbers, Americans were reaching the conclusion that the European imperial framework was no longer acceptable or even tolerable. Instead, the issue became how these New World regional societies would realign themselves. Those in English North America had been driven to the logic of independence and to the innovative assumption that they could join their regional societies into a large expanding republic through federalism. For Haiti's black majority, aligned with a mulatto minority, independence meant above all a social revolution through abolition of slavery and changes in land tenure.

Were these the only two alternatives for those elsewhere in the hemisphere? Could a confederational relationship with European states be created? A new round of external events beginning with the Napoleonic invasion of the Iberian peninsula in 1807–08 forced the issue in Spanish and Portuguese America. New political and cultural visions arose to address and answer these questions.

Notes

1. Bernard Bailyn, *The Origins of American Politics*, and *The Ideological Origins of the American Revolution* (Cambridge: Harvard University Press, 1967); Henretta and Nobles, *Evolution and Revolution*.

2. Herbert S. Klein, "Familia y fertilidad en Amantenango, Chiapas, 1785–1816," *Historia Mexicana* [hereafter, *HM*] 36 (October–December 1986): 282–84; Saeger, "Mission as a Frontier Institution," 497–99.

3. Michael Swann, *Tierra Adentro: Settlement and Society in Colonial Durango* (Boulder, CO: Westview, 1982).

4. John Tutino, "Provincial Spaniards, Indian Towns, and Haciendas: Interrelated Sectors of Agrarian Society in the Valleys of Mexico and Toluca," in *Early Provinces of Mexico: Variants of Spanish-American Regional Societies*, ed. Ida Altman and James Lockhart (Los Angeles: University of California, 1976), 182–87, 191–93; William B. Taylor, "Banditry and Insurrection: Rural Unrest in Central Jalisco," in *Riots, Rebellions, and Insurrections: Rural Social Conflict in Mexico*, ed. Friedrich Katz (Princeton, NJ: Princeton University Press, 1986), 226–31; David Cahill, "Curas and Social Conflict in the Doctrinas of Cuzco, 1780–1814," *Journal of Latin American Studies* [hereafter, *JLAS*] 16 (November 1984): 253–58.

5. Susan M. Deeds, "Rural Work in Nueva Vizcaya: Forms of Labor Coercion on the Periphery," *HAHR* 69 (August 1989): 447–48; Swann, *Tierra Adentro*, 65–71, 155–59.

6. José Cuello, "The Economic Impact of the Bourbon Reforms and the Late Colonial Crisis of Empire at the Local Level: The Case of Saltillo, 1777–1817," *The Americas* 44 (January 1988): 301–23.

7. John Hoyt Williams, "Observations on Blacks and Bondage in Uruguay, 1800–1836," *The Americas* 43 (April 1987): 411–27; Jane M. Rausch, *A Tropical Plains Frontier: The Llanos of Colombia, 1531–1831* (Albuquerque: University of New Mexico Press, 1984), 150–54.

8. David A. Brading, *Miners and Merchants in Bourbon Mexico, 1763–1810* (New York: Cambridge University Press, 1971), 14, 131; Robert J. Ferry, *The Colonial Elite of Early Caracas: Formation and Crisis, 1567–1767* (Berkeley: University of California Press, 1989), 48–77, 105–8; James Lockhart and Stuart B. Schwartz, *Early Latin America: A History of Colonial Spanish America and Brazil* (New York: Cambridge University Press, 1983), 370–83; E. Bradford Burns, *A History of Brazil* (New York: Columbia University Press, 1980), 77–81; Chance, *Conquest of the Sierra*, 103–22.

9. Taylor, "Rural Unrest in Central Jalisco," 225–29; Eric Van Young, "Moving Toward Revolt: Agrarian Origins of the Hidalgo Rebellion in the Guadalajara Region," in *Riots, Rebellions, and Insurrections: Rural Social Conflict in Mexico*, ed. Friedrich Katz (Princeton, NJ: Princeton University Press, 1986), 186–89; Rodney D. Anderson, "Race and Social Stratification: A Comparison of Working-Class Spaniards, Indians, and Castas in Guadalajara, Mexico, 1821," *HAHR* 68 (May 1988): 217–19.

10. Samuel Amaral, "Rural Production and Labour in Late Colonial Buenos Aires," *JLAS* 19 (November 1987): 237–52; Larissa V. Brown, "Port and Hinterland: Rio de Janeiro in the Internal Economy, 1790–1822" (paper presented at the American Historical Association Meeting [hereafter, AHA], San Francisco, December 27–30, 1989), 4–5.

11. Thomas Whigham, "Cattle Raising in the Argentine Northeast: Corrientes, c. 1750–1870," *JLAS* 20 (November 1988): 313–23; John Charles Chasteen, "Background to Civil War: The Process of Land Tenure in Brazil's Southern Borderlands, 1801–1893," *HAHR* 71 (November 1991): 737–55; Rausch, *A Tropical Plains Frontier*, 142–46, 150–54, 236–45; Stuart F. Voss, *On the Periphery of Nineteenth Century Mexico: Sonora and Sinaloa, 1810–1877* (Tucson: University of Arizona Press, 1982), 23–24.

12. George Gelman, "New Perspectives on an Old Problem and the Same Source: The Gaucho and the Rural History of the Colonial Rio de la Plata," *HAHR* 69 (November 1989): 715–19, 727–31; Ricardo Salvatorre and

Jonathan C. Brown, "The Old Problem of Gauchos and Rural Society," *HAHR* 69 (November 1989): 733–37.

13. Celia Wu, "The Population of the City of Querétaro," *JLAS* 16 (November 1984): 277–80, 292–300; Brading, *Miners and Merchants*, 17–18, 53, 232–33.

14. Sonya Lipsett-Rivera, "Eighteenth Century Agrarian Decline: A New Perspective," *HAHR* 70 (August 1990): 479–80; John E. Kicza, *Colonial Entrepreneurs: Families and Business in Bourbon Mexico City* (Albuquerque: University of New Mexico Press, 1983), 56–59, 84–85, 171–72; Linda Greenow, *Credit and Socioeconomic Change in Colonial Mexico: Loans and Mortgages in Guadalajara, 1720–1820* (Boulder, CO: Westview Press, 1983), 168; Margaret Chowning, "The Consolidación de Vales Reales in the Bishopric of Michoacán," *HAHR* 69 (August 1988): 455–56.

15. Kicza, *Colonial Entrepreneurs*, 23–24, 30–31, 187–205.

16. Brooke Larson, *Colonialism and Agrarian Transformation in Bolivia: Cochabamba, 1550–1900* (Princeton, NJ: Princeton University Press, 1988), 208–9, 212–31, 259–61; Van Young, "Moving toward Revolt," 193–94; Salvatorre and Brown, "Old Problem of Gauchos," 733–35, 740–41.

17. Dennis N. Valdes, "The Decline of Slavery in Mexico," *The Americas* 44 (October 1987): 170–71.

18. Ibid., 170–93; Donald Ramos, "Slavery in Brazil: A Case Study of Diamantina, Minas Gerais," *The Americas* 45 (July 1988): 47–60; Williams, "Blacks and Bondage in Uruguay," 413–27.

19. Rausch, *A Tropical Plains Frontier*, 138–39; Wu, "City of Querétaro," 277–80; Stern, "Feudalism, Capitalism, and the World System," 851–57.

20. Stern, "Feudalism, Capitalism, and the World System," 853; Chance, *Conquest of the Sierra*, 103–11.

21. Larson, *Agrarian Transformation*, 261; James S. Saeger, "Economic Trends on the Chaco Mission Frontier: Subsistance Patterns of Guaycuruans, 1700–1810" (paper presented at the Latin American Studies Association Meeting, Miami, December 1989), 21–37; Wu, "City of Querétaro," 292–302.

22. Silvia Arrom, *The Women of Mexico City, 1790–1857* (Stanford, CA: Stanford University Press, 1985), 26–29.

23. Henretta and Nobles (*Evolution and Revolution*) detail a remarkably similar pattern in which powerful families rise to dominate the regional societies of English North America.

24. Lockhart and Schwartz, *Early Latin America*, 369–79, 383–84; Mark Burkholder and Lyman Johnson, *Colonial Latin America* (New York: Oxford University Press, 1989), 244, 247–55.

25. Ferry, *Early Caracas*, 136–52, 157–60, 240–44, 248, 252–54.

26. Anthony MacFarlane, "The 'Rebellion of the Barrios': Urban Insurrection in Bourbon Quito," *HAHR* 69 (May 1989): 287–96, 303–4, 308–24.

27. Linda Arnold, *Bureaucracy and Bureaucrats in Mexico City, 1742–1835* (Tucson: Arizona University Press, 1988), 98–102, 112–24, 128; Cuello, "Saltillo," 302–3, 310–21; James S. Saeger, "Survivial and Abolition: The Eighteenth Century Paraguayan Encomienda," *The Americas* 38 (July 1981): 75–77.

28. Lockhart and Schwartz, *Early Latin America*, 252–53.

29. Arnold, *Bureaucrats in Mexico City*, 98–100, 107–9, 118–24; Burkholder and Johnson, *Colonial Latin America*, 261.

30. Brian R. Hamnett, *Politics and Trade in Southern Mexico, 1750–1821* (New York: Cambridge University Press, 1971), 64–71, 81–82; Cahill, "Curas and Social Conflict," 265–68.

31. José G. Rigau-Pérez, "The Introduction of Smallpox Vaccine in 1803 and the Adoption of Immunization as a Government Function in Puerto Rico," *HAHR* 69 (August 1989): 394–97, 414–19; Cuello, "Saltillo," 307–9.

32. Lockhart and Schwartz, *Early Latin America*, 383–94; Burns, *Brazil*, 107–9.

33. Arnold, *Bureaucrats in Mexico City*, 81–90; Ferry, *Early Caracas*, 244–52; Cuello, "Saltillo," 306–16; MacFarlane, "Urban Insurrection in Bourbon Quito," 285–88, 301–2, 306.

34. Cahill, "Curas and Social Conflict," 248–53, 265–68; Larson, *Agrarian Transformation*, 284–89; Louisa Stark, "The Role of Women in Peasant Uprisings in the Ecuadorian Highlands," in *Political Anthropology of Ecuador: Perspectives from Indigenous Culture*, ed. Jeffrey Ehrenreich (Albany: Center for Caribbean and Latin American Studies, State University of New York, 1985), 10–20.

35. Lockhart and Schwartz, *Early Latin America*, 388–97.

36. Saeger, "Mission as a Frontier Institution," and "Chaco Frontier"; Barbara Ganson, "The Evuevi of Paraguay: Adaptive Strategies and Responses to Colonialism, 1528–1811," *The Americas* 45 (April 1989); Voss, *On the Periphery*, chap. 1; and Rausch, *A Tropical Plains Frontier*, 107–21.

37. John B. Kicza, "Drinking, Popular Protest, and Governmental Response in Eighteenth and Nineteenth Century Latin America" (paper presented to the meeting of the AHA, San Francisco, December 1989), 8–9; Gary Miller, "Bourbon Social Engineering: Women and Conditions of Marriage in Eighteenth Century Venezuela," *The Americas* 46 (January 1990): 261–67.

38. John Fisher, "Imperial 'Free Trade' and the Hispanic Economy, 1778–1796," *JLAS* 13 (May 1981): 21–56; Fisher, "The Imperial Response to 'Free Trade': Spanish Imports from Spanish America, 1778–1796," *JLAS* 17 (May 1985): 44–48, 51–63.

39. See Cuello, "Saltillo"; Jackie R. Booker, "The Veracruz Merchant Community in Latin Bourbon Mexico: A Preliminary Portrait, 1770–1810," *The Americas* 45 (October 1988): 187–89; Saeger, "Paraguayan Encomienda"; Brading, *Miners and Merchants*, 140–45, 148–49, 159–68; Barry Danks, "The Labor Revolt of 1766 in the Mining Community of Real del Monte," *The Americas* 44 (October 1987): 150–55, 159–63; Stern, "Feudalism, Capitalism, and the World System," 856–57. See also Doris Ladd, *The Making of a Strike: Mexican Silver Workers' Struggles in Real del Monte, 1766–1775* (Lincoln: Nebraska University Press, 1988).

40. Ferry, *Early Caracas*, 249–51; Rausch, *A Tropical Plains Frontier*, 150–54, 236–43; Fisher, "Imperial Response to 'Free Trade,' " 62–63.

41. Rausch, *A Tropical Plains Frontier*, 121–30.

42. Larson, *Agrarian Transformation*, 241–58, 269.

43. Voss, *On the Periphery*, 18–32.

44. Lockhart and Schwartz, *Early Latin America*, 388–94; Brown, "Port and Hinterland," 4–7.

45. Jerry W. Cooney, "Oceanic Commerce and Platine Merchants, 1796–1806: The Challenge of War," *The Americas* 45 (April 1989): 509–24; Cooney, "Neutral Vessels and Platine Slavers: Building a Viceroyal Merchant Marine," *JLAS* 18 (May 1986): 32–39.

46. Larson, *Agrarian Transformation*, 258–68.

47. Lockhart and Schwartz, *Early Latin America*, 394–95.

48. Burkholder and Johnson, *Colonial Latin America*, 292.

49. Ibid., 292–93; Lockhart and Schwartz, *Early Latin America*, 351–52; Chowning, "Consolidación in the Bishopric of Michoacán," 451–54, 460–78. How widespread and deep the effect of the law of consolidation was on the church, on landholding, on the regional economies, and on public sentiment is not yet clear. Installment payments delayed the consequences for many, and many other properties remained untouched before the whole process was suspended with Napoleon's invasion of the peninsula in 1808.

2

The Kiln of Independence

By 1800 the Iberian monarchies increasingly confronted a twofold problem. First, the very policies designed to bind American subjects more tightly to the peninsula often had resulted in an acceleration and intensification of the economic and social changes within the colonial world that tended to foster American autonomy. The almost continuous series of European wars after 1790 was creating a second, potentially more insurmountable obstacle to Iberian efforts to reform the imperial framework. The transfer of more American wealth to the peninsula, in tandem with an enlarged and more direct supervision of the New World territories, was central to that reform. Expanding colonial economies had helped to disguise this royal gambit to alter the ratio of American to peninsular shares in the imperial relationship. However, for the Spanish empire in particular, the cost of the wars by 1800 was pushing the balance of New World and peninsular interests beyond the point of American forbearance. Crises in many regional economies in the first years of the nineteenth century aggravated the imbalance and intensified American perception of it.

By the turn of the century the Iberian monarchies' New World subjects had accumulated their own agendas pertaining to the imperial framework. They were responding to the internal social and economic changes that were beginning to refashion colonial life around them, to the growing royal intervention in their lives, and to other external realities that were impinging on their provincial domains (especially after 1790). Their grievances increasingly called into question the imperial framework: its guarantees of material security, reciprocity, and the balance and regulation of competing interests. Expressing concerns and grievances steadily gave way to envisioning new bases for the reconstruction of relations within regional societies, within the empire—and even outside it.

For many segments within the regional societies, the emerging visions of what was necessary (of what was possible) to resolve the growing disequilibrium in the colonial world were based upon the past. They sought to resurrect political and cultural patterns that tradition informed them had once been viable alternatives to the altered imperial framework that now prevailed over their lives. Others were guided more by present realities. For them, the political revolution in the United States, and the political and social revolutions in Haiti and France, placed the questioning of the imperial framework in a potentially more radical context. Most (especially the countless poor and nonwhite inhabitants) disputed the imperial framework only indirectly. Their visions addressed specific patterns and structures fostered or tolerated by the imperial framework that adversely affected their lives. Some, however, increasingly perceived the overarching imperial edifice as the proper basis of contention. Until that was restored, reconstructed, or even replaced (depending upon their particular perspective), the ills besetting them would not be overcome.

The events triggered by the Napoleonic invasion of the Iberian peninsula in 1807–08 brought the questioning of the imperial framework to a head, forcing its operation and rationale into a contradiction that could not be resolved. The succeeding struggle for independence served as a kiln for the transformation to a new society that had begun to form more than a half century before. The years of insurgency (1808–1825) were accompanied by extensive economic dislocations resulting from the wars' destruction and from an acceleration of the inroads of industrial capitalism emanating from the emerging North Atlantic sphere. Together, they brought the transformation of the Iberian colonial world to its consummation. The social and economic changes under way since the 1750s were solidified. A new political-cultural framework was negotiated.

Erosion of the Imperial Framework

Above all, assumptions of a common historical experience had bound the New World's regional societies to their respective European empires until the 1750s. The transplantation of European, Christian culture to America had succeeded. Colonization had been so substantial that in large portions of America the Amerindian peoples had been almost entirely replaced; and in the lands that straddled the western mountain chains from Mexico to Chile, they had been subordinated and partially acculturated into a subservient population. The Atlantic Ocean had become an ever increasingly traversed and connecting medium that joined the New and Old World territories that comprised the respective empires. However much American subjects of European origins might defer to the metropolitan centers as cultural trendsetters— and the condescending attitudes of their Old World cousins—they came to regard themselves as equal members of the larger imperial polity.

In Ibero-America, theory played an important role along with practice. Though without chartered regional self-government (as in English America), local officials had negotiated the accepted practice of declining to implement decrees from the peninsula that were deemed inappropriate to local conditions. This arrangement had given working confirmation to the legal concept of imperial polity that had originated under the Hapsburgs. For Ibero-Americans, parity within the imperial framework derived from and rested upon the sharing of not only a common heritage but also a monarch whose relation to each kingdom was the same: a parent ruler. The Spanish Bourbons (and the Portuguese crown to a lesser extent) resisted this accustomed role as they strove to centralize the empire. By the late eighteenth century their bureaucrats were referring to American territories in internal state papers as "colonies." Yet the patrimonial concept remained paramount among those in America, and the pretense of parity within the empire was maintained.[1]

For Ibero-Americans, the prime function of their parent ruler had been that of arbiter, ruling justly and in the subjects' interests, guided by the principle of parity in uniting the distinct territories of the transoceanic realm together. Hierarchy, in contrast, functioned to bind together the disparate elements within colonial society. Through separate laws, the patrimonial monarch protected and attended to specific segments of colonial society, fostering a special, personal tie with each. Then, as arbiter, the crown reconciled these competing interests. That which appears to have been most important to protect, promote, and reconcile was the access to resources, whether for survival or profit.

After 1750 a questioning of the parent ruler as impartial arbiter had steadily increased. As internal social and economic changes accelerated, as the Bourbon agenda for a more centralized, metropolitan-centered imperial framework was implemented, and as external circumstances reinforced both of these currents, to American subjects the imperial arbiter seemed less and less capable, and then more and more partisan: in regulating the intensifying competition of interests; in maintaining the balance of interests between the New World and the peninsula. The crown's growing intervention seemed to favor some interests at the expense or even survival of others and to convert kingdoms into exploited colonies, both of which were increasingly unacceptable. In American eyes the justness of the parent ruler was eroding. And with it, so too were the respect for and the confidence in the imperial framework over which their patrimonial monarch ruled.

Incomplete Reconstruction of the Imperial Regime

The customary, expected pattern did continue in specific cases, but the mounting number of exceptions were forcing American subjects to question the fairness of an imperial system that seemed increasingly to have gone awry. In Saltillo, in the far north of New Spain, the cabildo's dutiful appeal of the raising of taxes was granted by the viceroy. However, the customary arbitration system proved more arduous and somewhat less successful for mineworkers in the Real del Monte district in 1766. They sent petitions to both local and royal officials to reverse the mine owners' attempts to reduce wages and downgrade working conditions. When municipal and royal officials ignored the viceroy's directives meeting their demands, the workers employed selective violence. The viceroy immediately sent an experienced jurist as investigator and mediator (with ample troops), whose determinations in most of the grievances represented a compromise. By contrast, the miners who joined other groups in revolt in Guanajuato, San Luis de la Paz, and San Luis Potosí in protest of the expulsion of the Jesuits the following year found the imperial arbitration system amiss. José Gálvez, the inspector general sent out in 1765 to implement a whole series of reforms, suppressed the revolts with unprecedented severity.[2]

Though reformist royal bureaucrats concurred in the broad range of Bourbon policy initiatives designed to reorganize and redirect economic relations, they were not in agreement on how far the constitutional changes in royal government should go to accomplish those ends. For Gálvez (and those of like mind), imperial reform in its fundamental sense meant transforming royal government in the New World from a primarily jurisprudential institution into an activist state, one whose will was to be obeyed and fulfilled by its American subjects. "It is indispensable," he wrote the viceroy following the miners' revolt, "to establish and perpetuate in this great community the respect and obedience for the commands of the superior Government, which until now it has not known."[3] Implementation thus required concentration of authority in the executive, administrative function of government and limitation of the traditional influence of local society. As minister of the Indies (1776–1787), Gálvez strove to reorganize the governmental structure accordingly. The intendants he appointed embodied the concept of omnicompetent executives at the intermediary provincial level with no term limit, activists in policy initiatives and implementation to whom local and district officials were wholly subordinate. Finally, given that his confidence in the competence and loyalty of the crown's American subjects bordered on contempt, Gálvez worked determinedly to ensure that *peninsulares* predominated in royal offices.

Nevertheless, the constitutional revolution in the imperial framework remained incomplete. The crown remained above all a judge, an arbiter, rather than the chief executive of an activist state. Moreover, the bureaucrats held on to their power of adjudicating administrative law as it related to their content areas. Thus, the whole royal government from the monarch on down retained the ethos of a jurisprudential institution, even as many of its bureaucrats actively pursued policies that were decidedly metropolitan-centered and metropolitan-led.[4]

That was the rub and the source of growing conflict. The concept remained of the crown as impartial arbiter of the competing interests of its subjects within and among its diverse realms. But the accumulating experience of its New World subjects, amid dislocations arising from the economic and social changes then under way, led to the growing perception that the reality of royal government was otherwise. In its increasingly activist pursuit of changes in economic relations and political structure, the crown seemed to be taking sides on behalf of special interests, its own coffers, and the peninsula, especially its residents migrating to America. Of course, such complaints were not new in the Iberian colonial world. But the degree to which the perception was being pushed by the late eighteenth century was leading more and more American subjects to sense a change in kind was taking place: the royal arbitrator was becoming increasingly more arbitrary.

In Quito, the viceroy of New Granada apparently acted on his own initiative in 1764 in ordering that the *alcabalas* and the monopoly on the sale of aguardiente (liquor) should be placed under direct royal management. Moreover, in doing so he finessed the *audiencia* resident in that city. He also ignored petitions sent by various representatives to set aside the new fiscal measures. When in the resulting popular defiance of authority the following year, *peninsulares* (against the caution of Creoles) insisted on repressing such protest, anti-Spanish feeling came out into the open. The linkage of peninsular interests and royal government became firmly fixed. The expulsion of the Jesuits from the Spanish empire in 1767 later provoked similar reactions to the arbitrariness of royal rule among many American subjects. It came without consultation, without appeal, without even notice, as royal officials rousted the Jesuits from their beds and hustled them away. In several Mexican urban centers, commoners from various racial-cultural groups broke into revolt; their selected targets were *peninsulares*.[5] Paradoxically, the initial loss of faith in the imperial framework by communal villagers in the Peruvian sierra arose from the crown's inaction more than its intervention. Through the first half of the eighteenth century the royal government had steadily lost control of the economy. District officials manipulated the tribute collection and *mita* (Andean equivalent of *repartimiento* labor) labor recruitment and expanded the forced sale of goods for the private gain of themselves and their allies (including collaborators within the villages). With their subsistence security and internal cohesion eroding, the *mitayos* waged judicial struggles (and periodic violent resistance) against the corregidores' authority and mercantile practices. Instead of mediating on their behalf, royal bureaucrats sanctioned the alliance between corregidores and Lima merchants, calculating that the resulting revenues outweighed the abuses. As conditions grew more severe for the Indians, the legitimacy of the imperial framework disintegrated. Many turned to flight to escape the tribute and the *mita*. Many others, in the early 1780s, turned to rebellion.[6]

Mounting Economic Insecurities, Yet Greater Royal Exactions

After 1790 the dynamics weighing on the Spanish imperial framework began to shift. The crescendo of internal changes continued: demographic expansion; migration, especially to the growing provincial cities; commercialization of economic activity; rising proportion of free wage labor. In contrast, the pace of Bourbon economic and administrative reform slackened. Nevertheless, the pressures on the imperial framework—and on the ethos of a royal arbiter, a just parental rule—continued to mount.

Severe economic crises in older core regions of Peru and New Spain sternly tested commoners' ability and confidence to survive in the economic alterations that had taken hold since midcentury. In Upper Peru, drought, the exhaustion of slag heaps, and wartime interruption of mercury supplies induced a prolonged mining crisis beginning in 1801. That reduced demand, and crop failures cut tradable surpluses. Populations dispersed and labor supplies were disrupted, deepening the crisis. Hunger and pestilence spread among the poor, urban and rural alike. Still, royal officials maintained tax pressures at pre-crisis levels or even higher, aggravating the misery of urban and rural commoners. Accelerating vagrancy and violence marked these crisis years, culminating in the ferocious insurrection of the Chirguano Indians in response to food shortages.[7]

The two decades after 1790 were years of mounting insecurities for commoners in central New Spain. Rising maize prices, combined with static (at times, declining) wages, wrought falling real income for rural and urban laborers, whose ranks the continued advance of commercialized agriculture steadily increased. The rural and urban poor of the Bajío region appear to have felt the most threatened. Communal villages were much fewer in number and the rural poor more dependent. With crop prices rising, hacendados raised rents, forced evictions, and reduced payments in wages and kind to workers—all to gain greater control over the factors of production and enhance profits. In urban centers, weavers bore the brunt of the influx of imported textiles after 1802. In nearby mining districts after 1800, rising food and mercury prices led owners to suspend the *partidos* (shares acquired by workers) and lower wages to shore up declining profit margins. Then, in 1809–10, the Bajío's commoners faced economic crises on all fronts. A severe drought devastated crops and eliminated the mine owners' by-then-slim profit margins, leading to massive layoffs. A new wave of textile imports left cottage producers deeper in debt and without sufficient income for subsistence. Mounting popular grievances swelled to an outrage.[8] Many commoners began to question seriously the legitimacy of the colonial order itself. For among the Bajío's rural poor, textile weavers, and mine workers, Father Miguel Hidalgo y Costilla (leader of Mexico's first independence movement, in 1810) would draw his strongest support in his challenge to the entire imperial framework.

Spain's increasing entanglement in European wars in the wake of the French Revolution had more widespread repercussions for the imperial framework. Bourbon economic policies lost the permanence of their intention, as the necessities of war dictated first this course of action and then another. As detailed in Chapter 1, in the short run, certain regions prospered. However, in the long run the dislocations, instabilities, and bottlenecks in the trade networks of the empire destroyed the stability on which sustained economic enterprise depends.

The inconstancy of royal policy brought on by the near continuous European warfare was also felt in fiscal matters. Since the 1760s there had been a series of violent confrontations centered on Bourbon fiscal reforms, which had dislocated and threatened economic interests across the broad spectrum of society: commoners' already scant margin of subsistence and affluent Creoles' loss of profits and restrictions in some opportunities (particularly from royal monopolies). Moreover, American subjects generally had begun to link the intruding fiscal reforms with the growing number of tax collectors, soldiers, shopkeepers, professionals, and merchants arriving from the peninsula. Then, with the renewal of the Napoleonic Wars in 1804 and the royal treasury on the verge of bankruptcy, the Bourbons turned to more precipitous fiscal measures. Affluent Creoles began to feel the burden of royal levies with an unprecedented directness, pervasiveness, and consequence. Special taxes, loans cajoled or coerced, and emergency contributions were directed at the affluent and comfortable, especially in regions undergoing economic crisis where collections from the general populace were not meeting royal expectations.[9]

Were such escalating fiscal exactions fair when such regional economies were being pressed to the limit? Were they prudent? Creoles in particular raised and pondered these questions, as the mounting insecurities of subsistence provoked growing unrest and violence among urban and rural commoners, as racial-social privilege offered less and less immunity from direct royal taxation. The *consolidación de vales reales* (detailed in Chapter 1), threatening loss of property or bankruptcy and ruination of the principal long-term credit system in regional economies, constituted the most profound fiscal shock on the well-to-do. The balance, the reciprocity of peninsular and American interests was becoming badly skewed for the sake of the immediate needs of the metropolis. Ultimately, the colonial social order—and most particularly, the affluent Creoles' privileged place in it—was being put in jeopardy.

Paradoxically, that social order was also being destabilized by one of the few efforts by the crown after 1790 to arbitrate an intensifying conflict within Spanish New World society. Its decree of February 1795 allowed those of mixed blood to purchase legal whiteness, which meant the right to receive advanced education, marry whites, hold public office, and enter holy orders. The Bourbons were responding to the changing socioeconomic reality in the New World: the *castas'* increasing demographic weight, economic importance, and social aspirations for more mobility and equitable treatment. Yet with the intensification of war in Europe, the crown lacked the will and muscle to implement this attempt at social arbitration. Social tensions were heightened even more. *Casta* grievances and aspirations went unfulfilled; Creole fear of social upheaval was magnified, their confidence in royal support of the colonial hierarchy shaken. This frustration was especially high in regions such as coastal Peru and New Granada and above all Venezuela, where the *pardos* (those of mixed blood in northern South America) comprised a large or even principal segment of the population.[10]

By 1808 for Indians, *castas*, and Creoles alike, the Bourbon crown seemed no longer sufficiently protective of their separate interests as a parent ruler, nor sufficiently impartial in mediating conflicts and disputes as an arbiter. First the activist thrust of the Bourbon reformers and then even more the increasingly precipitous wartime policies after 1790 had made the royal government appear more partisan and arbitrary. Various segments of Spanish-American society also increasingly had come to perceive a parent ruler with weakening power and effectiveness. Confidence in the imperial framework was waning at a time when American self-consciousness and self-determination was on the rise.

New Cultural and Political Visions

Since the mid–eighteenth century social and economic grievances had been accumulating; changes in the colonial order had been accelerating. In reaction, New World subjects had begun to see their month-to-month, year-to-year concerns within the broader context of political systems and cultural patterns that constructed and maintained their whole way of life. The mounting immediate concerns of life—material subsistence or prosperity, social relationships and treatment—had reached the point at which Ibero-Americans were being forced to confront the prospect that their regional societies were on the verge of transformation.

Such a realization was far from uniform. It came to American subjects in disparate time frames, locations, social groupings, and family or individual experiences. They gave different weight to the causes for the momentous changes that were invading their lives: increased royal intervention, more fluid social relations, greater elasticity and uncertainty in economic activities, accelerating population growth, and the weakening of cultural norms. Despite the divergence as to cause, a common ground as to effect was emerging. The prerogatives that had maintained space within regional society and the understood and practiced autonomy within the imperial framework were breaking down. That space, that autonomy had previously left the disparate New World groups—in conflict over resources and lifestyles—room to maneuver, accommodate, and adjust among themselves and with the royal government.

Preserving Accustomed Autonomy

In core and transitional regions, the initial and predominant political response was to try to restore the long-accustomed autonomy (and the particular prerogatives it encompassed) that had evolved and accumulated over two centuries. This unwritten, quasi-constitutional arrangement that New World subjects had come to consider permanent, the Bourbons increasingly no longer seemed to honor. In response, growing numbers of Spain's American subjects looked to their past and to local polity to justify that autonomy and eventually to formalize the quasi-constitutional arrangement. Nevertheless, they diverged on the precedent and on the nature of the polity.

For Creoles of means, the precedent was the Iberian medieval *municipio*, in its larger sense, embodied in the *cabildo abierto* (a town/city convocation). The Hapsburg legacy of the sale of offices had made the cabildo itself factional and parochial (even familial) in its interests. Moreover, growing numbers of *peninsulares* were acquiring municipal offices, often with the cooperation of royal officials. The open convocation thus lent not only greater strength in Creole numbers but also greater legitimacy. Only *vecinos* (permanent, propertied residents) could directly participate. Still, all recognized population segments were represented (corporately) by members of the town's prominent families, signifying representation of the whole community.[11]

Iberian medieval towns had acquired charters (bestowing rights, prerogatives, and privileges) that manifested explicit definitions of rights and jurisdictions. In time, they had secured participation in royal policymaking itself, through representation in the Cortes (parliament). The rise of royal absolutism, beginning with the Catholic Kings and continuing with the Hapsburgs, had eroded these constitutional claims.[12] Yet distance and the declining power of the crown had allowed New World *municipios* to regain much of that autonomy in practice, though without formal recognition. The Bourbons were bent on making reality conform to absolutist theory. Creole leaders in American urban centers were being challenged to devise an ideology that would justify and preserve their de facto acquired autonomy.

Central to the Creoles' evolving legal argument was the need to establish limits on royal governmental power. On the one hand, they argued, implementation of royal decrees should take into account a particular locality's moral sensibilities, special circumstances, practices, and customs. On the other hand, royal decrees should be fully justified to the *vecinos* before implementation, through consultation. At the heart of the Creoles' constitutional formulations was the right of direct participation in royal government through negotiation. In this way, Creoles, representing the whole locality through the *cabildo abierto*, would carry its various interests directly to the crown, sharing in deliberations of policy and law when they pertained to local concerns.[13]

Urban common people also sought political participation and negotiation, but they did so from a different perspective. They had no distant "precedents"; they were the by-product of the colonial mixing of three races. Their ideology, as it was loosely propounded, was based on accumulated experience alone, which had nurtured a belief in a community that coexisted in two realms. As subjects of the crown, they recognized the imperial state and its overall authority over their locality, including its taxing power. At the same time, they believed that their community existed outside the imperial state, with its own customs and conventions. Their constitutional notions lay, above all, in their attitudes about the proper coexistence of these two realms.

The particular patterns of their community's life had been forged (or if imposed, then manipulated and adapted) to accomplish several ends: to secure access to local resources for subsistence; to maintain an adequate level of fairness and impartiality in resolving conflicts; and to express and celebrate a lifestyle that affirmed their identity as members of the community. When the imperial state imposed taxes too suddenly or onerously, when royal officials overstepped their bounds by compelling innovations or pursuing undue personal gain, when royal decrees sought to exert greater control over social behavior and cultural expression, then such intrusions crossed a threshold of forbearance that was unstated but understood by the urban populace. The threshold varied among communities (often among neighborhoods in the cities).

When the point of tolerance was passed, urban commoners acted with forethought and within defined patterns. Barred from formal political participation, they relied on intimidation and manipulation of those whom they viewed as responsible for restoring to acceptable bounds the unstated compact that linked their community to the imperial state. Above all, this meant local officials, whether royal or municipal. Assemblies of protest conveyed the commoners' numbers and hostility. Violence was employed discriminately, with damage more likely to be inflicted on property than on persons. Attacks against targeted people were generally aimed to intimidate and humiliate, not to kill or maim. Only when desired vengeance overwhelmed this strategy did wanton slaughter occur. Expulsion from the community was the most common severe sanction.[14]

After 1750, when the line was drawn in the commoners' minds between empire and community, Creoles were judged as local people, *peninsulares* as outsiders. Commoners preferred that prominent Creoles serve as intermediaries in resisting royal intrusion, deferring to their leadership or coopting them. When the alliance could no longer hold—almost always because Creoles feared that social controls were loosening beyond the danger point—urban commoners sometimes went on alone, which usually ended in the royal officials' harsh repression of their own leaders.[15]

Commoners in the Indian villages of the core regions of New Spain and Peru shared this ambivalence toward their social betters. Only there, race and culture were common ground, leaving the division largely the function of hereditary privilege and wealth. Mounting social and economic pressures on common villagers were aggravating the grudges and grievances they held against their leaders and noble families. Yet even as these three social elements of the village were being absorbed more and more into the commercial market and Hispanic society—commoners out of necessity, hereditary chiefs and nobles out of profit—they sought to uphold the autonomy and separate identity of the community as it had been passed down to them. All shared (to some degree) in dependence on the traditional, prescriptive rights to community resources, despite the growing inroads of privatization. Autonomy was their principal guarantee of control over those resources. A distinct racial-ethnic identity was the principal basis for the claim of hereditary chiefs and nobles as leaders of the community. For village commoners, it was the underpinning for maintaining autonomy and sociocultural solidarity.[16]

This more distinct racial-ethnic identity (compared to that of the far more Hispanicized urban commoners) and the countryside's greater isolation combined to magnify the villagers' sense of the externality of the imperial state. Community autonomy was closer to bordering on sovereignty. Yet villagers possessed an important measure of formal participation that set them apart from urban commoners. As direct members of a corporate body politic, they could engage in legal appeals—along with the resort to disorders—to challenge royal authorities.

The villagers' links to the past underlay this constitutional sense of their place within the imperial framework. A balance of rights and obligations had existed between Peruvian commoners and the Inca state (and lesser state societies before), through a hierarchy of *curaca* (Quechua term, used interchangeably with *cacique*, for governing hereditary native lords) intermediaries. The colonial world had only partially erased that memory. It had left the *curaca* hierarchy largely intact, making the Spanish imperial state appear more distant (even abstract). In New Spain, only local village leaders remained (increasingly as elected cabildo officials), and Hispanicization had made strong inroads through the course of the eighteenth century. The collective village memory tended to extend no further back than the sixteenth century, when villagers were given their grants of communal lands and right of self-government. In the midst of accelerating change, they sought to restore the balance of rights and obligations between their ethnically distinct, autonomous community (enshrined in royal law during the post-Conquest years) and the distant imperial state.[17]

Calls for reform of the imperial framework in Brazil were more forward-looking, but the numbers advocating them were more limited. The Portuguese crown had neither intervened as extensively nor placed nearly as heavy a fiscal burden. Yet economic stagnation in the late eighteenth century prompted a small but growing number of intellectuals to criticize the existing imperial arrangement. Their ideological foundation lay in the ideas of the Enlightenment that had been increasingly finding their way into Brazil. Although most called for an end to restrictions, monopolies, and taxes that burdened economic activities, all but a few remained vague in their support of alleviating the plight of Indians and African slaves. However, most did emphatically advocate ambitious plans for educational reform and expansion. Politically, there was near unanimity on one issue: Brazil's economic and demographic predominance, attained through the course of the eighteenth century, made imperative the improvement of its status within the imperial framework.[18] Though the limited evidence available suggests that such reformist sentiment was not yet widespread and did not arouse the militant protest that emerged in so many regions in Spanish America, radical visions for the future of Ibero-America did surface in Brazil as well.

Radical Visions

Though reformist sentiment dominated the political thought and actions of Ibero-Americans responding to what they perceived as a growing inequity in imperial relations and disequilibrium within colonial society, radical, even revolutionary visions were emerging, especially after 1790. Those conceiving and endorsing them wished to alter fundamentally the imperial framework that had long ruled them and relations within their regional societies. Some looked backward to recover what had been. Most looked forward to create what had never been.

In New Spain's peripheral regions, Indians were envisioning a New World without white people. They retained a strong tribal identity and had not been part of large state societies when the Conquest had taken place. Most had been pacified by missionaries and had faced accelerating encroachment of Hispanic settlers through the eighteenth century. None of these movements succeeded, but they aroused official concern and considerable fear among many whites. In some cases, they were precedents for the nineteenth century. For Indians in the northern areas that ringed the central core (from Tepic in the west to the Huasteca in the east), the ideological reference point was the prophesied coming of a millennium, not the restoration of a pre-Columbian past. There, the vision of an Indian messiah king became common among a large number of villagers. Replacing the Spanish monarch, he would lead the expulsion (or even vengeful murder) of whites. The long years of oppression, compounded by the recent economic crises, would cease. Yet many of these Indian villagers, ambivalent about those of European ancestry, focused their hostility on the relatively few and unprotected *peninsulares*.[19]

Such Indian visions of an alternative to colonial society were almost wholly self-generated and parochial. By contrast, the radical and revolutionary visions that surfaced among other racial-cultural groups were externally grounded and far more inclusive. Their demands for eliminating injustices included provisions for other groups and cut across status lines. The revolutions in France and the United States proclaimed universal and inclusive principles of legal and political relations. Of the two, the ideology of the French Revolution was more influential, in particular its Declaration of the Rights of Man. Moreover, Enlightenment ideas had been filtering into creole libraries, gatherings of literary salons and economic societies, and journalistic tracts. They provoked a growing chorus of criticisms of the Iberian imperial frameworks, as they engendered heightened self-awareness and self-confidence in things American and cognizance of and admiration for the "progressive" nations of the North Atlantic. University graduates played a pivotal role. Those from American universities were participants in or heirs to modern scientific education's successful challenge to scholasticism. Those who studied abroad were direct conduits for the revolutionary ideas permeating the intellectual circles of Europe, especially after 1790.

It was one thing to criticize the status quo, quite another to envision and proclaim a new political order. As individuals and more consequentially in small cells, a limited number of creole intellectuals elevated specific complaints—the lack of economic progress, of intellectual and educational advancement, of equality with *peninsulares*, and of access to political office—to constitutional issues. They did so on the premise that only independence would ensure the resolution of such grievances. Still, there was considerable disagreement about what was to take the place of the imperial framework and the colonial order it had fostered.

In Minas Gerais, intellectuals in Ouro Priêto tried to apply imported revolutionary ideology to the Brazilian reality. Some of the wealthiest Creoles feared the prospective collection of their sizable debts to the royal treasury. The two came together in the Mineira Conspiracy (the *Inconfidencia*) of 1789. In New Granada, an important group of radical intellectuals resented the entrenched occupants of university chairs (largely peninsular and defenders of scholasticism), especially since the latter had linked the accepted European view of America's ecological inferiority with the peninsular appraisal of Americans. They did gradually obtain academic positions, and royal botanical expeditions did support their research. But they came to view imperial institutional structures as the main barrier to scientific advancement, merging scientific and political independence. They dominated the conspiracy of 1794 led by Antonio Nariño.[20]

Though well-focused on the issue of complete self-government, these radical creole visions became blurred on issues of social justice. Not so for *casta* visionaires in transitional regions where African ancestry was the dominant element in *mestisaje* (racial intermixing). The French Revolution and the example of the Haitian Revolution firmly joined independence and economic freedom with legal equality and the abolition of all forms of servitude. The principles of "liberty, equality, and fraternity" had poignant meaning for those who sought inclusion and mobility within the larger American society.

The young mulatto leaders of the Bahia Conspiracy (1798) equated republicanism with equality for all and held abolition of slavery as a necessary prerequisite for both. A year earlier, in La Guaira (the coastal port for Caracas), *pardos* and poor whites, laborers and small proprietors proclaimed a broad-ranging program springing from the ideals of the French Revolution, including a republic, free trade, an end to egregious taxes, abolition of slavery and Indian tribute, land distribution to Indian villagers, and racial harmony. In another Venezuelan district (Coro, in 1794), free blacks were inspired by the Haitian example to lead a revolt by sugar cane workers, both slaves and free. For slaves generally, Haiti represented an important ideological reorientation. Previously, they had sought to re-create independent African communities by removing to more inaccessible areas. Now, this restorationist ideology was giving way to a vision of becoming full participants in a democratic, market-driven society. Haiti represented a uniquely African-American version (albeit in some facets distorted) of such societies then arising in the North Atlantic.[21]

Multistrata Resistance

Violent disorders had been a part of colonial society in Ibero-America from the beginning. The conquistadores had resisted royal efforts to control and then phase out encomiendas. Newly conquered or pacified Amerindians had tried to reverse increasing encroachment and control. Slaves had rebelled and sought refuge in *cimarrones* (outlaw camps) or independent maroon communities. Indian communities had staged uprisings to defend or reclaim lands or resist repartimiento exactions. Urban *castas*, poor whites, and Indians had rioted over food shortages and what they deemed unwarranted taxes. The novelty of the violent disorders after 1750 lay in their greater frequency, their enlarging purpose, and their altering composition.[22]

Most unique and significant was the social composition of a growing number of these disorders. Almost always before, violent action had been undertaken singularly by racial-cultural groups. But after 1750, there began to appear civil disorders whose participants were from different social strata. The leadership usually came from either a loose alliance of leaders from their respective groups or a hierarchy of these leaders deferring to Creoles at the top. But there were cases where the leadership core was of mixed racial and social background. The spatial dimensions of these multistrata disorders generally did not extend beyond the bounds of the community, but in the contexts of important urban centers such as Quito and Popoyán participants constituted quite a large number. Moreover, the potential for regional or multiregional rebellions was growing. In two instances they materialized.

The Tupac Amarú rebellion (early 1780s), which encompassed much of the Peruvian sierra, had a racially and occupationally diverse command. Most numerous among the followers were Indian villagers. The rebellion's leader, mestizo muleteer and provincial *curaca* José Gabriel Condorcanqui, who took the name of Inca ruler Tupac Amarú, appealed to them orally and covertly in a somewhat clouded vision of an Inca nationalism. But his public proclamations to recruit *casta*, Creole, and Hispanicized Indian followers called for imperial reform, especially in fiscal matters. In 1781, residents of towns and cities across the eastern sierra of New Granada and further eastward into the llanos joined a rebellion led by Creoles. The *Comunero* Revolt began as a cluster of riots against new controls over the production and sale of tobacco and aguardiente and the revision of the sales tax. Creole leadership then joined these community disorders into a multiregional revolt with a broad program of imperial reform, including the grievances of urban commoners and Indian villagers.[23]

In both major revolts (along with more numerous multistrata civil disorders at the local level), various racial-cultural groups found common ground. Opposition to increasing fiscal burdens and hostility toward *peninsulares* drew an important line that delineated royal officials and *peninsulares* more and more as aggrandizing outsiders. Nevertheless, this unity proved ephemeral throughout the first years of the nineteenth century. The disparities and contradictions of the groups' concerns and aspirations could be reconciled only temporarily. The breaking point for compromise was invariably short for Creoles. Less willing to bear the brunt of royal repression, even more they feared the social disorder that might ensue if control were lost.

Royal officials understood the danger of the centripetal forces bringing these social strata together to challenge Spanish domination over colonial life. But they also exploited the centrifugal pressures undermining these coalitions. They played upon creole fears of racially directed violence by highlighting acts of licentious barbarism verging on caste warfare. Royal authorities often met commoners' specific demands temporarily. Then, securing sufficient armed force, they imposed lenient punishment on creole followers (even their leaders) while brutally repressing nonwhite (or poor white) leaders. They sought to blur the American-peninsular line and heighten that which separated the white and well-to-do from the predominantly nonwhite general populace.

There were no more regional, multistrata rebellions after the early 1780s. The Bourbons increased their vigilance and military strength in the important economic and administrative centers of the Spanish empire. In regions where popular violence had exceeded their acceptable limits and confirmed their fears, affluent Creoles pulled back from taking direct action. Yet, creole criticisms and calls for reform continued to mount, as did the fiscal levies of the crown necessitated by years of almost continual warfare. The rising discontent of commoners—rural and urban—went on unabated. Radical visions gained more adherents. Revolutionary conspiracies appeared; and though scattered and ineffectual, they were increasing in number.

Still, most American subjects, though opposed to growing Bourbon intrusion into their lives, had not yet set themselves irrevocably against the imperial system. Their loyalty and test of the royal government's legitimacy came to rest increasingly on the monarchy itself. More and more, they questioned their parent ruler's impartiality and benevolence, even though they still separated the abuses of crown agents from the monarchy itself. Then, suddenly, in 1808 that critical link disappeared for Spain's New World subjects. Napoleon invaded the Iberian peninsula, forcing the abdication of first Charles IV and then of his son Ferdinand VII in favor of Napoleon's brother.

Most of Spain's American subjects were now at a crossroads, both ideologically and pragmatically. Should they seize this opportunity to expand the autonomy that the Bourbons had eroded and secure it formally through reform of the imperial framework? Or should they move toward complete separation? For Creoles, the basis for their answer rested upon the strength and confidence in their American identity, the degree of economic imperative, and their judgment on their ability to control the social order. Urban and rural commoners considered, above all, the desperateness of their material situation, along with their perceptions of the weakness of the imperial state and of the divisions among the prominent and powerful.[24]

Those in the New World seeking reform of the Portuguese imperial framework did not face this crossroads—at least not yet. Aided by the British navy, King John VI moved the royal court to Rio de Janeiro; Brazil became the center of the empire. Reform became more acceptable to the crown, even necessary.

The Imperial Contradiction

Spain's New World subjects were not alone in finding themselves at a crossroads. The vacuum at the top of the imperial framework created an opportunity for those in Spain who sought to apply to the monarchy the liberal political ideals deriving from the Enlightenment. But it had also left all Spaniards in a predicament: how to reconcile American demands for autonomy and parity within the imperial framework with the benefits of their colonial relationship with the New World, especially the trade monopoly. Both the opportunity and the predicament created deep, open divisions in the peninsula that compounded the disequilibrium in the imperial framework set in motion by Napoleon's invasion. They raised American expectations of the possibilities for either reform or separation, while they increased American frustrations through the inconsistency and uncertainty of the peninsula's response.

Peninsular and American Ambivalence

At least one reformer had foreseen this peninsular predicament and put forth a visionary scheme to circumvent it. In 1783, Pedro Pablo

Abarca de Bolea, the Conde de Aranda, one of Charles III's principal ministers, secretly proposed an imperial commonwealth. He did so fearing that an expansionist Anglo-American republic would pick apart the vast and overcentralized Spanish-American empire. His solution entailed the creation of three independent and sovereign American kingdoms, linked to Spain through royal marriages, commercial reciprocity, and military alliance.[25] The consensus among Bourbon policymakers—an enlightened, more active monarchy, controlling the entities within the empire more directly—was almost diametrically opposed to the Conde de Aranda's visionary scheme.

But in 1808, with the monarchy in abeyance, that governing consensus quickly disintegrated. Spanish liberals, suddenly making their presence felt, eagerly sought an end to the absolute, patrimonial monarchy, limiting the crown's power through an elected *cortes* and constitutionally guaranteed rights. Desperate for continuing American support in trade and revenues in the struggle against the French army, they successfully lobbied first the Junta Central and then the Regency Council to endorse the autonomy and nominal equality of territorial units within the empire.[26] In particular, they recognized the royal government's sudden vulnerability in the New World and Americans' growing resentment of the Bourbon imperial system. News from America between 1808 and 1810 readily confirmed these worries.

The by now widespread desire among Spain's American subjects to depose *peninsulares* in all levels of royal offices up to (and, in some cases, including) the viceroy quickly manifested itself. Creoles moved to oust them from cabildo offices, especially where they had gained dominance in recent decades. In some cities where higher royal officials sought compromise with Creoles, *peninsulares* staged preemptive coups of their own, most notably succeeding in Mexico City and Montevideo but failing in Buenos Aires and Santiago. The decisive turn came in the spring of 1810, when news arrived that the French had occupied most of southern Spain, including Seville. Whether in an initial attempt or where they had been previously thwarted, Creoles— through *cabildo abiertos* or outright revolt, backed by militias or popular forces—established governing juntas, most of which in turn set up representative assemblies, some drawing up constitutions. Only in New Spain, the Caribbean islands, Peru, and Upper Peru did royal officials retain control. There, royal troops and creole fears of social disorder were sufficient—for the time being.[27]

Yet, among the large numbers of those who were united in their desire to end the *peninsulares'* control of government in their localities and regions, there was fundamental disagreement. A minority of

Creoles, supported by many *castas*, opted for outright sovereignty. But they had prevailed only in Buenos Aires (and interior provinces) and New Granada, and even there, they did not proclaim outright independence. The majority of Creoles, with varying degrees of popular support, sought temporary self-rule until the monarch's return, using the principle of reversion of sovereignty cited by those in the peninsula as well. In the interim, they pursued negotiating a new imperial framework that would make autonomy formal and permanent, basing their hopes on a peninsular invitation to send representatives to a constituent *cortes*.[28]

At the opening of the Cortes in September 1810, American representatives called for a full constitutional commitment to the equality of territorial units within the empire. Within a month the Cortes declared a single monarchy and a unitary empire in which Americans were to be equal, not a federative empire in which they had guaranteed autonomy within their region and parity in imperial relations. That constituted a crucial change for Spain's New World subjects, not only from the Bourbons' imperial system most Americans despised but also from the pre-1750 de facto autonomous relations most sought to restore and expand. Not only relations within the new unitary empire but also the very structures of government, political and social rights, and economic policies within the American territories would be negotiated and settled by representatives in the Cortes. Elected representatives in a legislative body, not corporate petitions to an impartial absolute monarch, would determine the New World's future. The ramifications of that fact gave many Creoles pause to reconsider their constitutional position in the following years.

Representation, then, became the lynchpin on which rested American hopes for parity within the empire. The separate issue of autonomy was subordinated to the specific terms of parity. Implementation of equality in representation was immediately addressed by American delegates to the Cortes. But the peninsula's representatives were unwilling to risk losing domination over its American territories. New World population was about 50 percent greater than that of the peninsula (15–16 million, versus 10.5 million), but the Cortes' terms had left the Americans with only half as many delegates: one for every 100,000 inhabitants, versus one for every 50,000 for their peninsular counterparts. The peninsular rationale made the distinction between being free and equal inhabitants of the empire and being subjects. Full rights went only to those Americans whose ancestry could be traced to either the peninsula or the Spanish New World: Creoles, peninsular immigrants, and Indians. With such a large number of American inhabitants excluded (free blacks and *castas* with any African ancestry), peninsular delegates could then readily accept the principle that delegates on both sides of the Atlantic represented an equal number of "enumerated" citizens. Thus a minority at the drafting of the Constitution of 1812, creole delegates could only voice their strong objections. And even there, the underlying prejudices and fears regarding the *castas* tempered their argument and weakened their cohesion.[29]

The prejudicial resolution of the representation issue was the first of an unfolding series of manifestations of the inherent ideological contradiction of the imperial framework, despite its cosmetic reformation. For though parity had now been declared official, even constitutional, no succeeding peninsular government would implement it for fear of losing the material and psychological benefits of metropolitan control. Nor would any peninsular regime repeal that declaration of equality. That would have damaged American-peninsular relations irreparably. Even as popular insurgency became more widespread (beginning in 1810) and as retention of the support of moderate Creoles became increasingly imperative, peninsular bureaucrats and politicians would not budge.

The peninsular majority in the Cortes was simply unwilling to institute parity in appointments and economic opportunity (be it free trade or the abolition of restrictions on production). Ferdinand VII went the Spanish liberals one further. Though welcomed by most upon his return in 1814, he soon revealed his unwillingness to give up absolute power, returning the empire to its pre-1808 status. However, even he could not declare his American subjects officially inferior. Nevertheless, he made the reality clear enough. Hard-line bureaucrats were back in control by 1818. Widespread repression of insurgency was carried out by royal agents, reinforced by the large-scale commitment of royal troops freed by the new peace in Europe. A liberal revolt in 1820 briefly restored the constitutional monarchy. But that restoration and the second return to absolutism that followed in 1823 simply reprised the imperial contradiction.[30]

Delayed Contradiction in Brazil

The imperial contradiction confronted Brazilians in a delayed and more singular manner. The circumstances there were unique. The arrival of Prince John (ruling as regent until the death of his aged and demented mother) marked the first and only time that a European monarch ruled an empire from one of the colonies rather than the metropolis. John VI, recognizing that Brazil had become demographically and economically the dominant element in the Portuguese empire, readily agreed to the equal treatment of Brazilians. In the economic arena, free trade was declared (but with commercial privileges for Britain, his chief benefactor), the prohibition against manufacturing was lifted, the Banco de Brasil was established, and royal committees were created to promote economic activity. With regard to culture, institutes of higher learning were founded, primary education was expanded, and a library was inaugurated. As to government, Prince John declared Brazil a kingdom coequal in status with Portugal in the empire in 1815.[31] Brazilians had achieved largely through circumstance the constitutional parity coveted by Americans in Spain's empire. But not without a price.

Brazilians bore the royal court's expenses and its costly military expeditions against the Spanish-held and then insurgent Banda Oriental (1811 and 1816). British pressure to restrict the slave trade impaired the interests of sugar, cotton, and coffee producers. Portuguese immigrants continued to monopolize the royal bureaucracy. General prosperity and the new status of parity mitigated against these sources of disaffection. Radical Creoles in Recife did lead an unsuccessful insurrection (joined by those in Alagoas and Paraíba) to establish an independent republic in the northeast. But the successful challenge to the new imperial framework instead came from the metropolis, encouraged by and paralleling the Spanish experience. Liberals in Portugal, wanting to establish a constitutional monarchy, convoked a *cortes* (the last one having been adjourned at the end of the seventeenth century). With representation skewed in the metropolis's favor, the Portuguese majority dismantled the new imperial parity. They demanded that John VI return to Lisbon, abolished most royal agencies established overseas, established provincial governing bodies directly dependent upon Lisbon, and deposed the few Brazilians holding royal offices. They reintroduced restrictions on trade and reinforced Brazilian garrisons with Portuguese troops. When the Cortes ordered the return of Prince Pedro, who had been left by his father as regent, he and many creole leaders joined forces to declare an independent, constitutional empire in Brazil.[32]

Independence had largely been thrust upon Portugal's New World subjects. Unlike in Spain, the parent-ruler had endorsed parity within the empire, yielding to the practicalities of circumstance and the sentiments of Brazilians. And what peninsular parliamentary representatives in Spain granted nominally out of necessity, their counterparts in Portugal were quick to reverse, having seen the reality of imperial parity at work.

Dislocations

Whether victims of circumstance or shortsightedness, neither the Spanish nor the Portuguese were able to arrest the gathering forces of American self-determination. Except for the islands of Cuba and Puerto Rico, they lost all. For their former American subjects, becoming first autonomous and then independent after 1810, region by region, the struggles for self-determination had been both within as well as without. They resulted in dislocations that were economic and social as well as political, sought and unintended, desired and unwelcome. These dislocations both accelerated the transformation of colonial society that had begun in the 1750s and set in motion new currents and possibilities for altering the new societal order now crystallizing.

Direct Links with the International Market

The quarter century of war climaxing in Napoleon's invasion had steadily eroded the monopolistic Iberian trade networks. Out of expediency, Spain had acceded to trade with neutrals, the Portuguese crown in Brazil to free trade. Wherever Spain's American subjects achieved autonomy, the monopoly was broken temporarily. With independence, each American territory made free trade permanent, securing a direct link with the world market centered in the newly industrializing nations of the North Atlantic. Most commercial producers of primary products and merchants not directly linked to the peninsular trade had sought or welcomed this fundamental realignment of their regional economies. It offered the incentive of accelerating expansion of markets for agricultural production and the extraction of other primary resources, especially for regions on or easily accessible to the coast, and with adequate levels of security. For merchants, the growth in exports, enlarged source of imports, and lowering of import prices through more competition held out the prospect of an expanded volume of trade to distribute.

However, with the world market came those from the North Atlantic countries who dominated its credit and distribution networks. North American, English, French, and other European traders quickly established themselves in the ports, capitals, and other important urban centers. British merchants, in particular, forming sizable colonies in some ports, were able to offer more varied (and generally more reliable) shipping arrangements, more favorable credit terms, and better prices on imports. Ibero-American merchants found the opportunity to control the intermediary distribution and shipping trade rapidly slipping from their grasp. Moreover, they faced stiff, growing competition in the wholesale trade within their regions.[33]

The independence struggles also generated dislocations within the regional societies themselves. Existing economic patterns, whether holdovers from the colonial order or those that had emerged in the late eighteenth century, were disrupted. Capital was lost. Crops, livestock, mining equipment, and commercial inventories were destroyed or stolen. Many fleeing royalists took their money with them. Labor markets were disrupted through recruitment for military service, emigration from enemy-held areas, and escape from varying degrees of forced labor (most notably from bondage). Interregional economic relations that had begun to flourish after 1776 were undermined. With insurgents and royalists vying for control, regions were increasingly cut off from one another. This situation, combined with the proliferating foreign contacts, fostered the direct linkage of each region (whether with independent status separately or as part of a larger national entity) with the world market.

Weakened Lines of Status and Authority

Social distinctions among commoners were simplified and became less rigid and formal between them and those above. There was a commitment made to legal equality, either from the need to recruit soldiers or to secure popular support, from a sincere ideological belief in republicanism and libertarianism, or to prevent social unrest from boiling over (especially given the independence struggle's unleashing of racial caste antagonisms, with devastating consequences in some regions). The enslavement of Africans was abolished gradually in most regions, with some notable exceptions (in Peru and Venezuela after a generation; in Brazil in 1888). The legal inequities imposed upon those of mixed blood were removed. The *tributo* (a special poll tax) levied on most nonwhites was abolished (but was reinstated in Peru and Bolivia for several decades to rescue depleted treasuries). Among the wealthy and those of comfortable means, social mobility increased principally because of political dislocations.

Colonial political structures were dismantled during the independence struggles. The Spanish Constitution of 1812 established the precedent for division of governmental powers and election of a wide range of officeholders. These two fundamental alterations were carried to their fullest extent in most new nations with the adoption of republican representative government, operated concurrently at several levels. Politics replaced administration as the main dynamic of government. Politicians became the managers of the state apparatus. Bureaucrats became functionaries increasingly removed from decisionmaking. In the wake of these revolutionary changes in government, opportunity proliferated. Public posts multiplied. Governmental rules and controls loosened. Access to (and resulting competition for) resources and markets expanded rapidly. Not only was the whole idea of government and its purpose profoundly altered, but the personnel changed along with it. The large majority of veteran Spanish bureaucrats were gone from their posts within a few years following independence, voluntarily or not.[34]

Political dislocations also resulted from the militarization of society. The Bourbons, in creating a large colonial army comprising regulars and militia, had enhanced their prestige and influence by bestowing upon them the *fuero militar*, the right of trial by their superior officers over a broad range of criminal and civil charges. The insurgency enlarged not only the numbers of men under arms but also their power and influence in public affairs. The armies inherited by the new national entities were composed of men hardened by the experience of migration, conflict, and in many cases social mobility—veterans bound together largely on the basis of personal loyalty and mutual self-interest. A most important consequence of these political dislocations—in structure, personnel, and military power—was the greatly expanded opportunity they created for newcomers to enter the political arena. Some came as claimants to government office or to the political power over those who occupied such posts, often with the personal following or armed clout to back up their claims. Others simply sought to sway government to protect or promote their interests.

The independence struggles had also brought alterations in Ibero-Americans' larger sense of themselves. Their loyalty to an empire of peoples bound together through cultural ties, a shared historical experience, and a parent-ruler arbitrating disputes among them fairly, had steadily eroded. It had given way to a sense of nationhood that was clear to a very few, nonexistent to many, and vague at best to most.

What had remained constant—indeed, what had intensified—was the reality of their separate regional societies. Geography still divided more it united them. The intendancy administrative system imposed in the late eighteenth century had given formal recognition to these regional identities and loyalties. Though insurgent armies had swept back and forth across large imperial administrative territories, regional boundaries remained the most real in the ordering of people's lives. And contact with the larger world beyond no longer needed to be filtered through intermediary governmental realms. The world market and its agents were quickly making entrance and forging direct links with the regional societies, even those more remote if there were commodities that could yield a profit.

Notes

1. Timthy E. Anna, "Spain and the Breakdown of the Imperial Ethos: The Problem of Equality," *HAHR* 62 (May 1982): 254–56.
2. Cuello, "Saltillo," 307–16; Danks, "Labor Revolt," 150–65; Brading, *Miners and Merchants*, 233–34.
3. *Archivo General de Indias*, Mexico 1365, Gálvez to Croix, September 24, 1767, in Brading, *Miners and Merchants*, 235.
4. Brading, *Miners and Merchants*, 45–47, 63–92; Arnold, *Bureaucrats in Mexico City*, 28–47; Stanley J. Stein, "Bureaucracy and Business in the Spanish Empire, 1759–1804: Failure of a Bourbon Reform in Mexico and Peru," *HAHR* 61 (February 1981), 7–12, 21–27.
5. MacFarlane, "Urban Insurrection in Bourbon Quito," 285–91, 300, 309–13; Brading, *Miners and Merchants*, 27, 234–35; Kendall Brown, *Bourbons and Brandy: Imperial Reform in Eighteenth Century Arequipa* (Albuquerque: University of New Mexico Press, 1986), 156–58.
6. Larson, *Agrarian Transformation*, 123–32; Stavig, "Rural Cuzco," 741–62.
7. Enrique Tandeter, "Crisis in Upper Peru, 1800–1815," *HAHR* 71 (February 1991): 49–56, 66–69.
8. Arij Ouweneel and Catrien C. J. H. Bijleveld, "The Economic Cycle in Bourbon Central Mexico: A Critique of the Recaudación del Diezmo Líquido en Pesos," *HAHR* 69 (August 1989): 479–530, and the "Comments" of David Brading, 531–38; John Tutino, *From Insurrection to Revolution in Mexico: Social Bases of Agrarian Violence, 1750–1940* (Princeton, NJ: Princeton University Press, 1986), 79–100, 119–26; Eric Van Young, "Millennium on the Northern Marches: The Mad Messiah of Durango and Popular Rebellion in Mexico, 1800–1815," *CSSH* 28 (July 1986): 387, 407–10.
9. Anthony MacFarlane, "Civil Disorders and Popular Protests in Late Colonial New Granada," *HAHR* 64 (February 1984): 17–54; Cuello, "Saltillo," 316–21; Larson, *Agrarian Transformation*, 291–93; Burkholder and Johnson, *Colonial Latin America*, 290–93.
10. John Lynch, *The Spanish-American Revolutions, 1808–1826* (New York: Norton, 1973), 19–24, 190–94.
11. MacFarlane, "Urban Insurrection in Bourbon Quito," 287–293, 297.
12. Jaime Vicens Vives, *Approaches to the History of Spain* (Berkeley: University of California, 1970); Vicens Vives, *Manuel de historia económica de España* (Barcelona: Editorial Vicens Vives, 1965); and Richard Herr, *The Eighteenth Century in Spain* (Princeton, NJ: Princeton University Press, 1958).
13. MacFarlane, "Urban Insurrection in Bourbon Quito," 298.
14. Ibid., 307, 315–21, 327–29; MacFarlane, "Civil Disorders and Popular Protests," 37–43, 50–54.
15. MacFarlane, "Civil Disorders and Popular Protests."
16. Van Young, "Moving toward Revolt," 183–85, 197–99; Van Young, "Conflict and Solidarity in Indian Village Life: The Guadalajara Region in the Late

Colonial Period," *HAHR* 64 (February 1984): 67–69; Chance, *Conquest of the Sierra*, 131–46.

17. Stavig, "Rural Cuzco," 740–54, 767–70; Cheryl E. Martin, "Haciendas and Villages in Late Colonial Morelos," *HAHR* 62 (August 1982): 417–20.

18. Burns, *Brazil*, 132–39.

19. Roberto Salmón, "A Marginal Man: Luis of Saric and the Pima Revolt of 1751," *The Americas* 45 (July 1988): 61–77; Farriss, "Cosmology among the Maya," 575–79, 583–89; Van Young, "Millennium on the Northern Marches," 401–13.

20. Burns, *Brazil*, 122–24, 139–40; Burkholder and Johnson, *Colonial Latin America*, 256; Thomas F. Glick, "Science and Independence in Latin America (with Special Reference to New Granada)," *HAHR* 71 (May 1991): 310–33; Lynch, *Spanish-American Revolutions*, 232–34.

21. Burns, *Brazil*, 140–42; Lynch, *Spanish-American Revolutions*, 192–93; John H. Coatsworth, "Patterns of Rural Rebellion in Latin America: Mexico in Comparative Perspective," in *Riots, Rebellions, and Insurrections: Rural Social Conflict in Mexico*, ed. Friedrich Katz (Princeton, NJ: Princeton University Press, 1986), 56.

22. MacFarlane, "Civil Disorders and Popular Protests," and the contributors to *Riots, Rebellions, and Insurrections* stress the growing frequency in these incidents of collective violence.

23. Leon G. Campbell, "Social Structure of the Tupac Amarú Army in Cuzco, 1780–1781," *HAHR* 61 (November 1981), 679–92; MacFarlane, "Civil Disorders and Popular Protests," 18–22; John L. Phelan, *The People and the King: The Comunero Revolution in Colombia, 1781* (Madison: University Press of Wisconsin, 1978).

24. Tutino, *From Insurrection to Revolution*, 99–212.

25. Arnold, *Bureaucrats in Mexico City*, 12–13.

26. Ibid., 8, 15, 59; Anna, "Breakdown of Imperial Ethos," 256–57.

27. Larson, *Agrarian Transformation*, 290–94.

28. Lynch, *Spanish-American Revolutions*, 43–45, 49–55, 90–92, 106–7, 117–20, 131–33, 194–95, 235–39, 303–8. New Spain's popular insurrection, led by priests Miguel Hidalgo and José María Morelos y Pavón, was supported by some Creoles (including important leaders of the movement). But its excesses of violence and its socioeconomic reforms so alarmed most Creoles that they begrudgingly supported the royalist government for a decade.

29. Anna, "Breakdown of Imperial Ethos," 257–61.

30. Ibid., 261–71.

31. Burns, *Brazil*, 144–49; L. Brown, "Rio de Janeiro in the Internal Economy," 7–8.

32. Burns, *Brazil*, 142–44, 149, 151–57; Burkholder and Johnson, *Colonial Latin America*, 312–14.

33. Cooney, "Oceanic Commerce and Platine Merchants," 522–24; Hans Vogel, "New Citizens for a New Nation: Naturalization in Early Independent Argentina," *HAHR* 71 (February 1991): 126–27; Karen Racine, "A Community of Purpose: British Cultural Influence during the Spanish American Wars for Independence," in *English-Speaking Communities in Latin America*, ed. Oliver Marshall (London: Macmillan, 2000), 25–28.

34. Arnold, *Bureaucrats in Mexico City*, 47–49, 56–57, 67–80, 83, 109–11, 124–29; Vogel, "Naturalization in Early Argentina," 110–11, 117–25; Stanley Green, *The Mexican Republic: The First Decade, 1823–1832* (Pittsburgh: University of Pittsburgh Press, 1987), 140–48, 165–66.

3

The Regional Ethos

The colonial order that had governed and shaped the lives of Latin Americans for more than three centuries had broken down by the 1820s. For the better part of a century, that societal order had undergone radical economic and social change. Growing instability had culminated in a decade of successful insurgency. The penetration of a world market system centered in western Europe was now unfettered by imperial filtration and was intensifying through its own transition into industrial capitalism. In the midst of that disintegration, a new society had emerged, one quite distinct from its predecessor. There were continuities—most notably, the regional orientation and the strongly hierarchical ordering of society. But within these two larger constructs, the workings of society had been fundamentally altered, indeed, transformed. Latin American society—or, better said, societies—was no longer colonial, but neither was it modern. It was entering a Middle Period.

By the 1820s most vestiges of medieval Europe and pre-Columbian America had succumbed in the wake of the accelerating changes in the economy, governance, social relations, and cultural vision. The remnants of these colonial institutions and attitudes either clung precariously in defiance of the tide of societal change or were being forced to adjust such that by that very process of accommodation they were being transformed. These "outer shells" of colonial society—and the beliefs in and commitment to them by a declining minority of Latin Americans—belied the societal transformation that had taken place and the profound changes that were continuing apace.

Ibero-America's regional societies had been given political substance and identity in the creation of intendancies. As polities, they had become the organizing framework for the binding together of localities, whether concentrated in towns and cities and their environs, or more scattered in villages and hamlets in the countryside. At the center of these regional societies were urban centers, most having newly become state or provincial capitals. As their sources of economic and political power grew, they sought to bind the localities more firmly to them, to identify and promote regional interests, and to negotiate the retention (and, optimally, the expansion) of those interests in whatever "national" constructs of which they became a part.

The social foundation of these newly empowered regional societies had been in transformation since the mid–eighteenth century. Though still very much hierarchically organized, the basis of social stratification had undergone a metamorphosis. Identities changed, social relations were altered, and lines of division emerged. The ingredients of race, occupation, wealth, education, skill, and cultural behavior had been mixed into new social configurations that were distinct from either the colonial construct of racial estates or the modernizing North Atlantic stratification by class.

In the midst of this social metamorphosis and the consolidation of regional society was the "traditional" triad of the family, parish, and community.[1] Relatively self-contained, with varying degrees of autonomy, these institutions had embodied similar patterns of internal authoritarian relationships dominated by patriarch, priest, and local official. But the circumstances of daily life, markedly affected by the larger historical forces at work since 1750, in turn had begun to alter the inner workings of the local institutional triad itself, above all in the family and the community. Structure became more complex and authority more diffused.

At this microlevel of home, church, and greater neighborhood—and at the macrolevel whose hierarchy extended from locality up through province to nation-state (formerly empire)—a renegotiation of rights and obligations was taking place. The independence struggle had opened up practically the whole gamut of economic, social, and political relations within Ibero-America for reconsideration. Now, throughout the lands that in the merging of historical experiences were coming to constitute "Latin America," the prevalence of authoritarian dictation was giving way to an expanding negotiation of relations within the emerging Middle Period society. Enlightenment thought and French and Anglo-American revolutionary ideology were infusing the process and objects of negotiation with more formality and a more definitive articulation. The social, economic, and political leverage within society most assuredly had been altered. Still, the institutionalization of this new equilibrium of leverage had not yet been realized in either structure or mentality.

For all the enlarged stages on which the insurgent movements were fought, for all the conflicts within and among the nation-states that were beginning to ensue, the Middle Period society that had come into being by the 1820s found its spatial reference point at the regional level. The new layering of social groups, alterations within the traditional triad of local institutions and their articulation with the larger society, and negotiation of rights and obligations were being infused with a regional ethos.

The Consolidation of Regional Life

As the colonial order gave way to a new society in the late eighteenth and early nineteenth centuries, two important dividing lines had been established. For the vast majority of people living then in Ibero-America the empire and even the viceroyalty had been external, affecting their lives in varying degrees and frequency. The controlling dynamics that shaped their daily lives and ordered their world, giving them an ongoing sense of membership in a larger polity or social entity, rarely had extended beyond the boundaries of the regional societies that had come to comprise the empires.

In contrast, everyone had belonged to a community or parish. In the countryside, community had meant settlements of varied socioeconomic types. Some families lived in solitary ranchos or *granjas* (farmsteads), but the large majority of small farmers lived in *rancherias* (hamlets) or the more densely settled pueblos. Rural communities were also formed on haciendas, estancias, and *fazendas*, or plantations. *Reales* (mining camps) also constituted important settlements in many regions. In urban areas, communities consisted of the principal *cuarteles* (wards) that together constituted the central core and, depending on the size of the urban center, the separate barrios and *colonias* (community on the edge of the city) on its outskirts. Parishes (and vice parishes) encompassed one or more of these rural and urban settlements, reinforcing or extending people's sense of community.

In between community and empire lay a series of spatial levels that had come to constitute overlapping historical experiences for the vast majority of people. The fundamental spatial construct beyond the community was the *locality*. A small town of mixed population or a cabecera (head Indian village) served as a market and governmental center for outlying rural nucleated settlements. The political expression of this spatial entity was the *municipio*, governed by the cabildo in its primary population center and by subordinate officials in its nucleated settlements.

Several interrelated localities comprised a *distrito* or *partido*. Its size often depended on population density, creating considerable spatial variance among the districts. Frequently, similar geographical settings bound the localities together, such as being part of a river valley or a section of coastal plain, usually the basis of an even more important source of interrelation—economic activities and interchange. Districts came to specialize in certain kinds of economic production, and those of greatest commercial importance were supported by other sectors within the district. In areas with dense Indian population, tribal or linguistic divisions left their imprint on district boundaries. Economic and political power was centered in the *cabecera*, almost always the largest and most concentrated focus of population. Usually, these constituted genuine urban centers, unlike many municipal cabeceras that were little more than large villages.[2] The district was administered by the lowest level of royal officialdom.

The region came to embody the largest and most distant historical experience for all but a few in the Ibero-American colonial world. It was composed of districts linked together through bonds of economic interchange, usually of similar or complementary geographic settings but sometimes of common racial or ethnic patterns. The region frequently constituted a migration field, especially when migration to urban areas accelerated markedly. Administratively, depending upon geographic size and population density, a regional society encompassed one or more intendancies. In New Spain, for example, a single intendancy included the whole of the northwest. But the Bajío, that intermediate region north of the central core, comprised several intendancies.

With the political and economic decline of the Iberian crowns beginning in the late sixteenth century, dynamics within the regions themselves had become the controlling force acting upon the societies that emerged within their boundaries in varying spatial sizes and degrees of complexity. Prominent families, in alliance (but sometimes at odds) with royal and ecclesiastical officials, had manipulated legal, economic, and social structures to achieve a de facto autonomy. Imperial influence had been more by virtue of the homage, loyalty, and service rendered by these local powers-that-be than by an effective administrative apparatus of the crown itself.

The regional societies' cohesiveness and uniqueness had been manifested in the midst of Bourbon (and to a lesser extent Portuguese) efforts to reestablish more uniform, imperial structures. Demographic and economic growth, which the Iberian crowns' reforms had generally reinforced, had led to increasing regional complexity as settlements, markets, and communications multiplied. Primary urban centers that dominated their respective regions were the hub of this growth and complexity, reflected most distinctively in physical expansion, altered functional boundaries, more differentiated residential patterns, and more diversified economic activities. Many had been little more than small towns; some had sprung up seemingly overnight. Their place at the top of a regional settlement hierarchy—measured by population, the array of goods and services, and the concentration of civil and ecclesiastical authority—was greatly expanded and solidified.

The intendancy system had centralized governmental functions and increased royal presence. But the intendants' growing power to execute decrees and introduce policy initiatives had also infused the region with an expanded governmental function and a greater sense of polity. Their greatest impact was in the primary urban centers, where they were usually resident. Its municipal government was charged with more responsibility, in great part in response to the expanded size and greater structural complexity of the city itself but also as a result of its growing role in the functioning of the region as a whole. Networks of prominent families inflated their governmental horizons even as the reach and scope of their economic interests were expanding. Their enhanced sense of political awareness and regional identity, along with a similar feeling among those of lesser social station to a lesser degree as well, had manifested itself quickly with the outbreak of insurgent movements.

In the wake of independence, regional polities took several different forms. Some regions remained an aggregation of districts, but now with a complex state or provincial government that entailed divided functions and enlarged personnel. More numerous were the regions comprising two or more states (provinces). Their integration and unity were more geographic, economic, and cultural than political. Yet at times, movements, groups, or individuals would achieve political if not governmental integration within a region. Some regions became nation-states themselves, most notably Paraguay, Uruguay, islands in the Caribbean, and the republics of Central America. Indeed, the failure of the Central American Federation points to the overriding strength the regional societies had attained by the early nineteenth century. The "supraregions" of the colonial era—large economically integrated or administrative units—failed to hold together in the face of the centrifugal forces intensified by the independence struggle. Only Brazil, through its monarchy (and even then not without serious secessionist movements) remained intact. Mexico lost (through secession and conquest) its far northern frontier. Even in the nation-states carved out of the former viceroyalties of New Granada, Peru, and the La Plata,

regional conflicts made their status and boundaries uncertain throughout most of the nineteenth century.

The ordering of people's lives at the regional level had intensified
during the years of imperial reforms and independence insurgency.
Regional societies took on a more political character and governmental function. Their primary urban centers became hubs around which
a growing economic articulation and demographic integration ensued.
As imperial sentiments and loyalties (whatever their degree) weakened and then disintegrated, people's interaction and identification
with the regional context of their lives was strengthened.[3] A transformation of social relations was an important part of this gathering regional ethos.

Social Metamorphosis

After more than a half century of profound economic and social change,
culminating in the dissolution of a governmental framework that had
overseen people's lives for three centuries, the very structure of social
relations had undergone a metamorphosis. One could observe it in the
personnel and politics of Indian villages and see it in the homes, shops,
and factories where artisans labored. One could notice it in the changing composition of neighborhoods and hear it in the way people addressed each other on the streets. One could read about it in the debates
and pronouncements in the pages of the local gazette or watch it in the
celebration of public events. Few people could define the new social
structure with any precision, but new words to describe it had been
accumulating for several decades in the lexicons of the street, the shops,
the parish register, and the printed page.

The transformation was most noticeable in the city because the
general patterns of change there had been compressed in both space
and time. Yet one could observe it in the countryside too; if not very
clearly in one particular community or locale, then less ambiguously
in another not too far removed. The criteria that people a century before customarily employed in assigning and assuming their place in
the social order had been metamorphosed. Still recognizable in and of
themselves, their import and their use had been altered such that an
entirely new social structure had evolved.

In conquering America, Iberians had carried with them the medieval concept of estates in determining social rank, which entailed a
high degree of rigidity and predetermination. Law generally defined
each estate and gave it distinctive rights and obligations, largely determining occupation. Title solidified and marked the higher ranks.

Subordination—even enduring physical violence if commonly understood boundaries were crossed—governed and marked the lives of
those of lesser rank. Race, a lesser criterion in defining estates in the
peninsula, had been intertwined with religion and ethnicity in varying combinations.

However, in the New World, race had become the dominant factor
in the determination of the composition of estates so that estate and
caste became virtually synonymous. In time, miscegenation blurred
the simple racial categories and forced intricate categorization by caste,
with which the legal code was unable to keep up. The incentives and
necessities of economic pursuits fostered increasing exceptions in the
occupational attributes and standards of wealth of racially based estates. Yet even in the mid–eighteenth century, people continued to cat-
egorize each other by racial origin, appearance, and stereotyped
behavior. By the 1820s, race still was a factor in connoting social status.
But it was no longer dominant, not nearly so predetermining. Too much
had changed in those intervening years.

Forces of Social Transformation

Cumulatively and in aggregate, the marked demographic growth had
wrought profound change in the workings of colonial society. It had
altered the relationships of humans to resources, the relative supply of
labor, the potential of markets, the density and composition of urban
neighborhoods, and the physical and functional boundaries of towns
and cities. In part driven by this demographic growth, commercialization had forced people into new relations to the means of production
or, alternatively, had created new opportunities for them to do so. Concentration of control over resources had altered relations to land, of
labor, and to markets that had led to changes in the way people related
to and thought about one another. Widespread epidemics, agricultural
crises induced by natural disasters and compounded by the demographic changes, and the long years of imperial warfare and then insurgency had also disrupted the timing and recreation of families
and the social fabric and relationships of communities.

From these three underlying factors of change—demographic
growth, accelerating commercialization, and interrupted life rhythms—
derived social and economic alterations that had more directly brought
about the social structure's transformation. Spatial mobility increased
markedly. Agricultural crises, epidemics, overpopulation, and concentration of control over land use pushed people to migrate. The hope of
making a better living pulled others into migration, even at the cost of

changing language, diet, and occupation or living as a cultural minority. In New Spain's central core, Indians abandoning corporate village life for good were pulled by the attraction of employment opportunities to the barrios of that region's urban centers. There, they passed from the tribute lists, especially as they took on a *casta* lifestyle. In the intendancy of Arizpe, far to the northwest, the breakdown of the mission system after the Jesuit expulsion led to a twoway migration. Indians migrated to Hispanic settlements in mining camps, on haciendas, and alongside presidios. At the same time, non-Indians penetrated and usurped mission lands, backed by royal policy that sought to privatize more and more land to facilitate Hispanic settlement.[4]

Amplified spatial mobility had accelerated racial intermarriage. But the increase in intermarriage was also the result of calculated responses (enhanced by passion or tempered by family sentiment) to growing commercialization and to a more favorable set of legal privileges and obligations secured through a change in racial status. In corporate villages, non-Indians could gain access to land through intermarriage. Mission Indians could escape communal obligations. Those with African ancestry in particular gained from miscegenation. They were the only subgroup among the *castas* who paid the *tributo*, were barred from entering certain occupations (generally those of higher income and status), and carried with them the stigma of a family past that included enslavement.[5]

Alongside the expanding miscegenation among the racial estates was a growing social and economic differentiation within them. Among Indian commoners, vicissitudes of economic change expanded the differentiation of *originario* (original resident) from *forastero* (migrant to the village), tenants from landholders, seasonal wage laborers from resident *peones*. In rural Hispanic communities, especially in former frontier and peripheral regions undergoing extensive economic and demographic growth, heterogeneity in landholding, wealth, and status increased. In urban centers, especially cities, the numbers of whites in lower-status occupations was accelerating, whereas the number of *castas* (and even Indians) in middle- (and even upper-) status occupations expanded. Among whites, the distinction between Creoles and *peninsulares* intensified.[6]

Driven by the commercialization of the economy, the quickening pace of privatization had played a critical role in the growing differentiation within the racial estates. The colonial social structure had been buttressed by the wide-scale corporate organization (both formal and informal) of economic activity. Communal villages, guilds, kinship groups, and ecclesiastical bodies often had been organized along racial caste lines. Those oriented toward commercial production had employed such solidary relations to protect (and enlarge when possible) sources of supply and markets. Those preoccupied with subsistence had relied upon kin relations, mutual aid, and communal action to maintain access to resources and to mitigate against seasonal and cyclical fluctuations.

However, as population growth intensified pressures on access to (and control over) resources and created expanding possibilities for new markets, individual and familial confidence in such solidary relations had weakened. The boundaries and obligations of kin, community, and corporate affiliation were no longer either satisfactorily protective from outsiders or sufficiently supportive. Those possessing few of these ties readily responded to the changing economic realities. Guilds, for example, could no longer hold back the flood of nonwhite would-be artisans. *Forasteros* in Indian villages were quick to pursue access to resources that were opened to market forces. Nevertheless, more individuals and families reacted largely out of necessity, to make ends meet.

This adaptation had been especially true for women. In the growing urban centers as domestic servants, workers in craftshops and manufacturing establishments, or domestic artisans, they were increasingly in demand. They migrated from the countryside, left the confines of home and neighborhood, or changed the rhythm of life within their domiciles. In rural communities, networks of closely intertwined social and economic exchanges among kin and neighbors declined in importance to increasing numbers of them. Women joined the growing numbers of men who pursued market-oriented relations with outsiders. As domestic manufacturers, as petty commodity traders, and sometimes as widowed small-plot owners, their economic life became steadily privatized.[7]

The Spanish Bourbons generally had supported the expansion of privatization as a way to further their primary goal of increasing commercial production. There were important exceptions. In highland Peru, the crown had calculated (mistakenly) that restoration of the colonial economy based on forced communal labor for the mines and Indian tribute for royal coffers was preferable and feasible.[8] Moreover, when royal monopolies were expanded (most notably in the production and sale of tobacco), some economic sectors became less privatized. But in most regions and economic activities, Bourbon policy had supported private enterprise, sometimes through direct action. Jesuit holdings were broken up and most of their missions secularized after their expulsion. The crown looked favorably on the expansion of nonwhites and women in the craft industries, ignoring or overruling guild restrictions. In frontier and peripheral regions, vast areas of land were opened up for individuals to claim, a departure from the earlier prevalence of communal grants of land.

As individuals and families at all levels of society turned more and more to private economic relations, they also had sought to diversify the resulting economic activities. For some (especially those of substantial means), diversification brought expanding profits, property holdings, and wealth. For many more (especially commoners), it provided a way to mitigate the growing risks to subsistence security. As a consequence, with increasing frequency people of different racial castes crossed occupational boundaries that had previously been more restrictive, interacting more extensively with one another in the process.[9]

In a little more than a half century, the customary colonial social structure based on racial estates had broken down in the varied regional societies across Ibero-America. The task for their diverse citizenry was to understand and define the new social reality taking form in their midst. For those at the upper levels, the problem was redefining the social hierarchy, which benefited them most. For those beneath them, the issue was discerning and acting upon the changes in social mobility, space, and identity.

The Breakdown of Racial and Occupational Identities

With independence, constitutions, statutes, and civil registries manifested the changing social reality. Legal equality was widely proclaimed. Restrictions on civil status and occupation were removed; economic and social subordination was no longer enforced by law. Most tribal Indians in peripheral regions and many corporate Indian communities in older core regions sought to maintain their racial-cultural separateness by choice, but with more political autonomy and fewer obligations to the larger society. Nevertheless, for the remaining social groups the estate-based linkages among racial identity, occupation, and degrees of freedom had dramatically altered. The republican ideological environment spawned by independence formally worked against their reconstruction for the minority who might have desired it. More important, economic and social changes in the preceding decades had crossed a threshold that made a return improbable.

Racial identity as a guide to social rank had become noticeably blurred in all but the very upper and lower levels. "Passing" was based less on similar physical appearance than on assuming a different lifestyle (language, behavior patterns, material possessions, kind of work). With those circumstantial changes, growing numbers changed their racial identities, often formally at the time of marriage to secure a specific advantage, as noted previously. But available evidence suggests that a "racial drift" was at work as well, with people striving to bring their *calidad* (in its narrowest sense, racial identity) in line with their occupational status. Since the latter marked men more than it did women, women were more likely to alter their *calidad* at marriage. For both sexes, in comparative numbers the drift down the social ladder for whites was more extensive than the drift upward for people of color. Nevertheless, on the middle rungs, a "whitening" trend had begun as many of mixed racial ancestry were able to claim creole status.[10]

Although the Portuguese crown had encouraged racial intermarriage (officially, at least, between Indians and whites), the Spanish Bourbons had tried unsuccessfully to contain it. The Royal Pragmatic of 1776 required that minors (those under 25) obtain parental approval as a way to inhibit marriages between persons of unequal standing (particularly that based on race), but it lacked effective enforcement. The Spanish crown had also labored to maintain the race-occupation linkage in an occupation that could be narrowly defined and regulated. Its 1805 decree forbidding military officers' marriage to nonwhites sought to dispel all previous questions on their wives' racial origins. Still, the crown's allowance of those of African ancestry to purchase legal whiteness (1795) only added to the clouding of the distinct occupational attributes previously identified with race. More important, the logic of its economic goals had led to a pro-active (or at least neutral) response to the economic changes blurring the formerly distinct coupling of racial estate and occupation.[11]

Race was less and less a predictor of occupational status. What mattered more and more were effective ownership of or control over the means of production as the market economy spread. This control required a high degree of freedom, which the social system of racial estates had restricted. Coercion had been a vital force in the colonial economic order; leverage based on "natural" and market conditions had been minimized. Yet as the colonial order had evolved, freely contracted economic arrangements had steadily made inroads, often extralegally at first. What had made the post-1750 period distinct had been the pace and extent of this process. Everywhere, commercialization (supported frequently by Bourbon policy) was replacing coercion with freely negotiated relations. The remaining *repartimiento* labor was formally abolished, *repartimiento de mercancias* was attacked head on, most missions were secularized, and guilds and corporate communities were rendered increasingly powerless. Only slavery had maintained its accustomed role, even expanding in some regions. Its profitability still overrode its social and economic costs.

Economically, the ascendancy of free, market-governed relations had benefited those whose assets (personal or material) had been significantly restricted or rendered nonexistent under coercive institutions. For those possessing few such assets, the prior trade-off between opportunity and security was adversely altered. Socially, that ascendancy—reinforced by the insurgent ideology of legal equality—had resulted in a marked increase in fluidity and mobility. Subordination resting on the force of law and custom had been steadily replaced by that based upon the degree of one's economic control (or dependency), determined largely by natural and market forces.

In the countryside, commoners had sought to negotiate as much subsistence security and autonomy as they could obtain from large landowners, who negotiated to reduce risk and raise profit margins. Growing numbers of itinerant petty traders served as intermediaries connecting small producers and consuming laborers with one another and with larger market systems. Indian villagers, escaping coerced occupational roles, joined *castas* in moving from one job to the next. Privatization, concentration of wealth, and commercialization increasingly subordinated communal values based upon reciprocal exchange to the free seeking of individual advantage. Those same economic forces had undermined coercive subordination even more extensively in the city. Formal training or apprenticeship through entry into the guild system was being replaced by acquisition of property or capital as the key to occupational status in manufacturing. Large-scale merchants organizing craft production and master artisans diversifying into commerce employed both nonguild journeymen and cottage producers. In doing so, the value and prestige of skilled manual labor declined. At the bottom, more and more artisan laborers (especially Indians and *castas*) found easier access to less-skilled jobs. Above, the gap between journeymen and masters was narrowed as access to capital rather than guild regulations increasingly determined control over the means of production. In commerce, the parallel development was in the increasing separation of ownership from management. Merchants with ample capital were concentrating ownership at the retail level.[12]

Redefining the Social Hierarchy

Given the blurring of racial identities, the growing occupational differentiation within economic activities, and the disintegrating force of law to put and keep people in their economic and social place, by the early nineteenth century the colonial social order no longer effectively corresponded to the historical reality. Imposed racial estates and corporate distinctions had eroded since 1750 to the point at which, with independence, they were no longer even officially proclaimed. The number of claimants to white status had steadily risen. People of color, in their dress, occupation, residence, and manner, had become hardly distinguishable from the growing number of whites of poor and (increasingly) even modest means. Distinctions in the skill level of manual labor had narrowed, as its value and prestige as a whole had declined. How, then, were social distinctions to be drawn? To what rank could one lay claim or aspire? Where were the lines to be drawn that fostered mobility within but restricted its crossing without?

The answers to such questions that had emerged over more than a half century rested on notions of simplicity and respectability. Social labels became more simplified in the sense of being more inclusive, more generalized. The proliferation of racial categories had become so unmanageable by the mid–eighteenth century that there was a reversion to simplicity. Increasingly, a common term for those of mixed heritage was used (the term varying by region). The spreading use of the title of *don/doña* as a mark of respect among those of European descent by the late eighteenth century appears to have been reversed. With a few exceptions, that title of respect descended no further than the level of master artisan. Above all, the meaning and use of the term *calidad* had changed. Formerly, its close association with racial distinctions (color, purity of descent) had always connoted occupation, standard of living, honor, or even one's place of origin. After 1750, these connotations could less and less be taken for granted. Hence, the nonracial attributes of the term had come to the fore and individual assessment had become increasingly important. By the early nineteenth century *calidad* had become the inclusive impression of one's reputation and status, of which race was only one factor. The latter's importance varied but was increasingly in decline, often misread to align it with the other traits, thus "whitening" or "darkening" an individual.[13] Independence, with its accompanying formal commitment to legal equality, reinforced this changing use of *calidad*.

Calidad had come now to mean, above all, one's social quality, one's social importance, one's respectability. That quality was measured according to a number of criteria: the background of the family from which one came; the composition of the household to which one belonged and the residence that housed it; the formal training or manual labor involved in one's occupation; the economic empowerment one possessed; the stability of one's life; and, of course, the perceived color of one's visage. The standard had become increasingly whether one possessed a *sufficient* degree of this social quality, this respectability, to put one above what had become the most important social dividing line in an emerging two-tiered stratification.

Personas de calidad and *pleybeyos* constituted one pair of terms that expressed this emerging binary social stratification. Persons of quality were counterposed against persons who were plebian, who were common, with an accompanying connotation of crudeness or coarseness of manner. Other terms that had emerged to describe this basic social division were *gente alta* and *gente baja* and *gente decente* and *gente de pueblo*. The title *don/doña* appears to have settled along the line of respectability, denoting those above it. The vast majority of people who fell below the line were also referred to as *las masas* (the masses) and *las clases populares* (the popular classes).

Gente alta and *gente baja* seem most useful as a standard, working terminology. The former points most definitively to the essence of the distinction that had emerged. They were judged (above all, by themselves) to be those who possessed sufficient respectability to stand above the line. *Gente baja* most accurately describes the great remainder of the population that fell below the line of "respectability." They were commoners, plebes in the lexicon of ancient Rome. They were certainly of the small community in their spatial orientation (*de pueblo*). As an aggregate they were *las masas*. More explicitly, as collections of different social groupings—separated by geohistorical setting (rural versus urban), relations to the means of production, and cultural-ethnic orientation—they were the popular classes. But above all, they were people with insufficient respectability, people lacking decency, people below what was required—*gente baja*.[14]

A Simplified, Two-Tiered Stratification

The social line of respectability mattered most to the "decent" people above the line, for whom it served as a redefined barrier that preserved the social hierarchy, albeit on a modified basis. Whites positioned (or slipping) below the line by their color would not lower the line. People of color rising above the line over time would be "whitened," leaving the *gente alta* with the pretense of long-standing racial correctness. For nonwhites below the line, there was greater social space in which to redefine themselves as racial distinctions and occupational restrictions eroded. If they desired it, there were grounds for more hope of becoming respectable (though the odds were still unlikely).

The same criteria that divided the *gente alta* from the *gente baja* also formed the basis of important subdivisions within each. Family background, the level of wealth and the refinement of taste that it made possible, the degree of political influence, and the stability and security of one's lifestyle—these raised a group of families to a prominence that set them above the *gente alta* in general. They possessed "notability," a concept used and given social value by Iberian society. They were called by several names (*hombres acaudalados* [men of wealth], for example), but the one of most generic use was that of notables. What empowered them most over the long term was the web of relations and alliances that bound them together. The complexity, extension, and power of those networks of relations began to distinguish them from earlier such prominent families.[15]

The remainder of the *gente alta* can more properly be labeled by the more generic name for respectable—the *gente decente*, decent but not notable. Their lifestyle ranged from very comfortable to modest. They frequently were active in public life. The large majority were white; most of the remainder were recognized or claimed to be as such. They shared common aspirations, occupations, and manners with the notables. What they lacked were sufficient access to capital (or, in some cases, entrepreneurial acumen and vision), economic independence and security, family enterprise, and public influence for notability.

Gente decente in the countryside had separated themselves from the mass of small producers by acquiring property or use rights over sizable landholdings and employing a labor force outside their family or by managing the notables' large estates. Though they carried substantial economic responsibility, most were dependent on the notables for credit, leasing, or employment. The great majority lacked the capital to diversify; some, the business skill and sense to do so. Their network of family and kin were not sufficient in extent and accumulated wealth to share risks and pool capital. Their fortunes rested generally on a single enterprise or occupation. Unlike notable estate owners, they usually did not reside in the district *cabeceras* and provincial urban centers, where public influence could be attained and wielded to expand their interests.[16]

Those *gente decente* who did reside in Latin America's towns and cities were engaged in commerce, manufacturing, mining, and the professions. In commerce many *gente decente* fell into the general occupational category of *cajero*, who ranged from head administrators down to clerks. When they did not manage them for notables, other *gente decente* were the owners of all but the largest retail stores. Artisans among the *gente decente* were the successful masters who in the increasingly fluid, commercialized economy had become owners more than craft producers, securing access to the capital that allowed them to own large craft shops with flexible, inexpensive labor. Few urban *gente decente* engaged in manual labor. They enjoyed a relatively comfortable lifestyle, the most prosperous being able to acquire property (particularly their private residences), buy additional stores, or even invest outside their specialties. But the great majority were dependent on the notables for employee and supervisory posts (public as well as private), for the *companías* (contracted partnerships) that set them up as managers and co-owners of businesses, and for the credit with which they stocked their stores.[17] Their social advancement required, above all, a horizontal connection within the notable families' network of relations. Performance (often in combination with fortuitous circumstance) brought them the recognition and eligibility for such a connection; marriage secured it.

Among the *gente baja*, too, there was an important subdivision: those who might best be characterized as the *gente de profesiones*.[18] This term did not equate with the modern sense of professionals—those whose occupations (often termed the "learned professions") required specialized knowledge acquired through formal academic preparation. The *gente de profesiones* were practitioners of a trade or a skill, in a more limited sense akin to the "mechanics" of pre-industrial North America. The skill or trade (and personal property therein employed, such as tools, draft animals, stalls, or even small structures) that gave them more leverage and a measure of more stability in the marketplace set them apart from the *gente baja* in general. Indeed, they were the most connected to the market economy, and the least likely to engage in subsistence activities.

Within urban centers, the *gente de profesiones* worked primarily in commerce and artisanry. They were the master artisans who still depended upon the deteriorating protection of guild organization, especially those in low-ranking crafts. The worth of the goods they produced and the income that could be earned served as barriers to social mobility. Journeymen still associated with the traditional structure of artisan life were part of this substratum, though their skills had steadily declined in value (and their wages along with it) and their working conditions had become more unstable. So, too, were petty tradespeople, operating small stands and peddling wares, primarily in their neighborhoods. The most prosperous among them were the small shopkeepers. Women made up an important part of petty trade; generally, the more modest the store, the more common was their presence as owners and operators.[19]

Connecting the towns and cities with rural settlements were the *viadantes* (itinerant traders) and *arrieros* (muleteers). They were instrumental in the movement of goods, especially linking the rural *gente baja* to regional and more distant markets. The accelerating commercialization of agricultural production had created growing numbers of petty producers and consumers. The itinerant traders filled the gaps left by the merchants and estate producers. Frequently, they were the latter's agents, entering into short-term contracts on credit. But at times they were also competitors, offering the rural *gente baja* an alternative to the monopolistic control of the large local landowners in the marketing of crops and the sale of merchandise.[20]

In the countryside itself the substratum that paralleled the urban *gente de profesiones* was composed of two principal groups. Small producers who retained landownership beyond the subsistence plot level and who consistently produced for the market made up a large share of this stratum. They were usually dependent upon the notables (and, to a lesser extent, the *gente decente*) for the credit necessary to maintain production. *Servientes*—those who practiced specialized skills on the large and medium-sized estates, such as in the care of animals and in the processing of crops and animal by-products—were more directly dependent. Still, their permanent full-time work, with guaranteed rations and a monthly salary, set them apart from all other rural workers. The two groups within this substratum were increasingly becoming intertwined. Some family members worked their own small farms and ranches, whereas others plied their specialized trades on the *haciendas*. Individuals often moved between the two occupational groups and even pursued muleteering separately or in combination with agriculture.[21]

The *gente de profesiones*, both in the city and countryside, were the closest thing to a melting pot in the new Middle Period society. The economic and social changes since 1750 had greatly increased the absolute and proportional numbers of *castas* who fell into this substratum. Yet it was not simply a mixing of races but also of cultures. The *gente de profesiones* constituted the outer ring of Iberian culture emanating from its core among the notables. At the same time they brought into the melting pot the diverse cultural patterns of the popular classes (African, Amerindian, and European; rural and urban) and tempered the dominant culture with them.

The *gente de profesiones* were betwixt and between not only culturally but in their general social situation in the new Middle Period society. They were an integral part of the market economy, and yet they had more extensive economic relations with the popular classes than with any of their social betters. They shared with the popular classes the struggle to maintain subsistence, but their skills gained for them a distinct measure more of material security and of leverage with those above. They understood and partook of the plight of the popular classes, often being called to lead them in acts of resistance against the powers-that-be. However, increasingly they felt a part of the larger body politic and were pulled by the widening prospects of mobility that might enable them to cross the line of respectability. That required not only performance on the market economy's terms and a bit of good fortune. Even more it rested upon securing close client relations with the notables and *gente decente*.

A parallel but somewhat different social structure had emerged in those rural communities of Indians who had by and large maintained their closed corporate character (though, with few exceptions, they did so extralegally after independence). The colonial triad of hereditary caciques, *principales* (a legally privileged lesser nobility), and commoners had evolved into a two-tiered stratification that correlated with that of the larger society. As commercialization spread, caciques and *principales* both seized the opportunity to acquire a growing private hold on community resources and to tie landless and indebted commoners to them as dependent laborers, eroding their authority among the village commoners (especially that of the caciques). The cabildo became the forum for the commoners' demands for participation in the disposition of community resources. Independence completed this social transformation. Commoners acquired the vote, making cabildo posts more accessible. The caciques and *principales* lost their legal privilege. Access to community resources became more egalitarian. The result was the emergence of the cargo system, in which a hierarchical series of offices of public service elevated a now much smaller group to high status, one based far more on length of service and age. They constituted the elders of the village, within which they were "notables." In the larger society, depending on the size and wealth of the community and surrounding locality, as smallholders their status was that of *gente de profesiones*; some even of *gente decente*.[22]

Social and cultural distance and extreme disparity in economic well-being and security left notables and the popular classes quite removed from the fundamental line of respectability. But the *gente decente* and *gente de profesiones*, in the median of Middle Period society's social spectrum, were sensitive to its consequences. The market economy's fluidity and instability held out to the *gente decente* the dreaded prospect of a fall from respectability, even as it extended to the *gente de profesiones* the hope of crossing into it. The whiteness that provided the former with some insurance against that prospect also handicapped the latter. The microworlds and private lives of these four principal social components of Middle Period society—in residence, family structure, household composition, and community orientation—manifested their distinctness from one another.

The Traditional Triad: Family, Parish, and Community

Advancing commercialization of production and accompanying privatization and concentrating control over resources had wrought not only a metamorphosis of the macroworld of social relations. The private lives of people, shared in families and with neighbors, had been forced to make serious adjustments. This was especially true for the *gente baja*. Among them, life centered on subsistence production (and, to a lesser extent, production limited to the local market) had infused the relations of family, parish, and community with a set of deeply ingrained values and expectations.

Accommodating Reciprocal Relations

At the core of the *gente baja*'s moral economy was the concept of reciprocal exchange. The abundance or scarcity of subsistence-oriented production of the household drew it outward to kin and community, guided by generosity. The exchange was based on use and need rather than calculated value by which one sought increments of gain. In the immediate sense the reciprocal exchange was a gift; from a longer perspective, it was a promise of mutual aid. Independence was valued not so much in being separate or distinct as in being subsistently secure so as to be fully reciprocal in the exchange. Interdependence ensured a wider, more long-term security. Such reciprocity also fostered homogeneity nurtured in sociability and play and requiring ample discretionary time. Corporate entities—the communal village, *cofradía*, guild, and parish—constituted the largest embodiment and formal support of this set of values: the right to collective use and sharing of resources.[23]

The accelerating market economy had increasingly dislocated these reciprocal, solidary relations in the production and exchange of goods, undermining the set of values that had infused and underlay them. Whether forced or enticed, people had become more and more dependent on the market economy to fulfill their material needs (and desires). Social and corporate relationships as the guarantors of material needs were giving way to the reality of the marketplace, in which persons faced each other as independent buyers and sellers of their goods and labor governed by the value of the exchange being made. The more local the markets were, the more the traditional moral economy could accommodate the dislocations. The exchange of products, whether to replace commodities formerly self-produced or to add to them, tended to be seen in the eyes of both parties as equal. The long-term outcome of reciprocal exchange was telescoped to the immediate market transaction. However, as extralocal markets penetrated (often rapidly) and as value based on the local balance of supply and demand gave way to value functioning relative to those external markets, the advantage of accumulating money for use as capital (or simply for securing the greatest possible return) increased.

An intensifying and ever-widening process had been triggered on a scale unprecedented before 1750. The more advantage there was in accumulating capital, the more those able to increase production were in a position to concentrate control over resources. Those without access to resources to continue subsistence activities (or needing to supplement them) were, in turn, increasingly forced into the marketplace to sell their goods or labor, rather than to reciprocally exchange them with a declining number of kin and neighbors able to fulfill those customary obligations. The marketplace necessitated flexibility and mobility, which weakened homogeneity in family and community and eroded discretionary time.[24]

The large majority of the *gente baja* seemed to have preferred the relative security of the traditional solidary supports to their private lives over the uncertainties of the marketplace. When they could, in the margins of the countryside, they clung to subsistence. Otherwise, they tried to salvage their familial and communal livelihoods as best they could. But they did so on the marketplace's terms, which required increased mobility and a growing heterogeneity in household composition and community association. For the *gente baja*, accommodation of the traditional triad of solidary institutions to the pressures of the market economy was now ongoing.

For the *gente alta* generally, that accommodation had been increasingly welcomed. Solidary institutions had brought security and prestige for many of them (principally in the form of professional guilds and ecclesiastical posts) and considerable economic advantage and power for prominent families (above all, in the commercial and mining guilds and through purchased cabildo offices). Nevertheless, freedom from the obligations and limitations of those solidary institutions had proven increasingly profitable. Given their access to capital and control of resources, they were able to take advantage of the expanded opportunity and play of the marketplace. Paradoxically, among the *gente alta* (and especially the notables), advancing commercialization had fortified one side of the traditional triad. Family and kin relations were proving to be ever more important in the pursuit of enterprise and wealth in the marketplace.[25]

Family and Household

In the spreading market economy, diversification had become central to both survival and success. It lessened, when it did not overcome, the consequences of the unpredictable and sometimes catastrophic downward swings of that economy. It enhanced the ability to take advantage of opportunities presented by upward oscillations. Among the *gente alta*, diversification and the traditional family structure had become mutually reinforcing in the context of commercialization. Among the *gente baja*, as diversification had become more necessary to enhance survival, it had placed increasing pressure on familial and kinship relations, often weakening them.[26]

The patriarchal extended family had become typical of only a small minority of the population. The number of nuclear families had declined as a proportion of households, although the ratio varied among urban settings and especially between rural and urban communities. In rural settlements kin relations remained more extensive (though in decline) across the social spectrum. But among a growing proportion of the population, household (the shared responsibility for maintenance support among those residing together) increasingly did not correspond to family. Composition of the household had come to reflect the new social stratification.

Among notables, and to a lesser extent the *gente decente*, property interests and inheritance considerations created strong bonds. The expanding need for diversification made essential the maintenance and extension of kin relations within and beyond the household. Blood relatives and in-laws could be trusted and counted on more than outsiders. The scope of the family enterprise and its largesse could accommodate their talents and ambitions. Through careful nurturing, they came to identify their interests with the long-term benefits of that enterprise. Even relatives living in solitary households (those who had been single all their lives or were delaying marriage) generally had close continuing ties with the larger family. A growing manifestation of the division between notables and *gente decente* was the extent of their kinship networks (and household size). For both, marriage was crucial for securing the transfer, consolidation, and acquisition of property. As such, it was an essential mark of status.[27]

Marriage and family ties had become less important among the *gente baja*, but not because they desired it. Rather, the advancing commercialization of the economy had made these ties more difficult to retain and less essential in securing life's necessities. Though most true in urban centers, increasingly it was prevalent in rural districts where commercial production had been spreading and intensifying. Concentration and privatization of resources had left the *gente baja* with declining control, ownership, and access. Population growth and more unstable working conditions had reduced the leverage of their labor and with it the buying power of their wages. To sustain themselves, members of the popular classes found they had to be flexible in residence and occupation. That led them to move out of the household, migrate to other localities and regions, and lose contact with more distant kin. The same need to diversify led others, unrelated to them, to become part of their households. With marriage declining as a practical means of integrating into a network of reciprocal exchange, unrelated people were attracted (and found to be attractive) to other's households. In this changing economy, marriage also carried less status, whereas consensual union offered greater flexibility.

The result of these combined changes during the late eighteenth and early nineteenth centuries was that *gente baja* households functioned quite differently from the traditional institution of the Iberian family. Household size generally declined. Poor households that remained large did so because they retained the combined functions of production and consumption. The proportion of nuclear families in *gente baja* households diminished, while that of non–immediate family members (especially unrelated) increased. The number of children in poor households declined, and the abandonment of children increased, as did the number of those living with unrelated adults (including foster parents). The number of *gente baja* households headed by single people (both unmarried and widowed) rose, often dramatically in urban settings. Consensual unions became more prevalent, whether on account of the sacrament's costs, in recognition of the need for greater spatial mobility and occupational flexibility, or because of the heavier burdens of making lifelong commitments.[28]

One might conclude that there had been a disintegration of the family in the half century before independence. But that conclusion assumes that the *gente baja* had lost sight of the traditional paragon of the family and had drifted into a new model of private living. In fact, the struggle of *gente baja* families to maintain viable household units in the face of greater economic hardship and uncertainty can be seen from another, perhaps deeper perspective. They were reconstituting themselves to survive and endure until conditions permitted a return to the ideal they shared with the *gente alta* and with their ancestors.

Women's Pivotal Role

Women played a central role in accommodating the family to the growing commercialization of the economy. Among rural commoners, men had found work on estates and in mines, some nearby but often in other localities and districts. By contrast, female labor had become greatly sought in urban centers. *Gente baja* women migrated from the countryside (along with others seeking better opportunities) to become servants, craft laborers, domestic artisans, street vendors, and petty traders.

The result was a marked change in gender balance. In newer agricultural zones, men were more predominant. But in older rural settlements, a growing number of households (composed mainly of children and relatives but also of some unrelated people, such as orphans or child-servants) became headed by women, formally or consensually married, unmarried, abandoned, or widowed. In urban centers (especially cities), there was a nearly uniform imbalance on the side of women. Female-headed households commonly constituted 20–30 percent of the populace, in some cities even approaching half. Among *gente baja* women who headed these households, fewer had been formally married than their rural counterparts, and they were co-resident with more unrelated people. *Gente alta* women also headed households, but largely as widows. Respectability prevented all but a few from consensual unions. The vast majority of the unmarried lived with their close kin. The same resources that made that alternative possible also enabled "respectable" widows (especially notables) to avoid reliance on unrelated people for support of their households.[29]

The great majority of *gente baja* women, especially those among the popular classes, were the focal point of families and households whose cyclical character had become more pronounced and more complex. There were scarce resources to support young women in the home, especially in the long term. Single, those women faced living in a work-related dependency. Avoiding such servitude by securing a union with a man was thus a strong incentive. But in coping with impoverishment, high mortality rates, and the marketplace's dislocations in obtaining work, *gente baja* women found that such unions were often frequently interrupted and short-lived. Consensual unions were less costly and often more practical. Unrelated people who brought diversified sources of income and productive specialties were often essential to the survival of these women's households, particularly when they found themselves as head. Formal marriage often followed temporary unions that proved stable. This result was more likely for women who were *gente de profesiones* or who married men of that social substratum.[30]

Reconstituting the Ibero-American Community

The weakening of family ties and kin networks among the *gente baja*, joined by the erosion of racial estates, was reconstituting their traditional Ibero-American community as well as their families and households. For them, community was demarcated by the personal contacts that marked their daily life. In the colonial order the community had been best understood as an extension of kin networks that shared a common cultural lifestyle in a place with recognizable gathering points and boundaries. It was, in a very real sense, a greater "family" linked by solidary relations. This, for want of a better term, was the "small" community for which the *gente baja* felt great affinity, in contrast to the *gran* community, with which they felt a more distant affiliation. The latter generally corresponded to the locality, anchored in the cabecera (or parish center) in the countryside and to the central core in urban centers and their environs.[31]

Among Indian communities where the boundaries of race and tribal ethnicity had remained rigid (primarily in Andean, Mexican, and Central American regions), the colonial community (combining both Amerindian and Iberian traditions) had survived the most intact. Bourbon and independence reforms had sought to eliminate most forms of communal and corporate property. Though Indian villagers fought a continuing resistance, the legal underpinnings of solidary relations were eroding. Communal arrangements increasingly had to be worked out informally. A unified ladder of prestige and community service (emerging by the late eighteenth century) bound households together more and more. It integrated the posts of two community institutions: the long-standing cabildo offices (now open to villagers in general) and those of the *cofradías*. This cargo system was in the process of becoming the principal ordering force of these communities.[32]

Paralleling such Indian communities were those of rural commoners of African descent, where slavery and/or the plantation continued, and especially where their demise left such rural dwellers as small-holders in economically marginal zones. In much of Brazil, the Caribbean islands, and the Guyanas, African and European communal structures and religious practices were syncretized in varying mixes, depending upon the proximity and strength of the European overlay. In Ibero-American regions, the *cofradía* served as a vital center of community association.[33]

In many more districts and regions, the colonial constructs of rural communities had declined more extensively in the face of commercialization. Most community property was becoming privatized, in fact as well as law. Racial and ethnic barriers became blurred or deteriorated, and extensive kin networks narrowed and became more fluid as the growing necessity of geographic mobility encouraged family strategies of miscegenation and exogamous unions. Household and family action assumed growing precedence over collective action. Civil and religious offices did not become bound together in an intricate, consistent web of solidary relations. Nevertheless, amid this growing heterogeneity and relative atomization, the thing most sharable became the religious heritage and practice of a folk Catholicism. Here, too, the *cofradía* remained strong and served as a vehicle of community solidarity and interaction.

In the countryside the *cofradías* had become in varying degrees the principal expression of the popular syncretization of Indian (African) religious culture and Roman Catholicism and of *gente baja* autonomy. In many Indian regions, confraternities had arisen through the eighteenth century without legal recognition, coterminous with secularization. The *cofradías* had became first foci of resistance to parish priest abuses and then the institutional vehicle to fill the vacuum created by the clergy's increasingly declining presence in the wake of the insurgent struggles and independence. A weakened hierarchy, diminishing material support, and declining numbers were causing a steady clerical retreat to the parish centers and towns. And as community property became steadily privatized thereafter, *cofradías* proved more successful in retaining it than the cabildo.[34]

By the 1820s, such shared religious association had increasingly become the cement that bound rural commoners in Latin America into communities (especially where racial and kin boundaries had deteriorated). The most formal institution—the parish—coincided more with the larger locality of which they were a part. For them, the barrio (whether an isolated *ranchería* or component of a larger village settlement) was now more a religious association of people than a residential neighborhood. In function, it paralleled the *cofradía* to the point of becoming indistinguishable. Under the aegis of the *cofradías*, these "religious" barrios, each with their patron saint cult, served as centers of shared property, social activities, sentiment, and loyalty.[35]

In urban barrios, corporate bodies (especially guilds and *cofradías*, often joined) had usually formed the basis of association for daily contacts, organization, and collective action. This had been particularly true for the *gente de profesiones*. But as these corporate entities weakened, combined with the erosion of racial identities and kinship ties (more rapid and extensive than in the countryside), urban commoners' sense of community also became increasingly equated with their religious association. With population much more densely settled, barrio and parish came more to coincide in physical boundaries, routine personal contacts, and administrative space. The parish church and the adjoining (or nearby) plaza were strong centers of community activity and identity.[36]

The *gente alta*, too, had been changing their sense of community, but in a different direction than that of the *gente baja*. They had a different notion of what knit the community together and of the scope of the common space to be shared. For the *gente alta*, the community had always been understood as a polity in addition to being a network of solidary relations based on kin, racial caste, or corporate association. This understanding meant that they thought, above all, in terms of the *gran* community, the locality, which was composed of disparate groups of people sharing a common heritage and territorial space. To be cohesive it needed to be formally institutionalized and managed.[37]

The massive changes since 1750 had not altered the *gente alta's* broader spatial sense of community. Indeed, the expansion of public responsibility and representative government had given them an even firmer sense of the locality as *gran* community. Their sense of small community had been centered in the guilds (the affiliation of many professionally) and the cathedral church. The latter, located in the central core of the town or city where they resided, had been an important source of access (mediated through their own *cofradías* and the occupation of clerical posts) to economic resources and political influence. But the advance of the market economy and the influence of Enlightenment ideas had rendered these institutions increasingly less assets than obstacles. By contrast, the recent past had demonstrated the growing value of kin networks as vehicles for family enterprise. For the notables, in particular, the growing web of family relations was coming to constitute a small community within the *gran* community over which they presided.

The Coming Imperative: Negotiating Rights, Responsibilities, and Obligations

Articulating the small communities and the *gran* community in each locality—and relating the locality to new political constructs at provincial (state) and national levels—had become a critical issue facing *gente alta* and *gente baja* alike. The formal, legitimate basis of determining and enforcing rights and obligations had eroded. Accelerating economic change, social transformation, and political insurgency had left the old political order in tatters everywhere except Brazil. The challenge to long-standing lines of authority had not been just to an imperial regime. The traditional bonds of hierarchy within localities and regions as well had fallen into dispute, as graphically demonstrated by the popular movements led by Miguel Hidalgo y Costilla and José María Morelos y Pavón in Mexico and by José Antonio Páez and the royalist José Tomás Boves in Venezuela.

The twin foundations of colonial and imperial politics had been severely undermined. The mechanism of petition (satisfying needs and grievances by formal request to higher authorities) had been debilitated, first by the growing loss of confidence in imperial arbitration and then by the elimination of the legitimate royal patriarchal ruler altogether. In addition, the mechanism of corporatist representation had lost its clarity. Its carefully demarcated sets of privileges had become increasingly compromised. Its well-defined institutional-racial groupings had become more and more blurred. As these customarily dominant mechanisms had proven increasingly less effective and in time largely unworkable, the informal political devices of calculated disorder and negotiation had become ever more important. Late-colonial riots and rebellions had manifested this changing mechanics of politics, culminating in the insurgent movements. Revenge had sometimes escaped the bounds of calculated violence. But negotiation had played a crucial role in forging and accommodating coalitions, resolving conflicting demands, and terminating disorder.

On the surface it would seem that a new republican political order, guided by Enlightenment principles, was in the making, defusing the necessity for calculated disorder and making negotiation more institutionalized. In formal structures of governance and above all in republican rhetoric, a new equilibrium of rights and obligations was being heralded. However, as yet, there was little consensus on the specific political principles underpinning such an equilibrium: the degree to which authority should be centralized spatially and functionally; the role of the general public in determining political leadership; the legitimacy and basis of representation; the mechanisms for the redress of grievances; and the grounds for legitimate resistance.[38] *Gente alta* discussed and debated such questions in the formal parlance of the times and often in public forums. *Gente baja*, when they talked about such matters, mostly did so in terms far more simplified and bearing much more on the practical consequences for their daily lives.

One common republican idiom in which *gente alta* and *gente baja* had become commonly conversant was that of "citizen" versus "subject." Use of the term "citizen" by both had potentially revolutionary implications. In its republican context, citizen implied an association of free individuals with equal rights, not being bound to the authority and control of another who determined one's rights and obligations. Status and membership in the larger body politic was based on the individual alone, not on one's affiliation with an ethnic, racial, or corporate group. Moreover, that membership was volitional, with each citizen contractually related to the state.[39] The concept of citizen perhaps most epitomized the revolutionary potential of the new republican rhetoric and political models, for it had the potential to reduce dramatically the social, economic, and cultural space that existed between and among the *gente alta* and the *gente baja*.

In the colonial order, the crown had mediated and arbitrated the space and distance between racial estates and the factions within both. It had done so in the context of a hierarchy of privileges, obligations, and deference enforced through an elaborate system of formal governance in alliance with royally chartered corporate bodies. Nevertheless, the enforcement of those hierarchical relations had been compromised by the immense size of the Ibero-American empires and by the fluctuating fortunes of their royal governments. In the resulting gaps in royal authority, several informal sociopolitical practices had taken root to complement or temper that formal system of governance.

The Iberian medieval tradition of retainers (though without the rules and sanctions of feudalism) had come to America with the conquistadores. The existence and size of the band of dependent followers were a measure of a proprietor's prestige, influence, and de facto authority. The strong tradition of patriarchy had also come to the New World. Clientelism and patriarchy had created private circles of hierarchy (whose extension depended upon the size of a family's resources) that replicated the royally sanctioned societal hierarchy. They had also given rise to an informal pattern of leadership, strongly reliant on such linkages of kin and clients. Those with a forceful character, a knack for aggregating followers, an ability to articulate a common discourse, and a prior status (based on family or wealth) or acquired technical or administrative expertise had come to occupy such informal leadership posts in their communities.[40]

Nevertheless, such personalist, patriarchal leadership in the coming years could only partially fill the vacuum created by the demise of royal authority. It could not compel the deference that had formerly bound subjects of the colonial order into a formal hierarchy of societal relations. Gone was the royal authority that stood behind the proscribed rules and codes of etiquette, speech, dress, and general demeanor that translated deference into practice. Markedly diminished was the disposition toward deference that underlay and solidified its practice over time. Republican rhetoric declared that all were citizens, empowered to contract or give consent to the relations into which they entered. The tenets of the liberal capitalist marketplace echoed this new dogma.

Still, the realities of economic power and political force would compromise the republican empowerment that was being proclaimed and given formal structure, a fact understood more acutely as one descended the social ladder. From this would stem the considerable play in post-independence political and social relations. For hierarchical deference, as well as the just claim of consent—the one no longer sanctioned, the other formally declared—were clouded in uncertainty. As a result, deference on the part of those below became a strategy to be calculated far more than a code of conduct by which to abide in social and political relations. The need for consent on the part of those above would remain largely implied and unarticulated.[41] Herein, then, lay the boundaries of personalist, informal relations in Middle Period society, in which rights and obligations were being negotiated between members of families, patron and clients, and community leaders and their followers. Increasingly, the workings and limits of these personalist relations would infuse the formal public realm of government and officeholding.

Only in Brazil, among the independent territories within Latin America, did the monarchical authority remain to give formal sanction to the existing hierarchy of deference. But even that would be undermined. For rights and obligations were being negotiated in Brazil as they were elsewhere in Latin America (and as in some cases would be also done in the remaining European colonies in the Caribbean). That process was taking place on more familiar, formal, and restricted grounds in Brazil. Hierarchical deference was less clouded; consent more articulated and constricted. Yet the expansion of personal patriarchal relations continued apace there, too, though with less penetration of formal governance. More fundamentally, throughout Latin

America a new equilibrium in social, economic, and political relations needed to be institutionalized if Middle Period society were to be more than a transitory phase in Latin America's history.

Notes

1. James A. Henretta, *The Evolution of American Society, 1700–1815: An Interdisciplinary Analysis* (Lexington, MA: D. C. Heath, 1973), 23–25, 187–214.

2. Swann, *Tierra Adentro*, 91–97.

3. Taylor, "Rural Unrest in Central Jalisco," 235–36; Larson, *Agrarian Transformation*, 269–71, 292–94; Swann, *Tierra Adentro*, 389–92.

4. Arij Ouweneel, "Growth, Stagnation, and Migration: An Explorative Analysis of the *Tributario* Series of Anahuac (1720–1800)," *HAHR* 71 (August 1991): 555–65; Cynthia Radding, "Ethnicity and the Emerging Peasant Class of Northwestern New Spain, 1760–1860" (Ph.D. diss., University of California, San Diego, 1990), 246–86.

5. Wu's study ("City of Querétaro"), among numerous local and regional studies, demonstrates the expanding miscegenation.

6. Stavig, "Rural Cuzco," 754–62; Cahill, "Curas and Social Conflict," 253–59; Martin, "Late Colonial Morelos," 410–26; Van Young, "Conflict and Solidarity in Indian Village Life," 67–75; Carlos Mayo, "Landed but Not Powerful: The Colonial Estancieros of Buenos Aires," *HAHR* 71 (November 1991): 761–79; Anderson, "Race and Social Stratification," 220–37; John K. Chance and William B. Taylor, "Estate and Class in a Colonial City: Oaxaca in 1792," *CSSH* 19 (July 1977): 472–81.

7. Elizabeth Kuznesof, "Household Composition and Headship as Related to Changes in Modes of Production: São Paulo, 1765–1836," *CSSH* 22 (January 1980): 80–81, 94–100, 107; Larson, *Agrarian Transformation*, chaps. 4–5.

8. Larson, *Agrarian Transformation*, 115–32, 272–84.

9. Radding, "Emerging Peasant Class," see especially chaps. 4–7.

10. Robert McCaa, "Calidad, Clase, and Marriage in Colonial Mexico: The Case of Parral, 1788–1790," *HAHR* 64 (August 1984): 493–99; Ouweneel, "Growth, Stagnation, and Migration," 562–68; Radding, "Emerging Peasant Class," 268–86; Chance and Taylor, "Estate and Class in a Colonial City," 472–81; Anderson, "Race and Social Stratification," 231–37; Swann, *Tierra Adentro*, 323–74; Miller, "Bourbon Social Engineering," 261–67.

11. McCaa, "Calidad, Clase, and Marriage," 490–93; Lynch, *Spanish-American Revolutions*, 20–21.

12. Swann, *Tierra Adentro*, 357–74; Radding, "Emerging Peasant Class," 121–49, 259–76, 524–25; Anderson, "Race and Social Stratification," 217–19, 231–41; Larson, *Agrarian Transformation*, 115, 156–59, 194–98; Kicza, *Colonial Entrepreneurs*, 101–33, 170–72, 187–226, 233–34, 239; Lyman Johnson, "Artisans," in *Cities and Society in Colonial Latin America*, ed. Susan M. Socolow and Louisa S. Hoberman (Albuquerque: University of New Mexico Press, 1986), 245–47, 265–68.

13. Lockhart and Schwartz, *Early Latin America*, 317–18; Anderson, "Race and Social Stratification," 220–37; Swann, *Tierra Adentro*, 295–98; Ouweneel, "Growth, Stagnation, and Migration," 564–66; McCaa, "Calidad, Clase, and Marriage," 477–78, 499–500.

14. Robert Ferry, *Early Caracas*, 244, 249; McFarlane, "Urban Insurrection in Bourbon Quito," 306; Mark Szuchman, *Order, Family, and Community in Buenos Aires, 1810–1860* (Stanford, CA: Stanford University Press, 1988), 2–4; Anderson, "Race and Social Stratification," 220–27.

15. Diana Balmori, Stuart F. Voss, and Miles Wortman, *Notable Family Networks in Latin America* (Chicago: University of Chicago Press, 1984), 1–26 [Spanish edition, *Las aliances de familias y la formación del país en América Latina* (Mexico: Fondo de Cultura Económica, 1990), 9–41].

16. Juan Carlos Garavaglia and Juan Carlos Grosso, "Mexican Elites of a Provincial Town: The Landowners of Tepeaca," *HAHR* 70 (May 1990): 268–72; Mayo, "Colonial Estancieros of Buenos Aires," 762–77; Larson, *Agrarian Transformation*, 230–31; Tutino, "Valleys of Mexico and Toluca," 181–82; Radding, "Emerging Peasant Class," 335–49.

17. Kicza, *Colonial Entrepreneurs*, chaps. 4–6, 229, 233–35, 239–43; Johnson, "Artisans," 245–46.

18. Susan Deans-Smith suggested this nomenclature, based on her study of urban manufacturing in the Bourbon era, in particular the tobacco monopoly. See *The Making of the Tobacco Monopoly in Bourbon Mexico* (Austin: University of Texas Press, 1992).

19. Anderson, "Race and Social Stratification," 217–37; Kicza, *Colonial Entrepreneurs*, 110–14, 129–30, 207–8, 239; Johnson, "Artisans," 246; MacFarlane, "Urban Insurrection in Bourbon Quito," 300–308.

20. Kicza, *Colonial Entrepreneurs*, 96–99; Radding, "Emerging Peasant Class," 396–97.

21. Tutino, "Valleys of Mexico and Toluca," 187–89; Larson, *Agrarian Transformation*, 206–8.

22. Chance, *Conquest of the Sierra*, 131–50; Tutino, "Valleys of Mexico and Toluca," 182–86; Larson, *Agrarian Transformation*, 161–70; Cahill, "Curas and Social Conflict," 256–58.

23. Kuznesof, "Household Composition and Headship," 88–89; Radding, "Emerging Peasant Class," 1–6, 96–104; Johnson, "Artisans," 244.

24. Kuznesof, "Household Composition and Headship," 80–81, 92–94, 107–8; Radding, "Emerging Peasant Class," 142–49.

25. Balmori, Voss, and Wortman, *Notable Family Networks*, 26–35, 186–97.

26. Kicza, *Colonial Entrepreneurs*, 140–47, 239–43.

27. Ibid., 240; Anderson, "Race and Social Stratification," 233; Kuznesof, "Household Composition and Headship," 80–81, 101, 108; Donald Ramos, "City and Country: The Family in Minas Gerais, 1804–1838," *Journal of Family History* 3 (Winter 1978): 365–67; Szuchman, *Order, Family, and Community*, 198.

28. Kuznesof, "Household Composition and Headship," 80–81, 97–100, 106–8; Donald Ramos, "Marriage and Family in Colonial Vila Rica," *HAHR* 55 (May 1975): 207–16; Szuchman, *Order, Family, and Community*, 199, 203–4; Radding, "Emerging Peasant Class," 197–220.

29. Radding, "Emerging Peasant Class," 197–211; Kuznesof, "Household Composition and Headship," 99–100; Anderson, "Race and Social Stratification," 237–39; McCaa, "Calidad, Clase, and Marriage," 489–90; Swann, *Tierra Adentro*, 207–14; Sylvia Arrom, "Marriage Patterns in Mexico City, 1811," *Journal of Family History* 3 (Winter 1978): 382–89; Ramos, "Colonial Vila Rica," 218–20; Ramos, "Family in Minas Gerais," 370–72; Miller, "Bourbon Social Engineering," 279–89.

30. Radding, "Emerging Peasant Class," 211–19; Arrom, "Marriage Patterns," 379–89; McCaa, "Calidad, Clase, and Marriage," 484–90, 493–97.

31. Szuchman, *Order, Family, and Community*, 2–3, 236; Radding, "Emerging Peasant Class," 220, 244.

32. Chance, *Conquest of the Sierra*, 137–41, 146, 168–75; Van Oss, *Catholic Colonialism*, 109–15; Edward H. Spicer, *The Yaquis: A Cultural History* (Tucson: University of Arizona Press, 1980), 70–95.

33. Sidney W. Mintz, "The Origin of Reconstituted Peasantries," in *Caribbean Freedom: Economy and Society from Emancipation to the Present*, ed. Hilary Beckles and Verene Shepherd (Princeton, NJ: Marcus Weiner, 1996), 94–98; O. Nigel Boland, "Systems of Domination after Slavery: The Control of Land in the British West Indies after 1838," in *Caribbean Freedom*, 107–23; Roger Bastide, *African Civilization in the New World* (New York: Harper and Row, 1971), chaps. 2–3, 7.

34. Radding, "Emerging Peasant Class," 276–92; Chance, *Conquest of the Sierra*, 168–72; Van Oss, *Catholic Colonialism*, 109–15, 136–42, 149–52; Taylor, "Rural Unrest in Central Jalisco," 232–34.

35. Chance, *Conquest of the Sierra*, 171; Taylor, "Rural Unrest in Central Jalisco," 232–34; Swann, *Tierra Adentro*, 92–96.

36. MacFarlane, "Urban Insurrection in Bourbon Quito," 305–7; Szuchman, *Order, Family, and Community*, 4–6.

37. Ibid., 3–4.

38. Ibid., 12–13.

39. Vogel, "Naturalization in Early Independent Argentina," 108.

40. François Chevalier, "The Roots of Caudillismo," 28–30, Glenn Claudill Dealy, "The Public Man," 48–51, Hugh Hamill, "Hidalgo and Calleja: The Colonial Bases of Caudillismo," in *Caudillos: Dictators in Spanish America*, ed. Hugh Hamill (Norman: University Press of Oklahoma, 1992).

41. Szuchman (*Order, Family, and Community*) details the play and boundaries of these personal, informal relations in matters of criminal justice, education, public deportment, and caudillo politics. See also Mary Lowenthal Felstiner, "Kinship Politics in the Chilean Independence Movement," *HAHR* 56 (February 1976): 58–80.

4

The Regional Compromise
Vertical Collaboration

For nearly two decades, insurgency movements seeking independence from Iberian imperial rule had brought strife and turbulence. By the late 1820s their cumulative effect fostered a common desire among most inhabitants to reestablish order, in the formal sense of governmental authority but also very much in the realm of social relations and the stability of daily life. Many regions were still feeling the effects of demographic and economic dislocation, direct war losses, and the turnover of public authorities and policies. These conditions often had magnified in the first years after independence.[1]

Even more unsettling was the radical change in political vision and structure, particularly the rapidity with which it had come. Within two years the Napoleonic invasion had triggered a sudden political transformation. Subjects, hierarchically separated into groups with distinct rights and obligations, had become citizens equal under standardized law. Written constitutions spelled out the founding compact of a new political order. Representation was no longer by the most illustrious within the corporate bodies that had dominated the colonial world. Now representatives were elected proportionately from a given territorial unit, with all *vecinos* entitled to vote.

This vision of a modern republican politics drew from a remembered past and recent experience. The Spanish municipal reform of 1767 had partially revived the Iberian medieval tradition of representative municipal government, in which the vote was given to established male heads of household, "usefully" employed, and with no stain on their reputation. It set up an electoral system whereby all *vecinos* could elect a certain number of magistrates in the cabildo. The holding of open cabildo meetings in the formation of the first juntas after 1808 was an expression of a popular collective memory. Widespread popular support and sacrifice for insurgent movements bespoke the entitlement to widespread suffrage in the immediate circumstance. The drawing up of the first constitutions and electoral formats expressed the triumph of the radical visionaries, the political modernizers, who had found in the French Revolution the basis for a new political order that could restore the ancient freedoms and representative institutions.[2] The practical result was the sudden emergence of a potentially immense number of new direct participants in the public life of Ibero-America.

Still, the practice and tradition of representative government had not been carried out over a long period of time before independence, as in North America. There was only a remembered tradition. Territorial boundaries of sovereignty were far more uncertain and often remained unsettled. There was no singular, unifying pact among the sovereign states, and often what founding pacts there were among regional societies were imposed by one or some upon the others rather than freely negotiated. Finally, the ideological vision came first, tempered and blurred by the memory of a very old but little practiced premodern tradition of representative government. The practice was still to be worked out and institutionalized.

Thus, the transformation to a modern political system of representative government and sovereign nation-states in what became Latin America was far more sudden and compressed than in that part of Anglo-America that became the United States. As a result, conflict over the new political order's purposes and structure was far greater, with a ripple effect down from the nation-states through the localities into communities and households. Moreover, there was the uncertainty of how the new political order would correlate with the North Atlantic–driven international market, whose scope and penetration were accelerating rapidly as industrialization spread. Together, these two sources of disruption simultaneously expanded expectations for and bred threats to the lives and well-being of the new citizenry among the social strata that had come to constitute Middle Period society.

Possibility, Tempered by Fear and Accustomed Practice

For the *gente alta*, independence brought the opportunity to be free of the corporate bodies that had become more of an impediment than an aid in the pursuit of their private interests. The notables in particular, whose familial interlinkages were crystallizing into complex, expanding family networks, could most readily employ kinship ties to further their interests.[3] Yet alongside that reality of enhanced opportunity was the perceived threat of social disorder. *Gente alta* notions of and apprehensiveness about plebian proclivity toward crime seemed confirmed in the growing vagrancy, family incoherence, and disregard for traditionally accepted norms of behavior in social relations and public deportment that had grown in the last decades of imperial rule. The intermingling of banditry and popular vengeance with insurgency had intensified and politicized these trends. Combined with the new modern republican rhetoric and institutional models—and the fact of widespread suffrage wrought by the independence movements—the *gente baja*'s exercise of freedom and prerogative, now judged excessive by the *gente alta*, could become explosive.

The imperative of reestablishing social control had become a primal preoccupation, a common denominator, among those above the line of social respectability. It was so however much they might be split by the interests of family and locality and sometimes by ideological leanings. The political problem was how to transpose republican models and discourse into a new workable political order that would guarantee them social control over that line of respectability.[4] Beyond issues of law and practice, that meant reconciling long-standing obligations of hierarchy with modern republican notions of liberty.

Such republican notions were finding a response among the *gente de profesiones*. In calculating their private interests they weighed the declining support of corporate structures against their prospects of using increased freedom of individual action to maintain a small measure of stability in their lives or even improve their situation. The expanding marketplace, the experience of the independence struggles, the reality of widespread suffrage, and the promise of republican rhetoric had broadened both their freedom of action and their horizons. Some did embrace the tenets of marketplace entrepreneurship and republican citizenship. In so doing, they were forced to adjust their relations within their communities. The rest joined the popular classes in accommodating such tenets to the solidary relations of kin, corporate association, and community.

The aftermath of the independence struggles and the rise of the modern republican order did offer the *gente baja* in general new prospects. There was the possibility for greater prerogative and autonomy in their daily lives and in the shared patterns of thinking and behavior that cemented their communities. In particular, the revival of municipal life—and the vision of 'local democracy' that had become associated with the new modern politics and had been facilitated by the expansion of suffrage to all *vecinos* in practice—seemed to foster that possibility. Social and cultural space had expanded. The burdens of legal discrimination were in the process of being greatly reduced, if not eliminated. Economic leverage in labor relations and tenancy had increased. Nevertheless, those same republican values and political structures had reinforced the destabilizing forces of the marketplace, intensifying the potential threat to the *gente baja*'s subsistence and lifestyle. The imperative of reestablishing the security of their daily life had become even more pressing.

The *gente baja* sought security for their microworlds of household, community, and parish by expanding the social and cultural space between those small worlds and the larger society. Their ability to do so depended upon their economic leverage in the spreading market economy and upon their political power in local government in the layered republican political order that was being erected above them. The *gente alta* sought security as well, but far more to become than simply to be. Their social mobility required greater social order in the *gran* community and in the regional society upon which their private worlds depended. In turn, order required greater control over the microworlds of the *gente baja*. To maintain their social distance from the latter, the *gente alta* needed to contract the economic, social, and cultural space between them and to limit the *gente baja*'s political participation.

Both *gente alta* and *gente baja* faced the political reality that the independence wars and their aftermath had left the public realm of governance markedly weakened and formal authority dispersed. The legitimate mediator and arbiter had been eliminated, except in Brazil. Corporate bodies had been (or were being) undermined, if not expunged. The deference infusing prior social and political relations now lacked the guarantee of a formal government-sanctioned hierarchy. The opportunity and need for private, personal, informal patterns of control and leadership to inform whatever governing structures emerged to replace the imperial regime had grown proportionately.

The *gente baja* had little familiarity with the Lockean rule of constitutions and standardized statutes, now in modern republican guise. Nor had experience given them confidence in relying on the workings of the capitalist marketplace to increase the security in their lives. More and more, they were coming to see personal bonds as the most reliable guarantee for their livelihood and way of life. Though far more optimistic about the fortunes of the marketplace, the *gente alta* in general were beginning to reach a similar conclusion. For them, personal relationships had often proved to be a hedge against misfortune and an advantage for profit. Some ardently believed in the transforming power of modern representative institutions, and many more were willing to experiment with them, but their reliability in guaranteeing the social order was as yet unconfirmed or even untested. Nor was there common agreement on the most utilitarian selection and arrangement of these new constructs of governance. The notables, in particular, came to see the advantage (when not the necessity) of resorting to the traditions of patriarchy and personalism to reforge stable community and public links among the *gente alta* and with the *gente baja*. They had more to lose from social upheaval and more familial and clientalistic assets to employ.[5]

This openness to the private, the personal, in the conduct of public life—cutting across lines of social stratification—would prove central to the post-independence search of Latin America's Middle Period society for an equilibrium in negotiating rights and obligations and in the political structures that would formalize those relations. In this process, the *gente alta* (especially notables) generally set the political agenda. Nevertheless, in their reactions and adaptations, the *gente baja* not infrequently turned *gente alta* discourse and practice to their own advantage or shaped the boundaries of that agenda. From schooling and the circulation of Enlightenment thought, the "active citizenry" (as the *gente alta* saw themselves) chose among three classical options in trying to construct a system of government neither arbitrary nor despotic, but freely chosen and accountable. Though not without dispute in many of the new nation-states, monarchy was no longer seen as serving such ends. Paraguay did find a dictator for life in José Gaspar Rodríguez de Francia. His successor and nephew, Carlos Antonio López, converted the office into a hereditary presidency. However, with Brazil duly noted, such solutions were the exception.

Elsewhere, then, the choice was between the other two classical options: rule by the few or rule by the many. For those above the line of respectability, the choice would seem perhaps simple. But the problem lay in delimiting the "few." Networks of notable families were soon involved in struggles over the distribution of power at local, district, and regional levels. For the *gente decente*, the few had to extend considerably beyond notable families if the promise of modern representative politics was to be fulfilled and the notability most sought was to be attained. The whole of the *gente alta* might agree (and largely did) that the few should certainly not extend beyond the line of respectability. But the principles espoused and written into constitutions after 1808, combined with the aroused expectations and the political leverage gained by the *gente baja*, made the likelihood of any formal oligarchy most unlikely. The *gente de profesiones*, especially in towns and cities, had become a political force that could not be dismissed, and direct action by the popular classes was potentially more imminent and consequential. Given all of this, a caveat for the *gente alta* was that any form of modern republican government they might devise had to be based in popular sovereignty if it were to be legitimate.

Yet there was the rub for the *gente alta*: what if popular sovereignty came to mean democracy? For them that word connoted mob rule, which they deeply feared. Thus, the challenge the *gente alta* faced was to find a position of equilibrium between an "aristocracy" of the respectable (that could destabilize toward a closed oligarchy) and a democracy (that could destabilize toward mob rule, most likely ending in rule by a tyrant). They perceived Francia's Paraguay and the black republic of Haiti in just such latter terms. For their part, the popular classes, far from being a homogeneous social strata, possessed disparate cultural patterns. Although they despised oligarchy, their particular interests were not guaranteed by democracy. Their search for representation in the new nation-states would also settle between democracy and rule of the few.

The search for an equilibrium in representation in the new republican politics was not only a social question. It also entailed a spatial dimension, one upon which there was far less tradition and custom to draw. At what scale did sovereignty most appropriately lie? Modern republican government embodied in the nation-state did not give a definitive answer. Was the nation a uniform, standardized society of individual citizens, no matter how large the national territory? Or was the nation an association or federation of regional societies (usually dominated by a large urban center) whose relative autonomy took precedence in origin and priority over the mutually arrived at "national" goals and founding principles? And even within those regional societies, how free and autonomous were the localities embodied in the *municipios*?[6] *Gente baja* bias was toward the smaller end of the spatial continuum (as discussed in Chapter 3). The *gente alta* were divided, depending upon private economic interests (the power, relative independence, and connection to the international market of their locality, district, or region) and upon the ideological influence of a particular foreign model.

At first glance it would seem that Brazil alone among Latin America's new national entities achieved the equilibrium for which Middle Period society was searching after 1820 and that it had done so largely by maintaining pre-independence political tradition and practice. The authority of a European-bred monarch remained to give formal sanction to the existing societal hierarchy and a unitary government on a continental scale. At the top, a nonhereditary titled nobility, begun during the residency of the last Portuguese monarch, continued to expand. At the bottom, a large portion of the population remained rigidly held in the status of slaves for the foreseeable future.

Nevertheless, republican experimentation and regional resistance led to a paring down of the imperial hierarchy and limitations on aristocratic privilege in the first decades after independence. The emperor was obliged to surrender legislative power to a national assembly and provincial assemblies. A basic set of individual guarantees was established, including equality under the law (though voting rights were highly restricted). The entailing of estates was outlawed. Spatially, the power of *fazendeiros* (large estate owners)—heading *parentelas* (large informal networks of kin and clients) increased, overshadowing imperial governing structures at the local and district levels. In the 1830s and 1840s, several revolts for greater regional autonomy or for a federalist system erupted. Below, both socially and spatially, *gente baja* resistance was also manifest, in opposition to legal and racial discrimination, slave revolts, and resistance to imperial imposition.[7]

At the national level, the search for an equilibrium in representation had seemingly been resolved for two decades during the middle of the century. But underneath Brazil's imperial overlay, as elsewhere in Latin America, down at the local and regional level where people's lives remained centered, that search continued. For Brazil (though to a lesser degree) was also a fragmented nation-state society. There, too, though with less profile, modes of collaboration appeared in the search that cut across divisions of social strata and geopolitical scale.

The Fragmented Society

The daunting reality of a badly fragmented society made Middle Period society's search for an equilibrium in social and spatial representation more problematic. Though the half century before independence had blurred racial lines and weakened corporate identities, the reconfiguration of the social order had left deep cleavages on its own terms, especially the cleft of respectability. In addition, there were fissures within the new social strata, especially among the *gente baja*. There were also geopolitical fault lines, particularly given the fact that there had been no prior experience in linking locality, region, and nation-state in a spatial system of representation. Finally, there were those who could not accept the present limits of a middle ground in the search for representation. Their vision stretched too far to accommodate a negotiated search.

Visionaries on the Periphery

On the margins of Latin America's emerging bodies politic, both ideo-logically and spatially, were factions who lacked (or lost) faith in the negotiation of a workable system of representation. Some simply did not see themselves as part of the body politic and refused incorpora-tion. Others, facing the mounting detrimental consequences of eco-nomic and cultural change, felt driven to opt out. Still others, impatient with the pace of modernizing change, strove to force a new societal order, even if that meant destabilizing the very body politic they sought to lead expeditiously into the future.

On the edges of many of the new Latin American nations resided those who had come to be known (in the Iberian lexicon) as *indios barbaros*. These largely nomadic tribes, whose adoption of the horse had given them far greater mobility, had successfully resisted the Span-ish for nearly three centuries. The late Bourbons' twin policies of mate-rial rations and increased presence of presidial garrisons had produced a tentative peace and, in some cases, nominal allegiance. With the cre-ation of the new Latin American nations, *indios barbaros* declared their virtual independence, though the international community never ac-knowledged their status as distinct nations. Fiscal penury and politi-cal strife soon terminated the rations, undermined the missions, and weakened the frontier garrisons. In addition, the growing presence of foreign adventurers and traders in most of the regions enhanced these Indian tribes' separate status within Latin America's national bound-aries, at least in the short run. They acquired goods sought on regional and international markets, which were sometimes the result of their own production but more often were the result of raiding.

Into the late nineteenth century, the tribes of southern Chile and Argentina maintained their independence. With growing economic interchange and political consolidation among them (especially in Ar-gentina) and the lack of penetration among them by foreigners, they were able to establish a clear line of separation from the national enti-ties of which their lands were only technically a part. Only grudgingly and with fierce resistance did they allow that line to be pushed south. By contrast, on the Mosquito Coast and in the Mexican far north, for-eigners steadily penetrated the lands of these tribes. By midcentury North American traders and trappers, adventurers and immigrant set-tlers, British agents and merchants, and Jamaican black laborers had succeeded in eroding the *indios barbaros'* autonomy. Foreigners served as advance columns in the incorporation of Mexico's far north into the expanding United States. British–United States rivalry over trade and transit across Central America left Honduras and Nicaragua with titular control over the Mosquito Coast and the Mosquitos themselves with nominal autonomy. In reality, the non-Indians who were left controlled local government.[8]

In some other peripheral regions, principally in Mexico, a vision of independence also arose among Indian peoples who had been incorporated directly into the imperial system, though usually not without resistance and revolt in the face of the accelerating penetration of non-Indian settlement, royal administration, and the market economy. After independence, the circumstances surrounding external penetration of Indian community life had altered significantly. Government was at once weaker and yet operated on a radically new basis. The market economy was at once slowed by the aftermath of the independence wars and the failures of public policy and yet stimulated by new possibilities arising from increased and more direct contact with international markets. The subject Indian peoples within the new national boundaries differed in their response, depending upon their solidarity in scale and organization, their ability to find room to maneuver within the larger political and economic patterns, and their determination of the risks and imperative of total resistance. The large majority chose accommodation and collaboration with outsiders.

The vision of outright independence asserted itself in disparate parts of Mexico. In the northwest, the Yaquis and Mayos of southern Sonora rebelled in the 1820s in reaction to direct, geographically based rule by non-Indians, who demanded payment of taxes from which the tribes had previously been exempt and who sought access to tribal lands for commercial ventures. The tribes were unsuccessful in creating a pan-Indian confederation in the state, but decades of political turmoil helped them maintain a de facto autonomy until the late 1860s. In the Yucatán peninsula, the pressures of commercialization accelerated after independence. Mayan villagers in the eastern districts—who had maintained their local cohesion and control and who saw encroaching non-Indians almost uniformly as invaders—initiated the Caste War in 1847. Briefly, it looked as though the Mayans might drive non-Indians to the peninsula's western shores. But the need of subsistence farmer-soldiers to tend to their crops, lack of cohesion among villages, shallowness of commitment of the western Maya, and timely infusion of national and external support all led to the grudging retreat of the most defiant Maya to the southeastern part of the peninsula. They established a sovereign territory to protect their way of life and racial identity, infused with a new hybrid religion, the "Speaking Cross." The *Cruzob*, as rebel Maya called themselves, maintained their independence for almost a half century.[9] In regions long-settled by non-Indians and more closely tied to the core of Iberian rule and patterns of life, there is evidence that other Indian villagers may have shared such a vision of regional sovereignty. But in practical terms, their resistance was limited to securing as much local autonomy as was possible in a larger body politic controlled by outsiders.

These Indians' African counterparts could be found scattered through the Caribbean islands and in the Guyanas on the northeastern South American coast. First as slaves rebelling for freedom and then as freed slaves seeking refuge from the plantation regime, African Americans sought to reconstitute themselves in peasant villages with as little outside interference as possible. In marginal and hilly lands, many found such a lifestyle viable. In parts of the Guyanas, some maintained an independent existence.[10]

On another periphery of post-independence society were those whose visions threatened fragmentation from within, rather than erosion at the margins. Spatially, they were generally based in the very control centers of Middle Period society, the large provincial urban centers and national capitals. If they were not raised there, their education and political aspirations had led them to gravitate there. Their peripheral status was wholly ideological. They sought not independence or isolation from the new nation-states (or remaining colonies), as the *barbaros*, Indian villagers, and ex-slave African peasant visionaries did. On the contrary, they desired uncompromisingly to transform rapidly the body politic of their respective nations.

The independence generation of these visionaries were devoted followers of the Enlightenment. The ideological source of the succeeding generation was the social liberalism of mid-nineteenth-century Europe. It was not that either possessed their ideologies exclusively. Rather, the radicalness of their visions lay in their determination to push the tenets of freedom in modern republican government and society to their limits, or at least to limits beyond which the great majority of the citizenry dared to cross. Above all these radical republicans sought the elimination, rather than the adaptation or accommodation, of long-standing institutional structures. Taken individually, various segments within the active citizenry agreed with the radicals, especially as their interests were furthered by the elimination of obligations to such institutional structures or of obstacles to opportunity created by them. But for every segment that applauded such uncompromising action, there were others whose interests were impaired by it. Collectively, the result was the fraying of already tenuous lines of consensus and toleration and the intensification of factionalism.

Nowhere was the tension more evident than in relations across the social line of respectability. For radical republicans fully intended to transform the *gente baja*'s solidary relations and shared patterns of behavior. Whether it was the intention of Unitarians to replace the gauchos (cowboys) with small farmers and agricultural laborers on the plains of Argentina or the Colombian and Central American liberals' plans to "integrate" Indian villagers by breaking down their communities' isolation and protections, the *gente baja* were to be disciplined and acculturated to the ways of "progress" exhibited in Europe and the United States. At the same time, some radical republicans included an egalitarian resonance in their calls for transformation, which threatened to overwhelm the line of respectability. Ponciano Arriaga, a Mexican liberal, unsuccessfully proposed the confiscation and redistribution of idle hacienda lands. Bolivian president Manuel Belzú publicly railed at the aggrandizing evils of private property concentrated in the hands of the notables and then stood by as dispossessed rural commoners seized estate lands. He encouraged the organization of the first modern trade unions.[11]

Radical republican visions proved to be a two-edged sword, threatening to rend the fabric of Middle Period society. Egalitarian appeals encouraged abandonment of social deference while fostering belief in the possibility of greater control over economic resources and more direct involvement in political decisionmaking. This resonated most among the *gente de profesiones* (especially urban artisans) and among the dispossessed in the countryside. Meanwhile, radical republican intentions of "modernizing" the *gente baja* aroused hostility among the many who surmised that, in the process, they would be stripped of their cultural lifestyle and further subjugated economically and politically.

Geopolitical Fault Lines

At best, delineation of nation-state boundaries in independence's wake had been a tenuous proposition. From the 1820s through the 1870s, those boundaries were frequently adjusted through wars and an occasional treaty. Within the new national boundaries, demarcation of rights and responsibilities between the principal spatial levels of public life was on entirely new ground. Though differences over the extent of municipal powers and prerogatives arose, the fundamental fault line was that between the regions and the nation. Even in Brazil's constitutional monarchy these spatial divisions would be contested, though more sporadically and less officially. This regional-national dichotomy—expressed initially in the constitutional constructs of federalism and centralism—constituted the principal axis around which political movements of the independence generation formed. For the succeeding generation of liberals and conservatives, it was one of several such axes.

Complicating matters were vacuums that needed to be filled. Regionally, there already existed competing and dominant economic interests, along with common cultural patterns and historical experiences that had bound the various strata of regional society together. What was novel was the introduction of a formal body politic with an accompanying government. Sometimes encompassing a regional society but more often being one of several political entities within it, state (provincial) government became the formal instrument for pursuing interests within the region and beyond. Through this level of government, regional interests (either in competition or in coalition) sought to survive in the face of changing circumstances, to expand and absorb other localities or regions, and to use national political structures to further their interests. Some even pursued the projection of their regional interests onto the national level so as to dominate the nation.

The vacuum at the national level was great. The nation had only been declared. Economic interests that spanned and connected its various parts were still largely nonexistent. Customs and cultural affinities had yet to be created. Bureaucracies existed largely on paper, with the exception of an army inherited from the independence struggle. Identity with the *gran patria* (the nation) was spotty and shallow. In most countries by the 1860s, that national vacuum would begin to be filled by more than simply regional interests bent on extending their influence. Until then, however, regional societies clearly held the upper hand in the ordering of people's lives.

Most central to that ordering was the power of jurisdiction, the right and the authority to govern or legislate, to interpret and apply the law. The separation of powers, which came as an unfamiliar corollary of modern republican government, created a proliferation of opportunity in officeholding, whether for income or for employing public power to serve private interests. But jurisdiction determined the scope of that opportunity. A limited, consultative departmental assembly, alongside an appointed governor and revenue officers subservient to a centralized national government, presented far different political prospects for regional and district political interests than state governments with broad powers. Moreover, jurisdictional power decided the extent to which state and district officeholders could tackle pressing issues and pursue public policies. Who controlled access to and sale of public lands? Who granted concessions for large-scale public improvements and new enterprises? Who established the parameters of the church's participation in the economy and public services? How available and in what form would be education and health maintenance? Finally, central to the lifeblood of public decisionmaking was the question of who had the jurisdictional power to tax and spend. Without control over revenues, the prerogatives and benefits of public policies and officeholding were compromised.

Of major contention in jurisdictional control was the setting and application of economic policy. Contact with foreigners—whether primarily as entrepreneurs (particularly merchants) or less so as immigrant settlers—offered opportunities as well as structural alterations in local and regional economies. Laws had to be made governing their entrance and actions, and their degree of access to resources and markets had to be determined. Closely linked to foreign contact was the issue of the degree of trade freedom or restrictions, both vis-à-vis the international market and among regions. The level at which customs duties and other taxes on trade were set, along with the number of ports and land transit points opened to commerce, profoundly affected the economy.

Along with economic policy, control of military resources was a central issue in the geopolitical contesting for power. They provided a (sometimes the) crucial asset in deciding the distribution of power and prerogative, given the still quite liquid state of republican government in post-independence Latin America. The power to raise troops, secure revenues to maintain them, and employ them in the enforcement of policy was an issue dividing region and nation. In most new nations, the conflict took the form of the national guard (or state militias) versus the national army. Colonial militia had been organized locally, generally in urban centers. But in the new republican framework, military forces below the national level became organized by state governments. Indeed, more than any other institution they appear to have embodied state and regional power. Their existence and the degree of their autonomy vis-à-vis the national government in regulation and command were the central points of contention.

Although state militias (or national guard units) had no corporate immunity and were more directly subject to civilian authorities, they were also more republican and representative in their composition and functioning. Organized at the district level under the auspices of the corresponding state-appointed official, these citizens under arms elected their own officers, were exempt from various taxes, and had the prospect of receiving land for military services. Rather than subjugated conscripts, they saw themselves as the popular embodiment of the patriotic citizenry.[12] With such a strong popular base, many among the *gente alta* viewed them with alarm.

The Social-Cultural Dichotomy

Apprehension among the *gente alta* had been building since independence over the expanding involvement of the *gente baja* in public affairs. The most alarming manifestations of this were their acts of violence. The lesson of the Parian riot (December 4, 1828) remained fresh in the minds of Mexico City's *gente alta*. In the days before the riot, the support of thousands of the capital city's commoners had proved decisive in an electoral dispute among rival *gente alta* factions. The leader they chose to follow was of popular origins, spoke publicly in a populist style, favored the protection of domestic textiles (upon which many of them depended for their livelihood), and called for the expulsion of Spaniards (symbolizing for his plebian followers the riddance of a prime remnant of colonial rule). The riot, flowing out of victory celebration in the capital's central square, focused on pillaging fancy shops in the Parian building and spread to some neighboring establishments. Although the rioting was quelled by morning, complete order was not. For more than a week, the *gente baja* and victorious soldiers ruled the streets. The *gente alta* fled or stayed in their homes.[13] Appalled and shaken, they felt more intensely the sociocultural gulf that separated them from the *gente baja*, and they were not alone in such feelings.

In the southwestern region of what became the state of Guerrero, rural commoners of various backgrounds in the 1840s lashed out at the detrimental consequences of expanding commercial agriculture and external political control over their communities. They attacked private estates and recalcitrant local authorities with a vengeance and then carried the rebellion into districts of neighboring states. The *gente alta*, even those who sought to co-opt or compromise with the rebels, were alarmed at the caste-war character of the violence. In New Mexico, fearing a threat to their dominance, the united opposition of the province's prominent families foiled a popular rebellion in 1837. Another by various *gente baja* segments in the Sierra Gorda region in central Mexico in the late 1840s ended in defeat when they tried to attack towns. Violence also manifested the sociocultural gulf in Latin America's other large national entity, Brazil. A multiracial, multistrata insurrection for reform and regional autonomy in Bahia (one of four in the northeast in the 1830s) fell apart as people of color pushed their demands for an end to slavery and discrimination to a level of violence unacceptable to "respectable" whites. In suppressing the rebellion, the established order replied racially (and socially) in kind. In the years following, *gente alta* held up the *Sabinada* revolt as the danger of social and political revolution from below, emphasizing that they would brook no further challenges.[14]

Behind these manifestations of widespread violence by the *gente baja* and of their growing participation in public affairs more generally was an increasing divergence of identity, interests, and vision. This widening cleft of respectability was the product of the discourse and structural implementation of the modern republican politics of representation and of the continuing expansion of the market economy. The *gente baja* sought to reduce pressures to raise taxes now coming from two often uncoordinated extralocal governments—those of the state (or province) and the nation. They also strove to reduce other obligations, in particular the drafts of labor by local authorities and of military service. In addition, they aspired to secure greater control over the means of production, thereby increasing access to the resources upon which their basic livelihoods and lifestyles depended, especially those of the many commoners who were not independent small producers. Controlling production generally necessitated greater autonomy for their communities. Many *gente de profesiones*, small producers themselves customarily the leaders of these communities, understood most clearly the community's role in protecting the *gente baja* from outside exploitation and in fostering the common good, especially when resources were limited, even scarce.

By contrast, the vision dawning for more and more *gente alta* was of a society of boundless opportunity for advancement and accumulation, especially for those willing to experiment and to take on more risk. Increasing foreign contact fostered the vision. So, too, did the openings created by modern republican government to alter the laws and rules governing control over the means of production—in particular, toward privatization, deregulation, and the breakup of monopolies. For some, the vision entailed the social and cultural transformation of the *gente baja* to make them conform to the requirements for their subordinated participation in this emerging new order.

This social-cultural dichotomy can be seen in the struggle of freed slaves in the Caribbean islands to resist new forms of coercion employed by white propertied groups and to reconstitute themselves into independent or semi-autonomous communities, beginning in the 1830s. In New Mexico, new market opportunities arising from the growing interchange with the expanding economy of the United States enabled the *gente alta* (especially the notables) to exploit more the labor of the most vulnerable among the popular classes through peonage and servitude. New political offices created in the wake of independence allowed them to shift the burdens of taxation and militia service more to the region's *gente baja*. In southwestern Mexico, the press of commercialized agriculture (aided by state laws privatizing communal lands), the increase in taxes, and the elimination of small *municipios* threatened the aspirations of countless rural commoners. In pressing their vision, the *gente alta* largely provoked the *gente baja*'s growing public involvement, which often culminated in violent confrontation. This, in turn, prompted the *gente alta* to seek ways to limit their participation in the public realm and to curtail their aspirations to increased autonomy in the conduct of their lives.[15] The logical conclusion of such a process, if unmitigated, was an unbridgeable gulf.

Intrastrata Fissures

Further fragmenting Middle Period society were cleavages within the *gente alta* and *gente baja*. Divisions among notables centered on geopolitics, economic interests, and political ideology and were often inextricably intertwined. A fundamental split was the degree to which local sensibilities were regarded in the imposition of authority, cultural pluralism among the *gente baja* could be tolerated, and remnant colonial institutional patterns should be retained (in particular, those of the church). Certainly, notable families' economic interests were very often fused inseparably with these ideological leanings.[16] As the major players in Middle Period society, the notables were most prone to the fracturing arising from the geopolitical fault lines. Allied families vied with one another for control of district cabeceras. District networks struggled, even in armed conflict at times, over the state capital's location or over mastery of the state government. Notable cliques in a region joined together or split over whether to resist or cooperate with intruding agents of the national government or outside entrepreneurs. Some regional alliances of notables vied for domination over the national government to promote or guard their interests vis-à-vis other regional networks.[17]

Less frequently overt was the discord between notables and the *gente decente*. Aspiring to notability themselves and often beholden to notables, the *gente decente* were inclined to voice their grievances in private. Occupation and lifestyle underlay their respectability, but they understood that accumulation of property and capital, along with political influence and extensive kinship ties, were the requisites for elevation to notability.[18] They challenged the notables publicly only when they sensed that the latter's control was choking opportunity to the point of threatening their aspirations or when economic crisis threatened their maintenance of respectability. When they did and they were successful, their great reward was being co-opted by the notables. The great risk, if unsuccessful, was alienation from those whose acceptance was essential to fulfilling their aspirations.

Among *gente baja*, too, there were fissures. Race (and ethnicity) remained a divisive force, especially where slavery lingered (in Brazil, Cuba, Puerto Rico, Peru, and Venezuela) because of the denigration of status with which it had long marked those of African ancestry. In many regions, separation of communities by cultural race continued. The rebellion of rural commoners in southwestern Mexico in the 1840s was carried on separately by *casta* villagers on the Pacific coast, mestizo villagers in the foothill valleys, and Indian villagers in the sierra. Increasingly, however, socioeconomic differentiation fragmented the *gente baja*. Within rural communities, differences between the popular classes and the *gente de profesiones* not infrequently became sharply manifest. Pressures on the latter to exploit the advantages of their greater property holdings, special skills, and leadership position for their own private interests at the community's expense (often by making deals with the *gente alta*) could open deep wounds in their communities.[19]

In urban centers, artisans and petty tradespeople faced a similar situation vis-à-vis the urban popular classes, though the barrio structure was less formal. Widening prospects of mobility through entrepreneurship and the possibility of being active in public affairs exerted a strong pull on these urban *gente de profesiones*. For money and politics were the means to cross the line of respectability or at least maintain that measure of material security and social regard that elevated them above the popular classes. Fissures between rural and urban stemmed less from antagonism than from indifference and unfamiliarity. Nevertheless, when tensions rose and crises surfaced, they could translate into fears that left the *gente baja* guarded and unsupportive, if not combative.

Collaboration in the Midst of Pressing Concerns

In the colonial order, royal law had confirmed and sanctioned the fragmenting of society into racial estates and corporate bodies. Yet royal authority had striven to keep those divisions in check in its role as patrimonial arbiter. No new law or authority quickly arose to take the Iberian crowns' place, except in Brazil, and even there it was tenuous until the mid–nineteenth century. The public realm was in dispute, more so than at any time since the early sixteenth century. There were new governmental structures and tenets of law but no common acceptance of them, even less of those who attempted to implement and enforce them. The public realm was less and less predictable, which invited both growing ambitions to control it and expanding endeavors to avoid it. Both responses deepened the societal fragmentation arising from the colonial legacy and from the social transformation and breakdown of the imperial order during the prior half century.

Nevertheless, the reality of weakened public institutions, and of rules and regulations beset by experimentation and equivocation, led to collaboration as well as conflict. With so much uncertainty about the power and constancy of governmental institutions and of those who controlled them, collaboration served as a hedge against unacceptable loss and a calculated advantage in pursuing interests that temporarily coincided. Groups could challenge; they could threaten, even violently confront. When pushed too far or when they had miscalculated the strength of those against whom they sought advantage, they did so (as noted above). Yet there appears to have been stronger grounds for a predisposition to collaborate. In a weakened public realm, courses of action could be more improvised and discourse more pliable. That, in turn, made negotiation of interests more feasible and more desirable, both within the strata into which Middle Period society was divided and between them.

Within Social Strata

Reading legislative debates, official reports, and newspaper columns, one could easily be struck by the conflicts among (and even within) the notable families, who had the most influential role in the uncertain public realm of the post-independence decades. However, alongside, often underneath these public disputes and confrontations, was a parallel strategy of collaboration. Notables hedged their political bets by making sure kin were present, through marriage and godparentage, in the families of their opponents. They were also careful to use business ventures as a means to widen the circle of family connections, at times including potential or actual rivals. Those same strategies were especially productive when notables faced challenges from the *gente decente*, given the latter's strong proclivity to seek notability themselves.[20]

At the microlevel (within notable families and within the networks of families they formed at the local level), common ideological sentiments and political cooperation were the rule. But when sides were taken, existing kinship ties and interlocking economic interests mitigated these conflicts. For example, the Prado family of São Paulo, Brazil, was split over the issue of the monarchy by the 1860s. Two brothers were influential in the Conservative Party and served in the imperial government, whereas a third was a provincial deputy for the Republican Party. Nevertheless, their economic interests were closely intertwined, and they used their public positions to work together in fostering the replacement of slavery with immigrant labor.[21]

Beyond the local level, prevalence of ideological disagreement and political antagonism was greater. Economic interests became more divergent and political relationships more tenuous. Yet, here too, notables were inclined to seek collaboration. After 1830, Chilean notable families increasingly joined their interests across regional-sectoral divisions through joint business ventures and marriage to minimize the risks of fluctuations in mining in the north and wheat growing in the center and south and to enlarge their investment capital. Then, in the 1870s they faced mounting economic crisis. When changes in Bolivia's policy injured or threatened nitrate interests of one segment of the notables, in a public campaign it successfully appealed to notables in general for support. A united resistance formed, the War of the Pacific ensued, and economic expansion was renewed.[22]

Collaboration also overcame fissures among the *gente baja*. In Bolivia's highland communal villages, for example, social and political divisions were tempered by the necessity of economic cooperation in the face of the penetration of the market economy, with its rising demand for labor and foodstuffs. *Originarios* provided *forasteros* with access to land for rent or as wage laborers and other benefits. This cooperation allowed these permanent village landholders to expand cultivation or be free to gain supplemental income from part-time work in mines, construction sites, and urban centers—all the while retaining exclusive political control. After 1850 in Mexico's Sierra Gorda districts (Puebla state), mestizo communities supported the liberal reform laws, whereas Indian villagers focused on gaining greater local autonomy and regaining land. Still, they found common cause in breaking the power of the conservative notables and clerical interests of the central plain. In Peru's urban centers before midcentury, artisans had incessantly demanded higher prices through protectionism and the revival of guild monopolies. But the shock of the ensuing inflation in the wake of the booming guano trade led them to join the popular classes in calling for free trade policies that would provide inexpensive goods and thus ensure subsistence security.[23]

Across the Line of Respectability

Collaboration was born of necessity. But especially in bridging the dichotomy between those above and below the line of respectability, it required leverage. The very traits that gave *gente alta* superior status in society also conferred considerable leverage, though it varied in time and circumstance. Without leverage, *gente baja* were doomed to subservience. That was the fate former slaves in Peru found themselves in following abolition in 1855. Long-standing denigration of those with African ancestry combined with the reintroduction of Chinese coolie labor to limit severely their occupational options and their bargaining power within those traditional sectors available to them. Lacking leverage, those of African descent sought to alter their identity and status through whitening, resulting in a steady erosion of both the black population and the presence of African culture.[24]

Yet most *gente baja* found that the climate of weakened government, republican discourse, and fluctuations in economic opportunity provided greater room to maneuver in their relations with the *gente alta*. The weakened public sector and republican ideology eroded coercive labor (either through its outright abolition or inability to compel it), which left *gente baja* with more leverage in negotiating for their labor. So, too, in many districts and regions did the disruption of the labor supply from the independence wars. Already expanding their role as small producers before independence, the *gente baja* thereafter strove increasingly to do so wherever and whenever economic and political circumstances permitted them to do so. That made their material concerns—land use, labor, and subsistence—more negotiable vis-à-vis the *gente alta*.

Central to the leverage of Bolivia's highland Indians in their various socioeconomic roles in the post-independence decades was the continuing dependence of the government upon tribute revenues. In return the Indians secured protection of their communal lands. This enabled them to adapt to the penetration of the market economy (which began to accelerate after midcentury) and to turn it to their advantage, whether as producers or laborers. Though not subject to the tribute, the Chiriguano Indians on Bolivia's eastern frontier also benefited from the government's weakness until the late 1850s. The government paid members of the tribe money and goods (and withheld support of settler encroachment) to curtail their raids on settlers. It also depended on the Chiriguanos as a supplemental armed force against tribes further to the east.[25]

Gente baja of varying stripes took advantage of the widespread availability of public land in many frontier regions to pursue independence and material improvement. In Colombia, public lands still constituted an estimated 75 percent of the national territory in 1850. Landless workers, impoverished small landholders, dispossessed communal Indian villagers, and refugees from civil wars moved to vacant districts of that nation's Caribbean plains, interior river valleys, and interior lowlands. They formed nucleated settlements, soon joined by artisans and shopkeepers. In some cases, they were encouraged by notable entrepreneurs acting as merchants and providers of public services (especially roads). In the western Andean region of Venezuela after 1860, notable entrepreneurs supplied small producers moving onto public lands with credit for coffee production and invested in transportation improvements. In many other locales in post-independence Latin America, *gente alta* held the upper hand in the negotiations over economic livelihood, above all with the popular classes.[26]

Possessers of a skill, job-related personal property, and often real property, the *gente de profesiones* generally held the best prospects among *gente baja* in the collaboration in material interests across the line of respectability. Then, too, as cultural intermediaries and with more ambition toward social advancement, they were more inclined to cooperate. They were more attuned and accustomed to the mechanisms of the market economy. Such was the case with their response in Bogotá and other main Colombian urban centers to the establishment of savings banks in the late 1840s. Working through state legislatures for their creation, notables (who as volunteers controlled these institutions) were pushing a social mission, promoting thrift among the general citizenry as well as manufacturing activities among the more industrious. *Gente alta* proved to be the largest group of depositors and even more of the borrowers. But among *gente baja*, only the artisans and small shopkeepers participated equal to their proportion of the population. They were not as alienated by directed social improvement from above as the popular classes. More important, they had greater capacity to use the bank. Borrowing to meet pre-sale expenses, artisans (especially those owning their own shops) could obtain an interest rate of 12 percent (one-half to one-fifth that of private sources).[27]

Utilitarian and sociocultural concerns also made the *gente de profesiones* more inclined to collaborate in the expansion of education. The popular classes tended to weigh public schooling on the basis of whether it directly supported subsistence survival and whether it undermined their existing supports of community control and popular culture. The *gente de profesiones*, it appears, perceived the link between literacy, economic skills, and social mobility, something *gente decente* understood out of necessity to maintain their respectability and even more to advance to notability. That is why they sent their children to school in growing numbers and supported public efforts to expand schooling.[28]

Education was only one of many juridical matters that had an impact on social relations. Maintenance of order, freedom of expression, regulation of economic activity, and determination of legal status—all were bound up in the way people of all social strata carried on their daily life. The pre-independence social transformation had unsettled such issues; republican ideology had disarranged them still more. The *gente baja* generally placed more stock in traditional Iberian juridical principles embodying notions of localism, particularism, and personalism. Still, they also saw in modern republican legal structures means to check arbitrariness and undue unfairness by those in authority, almost always *gente alta*. The latter, particularly *gente decente*, increasingly accepted the economic and political advantages of a modern, uniform juridical system, but most did not trust its social consequences. Involving *gente baja* officially and directly in the judicial system, they feared, would threaten the social control and hierarchical deference they relied on to maintain the line of respectability.[29]

In Mexico City by the late 1820s, prisoners (the large majority *gente baja*) were requesting individual protection and respect for their rights. Soon after, petitions began coming from those of varying social strata seeking protection from abusive military acts. *Gente alta* jurists lobbied the national congress to devise a uniform legal code that defined individual and corporate rights and particularly pushed to institutionalize the court's power to protect individual rights through the petitionary procedure of *amparo*. However, although their congressional counterparts affirmed their republican commitment to such legal guarantees in legislative and constitutional preambles, they dragged their collective feet, worried about the political fallout. Only with the triumph of the liberal Reforma (1860s) did they summon the political will to codify these juridical provisions sought by ordinary people in collaboration with jurists.[30]

By contrast, in Buenos Aires the resolution of such issues leaned firmly on the side of Iberian legal traditions throughout this period. *Gente alta* initially were taken with the idea that implementing uniform modern juridical structures could reverse the growing trend of autonomous popular behavior. But the "disorder" continued, especially given the frequent civil strife and economically driven urban migration. *Gente baja*, increasingly interpreting these juridical programs as threatening their way of life rather than securing protection of their rights, resisted such impositions from above, holding firmly to Iberian legal practice and custom. In varying degrees, the *gente alta* fell back upon barrio initiative, autonomy of local authorities, and Iberian tradition to reestablish social control and deference. As a consequence, arrests and punishments were determined largely by social-racial considerations and by political expediency. Exercising the local option in dispensing justice was given preference. All social strata then sought to circumvent the arbitrary effects of such a judicial system, using family, kin, and friendship. Where social relations were unequal, they collaborated in common cause through clientelism.[31]

The Mechanics of Politics

At issue throughout Latin America in the post-independence decades was how to stabilize public affairs at each of the different geopolitical levels: local, regional, and national. With civil wars numerous, political institutions proving ephemeral, and representation unsecured by law, no social stratum was able to impose its will wholly and permanently. A politics of absolutism—whether by one, the few, or the many— was no longer possible under the circumstances. Yet, neither did a politics of compromise emerge because it requires an ongoing, formal framework in which settlements resulting from mutual concessions can be consistently hammered out and implemented. Not all strata were recognized as legitimate, permanent participants in the determination of public affairs. Political compromises were made intermittently but not as part of a persisting arrangement in which fixed rules governed the exchange of concessions and the commitments to abide by them.

What emerged during the post-independence decades in Latin America's Middle Period society was a politics of collaboration. More often than not, the transacting of public affairs took place between social strata (and among groups within them) who had no immediate, lasting, and formal political connection and who at times considered each other adversaries, even enemies. They transiently cooperated with one another when their private concerns intersected, but there were few enduring settlements of their interests. There were patterns to this politics of collaboration. They simply did not take on a formal, legal character.

Modes of Collaboration

A precedent of sorts for this political mechanism can be found in the multistrata coalitions that challenged the Iberian crowns in the last decades of imperial rule. The resurrected *cabildo abierto* had often served initially as a formal structure for such joint action but was only a temporary device. The ensuing republican constitutional structures created by the newly independent nations were intended to be enduring. In some cases they did continue to exist, at least on paper, in lofty flights of rhetoric, and in the minds of political idealists. The political reality, however, was otherwise.

The law—as embodied in formal constitutions and legislation to implement them—was neither respected nor trusted enough to form the primary basis of reconciling conflict and establishing an equilibrium in Latin America's public realm. There was neither a duly accepted body of law nor cohort of authorities to enforce a firm social hierarchy or to ensure freedom and egalitarianism in the pursuit of private well-being and happiness. Instead, what came to infuse post-independence politics was the notion and practice of deference, but a deference bounded and qualified by an implied principle of consent.[32] Socially, that deference went upward. Spatially, it moved downward through the district to the locality and community. In the colonial tradition of "I obey but cannot comply," royal law had been adjusted to local interests and sentiment. Now, the weakened state of government only strengthened such spatial deference.

Families, households, and communities transacted the major portion of their public business through local politics, through authorities both official and unofficial. The *municipio* and the district official—the only two legacies and constants in their public life—provided people of all strata with a measure of formal political structure. But the rule of law and adequate, systematic representation, as embodied in modern republican government, failed to infuse these old structures. People generally went outside or around such formalities, though they often dealt unofficially with those who presided over these political institutions. Electoral manipulation, extralegal transactions, and subjective implementation of justice were the rule.

"Local" politics, in fact, encompassed both the localities and the districts. Depending upon the sparseness of population, the degree of urbanization, and the political interests and ideology in force at the time, that politics could be quite dispersed or quite concentrated within the boundaries of a given district. In those with large regional urban centers the city was the district. At times, the cabecera town could be the only *municipio* in the district, whether because of sparseness of population or by law. In that case, all officials of other communities in the district were beholden to the town's ayuntamiento (post-independence nomenclature for the traditional cabildo). In many cases the economic interests of the notable network that dominated the cabecera so penetrated the district that its other *municipios* were greatly influenced, if not dominated, by the network. In districts with large rural populations (especially with numerous corporate communities), the numbers of *municipios* could be large and their independence considerable.

Whatever the particular construct of local politics in a given district, the authorities of the localities and district served as intermediaries between the local citizenry and state, regional, and national authorities. The only exceptions were among notables who had special connections with higher authorities. Especially where no large urban centers were present, the key public officials were the district judge and district executive (*jefe político* or *prefecto*), there being no legislative body at that level. The former dispensed justice in criminal matters, in the adjudication of land, and in protection from official actions. The latter's principal task was to preserve order. Usually appointed, they were in a tenuous, often conflictive position. They were at once agents of the state or provincial government and yet leaders and emissaries of the local citizenry. Within their district, they could be representatives or agents of notable networks or much less frequently tribunes of nonnotables. Generally, though aligned with one element, they were pushed toward conciliation and collaboration to maintain an equilibrium among local interests. When they could not, they lost their position.

Caught in the middle, too, were state or provincial politicians and bureaucrats. In the wake of independence there was power to be accumulated at that governmental level, either at the expense of the localities or of the national regime. Some of these politicos equated their interests with those of the nation and sought to dominate it. Others subordinated themselves to the national government, narrowly to obtain or preserve their hold on power or more broadly to face challenges from forces from within their region (such as autonomous Indian groups, slave rebellions, or foreign adventurers). Still, most state or provincial politicians during this period sought to maintain a distance from the national government, collaborating with both those at the local and national levels to do so. Spatially, both the state and national politicos found that in most cases they had to defer to those below them. They lacked either the force to impose their will or the implied consent to do otherwise. Collaboration across these geopolitical levels was thus a prerequisite in post-independence politics.[33]

Personal relationships permeated these geopolitical interconnections. Often, they were carried over from private relationships and concerns. Especially for notables, family and kin undergirded political ties. In the state of Sonora in northwestern Mexico, for a half century every governor was the brother-in-law of either the military commander of the state or the secretary of government (the most important state bureaucrat).[34] Not infrequently, *gente decente* who were poor relations of notables made use of that status in pursuing their public concerns. For the *gente baja*, the web of community, neighborhood, and parish relations was interspersed with personal ties, though more based on household and godparenting than on extensive, complex familial linkages.

A whole series of client relations connected the various social strata. They, too, frequently formed the basis for collaborative political action, depending upon the necessity and leverage of patron or client. Emergency assistance, personalized social security in the form of godparent commitments, extension of credit based upon personal trust and obligation, grants of access to land, and acceptance of a youth as servant or trainee all constituted personalized economic relations that could be and were carried over into public affairs. Francesca Pérez Gálvez, a widowed mine owner and hacendada in the Mexican state of Guanajuato, accepted numerous solicitudes from her workers and subordinates for godparenting and direct assistance and served as a benefactress to the *gente baja* more generally when they found themselves as prisoners and hospital patients. Such client relations assisted her in exercising considerable political influence in the district.[35]

These private, personal relations within and across the social strata were juxtaposed with the contractual relations implicit in modern republican constitutional government (and in the workings of the market economy). Although political discourse and formal governmental affairs centered around the latter, the politics most practiced during this period pivoted around the former. Those informal relations formed the basis of a collaborative politics behind and underneath the formal political structures created following independence.

For the *gente baja*, unschooled in the formalities of republican government and unwelcome as full and equal participants in it, a politics rooted in deference usually proved more practical and advantageous. And if it did not yield results and they found themselves pushed too far, their way of life threatened, they could resort to withholding consent and then defying authority to reestablish an equilibrium. The *gente alta* neither trusted in the guarantee of order proclaimed in republican constitutional government, nor were they consistently willing to abide by its results in the public adjudication of competing private interests, especially those among the *gente alta* themselves. For them as well, a politics grounded in deference and employing personal, informal relations proved more effective and profitable. The result was a politics in post-independence Middle Period society that was highly personalized and privatized, one in which collaboration superseded compromise or domination.

The Case of Brazil

Though a constitutional monarchy until 1889, Brazil's post-independence politics was also rooted in collaboration. Prior to independence, notables heading patriarichal clans (*parentelas* based broadly on ties of kinship and clientelism) had dominated most localities, controlling municipal elections and the actions of local officeholders, as well as leading the militias upon which internal order depended. Political instability at the national level from 1822 to midcentury left this political pattern largely in place. But alterations were beginning to emerge. The spread of elective office and representative government, especially beyond the district level, led these notables to move more directly into the formal structure of politics. They increasingly dominated the main provincial cities and sought provincial and imperial posts to ensure their control, especially in areas of significant economic expansion. The *parentelas* seem also to have been gradually reconstituting themselves from within, becoming networks linking notable branches from different *parentelas* together through marriage and business ventures. The prior, predominantly vertical, patriarchal lines of control between father and sons were yielding to horizontal cooperation among sets of brothers-in-law. In contrast, other social strata were tied to these notable networks more and more through client relations alone.

Stabilizing politics at the national level at midcentury, however, resulted in a greater need for vertical collaboration in Brazilian politics. His authority firmly acknowledged, young Dom Pedro II began to use and enhance the extensive appointive powers given to the emperor by the Constitution of 1824. In particular, he employed the "moderating power," through which he could replace cabinets and force new elections, maintaining his predominance by alternating control of national government between liberals and conservatives. The impact of this change in national politics was soon felt at the district level. The two national "parties" were, in fact, loosely coordinated alliances of political cliques, sometimes provincial or regional in scope but generally centered at the district level, where they were cemented by kinship and client ties. Ascendancy in the imperial government by either party connoted control of patronage (and elections) at the district level through the provincial governors, making affiliation with one of the two parties imperative for rival notable networks and their clients. This vertical collaboration brought increased penetration of imperial authority into local politics. Yet enduring kinship and client ties embodied in the old *parentelas* were employed collaboratively by all social strata to obstruct agents of imperial authority in the administration of justice and enforcement of laws when rival cliques held office. Noteworthy in this regard were the private armed forces used to pressure, extort, and terrorize (if need be) judges and officials.[36]

In Brazil's collaborative politics, non-notables were at a comparative disadvantage, especially in the countryside. Slavery remained entrenched, removing a large proportion of the popular classes from public affairs except in times of rebellion. Concentration of land ownership, combined with slavery's prevalence, left the large majority of the remainder dependent upon notables for land to work or a job. Moreover, suffrage was very restricted. Patron-client relations were the way most among the popular classes managed to get by or possibly get ahead. Such circumstances also limited independent political action by *gente de profesiones* and *gente decente*, especially in districts where lack of marked economic growth blocked expansion of their numbers and economic leverage. Many of the latter were dependent upon public employment, which notables controlled through patronage. Still, notables discerned that their ability to maintain control locally and engage in politics regionally and nationally depended upon collaboration with other social strata. In such collaboration, admittedly, they held a stronger hand than their counterparts in most other regions in Latin America.

That post-independence politics in Latin America was anchored in vertical collaboration did not mean an absence of civil strife or armed conflict; far from it. What it did signify was a tenuous political equilibrium in the renegotiation of rights and obligations, both among the social strata within a district and region and among the regional societies that constituted the nation and ordered people's lives. Most among the various social strata of Middle Period society acknowledged that political equilibrium—both as an opportunity to exploit and an advantage to maintain. No ideological system, no body of law was found to sustain it. Instead, private kin relations, godparenting, patron-client ties, and personal followings were taken into the public realm to facilitate it.

Notes

1. Szuchman, *Order, Family, and Community*, 12, 16.
2. Francois-Xavier Guerra, "The Spanish-American Tradition of Representation and Its European Roots," *JLAS* 26 (February 1994): 2–11, 13–17, 24–27.
3. Balmori, Voss, and Wortman, *Notable Family Networks*, 9–10, 27–35.
4. Szuchman, *Order, Family, and Community*, 16–19, 100; Guerra, "Spanish-American Tradition of Representation," 9–11.
5. Szuchman, *Order, Family, and Community*, chaps. 1–2; E. Bradford Burns, *The Poverty of Progress: Latin America in the Nineteenth Century* (Berkeley: University of California Press, 1980), chaps. 1, 4–6; Barbara A. Tenenbaum, *The Politics of Penury: Debts and Taxes in Mexico, 1821–1856* (Albuquerque: University of New Mexico Press, 1986).
6. Guerra, "Spanish-American Tradition of Representation," 24–25.
7. Burns, *Brazil*, 158–56. Several regional studies have revealed the extensive informal power and prerogative of the patriarchal clans (*parentelas*) vis-à-vis the imperial government, including Billy Jaynes Chandler, *The Feitosas and the Sertão Inhamuns: A History of a Family and Community in Northeast Brazil, 1700–1930* (Gainesville: University of Florida Press, 1972); Linda Lewin, "Some Historical Implications of Kinship Organization for Family-Based Politics in the Brazilian Northeast," *CSSH* 21 (April 1979): 262–92; and Marc J. Hoffnagal, "From Monarchy to Republic in Northeast Brazil: The Case of Pernambuco, 1868–1895" (Ph.D. diss., University of Indiana, Bloomington, 1975).
8. Michael Olien, "Micro/Macro Level Linkages: Regional Political Structures on the Mosquito Coast, 1845–1864," *Ethnohistory* 34 (Summer 1987): 257–82; Daniel Weber, *The Mexican Frontier, 1821–1846: The American Southwest under Mexico* (Albuquerque: University of New Mexico Press, 1982), 83–105, 122–45; Kristine Jones, "Conflict and Adaptation in the Argentine Pampas, 1750–1880" (Ph.D. diss., University of Chicago, 1984).
9. Evelyn Hu-DeHart, *Yaqui Resistance and Survival: The Struggle for Land and Autonomy, 1821–1923* (Madison: University of Wisconsin Press, 1984); Voss, *On the Periphery*, 41, 48–67, 99–107, 148–59, 179, 191–92, 284–85; Nelson Reed, *The Caste War of Yucatan* (Stanford, CA: Stanford University Press, 1964); Enrique Montalvo Ortega, "Revolts and Peasant Mobilizations in Yucatan: Indians, Peons, and Peasants from the Caste War to the Revolution," in *Riots, Rebellions, and Insurrections: Rural Social Conflict in Mexico*, ed. Friedrich Katz (Princeton, NJ: Princeton University Press, 1986), 296–308.
10. John M. Hart, "The 1840s Southwestern Mexico Peasant War: Conflict in a Transitional Society," in *Riots, Rebellions, and Insurrections: Rural Social Conflict in Mexico*, ed. Friedrich Katz (Princeton, NJ: Princeton University Press, 1986), 249–68; J. H. Parry and Philip Sherlock, *A Short History of the West Indies* (New York: St. Martin's, 1956), 188–201; Franklin W. Knight, *The Caribbean: Genesis of a Fragmented Nationalism*, 2nd ed. (New York: Oxford University Press, 1990), chap. 6; Hilary Beckles, "Divided to the Vein: The Problem of Race, Colour and Class Conflict in Haitian Nation-Building, 1804–1820," in *Caribbean Freedom: Economy and Society from Emancipation to the Present*, ed. Hilary Beckles and Verene Shepherd (Princeton, NJ: Marcus Weiner, 1996), 494–503.

11. Frank Safford, "Race, Integration, and Progress: Elite Attitudes and the Indian in Colombia, 1750–1870," *HAHR* 71 (February 1991): 11–23; Burns, *Poverty of Progress*, 46–97, 106–9.

12. Pedro Santoni, "A Fear of the People: The Civic Militia of Mexico in 1845," *HAHR* 68 (May 1988): 270–88; Guy P. C. Thomson, "Bulwarks of Patriotic Liberalism: The National Guard, Philharmonic Corps, and Patriotic Juntas in Mexico, 1847–1888," *JLAS* 22 (February 1990): 31–48.

13. Sylvia Arrom, "Popular Politics in Mexico City: The *Parian* Riot, 1828," *HAHR* 68 (May 1988): 245–62.

14. Hart, "Southwestern Mexico Peasant War," 249–50, 256–57, 268; Leticia Reina, "The Sierra Gorda Rebellion, 1847–1850," in *Riots, Rebellions, and Insurrections: Rural Social Conflict in Mexico,* ed. Friedrich Katz (Princeton, NJ: Princeton University Press, 1986), 286, 294; Weber, *American Southwest under Mexico,* 261–65; Hendride Kraay, "As Terrifying as Unexpected: The Bahian *Sabinada, 1837–1838,*" *HAHR* 72 (November 1992): 501–7, 519–25.

15. Bonham C. Richardson, "Nineteenth Century Labor Mobility in the Eastern Caribbean: A Three-Fold Typology" (paper presented at the LASA Meeting, Miami, December 4–6, 1989), 2–8; Knight, *Caribbean,* chap. 6; Weber, *American Southwest under Mexico,* 208–18, 261–65; Hart, "Southwestern Mexico Peasant War," 249–50, 254–63, 268; Peter Guardino, "Barbarism or Republican Law: Guerrero's Peasants and National Politics, 1820–1846," *HAHR* 75 (May 1995): 187–97; Szuchman, *Order, Family, and Community,* chaps. 2, 4, 5, 7.

16. Ibid., see especially chaps. 4–7; Fernando López-Alves, *State Formation and Democracy in Latin America* (Durham, NC: Duke University Press, 2000), chaps. 2–5.

17. Santoni, "Civic Militia of Mexico," 270–273; Tenenbaum, *Politics of Penury,* 76–85, 115–17.

18. Mark Szuchman, *Mobility and Integration in Urban Argentina: Cordoba in the Liberal Era* (Austin: University of Texas Press, 1980), chap. 3.

19. Hart, "Southwestern Mexico Peasant War," 254.

20. In *Notable Family Networks,* Balmori, Voss, and Wortman analyze and detail the strategies employed by notable families in Latin America through the course of the nineteenth century.

21. Darrell Levi, "The Prados of São Paulo: An Elite Brazilian Family in a Changing Society, 1840–1930" (Ph.D. diss., Yale University, 1974), 160–217.

22. Luis Ortega, "Nitrates, Chilean Entrepreneurs, and the Origins of the War of the Pacific," *JLAS* 16 (November 1984): 338–47, 354–72; Diana Balmori and Robert Oppenheimer, "Family Clusters: The Generational Nucleation of Families in Nineteenth Century Argentina and Chile," *CSSH* 21 (1979), 231–61.

23. Herbert S. Klein, *Haciendas and Ayllus: Rural Society in the Bolivian Andes in the Eighteenth and Nineteenth Centuries* (Stanford, CA: Stanford University Press, 1993), 128–32, 162–65; Thomson, "Bulwarks of Patriotic Liberalism," 40–47; Paul Gotenburg, "*Carneros y Chuno*: Price Levels in Nineteenth Century Peru," *HAHR* 70 (February 1990): 38–42.

24. Peter Blanchard, *Slavery and Abolition in Early Republican Peru* (Wilmington, DE: Scholarly Resources, 1992), 218–22.

25. Erick D. Langer, "El liberalismo y la abolición de la comunidád indígena en el siglo XIX," *Historia y Cultura* 14 (October 1988): 61–63; Langer, "Las 'guerras Chiriguanas': Resistencia y adaptación en la frontera surboliviana (siglo XIX)" (paper presented at the First International Congress of Ethnohistory, Buenos Aires, July 17–21, 1989), 11–19.

26. Catherine LeGrand, "Labor, Acquisition and Social Conflict in the Colombian Frontier, 1850–1936," *JLAS* 16 (May 1984): 29–32; Doug Yarrington, "Public Land Settlement, Privatization, and Peasant Protest in Duaca, Venezuela, 1870–1936," *HAHR* 74 (February 1994): 33–42. Peones and domestic servants were generally the most vulnerable among the popular classes. For examples, see Montalvo Ortega, "Revolts and Peasant Mobilizations," 303–14; and Szuchman, *Mobility and Integration in Urban Argentina*, 31–32.

27. David Sowell, "*La Caja de Ahorros de Bogotá*, 1846–1865: Artisans, Credit, Development and Savings in Early National Colombia," *HAHR* 73 (November 1993): 616–37.

28. Mary Kay Vaughn, "Primary Education and Literacy in Nineteenth Century Mexico: Research Trends, 1968–1988," *Latin American Research Review* (*LARR*) 25:1 (1990): 36–37, 39–42; David Sowell, *The Early Colombian Labor Movement: Artisans and Politics in Bogotá, 1832–1919* (Philadelphia: Temple University Press, 1992), 84, 86, 96, 103–4, 159.

29. Szuchman, *Order, Family, and Community*, chap. 2.

30. Linda Arnold, "Vulgar and Elegant: Politics and Procedures in Early National Mexico," *The Americas* 50 (April 1994): 481–500.

31. Szuchman, *Order, Family, and Community*, chap. 2.

32. Ibid., chap. 1.

33. López-Alves, *State Formation and Democracy*, chaps. 2–4.

34. Though unpublished, this compilation is drawn from varied sources used to analyze the extensive connections between family and politics, as found in Voss, *On the Periphery*; Balmori, Voss, and Wortman, *Notable Family Networks*, chap. 3.

35. Carlos Macias, "El retorno á Valenciana: Las familias Pérez Gálvez y Rul," *HM* 36 (April–June 1987), 646–50.

36. Hoffnagel, "From Monarchy to Republic," 1–48, 259–60; Chandler, *The Feitosas*, 43–44, chaps. 3–4; Lawrence J. Nielson, "Of Gentry, Peasants, and Slaves: Rural Society in Sabará and Its Hinterland, 1780–1930" (Ph.D. diss., University of California, Berkeley, 1975), 22–41, 113–15, 124–52; Levi, "The Prados," 62–66, 193–220; Lewin, "Family-based Politics in the Brazilian Northeast," 265, 274–77, 285–90.

5

A Mixed Economy

Paralleling politics, Latin America's economy in the post-independence decades manifested an uneasy equilibrium. Examined at the national level, it has been characterized as one in which large estates dominated the countryside, controlling production and marketing and subordinating labor to their interests. Towns and cities (with some noteworthy exceptions) were dependent upon a reduced commerce. Mining was in marked decline, and there was little manufacturing. Overall, the economy was stagnant because of receding contacts with the international market. This condition began to reverse itself, beginning in some countries in the 1850s and then spreading to the remainder in the 1860s and 1870s.

There were regions where such a characterization of the economy was largely the case, and some nations where, in the aggregate, some of these conditions were prevalent. However, scrutinizing Latin America's economy during this period from a regional perspective yields a considerably different picture. One finds considerable variation in the organization of production and in the degree of contact with the international market. There was more extensive market production at the local and regional level than previously thought. In addition, the *gente baja* and women of all social strata played a considerable role in that market production, beyond the customarily assumed position of dependent laborers. At times they engaged in export production. The independence wars' impact has generally been seen as a depressant on economic activity, resulting in a general stagnation that lasted until at least midcentury, with a few exceptions. Their devastation and dislocations (and uncertainties unleashed with imperial rule's end) did reduce assets, disrupt labor and commodity markets, and curtail public support mechanisms. Still, those same conditions forced adjustments and opened new avenues in the production process. Recent local and regional studies seem to indicate that recovery was soon under way in the 1820s and 1830s and that in many sectors pre-1810 production levels were attained by the 1840s and surpassed thereafter.[1]

The basic economic patterns emerging in the 1750–1810 period continued, fed by a series of circumstances that the wars of insurgency affected minimally: the emergence of secondary regions, population growth, significant urban growth that stimulated internal markets, the redirection of foreign trade toward the North Atlantic, and the greater diversification of and articulation among economic activities.[2] What had changed were some of the circumstances in which those general economic patterns were evolving. The international context was now more variable, not only in the movement of trade but also of people. Furthermore, the balance of economic leverage among the social strata had been altered. The *gente baja* had clearly gained in leverage, although only in rare instances were they dominant. It appears that *gente decente*, too, found more latitude in pursuing their interests. Accustomed governmental power and authority—previously favoring notables' interests as a whole—had been weakened. State or provincial government was trying to define itself in its powers, personnel, and resources. National government had the added burden of being more spatially removed. In practice, its effective power was limited to only some regions within its boundaries.

Nevertheless, the public sector's weakness also opened more economic opportunities for the *gente alta*. Notables, in particular, through expansion of their family networks and increasing diversification of their family portfolios, were able to enlarge their holdings. Central to these family networks were the merchant-capitalist entrepreneurs. Either as patriarchs or with increasing frequency as brothers or brothers-in-law in partnership, they guided the family fortunes. In so doing, they became the principal protagonists of Latin America's post-independence economy.

The General Economic Milieu

To speak of a "Latin American" economy is a misnomer. There were common patterns and processes among the newly independent nations but not an integrated system of producing and distributing goods and services. In fact, no truly national economies existed during the post-independence decades. What primarily shaped people's material lives were regional economies, those that had emerged in the colonial society and had been energized (and proliferated) after 1750.

In some cases their scope had been reduced in the wake of independence, as some of the larger imperial market units into which they had been integrated had been fractured (above all, that encompassing much of the viceroyalties of Peru and the La Plata). National political leaders devised reforms to redirect, alter, or transform economic structures. But they quickly found themselves lacking the fiscal capability, common agenda, and political cohesion to implement them. Consequently, economic policies were often left unenforced or without implementation. Nowhere was this more true than in the control of contraband, which in many coastal and frontier regions became rampant (Chile and especially Paraguay were noteworthy exceptions to this rule).

In contrast, the influence on regional economies of two other forces had been heightened. From without, direct contact with immigrants, foreign interests, and the international market conspicuously expanded, especially in peripheral or coastal regions. From within, small producers (and those seeking to be so) among the *gente baja* used their greater economic leverage to turn the regional economy to their advantage. The specific weight of these influences—centralized governmental direction, foreign contact, and small producers—varied from region to region.

The International Context

Externally, the post-independence decades can be divided into subperiods, generational in time frame and character. Abroad, they marked two phases in the development of the industrialized nations of the North Atlantic and of the international market they dominated. They also reflected two loan cycles connecting Latin America with the North Atlantic. At home, the subperiods denoted a shift in economic policy spurred by the rise of a new generation of politicos, foreign immigrants, and domestic entrepreneurs.

The peoples of Latin America did not automatically or necessarily fall from a dependent relationship in an imperial, mercantilist framework to one in a complex international market system. The macrodecisions of national and provincial political leaders, combined with the countless microdecisions of well-to-do entrepreneurs and small producers as well, determined the terms and extent by which Latin America's regional economies became articulated with those of North Atlantic nations. But the external weight on those decisions rose between 1820 and 1880, significantly so after midcentury. Direct foreign presence increased. The ratio of incentives over disincentives to participation in the North Atlantic–led world market system grew. The change in political leadership after midcentury was partly a consequence of this shift in external circumstances and even more a force behind its intensification.

Free trade for the independence generation meant an end to mercantile restrictions, the ability to trade with anyone abroad under negotiated terms. It did not denote removal of commercial restrictions and tariffs in Latin America (nor in Europe and the United States). There were voices then calling for such a revised definition of free trade, but they did not become ascendant until midcentury. On that existing basis, then, free trade broke forth in Latin America, almost wholly free of coercion in world markets. Though Britain had the advantage—in its lead in industrialization, its naval strength, and its shipping and financial resource capacity—no single country monopolized Latin America's trade.

After several decades of warfare, Europe was flush with economic activity. The United States rushed into the development of its western lands and infant industries after the conclusion of the War of 1812. A wave of foreign merchants, most notably British, spread into the seaports, national capitals, and some inland provincial cities of Latin America, backed by their respective nations' accelerating industrial production, credit markets, and shipping. The money to be made was in supplying imports in exchange for hard currency and precious metals, which could then be used to purchase commodities in other world markets, especially Asia. Except for sugar, coffee, cacao, and hides, there was little else they were then interested in acquiring. In the regions to which they were drawn, foreign merchants grabbed a large, if not predominant, share of wholesale commerce. They drained away hard currency and extended credit.[3]

Some of the enlightened reformers who controlled many national governments during the 1820s sought to carry foreign presence one step further. Mexico succeeded in attracting immigrants from the United States to the far north, but the end result was far from what was intended. In Argentina, the Unitarians' grandiose plans to transform the countryside through immigration merely intensified the federalist, traditionalist opposition that soon removed them from power. Elsewhere, reality never moved very far beyond intentions. Market and state-sponsored inducements were inadequate compared with the volume of immigrants and the attraction of North America.

National political leaders in the 1820s did succeed in substantially augmenting foreign influence in another area, though they received less (and at the same time more) than what they had bargained for. Surplus capital accruing from the investment boom in the North Atlantic supplied a series of loans to Latin American governments in the mid-1820s. Britain's entrepreneurs and politicians were best able to seize the advantage, hoping to increase their share of trade, secure more specie, and enhance British diplomatic influence. For Latin American politicians, the loans had become a necessity. Customs duties and tax reforms were failing to meet rising expenses to maintain military forces, fund the expanded layers of officeholders, and initiate public improvements.

But quickly, the external force initiating the loan infusion set in motion a loan crisis. A European commercial and banking crisis in 1825 spread to Latin America the following year. Many mining ventures failed; trade contracted. National governments faced drawn-out debt negotiations but survived and resisted through an effective debt moratorium. However, that and the immediate effects of the economic downturn forced them to turn more and more to domestic moneylenders and colonial revenue sources (including monopolies, sales taxes, and head taxes). Popular protests broke out against the consequences of overborrowing, principally in taxation and a decline in economic activity. Reformers fell from power within the next few years, replaced by politicians inclined to fall back from the enlightened model for progress to late imperial economic policies. They were also more wary of being drawn into the orb of the North Atlantic economies. In turn, observers in creditor nations, placing blame for the financial crisis on Latin Americans, dampened interest in Latin America.

Despite this economic crisis and retreat by both Latin America and the North Atlantic, overseas trade soon stabilized. There was a shaking out of foreign firms into a smaller number of large commercial houses. Indeed, trade soon began to expand, especially in coastal areas and in regions with navigable river outlets to the sea. A downward trend in freight rates began, generally preceded by a dramatic rise in the demand for and supply of maritime transport, depending on the commodity and region. By the 1840s, larger ships and cargoes were permitting maximum advantage from existing technologies.[4]

In the 1850s a second round of accelerating economic growth began in the North Atlantic, with a greater ripple effect than that a generation before. The industrial revolution had spread to a growing number of nations. Gold rushes in California and Australia provided an infusion of precious metals, intensified Atlantic-Pacific exchange, and renewed optimism and zeal for overseas investment. Rising incomes, expanding populations, and technological innovations in the production process created new demands for raw materials. The same technology produced advances in communications and transport that enabled supply to meet rising demand. The decline of freight rates quickened. Increasing competition, the introduction of steam-powered iron-hulled ships, and the new railroad's facilitation of inland production all permitted the shipment of lower unit value commodities in ever larger ships, thereby expanding the industrial base.

A concomitant advance in shipping revealed a quantum difference in the international context facing Latin America. A comprehensive web of naval treaties was negotiated (led by Britain's navigation acts in 1849), establishing the principles of multilateralism and nondiscrimination in international shipping. An effective, integrated world market system was now becoming a reality as main markets were being woven together. Different climates and production seasons were being integrated, with sources of supply for cargoes governed by an annual rhythm, especially between the Northern and Southern Hemispheres. Financial markets were more interconnected and intertwined, with capital organization on an ever-larger scale, more centered in the modern business corporation.

Buoyed by expanding trade possibilities, a new wave of foreign merchants established themselves in ports and many inland urban centers, joined by many more other entrepreneurs than previously and the beginnings of large-scale immigration of laborers from Asia as well as Europe. A new generation of political leaders received them more openly and warmly. A majority embraced the liberal economic model for progress, accepted the revised definition of free trade (denoting removal of restrictions and excessive tariffs), and also were not averse to participating in a new loan cycle, eagerly offered and then pushed by European bankers. Debts could be refinanced. Arms could be secured for a spate of civil conflicts and wars with neighbors that broke out during these decades. Above all, large infrastructure works could be initiated, railroads in particular.

A trade boom ensued, especially in western and southeastern South America. And as earlier in the century, the same external economic impulse that initiated the commercial expansion and infusion of loans also brought about its bust, causing the depression that spread throughout the North Atlantic economies beginning in 1873 and lasting for the better part of a decade. The impact on Latin America was more pervasive than that in the 1820s.[5] Yet this time there would be no pulling back from the advancing world market system and the North Atlantic world that animated it.

The Roman Catholic Church was an additional, though indirect, external force affecting regional economies. The breakdown of relations between the Vatican and new national governments, which claimed the special prerogatives that Iberian monarchs had held over ecclesiastical affairs, weakened church administration. The large number of foreign priests who had helped staff many branches of the church dwindled rapidly. Most governments carried further the Bourbon policy of reducing church influence in civil affairs. Convents and monasteries were closed or severely restricted. Sometimes, governments claimed tithe revenues for themselves and ceased to sanction the collection of ecclesiastical fees. In frontier regions (especially Mexico's far north and the Andes' eastern slopes), government support for missions was curtailed and then terminated. In response, the church contracted its once diverse economic activities, principally falling back on the rental of urban real estate holdings. A more sweeping phase of secularization carried out by liberals in most countries after midcentury led to a further reduction in its economic activities, as properties were forced into sale or, less often, confiscated. Notable families in particular, having previously found economic articulation with the church vital, now increasingly found other partners and mechanisms in pursuing their interests. Correspondingly, fewer of their members took ecclesiastical office.[6]

The impact of contact with immigrants, foreign interests, and the international market varied among Latin America's regional societies. Perhaps none was affected more profoundly than Mexico's far north, where, overnight, independence brought a burst of commercial activity. Both sea and land became avenues for the passage of a growing volume of goods and people. Whether directly as settled immigrants or less directly as merchants, trappers, and adventurers, foreigners predominated in the provision of capital, means of transport, and access to the international market. In general, this inflating foreign presence brought a measure of prosperity to the region, especially for notable families. Despite some good intentions in trying to limit and regulate this growing foreign presence, the instability and inefficacy of the government in Mexico City tipped the balance of opinion and power increasingly toward those in the region who benefited most from foreign contact and identified least with the nation. Texas seceded. Then the United States, moving to acquire the region in the 1840s, encountered the active collaboration of North American immigrants and little resistance from what had become an ambivalent Mexican frontier population.[7]

In northeastern Brazil, the external impact was owing to a decline in, rather than an influx of, direct foreign presence in the first decades after independence, which contributed to a deepening recession. The flight of Portuguese capital arising from conflicts over independence, restrictions on the slave trade imposed by Britain, and the burgeoning production of competitive Cuban sugar combined to deflate the economy. By contrast, the highland region centered around the Colombian capital of Bogotá was only sporadically affected by the international context. Relative geographic isolation, the protectionist character of customs duties up to 1850, and then the turmoil of civil war and succeeding recession together limited significant foreign trade and contact until the latter part of the century.[8]

The international context had distinct sectoral repercussions. Depending upon the stability and confidence of North Atlantic financial markets, foreign investment was most readily attracted to mining. The California Gold Rush drew thousands, running the entire gamut of related occupations and functions. In the rest of Mexico and some western South American districts, foreign companies, managers, and skilled laborers often played important roles. Certainly, foreign merchants were quick to extend credit to such operations to control marketing of precious metals. Before midcentury, where transportation was feasible and demand sufficient, foreign merchants used credit to expand agricultural export production and the sale of imports to producers and their employees and laborers. Thereafter, foreigners came in growing numbers as producers (estate owners, small farmers, tenants) and laborers, most heavily concentrated in regions in southeastern and western South America.

Throughout the post-independence decades, external forces depressed rather than stimulated manufacturing. Poor transportation networks, political instability, and more tangible returns in other sectors discouraged both foreign and domestic entrepreneurs from investing in large-scale manufacturing for the domestic market. In addition, most governments lacked the political will to institute a cohesive policy promoting industry in the form of short-term monopolies, restrictions on imports, and subsidies. Contraband, especially in coastal areas and the hinterlands they serviced, undercut both private initiatives and protectionist policies. Even in inland regions, only a marked degree of geographical isolation sufficient to limit volume and make transport costs excessive seems to have proved effective in curbing the inroads of foreign manufactures.

Artisans faced declining opportunities, especially in trades more susceptible to foreign competition and the beginnings of factory mechanization (such as textiles). In some districts such as Mexico City, that resulted in significant loss of jobs. More generally, it meant that many had to sacrifice income in the face of price competition to remain in their trades. Very few could create or sustain the large workshops and technological innovations that movement along the road to industrial manufacturing required. A few merchant-entrepreneurs did invest in large factories (some including mechanization), but success, if any, was usually short-lived. More attractive investment alternatives lay in producing primary exports and in the import trade. This growing predisposition was prevalent among the *gente alta* as a whole. The triumph of liberal political economy after midcentury only strengthened the external forces working against the evolution of domestic manufacturing.[9]

Gente Baja *Initiative*

Customarily, commoners during the half century after independence have been portrayed economically in two ways: either as passive subservient workers laboring miserably on behalf of their social betters or as subsistence producers disinterested in and disconnected from the market. Among certain segments and in some locales that picture is accurate. However, the recent, growing body of local and regional socioeconomic studies suggests that *gente baja* were very much active players in the post-independence economy—mostly out of necessity but with some vision of improvement and even mobility. They often did so with considerable initiative and increased leverage.

In the countryside, their leverage depended upon a number of variables whose particular combination produced differing outcomes: degree of access to land and its productivity; relative population density and availability of alternative labor supplies (migrants and imported contract labor); profitability of markets; the level of public security and the degree to which *gente baja* could determine it; and government policies. The leverage of Caribbean ex-slaves varied markedly. In Haiti, a combination of these factors produced widespread ownership of land by smallholders. In Jamaica, Grenada, St. Vincent, and Surinam—where land was available and sugar productivity was in relative decline—planters had to negotiate complex work arrangements to attract ex-slaves as laborers. Yet in Barbados, St. Kitts, and Antigua, limited land availability and population increase gave the advantage to the planters. Even those with minimal leverage found a mechanism to enhance what little they had. Blacks created a network of small sailing vessels that gave ex-slaves mobility in negotiating with employers and labor recruiters, especially the ability to work only part-time and then return home despite considerable distances.[10]

Other than slaves retained in some countries throughout much or most of the post-independence decades up to 1880, rural laborers (especially *peones*) were the most passive, controlled, and vulnerable among the popular classes. At the other end of the spectrum were the rural *gente de profesiones*, whose skills and scale of property ownership provided them with the basis for considerable independence in decisionmaking and incentive for engagement with the market economy. In between were a range of communal villagers, small-holders, tenants, sharecroppers, and drifters. Chilean *inquilinos* (service tenants) faced increased vulnerability when wheat production began to boom in the central valley at midcentury. With ample underused land, an abundant rural population, expanding export and urban markets, and a supportive centralized government, hacendados were able to expand *inquilinaje* (by converting day laborers into *inquilinos*) and add to their advantage in this labor relationship. Overall, the *inquilinos'* obligations in labor service rose, while their perquisites in land allotments decreased.

Despite such vulnerability, even the most subservient rural commoners often took the initiative in engaging the market to improve their material lives, above all to better their chances of survival. An 1855 Chilean census recorded more than 80,000 female spinners and weavers, much of their production being sold in local markets. Many were from *inquilino* families. Even slaves on large estates pursued market activities. In Brazil's coffee districts, they exchanged produce from their subsistence plots for a variety of goods through traveling peddlars.[11]

Resident estate laborers in more favorable circumstances seem to have taken even more initiative. The strength of ayllu (kinship group) communities in Bolivia's highland districts increased the leverage of hacienda workers. Seeking to enhance subsistence through pursuit of market opportunities, they looked for land arrangements whereby they could produce commercial crops, made themselves available for part-time labor elsewhere, and even at times hired migrating workers for their own land parcels. At the same time, a far larger number of Indians—*originarios* and *forasteros*—integrated themselves more extensively into the market economy. They did so to enhance subsistence, but even more to maintain their communities' independence and viability in the face of increasing demands for labor and foodstuffs in the mines and growing urban markets (principally La Paz). If Indian communities did not supply labor and foodstuffs, competing haciendas would do so at their expense. So, *originarios* used offers of idle lands and other benefits to attract *forasteros*, the highlands' most mobile Indian segment. Their labor met external demands and those within the community, enabling *originarios* to expand cultivation to meet the growing demands for foodstuff and cover the rising tribute quotas. In addition, they themselves were freed to work outside the community part-time for supplemental wages. Through this symbiotic relationship, until the 1880s the *ayllus* were able to best the haciendas in both population growth and response to the expanding market economy, thereby preserving their integrity and independence. Indian communities in the central Andes of Peru also responded to the market, supplying the Cerro de Pasco mines with an expanding variety of commodities and, along with mestizo teamsters, managing the llama teams that transported them.[12]

Alongside these large estate laborers and communal villagers were a growing number of independent small producers. Their expansion in numbers came in three principal ways after independence. In many sparsely populated regions, growing populations (from internal increase or migration) seized the opportunity to occupy or claim what had become public or "vacant" (as versus royal) land. Whether encouraged by governmental policies and authorities or doing so without official sanction or in defiance of governmental prohibition, almost all strove to improve subsistence living; a growing body of evidence suggests that most also sought to enhance their material well-being through additional production for the market. The rise of coffee production in districts ranging from southern Mexico to central Costa Rica and interior valleys of Colombia and Venezuela provided just such an opportunity for the expansion of private landholding.[13]

New landholdings also became available through the liquidation or confiscation of corporate properties. Communal villages were increasingly threatened during this period, but in most cases legislation went unenforced (or was withdrawn) in the face of stiff resistance. Most corporate holdings transferred into private hands were ecclesiastical. Frontier missions were liquidated. Anticlericalists forced the sale of other church properties in several countries, most notably Mexico. Various church segments divested themselves of rural properties, either under political duress or because they needed to consolidate their assets into more profitable, less risky ventures. The availability of such ecclesiastical lands to rural *gente baja* (and public lands as well) depended in part on the power and policies of politicians and bureaucrats. The latter's disposition in Brazil, Argentina, and Chile was to distribute frontier land in large, concentrated holdings, and there was sufficient power in the national government to enforce it.

Private considerations alone shaped a final avenue for would-be small producers to gain access to land. Whether to secure income from otherwise unused land, to avoid risks of production and gain greater profits in marketing it, or because they lacked sufficient labor to exploit a commodity now profitable, *gente alta* landowners (especially hacendados) offered land for sharecropping and tenancy. In central Chile, they supplemented the *inquilino* system by using sharecropping on poorer, marginal lands in the coastal range and Andean foothills. These arrangements were generally with the "more elevated" segment of the rural populace, the farming segment of the *gente de profesiones*.[14]

Such differences reflect an important economic reality—the increased social differentiation caused by the *gente baja*'s participation in the spreading market economy. Partible inheritance added to the uncertainties of nature and the marketplace. Maintaining one's position of small producer with as much independence as possible depended upon a multiplicity of economic activities: securing part-time work in a nearby estate, town, or extractive center; with other family members, producing household manufactures for sale in local markets; or sharecropping or renting land if rural commoners could exert enough leverage in a given region.

Indeed, what enabled the rural *gente de profesiones* to achieve and maintain their status, even at times rise above it into respectability, was their ability to multiply their economic activities. The purchase of other smallholdings and the increase of production by renting or sharecropping additional land (or by hiring labor) expanded their interests horizontally. They also diversified into part-time artisanry or commodity distribution. In southern Bolivia, for example, some landowning *gente de profesiones* added commercial activities. As petty retailers, they purchased goods in the regional capital and then sold the merchandise in small towns and villages of neighboring districts and to settlers, soldiers, and independent tribal Indians on the frontier.[15]

In urban centers, *gente baja* leverage was more circumscribed from the 1820s through the 1870s, and the variables determining it were more limited. Almost all were involved in the market economy one way or another, usually as wage earners. What mattered was the degree of choice, mobility, and control they exercised in the often complex workings of that economy. That was determined by three basic variables: the local economy's general health (above all, the flow of migrants), the scale and kinds of imports (and, increasingly, foreigners themselves), and the type and effectiveness of governmental policies affecting economic opportunities.

The urban counterparts to *peones* on rural estates were domestic servants. They comprised a large component of the labor force, constituting as they did an important criterion of status for the *gente alta*. Their wages were paltry, and their lives were controlled to a great degree by their employers, who considered them to be lowly, subordinate members of the family. Economic hard times simply made their plight worse.[16] Workers who could avoid falling into the necessity and confines of domestic service were beset by two forces. Both tended to limit their leverage vis-à-vis employers and their prospects for material improvement. The urban migration that had accelerated greatly after 1750 continued apace. *Gente baja* (perceiving more economic opportunities in urban centers) came from rural communities but also, it increasingly appears, from other towns and cities. This placed urban workers, long-time residents and newcomers alike, at a worse competitive advantage in finding and holding jobs and in maintaining subsistence wages. Compounding this problem was the elimination of jobs (or decline in wages) caused by the inroads of foreign manufactures. Spinners and weavers were especially hard-hit. The reverse side of the coin was that those same urban migrant competitors for jobs were also potential consumers of necessities. Artisans in crafts related to construction (or not in direct competition with foreign goods) found that in times of an upsurge in economic activity, they stood to gain.

Whether their impact was positive or negative, urban migration and the influx of foreign goods stimulated more initiative by urban commoners in the marketplace. As workers lost jobs in artisanal and factory workshops, they turned to petty vending in subsistence commodities, often as self-employed producers. Even better, gaining access to a piece of land in suburban barrios (either by squatting or renting) afforded them the opportunity to enhance subsistence independence and prospects for selling foodstuffs, fresh or prepared. But in more established urban wards, property in general (and housing in particular) was often scarce, too expensive for the popular classes to do more than find crowded rooms in which to eat and sleep. Access to credit was key to keeping one above meager wages and measly sales, as petty traders and artisans who comprised the bulk of urban *gente de profesiones* knew only too well. Both required credit to cover the costs of inventory and materials before sales. As private individuals absorbed even more of the church's lending role, as republican governments abandoned colonial restrictions on usurious interest rates, and as price competition from imports ate away profit margins, access to credit was at once more tenuous and more necessary.[17]

Women: Vital Players in the Economy

Customarily seen as marginal economic participants at best, women were (as accumulating monographic studies reveal) players of important consequence in most sectors of the economy. In some sectors, in some regions, they were the dominant players. Their fortunes, however, differed noticeably depending upon several variables: social strata, degree and type of penetration of external markets, relative prosperity or stagnation of the regional economy, and the impact of public insecurity (wars, civil strife, political persecution) on family stability and economic activity.

Underlying women's economic role was the stark fact that they headed a large minority of households. Unmarried, widowed, or not infrequently an independent partner in a consensual union, they had themselves and usually children to support. Such households were more numerous in urban areas than in the countryside. In Costa Rica's central highlands, nearly 40 percent of urban households were female-headed; in villages that figure was around 20 percent, still a substantial number. Whereas widows predominated in such rural households, single mothers in urban households were nearly even with widows in distribution. One might expect substantial numbers of female-headed households in *gente baja* neighborhoods, but even among the *gente alta*, their numbers were significant.[18]

This sizable proportion of female-headed households was an important consequence of the social transformation begun in the mid–eighteenth century and seems generally to have increased after independence. So, too, were the growing possibilities and necessity for women to participate in the pre-industrial, early modern commercializing economy that had been the prime factor in that social transformation. There were goods to be crafted in homes and workshops, marketable crops to be produced and tended, and a range of merchandise to be retailed in shops, in stalls, and on the street.

Unless they possessed adequate land and labor for independent subsistence (a clear minority), women entirely on their own had to engage the market economy. For the *gente baja*, marriage did reduce the chances of such engagement. But the dislocations and fluctuations of the market economy frequently necessitated the participation of a noteworthy proportion of married women to secure sufficient supplemental income for their families (in Mexico City, one-fourth of married women were so engaged).[19] Then, too, there were some women (precisely how numerous is difficult to determine) who pursued openings in the market economy for the increased independence or satisfaction it brought them. They were mostly widows and spinsters of means and owners of real property.

The most prevalent and long-standing occupation among women was that of domestic service. A requisite of respectability (whether achieved or aspired to), servants were always in demand. A steady stream of migrants from the countryside and a residue of penniless longtime urban residents provided a continuing supply. A job most paternalistic, most limiting of freedom, and quite vulnerable to abusive treatment and degradation, domestic service was generally the province of impoverished girls, young women, and destitute older women with no other alternatives. Its undesirability led women to seek alternative work whenever and wherever they could.[20]

The cottage industry was the second most identified work in which women were engaged, especially the apparel trades. They were spinners, weavers, and seamstresses in the thousands in most regions, working out of their homes. Still others found jobs as craft laborers in workshops. From Chile's central valley to Costa Rica's and Colombia's highlands, they dominated the cottage industry in small towns and villages. In large urban centers they constituted a sizable portion of those engaged in such crafts.[21] But mechanization and imports undercut female employment in the craft industries (as it did to artisans in general). Spinners and weavers were most vulnerable. They simply could not compete as prices lowered; their numbers dropped continually, often precipitously. One alternative, which growing numbers of women seized upon, was becoming seamstresses, using foreign-made and domestically manufactured cloth. In Mexico City, there were five times as many seamstresses at midcentury as in 1810. But excessive supply diminished earning power, a problem women faced in most economic sectors in which they participated.

Limited available evidence, however, suggests that mechanization did offer another area of employment to women. Textile factories that drove female spinners and weavers from the market also provided some jobs. In parts of Mexico, women comprised a substantial part of the textile mill labor force, including those in the villages and neighboring provinces around the national capital, though in the latter, mills (established mainly by French investors) employed mostly foreign workers. In Bogotá, the numerous small factories opened in the 1870s (chocolate, cigar/cigarette, and china factories most notably), using low technology and unskilled labor, hired large numbers of women.[22]

Retail trade was the other principal economic sector in which women were engaged in large numbers. In some regions, rural women were the dominant players in petty trade, marketing the production of small farms and household crafts, often their own, in villages and towns. Urban *gente baja* women, working out of their homes and on the streets, could combine their work with household chores and child care, especially in food vending. This also explains why this sector involved so many married women. But like most economic activities engaged in by *gente baja* women, there were no formal contracts, no security in case of sickness or old age. Moreover, remuneration was meager, owing to illiteracy, low skill levels, and an abundant supply of women seeking work.[23]

Gente alta women were also engaged in market activities, though in fewer numbers and in different sectors (with the principal exceptions of retail trade and sewing). Especially during times of economic recession and political conflict, *gente decente* women found themselves with husbands out of work, in jail, or in exile. They joined the significant number of widowed and divorced women of means in having to produce their own income. The least affluent were most likely to be involved as shopkeepers (often operating from their residences) and as managers. These enterprises ranged from the more numerous general merchandise establishments, taverns, apparel shops, and restaurants to some hotels and printing shops. The spread of education and the growing professionalization of teachers (and midwives) appear to have opened up a growing avenue of employment for *gente decente* women. The growth of social service institutions (foundling homes, poor houses, and municipal hospitals) did the same.[24]

Some *gente decente* women were engaged in the management of investments and inheritances; much more so were notable women. In a partible inheritance system in which property was divided evenly between sons and daughters, these women had considerable sums at their disposal, and their management was seen as an acceptable extension of family responsibilities. Many husbands, sons, and brothers often did manage the assets of notable women (a wife's inheritance legally became part of the community property to be managed by her husband). But spinsters and widows made up a considerable portion of notable women (and of the *gente alta* generally). One only has to scour notary archives to see the extent to which notable women were engaged in the buying, selling, and renting of urban property, rural estates, and profitable businesses. In Mexico City, they held title to one-quarter of all privately owned buildings in 1813, their proportion of notarial transactions increasing thereafter. In Bolivia's central highlands, from the end of the imperial period to 1880, the percentage of haciendas owned by women increased from 17 percent to 25 percent. *Gente alta* women in Bogatá were major users of the savings banks, usually as depositors. Notable wives appear to have been not infrequently involved in the day-to-day operation of various family enterprises, including general merchandising, agricultural production, and mining.[25]

Regional Variation

The mix of variables influencing the configuration of the post-independence economy—centralized governmental direction, foreign contact, and small producers—varied from region to region. Several factors shaped those variables. Ample studies have demonstrated the marked population growth during the last century of imperial rule. Recent regional studies have begun to reveal that population growth, which was generally negatively affected by the independence wars, resumed in a number of areas. This finding could manifest a changing ratio of land to labor that reduced the leverage of the *gente baja* and intensified their struggle for survival. But likewise, it could indicate their success in increasing their role in the economy, especially in formerly sparsely settled regions. Their numbers could have increased because of opportunity rather than necessity.

Given the existing state of transportation systems and technology, the pervasive commitment to open trade following independence, and generally ineffective national governments, linkage with the international market depended in great part on location. Formerly marginal regions located near the coast or a navigable river often experienced a marked shift in external contacts. But the extent of those contacts also depended upon a given region's production of, or perceived potential for, a commodity marketable abroad.

Economic policies of the central (or federal) government, though failing to create integrated economies on a national scale, nevertheless had an important influence on regional economies. Specific policies favored some groups and regions at the expense of others, altering advantages of location and population density. Still, those policies' impact depended greatly on implementation and enforcement, which varied according to the support and unity of important constituencies, the strength of opposition resistance, fiscal resources, and the resolve and integrity of officeholders.

In one sense, labor systems reflected the degree of leverage socioeconomic groups possessed vis-à-vis one another, the ability of the state to maintain and sanction those relationships of economic power, and the impact of demography (land-population ratios and composition). Yet they also acted as inhibiters and stimulants for foreign contact and small producers.

The highlands of Peru and Bolivia do not fit the models of Indian communities on the defensive and in decline or those of stagnant economies. In some regions the Indians actually increased their majority among the general population, reflecting their ability to increase their economic, political, and cultural autonomy, thus strengthening their communities. An ample land-person ratio remained, and they expanded traditional relations of reciprocal exchange, more efficiently exploiting extensive resources. At the same time, the Indians moved into spaces in the market economy either vacated or left unexploited by non-Indians. They replaced intermediaries and gained control over the production and distribution of goods, aided greatly by the employment of district and regional trade fairs. Foreign contact remained limited, and the national government was weak at least until the 1860s.[26]

In the middle-altitude highlands of Costa Rica, Colombia, and Venezuela, there was also an expansion of small producers. In this setting, though, the cause was the migration of non-Indians (and some dispossessed Indian villagers) into sparsely settled districts, creating new communities. In addition, the rise of coffee export production in its early stages held an important place in these expanding regional economies in which small producers played such a significant role. By contrast, the same stimulus strengthened the leverage of *gente alta* producers in other regions. Strong central governments and existing concentrated land ownership enabled large producers with controlled labor supplies to expand coffee exports. In Brazil, slavery was employed in the expansion of coffee in the Paraíba Valley and the São Paulo region. In Puerto Rico (still a colony), the declining use of slaves induced by the slave trade's abolition was supplanted by the use of debt peonage to control labor mobility and maintain a dependent rural population.[27]

In Chile, the population-land ratio was such that it enabled hacendados' to so dominate rural commoners as to withstand emigration to the northern mines and the commercial centers of Valparaíso and Santiago. It also made possible a boom in grain export production for two decades with few technological or capital improvements. Cumulative population growth from the eighteenth century, combined with an excessive concentration of landownership, had converted most of the rural popular classes into a floating population by the mid–nineteenth century. Only a minority could be absorbed as labor service tenants. When an opportunity to produce grain for export opened in the third quarter of the century—one that was profitable but uncertain in its longevity—hacendados used ample underused lands and their considerable leverage over rural commoners to respond quickly and inexpensively. Wages remained stable or declined slightly. *Inquilinaje* was extended, but with land allotments reduced and labor obligations increased. Chile's central government, one of Latin America's most stable and strong after 1830, provided firm backing for the hacendados' interests.[28]

Though a mountainous interior area, the district of Tarija in southern Bolivia was transformed after 1820 from frontier outpost into a commercial entrepôt. It became a center for the transshipment of goods between the region's stagnating silver mines, the eastern Chaco frontier, the Pacific coast (especially new mining centers opening up along it), and northwestern Argentina. Imported cloth and clothing dominated the trade, with more than half of sales going to the eastern frontier region, where these imports were exchanged for cattle. By 1880, a growing portion of the district's population had also been incorporated into this commerce. Customers from all social strata acquired imported goods through the extension of credit repaid with earnings from the internal market.[29]

No greater exception to the customary portrayal of Latin America's post-independence economy existed than in Paraguay until the War of the Triple Alliance in the late 1860s. For nearly a half century under an authoritarian but popularly based government, *gente baja* dominated the economy, with consistent and considerable governmental support and a controlled and beneficial relationship with external markets. Population steadily grew, and production expanded significantly (especially in agriculture). Moreover, women played a prominent role in most economic sectors.

Most important, landownership and tenancy was widespread. The large majority of the *gente baja* were small producers, whether in urban centers or the countryside. There was an abundance of farmland and ranch land in relation to the population. Distance from major markets also helped keep land values low. The government, especially under José Gaspar Rodríguez de Francia (1811–1840), provided assistance for land purchases and even gave away land to soldiers as payment for service and to individuals (largely commoners) it deemed deserving. The state, which owned more than half of the land by midcentury, rented out a large portion at low rates. Squatters on state lands were numerous; fines were minimal when infrequently collected.

Other governmental policies also played a substantial role in the success of the many small producers. They discouraged foreigners from purchasing land while promoting crops and improving production.

Francia focused on self-sufficiency: lessening the export trade in tobacco and yerba maté tea; and urging farmers to move from one crop to two a year and to focus on crops more suitable to the region's climate and terrain. His successor, Carlos Antonio López (1841–1862), sought to expand the production of tobacco and cotton for export. He used newspapers to spread better techniques, distributed seeds, built reservoirs, and improved roads. Small producers preferred tobacco because it earned twice as much per acre, and the government assisted them by making advantageous purchases and by grading for quality. Tobacco production increased tenfold between 1829 and 1863. Food producers, meanwhile, found expanding local urban markets.

Women were the primary beneficiaries of the latter opportunity. In the districts around Asunción, women constituted nearly one-fifth of the renters on state lands; within the nation's capital proper, they worked two-thirds of the small plots. Nationwide, they made up about one-fifth of the buyers and sellers of real estate. The ready availability of land in both city and countryside meant that single women (who headed 34–40 percent of households in 1846) could support themselves selling surplus production. And in households headed by men, women and girls were essential to farm operations in which the family was the basic unit of labor. Moreover, with men away in the yerba fields and in military service, women maintained many of these farms. They also held a significant position in the craft industries and as retailers in local markets.

With access to inexpensive and abundantly available land and favorable government policies, Paraguay's *gente baja*—both men and women—gained a subsistence security and the opportunity for additional material improvements in their lives equaled by few of their counterparts elsewhere in Latin America. Largely homogeneous (culturally mestizo and to a large extent biologically as well), their economic position reinforced a popular culture that characterized the whole regional society.[30]

The Merchant-Entrepreneur: Economic Protagonist

Though indicative of the extent to which the *gente baja* could be involved in regional market economies throughout Latin America—in this case, even dominate the economy—Paraguay was the exception. Elsewhere, their influence varied over a considerably lower range of degree. Instead, the protagonist was the merchant-entrepreneur. The economic transformation initiated in the 1750s had opened up new opportunities for merchants, and independence expanded their range even further. Corporate burdens on (and barriers to) private entrepreneurship were markedly weakened. The church was economically in retreat. Guild regulations were disappearing. Communal ownership was on the defensive, challenged by the new republican legal ethic. The state was increasingly deficient in both legitimacy and finances. Into this expanded economic space moved the merchant, now, above all, an organizer of a broad range of business ventures, an entrepreneur.

The merchant-entrepreneurs who rose rapidly as central players in the post-independence economy came from several different strands that had become increasingly intertwined. Most numerous were the merchants of prominence in their localities and districts, whose horizons were broadened by greater and sometimes direct contact with external markets. A smaller number owned large commercial houses in the regional urban centers. They were joined by foreign merchants of various nationalities, who set up operations in commercial centers that ranged from small district seats to provincial cities and capitals to national capitals. Gradually, such merchant-entrepreneurs diversified from their commercial base. The first step usually was to convert the dynamic core of their business activities from commercial capital in the form of goods to financial capital in the form of credit and loans, thus becoming extenders of credit, granters of loans and mortgages, exchangers of money, and discounters of bills of exchange. The largest of them—expanding into receivers of deposits, lenders to governments, and traders in domestic and foreign bonds and securities—became the functional equivalent of North Atlantic banking institutions at the time.

Through the leverage of this array of financial services, these merchants steadily penetrated the whole of the economy as recipients of foreclosed mortgages and collateral from defaulted loans and as partners in enterprises. Increasingly after 1850, they took the initiative in a broad range of economic activities. In part this was a response to external stimuli: an expansion of foreign trade, especially in agricultural exports; a new wave of enterprising immigrants interested in joint-stock ventures with local investors; and the emergence of modernizing state bureaucracies committed to expanding public services and public improvements through growing revenues and a new cycle of foreign loans.[31] The merchant-entrepreneurs became the hub linking the economy's various sectoral spokes.

These *empresarios* also provided spatial linkages in the economy, especially in the first decades following independence. They were at the center of local-district networks of indebtedness, credit, and market exchange in small towns and district seats. Through their control over the lines of credit and frequently over commercial outlets for agrarian production, they tied many small producers in their respective communities dependently into the larger economy of the locality and district. Among small producers, but even more so among *gente decente* and fellow notables, merchant-entrepreneurs also rendered services as executors of wills and powers of attorney. This role often gave them effective control over economic activities and resources they did not formally own. Not surprisingly, then, within the larger regional economies they functioned as commercial intermediaries, facilitators of credit exchange, and collectors of outstanding debts (through powers of attorney). In regional urban centers (especially in major ports, important state capitals, and national capitals), they served as bridges to extraregional and international markets. In addition to processing investments and loans made within their region (especially in their city's environs), they served above all as commission agents in shipping and commercial transactions. They also traded in bills of exchange, made advances and loans, and maintained current and deposit accounts for clients.[32]

Social connections also contributed to the pivotal role of merchant-entrepreneurs in the post-independence regional economies. Their business interests were enlarged and consolidated through marriage into one another's families, through serving as formal witnesses at such nuptial events and as godparents for resulting progeny, and through functioning as powers of attorney. Weddings, funerals, local celebrations, and personal social calls all became occasions to help cement business relationships. Family ties and social interchange bred familiarity and trust as they linked the merchant-entrepreneurs to one another and to other players in the economic sectors.[33]

Generators of Agricultural Production and Trade

The linkage of agricultural production and trade was the initial fundamental base for the merchant-entrepreneurs' expanding economic activities. For several centuries, profits generated in urban centers by merchants had been poured into large-scale agricultural pursuits, usually as a one-way passage to social notability. But with the economic transformation after 1750, merchants had increasingly realized that landed wealth without access to commercial resources and other urban sources of profit was destined to economic insecurity, even ruin. Tadeo Díez de Medina possessed such foresight, investing heavily the capital accruing from trade in agricultural ventures in the province of La Paz (central Bolivia), particularly coca estates, and then plowing the returns from these estates into his urban activities as well. More tellingly, he married three of his four daughters to up-and-coming merchants to cement commercial relations while securing a legal education for both of his sons to facilitate their taking over the active management of his diversified portfolio.[34]

With barriers to international commerce greatly reduced after independence, fortunes could be made by articulating sources of supply with newly opened (or expanding) markets. Yet these entrepreneurs learned that less direct control over rural production often brought greater gain and less risk in the long run. Merchant-producer partnerships were one avenue of investment in agricultural production without landownership. The former provided the financial capital, while the latter supplied the land, labor, and equipment, with profits split according to various arrangements. As important, the resulting trade was funneled through the merchant-entrepreneur's commercial enterprises. A less direct strategy was to provide loans or advances of cash or goods to finance production, with crops and land as the collateral. Depending upon their leverage (based upon degree of risk, need for capital, and extent of economic and political influence), merchant-entrepreneurs sought to secure exclusive rights to furnishing supplies and marketing production.[35]

By maintaining varied strategies, merchant-entrepreneurs could adjust their involvement in rural production according to market risks and opportunities (and political circumstances). That they accumulated and lost considerable capital from agricultural ventures during this period is evidenced in countless individual and regional studies published since the 1970s. What is less evident is the extent to which through those ventures, they increasingly shaped this important sector of the post-independence economy.

Manipulators of Public Finance

Provision of loans to governments proved to be far more rewarding than other investments in terms of returns and concomitant opportunities. In some regions and nations, where consistent economic expansion or a valuable commodity for export was attained by midcentury (wheat and copper mining in Chile or guano collection in Peru, for example), revenues could begin adequately to support administrative expenses and public improvements. Nevertheless, these successes were the exceptions to the general rule of fiscal penury that most governments confronted until the 1870s. In such circumstances, they turned more and more to those who could provide them with ready cash and credit. Merchant-entrepreneurs, with greater access to liquid forms of capital, seized the opportunity. From time to time, they fell victim to forced loans by desperate or dictatorial politicians. But more often than not, they collaborated with public officials, developing ongoing fiscal arrangements to keep governments afloat. As governments found themselves backed into fiscal corners, merchant-entrepreneurs incesssantly sought much shorter terms at much higher interest rates and with more substantial collateral than had been the case before 1820. For these moneylenders, collateral ultimately translated into a share of customs revenues.

Using these loans to governments as leverage, merchant-entrepreneurs pursued ancillary opportunities in public finance. Facing a growing inability to meet their commitments in hard currency, governments turned to payment in a variety of paper credits and securities. Moneylenders frequently bought up these issues of credit at a discount (often steep) and then used their influence with public officials to secure priority of repayment, with a high percentage in cash. When governments sometimes resorted to the colonial policy of tax farming or authorized bondholder agents to collect certain portions of the customs revenues, merchant-entrepreneurs snapped up the opportunity. In such capacities—or even receiving appointments to customs or treasury posts themselves—they were able to manipulate public finance with even greater effect.[36]

Contractors of Public Improvements and Services

Connections with politicians and bureaucrats through public finance often led merchant-entrepreneurs to become recipients of contracts awarded for the provision of public services and the construction of infrastructure. More and more after midcentury they began to expand into this sector with the assistance of a new wave of external loans that followed the surge of a trade boom in Atlantic commerce and through use of corporate business structures.

Strapped for funds, some governments turned to contracts with private individuals and firms to supply state services. Enterprising merchants discerned that managing such services as public transportation (principally stagecoach and shipping lines), mail delivery, and road maintenance could readily support other business activities. Such contracts could also deepen the dependency of public officials, providing increased leverage in gaining access to public finance deals. Contracts for public improvements also awaited merchants with the foresight to diversify: port works; roads; water and sewer systems; public buildings; and railroads, at once the symbol and prime vehicle of the new age of progress dawning with varying time lags in Latin America after midcentury. The international trade boom made infrastructure works all the more imperative. And where national politics first stabilized and when external loans became abundant (culminating in the lending frenzy of the 1860s and early 1870s), ample public resources could fund the desired public improvements fully through contracts or supplementally through concessions. In particular, merchant-entrepreneurs increasingly set up joint corporate ventures to invest in railroads and port works that moved the expanding production of the immediate hinterland and more interior regions to the coast or major cities.[37]

Tentative Pioneers in Industrial Manufacturing

Since the late eighteenth century, either as owners of large workshops or more frequently as organizers of cottage industries, merchants had come to play an important role in the finishing of goods. However, growing competition from foreign industrial manufacture, combined with a series of internal conditions (noted above), discouraged the initiation of large factories, especially given more attractive investment alternatives. Merchant-entrepreneurs in Chile had shied away from manufacturing from the beginning. Few had financed household production or opened workshops before independence. Erosion of small-scale production by industrially manufactured imports only confirmed their prior inclinations to diversify into land and mining. The growing interlocking network of these interests committed the country to policies that fostered production of primary exports and consumption of imported manufactures that endured into the twentieth century.[38]

Elsewhere, the far more typical case was that of merchant-entrepreneurs taking the first hesitant steps in introducing industrial manufacturing, beginning in the 1830s in some countries with very limited success and accelerating somewhat after midcentury with moderate success. In the latter case, a considerable number of foreigners, both of long residence and newly arrived, took the lead. In Rio de Janeiro, for example, they comprised the large majority of wealthy merchants engaged in such manufacturing. Their counterparts in Bahia, however, vigorously opposed it.[39] For industrial manufacturing cut the large-scale merchants, foreign and native alike, like a two-edged sword. In a given commodity, investment in factory production undercut imports and vice versa. The critical judgment was in discerning which commodities in which particular districts and regions stood a reasonable chance of success in being domestically fabricated.

In Venezuela the Casa Boulton operated a soap- and candle-making factory and flour mill to process its tallow and wheat imported from the United States. In Mexico the textile sector proved the largest attraction to merchant-entrepreneurs. Funds and support from the government's Banco de Avio coaxed the first investors into establishing factories in the 1830s. The industry became firmly established in the next decade, as the largest merchant houses, having triumphed in the speculative frenzy in public finance, began investing heavily in textile manufacturing, generally buying up existing firms and greatly expanding production. But they were soon hampered by changes in government, changing public policies on imports, unstable demand, and the need for much improved transportation. These problems did not begin to be resolved until the 1880s.[40]

Accumulators of Property

If the establishment of industrial factories was a risk-laden venture during this period, by comparison the acquisition of property seemed almost a sure thing, and nothing more so than urban real estate. Given the uncertainties following independence in many regions, urban property offered a steady income with low risk. Thereafter, because of expanding economic activities and population, urban rents often produced handsome returns. In Buenos Aires, with the growing influx of immigrants and migrants from the interior after midcentury, patio-style homes were converted into *conventillos* (multiple-unit tenements), along with smaller boarding houses and narrow two-story residences. In the 1870s, one local newspaper placed the annual return on such investments to tenement owners (whom it characterized as the port's richest and most respectable men) at 30–36 percent. Such profits led merchant-entrepreneurs to build 300 new *conventillos* by 1880.[41]

In such economic and demographic circumstances, urban property was also a good investment for other purposes. Choice real estate was essential for these *empresarios'* expanding enterprises, whether for the establishment of enlarged commercial operations, factories, or public services. It was also the basis for speculative profits. Rural properties, too, were avenues for speculation. However, merchant-entrepreneurs seemed to have accumulated land in the countryside more for large estate production or rental income, depending upon the risks and potential returns. They also increasingly discerned the valuable use of rural landholdings as collateral for raising investment capital for other enterprises.[42]

Founders of Banking Institutions

Consolidating their hold on credit through networks of personal loans and credit alliances, before midcentury merchant-entrepreneurs had little incentive and less foresight to experiment with corporate financial structures. But first in those countries where economic expansion and political stability had been most prevalent after 1840 and then spreading through most of Latin America in the 1860s and 1870s, they began to employ part of their accumulating capital in the establishment of formal, corporate financial institutions. Profits from the trade boom then under way compounded the sizable amounts of capital accumulated from moneylending and urban real estate since 1820. Many merchant-entrepreneurs derived additional profits by diversifying into agriculture, public services, mining, and manufacturing. They also became increasingly aware that formal, corporate financial structures could reduce legal liabilities and provide a large pool of investment capital. At the same time, liberal economic theory from the North Atlantic began to take hold among the now generally liberal governments. Unfettered corporate enterprises (including financial institutions) were encouraged as stimulants to the economy, with appropriate legislation drafted to support them.[43]

The founding of the Banco de Cauca in 1873 brought together the diverse patterns of economic change set in motion at midcentury in this region of west-central Colombia. During the 1850s and 1860s, beset by the risks of civil unrest, merchant-entrepreneurs had shifted from forced-labor, large-estate agriculture into the redemption of ecclesiastical assets and investment in urban real estate. The revival of extralocal trade by the early 1870s added to their profits. Along with other local investors, they saw the bank as a haven for accumulating liquid assets, an adjunct to existing internal credit networks, and a resource for future investments. Most were the representatives of the principal families of the city.[44] For the financial institutions spreading through Latin America after midcentury were not merely the vehicle of adjustment for merchant-entrepreneurs as individuals, but for the diversified portfolio of economic interests accumulated by their notable families, portfolios that they generally managed.

Managing the Family Portfolio

The rise of formal banking institutions after midcentury represented the culmination of a reorganization of notable family wealth that had been going on for two generations. Investment initiative and control of wealth were being shifted from individuals and partners within families to formal corporations. Until then, notables largely had relied upon informal alliances to link their expanding economic activities. Various family members (together, increasingly, with kin relations) supplied one another with credit, created vertical and horizontal integration for their enterprises, and retained assets. Since the late 1700s the joining of trade and primary production (of merchant house and large landed estate) had been the foundation of their family portfolios. In various combinations as direct partners or in a more loose cooperative arrangement, family members managed these twin pillars of the family enterprise: father and son(s), uncle and nephew, mother and son(s), brothers, brothers-in-law. When family members fell deeply in debt, other members loaned them money or bought them out. When left without an heir or to join together properties previously divided through probate or newly acquired, uncles married nieces, aunts wed nephews, and cousins united in marriage—all with the necessary dispensations from the church.

In the post-independence years, merchant-entrepreneurs generally emerged as the central figures in this growing web of family business connections. They possessed the largest reserve of (and access to) credit and other forms of liquid capital. Their commercial ties gave the family its broadest economic connections. Their growing involvement in public finance, infrastructure, and services gave them considerable leverage in the family's dealings with government, especially at the state and national levels. If not the family patriarch, they were usually the first among equals.

However, for Latin America's most successful prominent families—those who kept pace with the rising prerequisites of notability—diversification came not simply through its principal *empresario*. In their individual activities and roles, family members came increasingly to constitute the family's diversity. Those coming of age at midcentury began shifting away from occupations directly supporting the family's commercial-agricultural base. Usually younger sons trained in learned professions. They chose military careers, went into government service, became educators, and ran for public office. In such posts, they lent support to the family enterprise—almost always valuable, often vital, sometimes critical. Moreover, they were becoming more entrepreneurial, supplementing salaried and professional incomes with business ventures, which not infrequently linked them with those on the edge of or outside the family circle. Distant relations, members of other network families, those of lesser station with rising political or economic fortunes, and enterprising immigrants became likely partners, with ties often sealed through marriage. The family circle widened. Diversification expanded. Networks within notable families were evolving into networks among them.

Female members played a crucial role in this process of expanding linkages. Sometimes they owned important assets in the family's portfolio; less frequently they managed them. Yet their most important economic role derived from their serving as "human investment capital." Their marriages often served to preserve, solidify, or merge various family assets or working business relationships. That is why, principally, they married their uncles, nephews, cousins, or the business partners of their male relatives. Perhaps more importantly, as notables sought to expand their networks, women constituted an important source of risk capital. They bore the risk almost alone; the whole family amply shared in the returns, if they were forthcoming. Through their marriages, notable families invested in the rising career of a politician or military figure; a prospering large estate owner or one whose land could be integrated into the family's holdings; or a foreign owner of a merchant house, factory, or mine. If her husband's success was lasting, then the investment could be secured through the marriage of their children back into the family, to cousins. If her spouse's good fortune proved fleeting, then the family divested itself, and the children became poor relations. Of course, there was always the chance that one of those children would make a name for themselves. In a succeeding generation, they might very well rejoin the family or another notable family. Not a few eventually did.

Notable families also came to depend on female members as diplomats, counselors, and negotiators. For the growing web of family relations was neither of one political mind nor free of the customary personal rivalries and conflicts. By organizing and managing family celebrations, remembrances, and less poignant social occasions, notable women soothed hurt feelings, defused political conflicts, and provided opportunities for family business to be transacted in a supportive atmosphere. At times, their counsel was sought or given on economic matters (particularly assets they had brought to the family). Less often, but crucial to family fortunes, they negotiated and pleaded with blood relations and in-laws on behalf of family members who had lost in a political struggle.[45]

By the 1850s, then, an increasingly intricate network of relations had been forged within and among notable families in Latin America. Corporate structures concentrated management of the family portfolio capital in the hands of a few members, usually merchant-entrepreneurs. Liabilities were limited; the wide range of enterprises could be better coordinated and integrated. Through banks in particular, family members with occupations not directly connected to business activities could count on secure supports to their income, whereas those wishing additionally to engage in entrepreneurial ventures had a ready vehicle to do so. Pooling individual family members' wealth, such a financial institution could redistribute it (more rationally and with greater protection) in the form of loans, mortgages, commercial credit, and investment ventures. Stock transactions and managerial posts ensured that notable families had sufficient control over corporate financial decisions.[46]

With members spreading out into the gamut of important economic activities in regions across Latin America, coordinated and integrated more effectively through the growing adoption of corporate structures, networks of notable families were positioned to dominate their regional societies. In some cases, their sights were becoming set on the national level. Both threatened the equilibrium of Middle Period society that had been present since the early nineteenth century. So, too, did a set of other historical forces coming into play after midcentury.

Notes

1. Margaret Chowning, "The Contours of the Post-1810 Depression in Mexico: A Reappraisal from a Regional Perspective," *LARR* 27:2 (1992): 119–36; Chowning, *Wealth and Power in Provincial Mexico: Michoacán from the Late Colony to the Revolution* (Stanford, CA: Stanford University Press, 1999), chap. 4.

2. Chowning, "Post-1810 Depression," 130–36; John Kicza, *La vida social en hispanoamerica* (Caracas: Academia Nacional de la Historia de Venezuela, 1998), chap. 1; Sowell, *Artisans and Politics*, 15–18.

3. David Bushnell and Neil MacCauley, *The Emergence of Latin America in the Nineteenth Century* (New York: Oxford University Press, 1988), 40–45; Carlos Marichal, *A Century of Debt Crisis in Latin America: From Independence to the Great Depression, 1820–1930* (Princeton, NJ: Princeton University Press, 1989), 3, 13–26.

4. Marichal, *Century of Debt Crisis*, 4–14, 26–67; Juan E. Oribe Stemmer, "Freight Rates in the Trade Between Europe and South America," *JLAS* 21 (February 1989): 25–27, 33–34, 56.

5. Oribe Stemmer, "Trade," 27–29, 33–34; Bushnell and MacCauley, *Emergence of Latin America*, 181–87; Marichal, *Century of Debt Crisis*, 68–109.

6. Jane M. Rausch, "Frontiers in Crisis: The Breakdown of the Mission in Far Northern Mexico and New Granada, 1821–1849," *CSSH* 29:2 (1987): 340–59.

7. Weber, *American Southwest under Mexico*, chaps. 7–11.

8. Kraay, "Bahian *Sabinada*," 503; Sowell, *Artisans and Politics*, 15–21.

9. Sowell, *Artisans and Politics*, 17; Arrom, *Women in Mexico City*, 191; Arnold J. Bauer, "Industry and the Missing Bourgeoisie: Consumption and Development in Chile, 1850–1950," *HAHR* 70 (May 1990): 227–52; Albert Berry, "The Limited Role of Rural Small-Scale Manufacturing for Late-Comers: Some Hypotheses on the Colombian Experience," *JLAS* 19 (November 1987): 295–322.

10. Herbert S. Klein and Stanley L. Engerman, "Del trabajo esclavo al trabajo libre: Notas en torno a un modelo económico comparativo," *Centro Latinoamericano de Historia Económica y Social* 1 (1983), 41–55; Richardson, "Labor Mobility," 8–10; Knight, *The Caribbean*, chap. 6.

11. Arnold Jacob Bauer, "Chilean Rural Society in the Nineteenth Century" (Ph.D. diss., University of California at Berkeley, 1969), 17–18, 29–35, 132–66; Stanley Stein, *Vassouras: A Brazilian Coffee County, 1850–1890* (New York: Atheneum, 1970), 87–90.

12. Klein, *Haciendas and Ayllus*, 14–16, 108–32, 162–65; José Deustua, "Routes, Roads, and Silver Trade in Cerro de Pasco, 1820–1860: The Internal Market in Nineteenth Century Peru," *HAHR* 94 (February 1994): 10–21.

13. For regional case studies, see LeGrand, "Colombian Frontier"; Yarrington, "Public Land Settlement"; and Lowell Gudmundson, *Costa Rica before Coffee: Society and Economy on the Eve of the Export Boom* (Baton Rouge: Louisiana State University Press, 1986).

14. Bauer, "Chilean Rural Society," 128–31. See also David A. Brading, *Haciendas and Ranchos in the Mexican Bajío, 1680–1860* (Cambridge, England: Cambridge University Press, 1978).

15. Eric D. Langer and Gina L. Hames, "Commerce and Credit on the Periphery: Tarija Merchants, 1830–1914," *HAHR* 74 (May 1994): 288, 291–95.

16. Szuchman (*Mobility and Integration in Urban Argentina*), Arrom (*Women in Mexico City*), and Gudmundson (*Costa Rica before Coffee*) derive similar portraits of the plight of domestic servants.

17. Sowell, "Artisans, Credit, Development," 617–18, 624, 630–34.

18. Gudmundson, *Costa Rica before Coffee*, 96–98.

19. Arrom, *Women of Mexico City*, 196.

20. Gudmundson, *Costa Rica before Coffee*, 116–17; Arrom, *Women of Mexico City*, 161, 165, 187–89.

21. Bauer, "Missing Bourgeoisie," 232–33; Berry, "Rural Small-Scale Manufacturing," 297–302; Gudmundson, *Costa Rica before Coffee*, 99–100.

22. Arrom, *Women of Mexico City*, 189–92, 196; Gudmundson, *Costa Rica before Coffee*, 100–1; Sowell, *Artisans and Politics*, 21.

23. Arrom, *Women of Mexico City*, 192–93, 200.

24. Ibid., 166–72, 197–98.

25. Ibid., 172–74; Klein, *Haciendas and Ayllus*, 154; Sowell, "Artisans, Credit, Development," 632–33; Gudmundson, *Costa Rica before Coffee*, 99; Macias, "Las familias Pérez Gálvez y Rul," 646–47, 651–54.

26. Paul Gootenberg, "Population and Ethnicity in Early Peru: Some Revisions," *LARR* 26:3 (1991): 109–57; Klein, *Haciendas and Ayllus*, 102–8, 112–32, 162–65; Deustua, "Internal Market in Nineteenth Century Peru," 14–29.

27. LeGrand, "Colombian Frontier," 28–35; Gudmundson, *Costa Rica before Coffee*, chaps. 1–2, 4; Stein, *Vassouras*, chaps. 1–3; Tom Brass, "Free and Unfree Rural Labor in Puerto Rico during the Nineteenth Century," *JLAS* 18 (May 1986): 181–94.

28. Bauer, "Chilean Rural Society," 135–65.

29. Langer and Hames, "Commerce and Credit," 287–95, 309–16.

30. Vera Blinn Reber, "Small Farmers in the Economy: The Paraguayan Example, 1810–1865," *The Americas* 51 (April 1995): 495–524; Blinn Reber, "The Demographics of Paraguay: A Reinterpretation of the Great War, 1864–1870," *HAHR* 68 (May 1988): 315–17.

31. Rosa María Meyer Cosio, "Empresarios, crédito y especulación (1820–1850)," in *Banca y poder en Mexico (1800–1929)*, ed. Leonor Ludlow and Carlos Marichal (Mexico: Editorial Grijalbo, 1986), 102–15; Tenenbaum, *Politics of Penury*, 69–73; Marichal, *Century of Debt Crisis*, 68–96.

32. Radding, "Emerging Peasant Class," 390–94, 400, 423–25; Susan Bergland, "Mercantile Credit and Financing in Venezuela, 1830–1870," *JLAS* 17 (November 1985): 371–73, 384–91.

33. Rolf Engleson, "Social Aspects of Agricultural Expansion in Coastal Peru, 1825–1878" (Ph.D. diss., University of California at Los Angeles, 1977), 309–21, chap. 7. For a comprehensive, systematic study of these social linkages see Balmori, Voss, and Wortman, *Notable Family Networks*.

34. Klein, *Haciendas and Ayllus*, 33–55.

35. Chowning, "Post-1810 Depression," 128–31; Mario Cerruti, "El préstamo prebancario en el noreste de México: La actividád de los grandes comerciantes de Monterréy (1855–1890)," in *Banca y poder en México (1800–1929)*, ed. Leonor Ludlow and Carlos Marichal (Mexico: Editorial Grijalbo, 1986), 128–34.

36. Tenenbaum, *Politics of Penury*, 30–34, 56–69; Bergland, "Credit and Financing," 381–84; Cerruti, "Préstamo prebancario," 120–24; Sowell, *Artisans and Politics*, 17.

37. Tenenbaum, *Politics of Penury*, 34, 59–60, 65; Marichal, *Century of Debt Crisis*, 77–97; Robert Oppenheimer, "From Family to Corporation: Merchant Family Organization in Nineteenth Century Santiago, Chile" (paper presented at the AHA Meeting, Washington, DC, 1980), 8; James R. Scobie, *Buenos Aires: From Plaza to Suburb, 1870–1910* (New York: Oxford University Press, 1974), 39–40, 71–77, 165–66.

38. Bauer, "Missing Bourgeoisie," 227–53.

39. Eugene W. Ridings, "The Foreign Connection: A Look at the Business Elite of Rio de Janeiro in the Nineteenth Century," *The New Scholar* 7 (Spring 1978): 169, 177.

40. Bergland, "Credit and Financing," 371–96; Tenenbaum, *Politics of Penury*, 37, 70–73, 111–12, 137.

41. Scobie, *Buenos Aires*, 146–54.

42. Chowning, "Post-1810 Depression," 125–28, 140–41; Richard P. Hyland, "A Fragile Prosperity: Credit and Agrarian Structure in the Cauca Valley, Colombia, 1851–1887," *HAHR* 62 (August 1982): 388–98; Bauer, "Chilean Rural Society," 86–87, 197–214.

43. Steven S. Volk, "Mineowners, Moneylenders, and the State in Mid-Nineteenth Century Chile: Transitions and Conflicts," *HAHR* 73 (February 1993): 73–96; Sowell, "Artisans, Credit, and Development," 615–22.

44. Hyland, "Credit and Agrarian Structure in the Cauca Valley," 388–404.

45. The above analysis of the workings of the notable family is based on the array of sources consulted for Balmori, Voss, and Wortman, *Notable Family Networks*. Subsequent case studies have confirmed these findings.

46. Oppenheimer, "From Family to Corporation," 7–10.

6

Portents of Destabilization

A considerable degree of balance characterized Middle Period society as it crystallized and then matured through the first half of
the nineteenth century. Within and between the regional societies that
joined in various combinations to constitute Latin America's new nation-states, there was ample space for the social strata to preserve things
held dearly and to pursue visions of a better future while attending to
matters of daily life. The colonial order's transformation and imperial
rule's dismantling had created this broadened historical space. The
challenge—for notables, *gente decente, gente de profesiones,* and the popular classes alike—was the degree to which they could control and use
it. That required articulating local and regional practice and discourse
with the larger forces that were opening up the new historical possibilities. Existing structures limited, accommodated, or gave way to these
forces of change. Ways of understanding the world were reaffirmed,
redefined, reinterpreted, or replaced.

Economically, the market economy's elastic but steady expansion
had been breaking down the rigidities and barriers into which the
means of production had settled under the colonial order. One was
freer to move within the economy. Yet the economic space one occupied could be more easily penetrated by others. Leverage—the ability
to negotiate that more flexible economic space—had become more diffused. So, too, had the distribution of political power and authority.
The Enlightenment-derived principle of legal equality, combined with
the modern republican tenets of universal citizenship and broadened
representation, had greatly amplified the political space in which individuals and groups could pursue their interests. In addition, military
force was more disseminated. Socially and culturally, there was less
imposition from above and more prerogative from below, as political
and economic sanctions were more difficult to enjoin.

The state's character after independence reflected and embodied this broadened historical space. In most countries, the nation-state was authoritatively weak, fiscally feeble, inconsistent in legislation and policy, and far from monopolizing military force to impose its will. Even where it did achieve a firm footing (as in Brazil and Chile), its ability to implement policies and mold society on a national scale was limited. Provincial governments, often the repositories and defenders of regional interests vis-à-vis the national state, were also frequently the forum for struggle among competing local-district interests. The resulting discontinuities in government and the general shortage of public funds and coercive force left power and prerogative considerably dispersed. Even at the municipal level, dominated by notables and their clients among the *gente decente*, other social strata enjoyed considerable autonomy in their barrios and communities. Except in the principal urban centers, public funds and administrative organization were woefully inadequate; police forces barely existed.

Middle Period society's four social strata contested the limits of representation and autonomy versus those of exclusion and conformity, the decentralization or concentration of power, the weight of public sanctions on behalf of or counter to access to material resources and the rigidity or fluidity of hierarchy and degree of deference it could command. In its bureaucratic immaturity, discontinuities of policies and personnel, and fragmented power, the state was a virtual "condensation" of the relationships among the social strata in these conflicts.[1] None was able to establish hegemony in alliance with or through state power. The *gente alta* generally predominated in the discourse that sought to define Middle Period society clearly and guide its direction. But they could not monopolize it or contain its considerable variation. Besides, practice often did not square with discourse. The division between plan and implementation, word and deed, vision and actuality became wonted.

The state's weakness and instability constituted one by-product of this sociopolitical reality. The other derivative was the necessity of collaboration and alliance among the social strata. Overall, the result was an expanded historical space in which balance (though not equality) among the social strata was considerable and in which an equilibrium existed, though uneasily. By the 1870s, however, portents of destabilization, of disequilibrium, had begun to emerge.

As notable families became more extended and complex, they exhibited a marked degree of autonomy vis-à-vis the state at whatever level. Indeed, their private world was increasingly encroaching on that of the state. At the same time, a liberal-national initiative was advancing in the conflict over discourse. Liberals generally triumphed in the civil wars after midcentury, national bureaucracies and identities solidified in the many countries involved in external conflicts, and an expanding number of those whose economic and political interests transcended the regional ordering of life emerged. This initiative was abetted by a quantitative leap in the presence of foreigners, sometimes in sheer numbers but more generally in the scale of their impact. Despite these portents of destabilization, an alternative discourse was emerging in some regions. Its pluralist-federative orientation sought to institutionalize the uneasy equilibrium that had characterized Middle Period society since independence.

The Growing Power of the Notables' Networks

The cumulative effect of the notables' response to the expanding opportunities of a market economy and of modern republican politics had reached a critical turning point by the 1870s. Their large and well-structured families enabled them steadily to broaden and deepen their involvement in the economy and public affairs. What had held them back to a marked degree were the divisions among them—economic, ideological, and cultural in nature. These ended in political stalemate, discontinuity, and periodic armed conflict. The *gente baja*'s resistance also checked their expanding power. Indeed, the notables' tendency to resort to multistrata coalitions in the fluid and often turbulent political arena both manifested and contributed to these limitations.

By the 1870s, however, the notables had begun to overcome those confines. Intermarriage, godparenting, and economic association over two generations had spun intricate webs of relationships linking notables to one another. Moreover, they increasingly realized that the degree of their interconnection correlated with and was even responsible for their success. Of course, personal preference and individual attributes weighed importantly on life decisions. Yet behind those decisions was the ever-present force of the collective familial good. Kinship ties fostered trust, empathy, and forbearance. Individual family members had to appraise the value of their own predilections against the mounting evidence of the benefits of family solidarity.

Economically, family networking secured accumulated assets against unwanted alienation. Parcels of property and working capital were transferred in cases of default, joined in the face of probated divisions, and pooled to create larger enterprises. Vertical and horizontal integration led to greater efficiencies in production and distribution and to enhanced influence in markets. Family connections opened doors of opportunity for individual members: apprenticeships for ascending the ladder in a given enterprise, loans to start a business, posts in a firm to support one's profession, or investment shares to supplement it.

Politically, family networking was proving to be of immeasurable value. Modern republican government and politics fragmented the imperial order's highly centralized authority, giving individual family members more openings to turn governmental posts to the service of their interests. At the same time, it put a premium on interfacing those fragmented governmental functions. Within and among notable families, members in the differing branches of government could coordinate with and support one another. Kinship ties were also a form of political insurance at a time (especially after midcentury) when conflict was marked. Among notable families and often within them, disputes were intense and divisions deep (as noted in Chapter 4). Forbearance and recognition of mutual interests nurtured tolerance, reconciliation, and inclusion. One could impose penalties of a temporary nature but had to undertake assiduous thought before levying material ruin, political extinction, or the pain of death. Indeed, there emerged an informal code of honor among notables that disavowed such extreme measures. Women were often the political intermediaries guaranteeing and enforcing this familial form of political insurance.

After a half century, notables had learned a critical lesson: protection and promotion of their economic and political interests in large part depended upon the degree to which kinship ties were intertwined. Indeed, by taking the family network into public affairs, they could increasingly control government and employ it to advance the family portfolio. Political clubs that selected and promoted candidates for office were composed mostly of their families' representatives. Elected and appointed officials worked closely with kin and in-laws engaged in business, often blurring the lines between private and public enterprise. Legislators passed favorable laws, judges made approbatory rulings, military officers provided protection, and customs officials enforced tariffs selectively. Such practices were hardly unknown in the colonial order. The difference was the degree to which governmental authority and power were fragmented and open to participation and the extent of family networking. By the 1870s, through their family networking, notables were giving full testament to the premise that the public realm and their economic portfolios could and need be inextricably intertwined. They were joined by some *gente decente* (and a few *gente de profesiones*) who, through their own acumen and fortuitous circumstance, had been drawn into the networks as colleagues or important clients.

By 1880 the network headed by the Terrazas family, based in the capital of the northern Mexican state of Chihuahua, was well on the way to establishing an economic hegemony. Yet theirs was the exception rather the rule among notable families in Latin America. Nevertheless, their example carried great import in the development of Middle Period society. It manifested notable families' potential to employ interlocking networks to break the limitations imposed on them by the equilibrium among the social strata that had existed since independence. The Terrazas took advantage of the expanding foreign presence, incorporating talented immigrants into the family and pursuing the growing opportunities of external markets. Their participation in national conflicts enhanced their political power and authority.[2] Perhaps above all, they articulated their interests with the liberal-national initiative that was becoming increasingly predominant in most regions within Latin America.

The Liberal-National Initiative

The words "liberals" and "conservatives" comprise the commonly accepted nomenclature for the principal political movements that emerged at midcentury. But scholars have as yet found no common agreement in labeling the political groups that emerged prior to that. Some project the liberal/conservative labels back through the immediate post-independence years into the insurgency struggles against the Iberian crowns. Others project the Enlightenment of the eighteenth century forward to characterize the initial generation of reformers after independence. Opponents of such reforms are given various names implying retention of a colonial mindset.

What seems clear is that the Enlightenment and a "liberal tradition" (both arising in the eighteenth century) were part of a larger historical phenomenon dating back to around 1600 that recent scholarship has encompassed in the term "democratic-national revolution." A new discourse on liberty, equality, and progress arose in opposition to the medieval worldview and practice in the wake of a series of revolutions: the creation of a market economy, the rise of nation-states, the development of an accelerating technology, and the formation of a European-centered world economic and political system. In Latin

America, much of medieval tradition had taken root alongside nonmodern Amerindian traditions. Thus, it had come late to this dynamic historical process, though its conquest and colonialization had helped bring about these revolutions elsewhere.[3]

Until the 1850s, political discourse—born out of varying combinations of adapting long-standing Iberian traditions, articulating colonial experiences, and absorbing external intellectual thought—centered on five principal issues. First, the imperial regime's demise raised the issue of the spatial distribution of political authority and power, manifested in the cleft between federalists and centralists. Second, the insurgent struggle had challenged royal monopolies and restrictions on trade (especially overseas) but thereafter had rarely moved beyond sectoral disputes, channels for the movement of trade, and tariff levels. Far more universal in post-independence discourse was the issue of citizenship and representation, but no political movements arose with a clear-cut program. In general, those with the upper hand in political competition and conflicts worked pragmatically to limit effective representation and to compromise selectively the rights of equal citizenship. The principal social question was how hierarchical society should remain and the degree of deference that should be maintained. Except in the *gente alta*'s preoccupation with maintaining order, this issue played itself out more in the streets than in the halls of government. A final issue involved cultural orientation. While intellectuals debated the degree of progress (modernization in contemporary parlance) and the utility of cultural pluralism, politics focused on the role of the Roman Catholic Church in the society and the religious versus the secular basis of belief and behavior.

At midcentury, this fragmented political discourse gave way to Latin America's first cohesive ideological projects, formulated within the context of the universal democratic-national revolution and both very much shaped by the experiences of the post-independence decades. Europe and North America by then offered mature, well-formulated conservative and liberal responses to the realities of the new era permeating much of the world. In Latin America a new generation was coming of age. Some were trained specifically in North Atlantic political thought; others were acquainted with it. All were schooled in the ambiguities, selective advancements, disappointed expectations, and yet visionary potential of Middle Period society following independence. Among the new generation, *gente alta* were largely the protagonists in ideological formulation. Still, many *gente baja* participated in the political struggles enjoined by the competing ideological projects and responded often forcefully to their implementation (whether affirming or contesting). In doing so, they not only spurred modifications but in some regions formulated alternative projects.

The conservative initiative centered on the maintenance of order and measured, controlled progress. The lesson for its proponents was that order in the postcolonial world in which they lived required, above all, centralized authority and social-cultural continuity. Politically, that meant limiting the rights and prerogatives of much of society, distancing them from governance through indirect participation and representation, and limiting regional and local self-government. Brazil's monarchy was at its zenith. Mexican conservatives became convinced that only a monarchy could hold its many and disparate regions together as a nation. Elsewhere, conservatives moved toward more authoritarian or oligarchic arrangements within a republican framework. Economically, the conservative initiative sought to regulate and select both the currents of the world market penetrating their society and the structures carried over from the imperial order. To maintain adequate revenues in the face of fiscal penury, they tolerated (if not endorsed) the retention of numerous long-standing economic practices: direct operation or leasing of monopolies, tribute tax on Indian corporate communities, substantial tariffs, and the tithe.

There were social reasons for retaining many of these economic structures as well. Prior to independence, they had embodied the assumptions and practice of the strong hierarchical ordering of colonial society. Corporatist bodies, in particular, had protected the individual's place in society while at the same time limiting it, with the ratio of protection to limitation growing as one ascended the social ladder. Culturally, conservatives viewed the Roman Catholic Church as a universal reference point for all in society and the primary agent bonding together the various social groups. Maintaining the preeminence of such a dominant, state-sanctioned religion necessitated extensive legal protection. Nevertheless, conservatives as well countenanced a diversity of cultural expressions socially and spatially, especially among the popular classes' varied patterns of belief and daily life.

The liberal initiative was far bolder. It sought to test the limits on participation in modern republican politics, on the freedom of individuals in pursuing their economic interests, and yet on the uniformity of the citizenry in their loyalty to the civil state and its efforts to improve the general welfare. However, in testing these limits, liberals found themselves increasingly reliant on an enlarged and invigorated state at the provincial and national levels.

Secularization, Privatization, and a Pro-Active Civil State

Liberals, in varying proportions, were driven by immediate material self-interest and by a more long-term vision of an open, progressive society. Above all material, that progress also denoted the general improvement of the citizenry's education, mores, and demeanor. To advance both, liberal thinking held, required freeing the individual from all the restrictions accumulated over the previous centuries in Ibero-America. Reformers in the preceding generation had chipped away at those constraints (most prominently coerced labor, especially slavery). However, their structural and institutional bases remained. Liberals regarded them as colonial anachronisms. Only their wholesale destruction would sufficiently unfetter the individual.

Market forces had been privatizing economic life for more than a century. What remained was a legal structure buttressing individual and corporatist privilege at the expense of responsibility and initiative. Liberals moved to eliminate monopolies and markedly reduce the plethora of governmental regulations. In their place, legal guarantees and civil codes were enacted to protect the individual's access to land, labor, and capital. Similar constitutional and statutory provisions ensured the individual's ample participation in public life and legal protection against arbitrary acts.[4]

A major target of the liberals was the Indian corporate community. From Mexico down through Central America and the nations straddling the Andes, this communal landholding institution was under attack as the antithesis of the liberal ideal of the individual proprietor. Behind that universal paragon was the far more narrow concern of access to often productive land denied to the more enterprising in society—namely, people like themselves. A consensus did exist on the necessity of abolishing the corporate community. But liberals disagreed over whether all village lands should be divided among the inhabitants or surplus lands be claimed by the government and auctioned publicly, and whether the goal of this reform of land tenure was the creation of a productive group of independent small farmers or an expanding number of docile wage laborers on large estates. Indian villagers themselves were critical to the resolution of these issues. Their general resistance and tactical alliance with liberal factions frustrated and delayed implementation of legislation.[5]

Radical liberals viewed the Roman Catholic Church far more comprehensively as a target for radical reform, regarding it as the chief obstacle to Latin America's economic, social, and moral progress. The issue was not simply privatization of ecclesiastical property but also secularization, breaking the church's undue influence (in some cases, hold) on the various arenas of public life. Moderate liberals tempered their view of the extent of secularization required. Through legislation—and armed conflict when it came to it—liberals strove to remove the church from civic matters, whether in education, determination of civil status, economic policy, or the formal workings of government. They also labored to sever all governmental financial support to the church and end its official status. Their success varied: it was most notable in Mexico and least so in Guatemala and Ecuador.[6]

In place of the church, liberals proposed a civic religion (centered around the concept of *la patria*) as the cultural cement and beacon of virtue in public life. Notions of a native land had evolved over centuries in Latin America, having generally come to be identified with one's region or locality (*patria chica*). Liberals, however, transformed the political meaning of this concept. Harkening back to the ideals of the French Revolution and republic, their discourse translated *la patria* as the liberal republic. Their movement fulfilled the role in this civic religion that the church did in Christianity. Liberals proclaimed that only as citizens of a free, liberal *patria* could people enjoy liberty and realize their full potential as virtuous human beings. They recognized that individual self-interest was the chief motivator of material progress. At the same time, they maintained that civic virtue required that public action have priority over private concerns.[7]

For the cultivation of that civic virtue, liberals singled out universal education. Not only was it the source of individual success in a progressing society. Primarily through it, in a form of "civic apprenticeship," the *gente baja* could be socially integrated, cleansed of what liberals considered their untoward popular attitudes, and become effective citizens of the liberal republic. Only as conformity to liberal tenets spread over the national space and down through the social order could the liberals' *patria* be secured. The particularity of barrio, village, and locality and of race and ethnicity undermined such a universality of discourse and practice.[8]

The liberals' concept of the utility of universal education revealed a fundamental paradox in their political discourse and practice. They were intent on clearing away obtrusive restrictions on individual initiative and freedom. That implied a more open political system, a wider involvement in public affairs. Certainly, electoral participation (among males) was expanded; a broader range of officials were subject to electoral accountability and to more exacting codes of law. In most nations, federalism was instituted (or reinstituted). Yet, as the liberals emerged victorious, the power of the state (at all levels) was enhanced.

The institutional power of its competitors (most notably the church and the military) decreased. The expansion of trade after 1850, especially in export markets, provided the state with additional revenues. So, too, did a new cycle of foreign lending. But evolution of thought among liberals also played a crucial role in the enhancement of state power.[9]

Liberal officeholders and bureaucrats at all levels soon found that to implement their radical program of change, the state needed increased power and authority to carry out the alienation of lands held by corporatist institutions, to set up and direct an expanding system of formal education, to establish civil registries, and to realize improvements in infrastructure. This imperative was compounded by the exigency of resisting the reaction that such radical reforms inevitably provoked, including civil war. Moreover, hierarchical tradition still influenced the thinking of most liberals. That hierarchy was no longer based, in their minds, on inherited or legal privilege or membership in corporatist bodies. Rather, it was based on moral and intellectual superiority (along with material achievement), which evinced in its exponents political action that was prudent, rational, and upright. Weighing as well on liberal minds was the memory of nearly a half century of a tenuous social order, in which, from their viewpoint, the *gente baja* had given themselves over to calculating political patrons who used that support to further their own ambitions. The *gente baja* were still political wards, requiring political tutors to school them in the rights and obligations of republican citizenship in the liberal *patria*. Officeholders and bureaucrats embued with liberalism's tenets and backed by the state's expanded powers were increasingly seen as the agents of liberalism's democratic-national project.[10]

Nationalizing Conflicts

In practice, liberals quickly found that in the near term it was not formal schooling but rather armed conflict on a nationwide scale that mobilized the *gente baja* beyond their localism and regional identity. Leaders of coalitions seeking to span the national territory needed a broad base of popular support to counter opponents, be they domestic or foreign. War came to communities and localities on a scale and with an intensity rarely seen since the independence struggle, forcing them to choose sides in the face of retaliation or possible reward. Moreover, *gente baja* began to take the initiative as competing broad political coalitions vied for their support. They decided to pursue the inclusion of their concerns and the resolution of their grievances in a much broader political arena. In the process, many increasingly came to see themselves as included in a national polity in the making. This was true, above all, in the case of international wars, especially when foreign troops were engaged. Only one generation removed from liberation from imperial rule, resistance to foreign armies on one's soil was most compelling for common folk, who had largely seen their sovereignty as local or regional in breadth. It also affected those sending their sons beyond the nation's borders or rendering material support in what was viewed as a defense of the nation. In a way no classroom could convey, the *gente baja* were exercising their civic responsibility and claiming the rewards of full citizenship. And the *gente alta* recognized their inclusion, whether by welcome or concession.[11]

Military units fighting on behalf of the nation (or national projects) became important intermediaries in this process. In countries faced with foreign armies of occupation—most notably Mexico and Peru—national guard units played instrumental roles, conveying local concerns to the broader arena and embodying the idea of an armed citizenry close to their communities. In some areas, their organization reflected hierarchical patron-client relations infused with deference. But in others, units operated in a more democratic, communitarian fashion. The latter, especially, took into account the grievances and expectations of *gente baja* families and communities, from which the bulk of the units' forces came. *Gente alta* leaders of the national projects understood that these units were often decisive in bringing them to power. At the same time, national guard soldiers absorbed much of the liberal discourse and articulated it with local, popular notions and concerns.[12]

Soldiers in regular military units also occupied intermediate political space between national projects and localities. In the War of the Triple Alliance (1865–1870), the Paraguayan army (then South America's largest) combined a broad popular base with a firm loyalty to the nation, which enabled it to resist the combined forces of three nations for five years. By contrast, the major partners in the alliance (with Uruguay) had entered the war ill-prepared militarily. Yet from the conflict their soldiers became part of empowered national institutions and advocates of an agenda that was national in scope and liberal in tenor. Brazil's military had been weak and inconsequential in the half century after independence. Five long years of war changed all that. The greatly enlarged officer corps was composed mainly of urban *gente decente*; many, if not most, of their troops were drafted or recruited from Brazil's towns and cities. Among them were some 6,000 slaves who gained their freedom in exchange for service to the nation. The war engendered a newfound public respect for the military while discrediting the imperial regime. A growing movement for change resulted, culminating in the end of slavery and the monarchy (1888–89), in which the military played a central role. An Argentine army had never really existed before the war. Soldiers from provincial military units, having fought one another since the 1810s, were molded into a truly national army. They waged war not only against Paraguay but also against the tradition-oriented, confederative federalism that had stymied the national agenda of Buenos Aires liberals and their provincial allies. In the process, the army became the arbiter of a new liberal-national political order.[13]

Foreign wars also often fortified the national state. They generated increased public revenues from new or expanded markets for supplies. In addition, a new cycle of foreign loans provided funds to pursue the war effort and carry on public improvements. In Argentina, public spending grew by 120 percent. Most financed the war effort, but the remainder enlarged the government's scope and the bureaucracy's size, setting a precedent for the postwar years.[14]

Nationally Oriented Politicos, Professionals, and Entrepreneurs

Officers and soldiers were not alone in coming to see themselves as having a shared interest in a national political project, in particular the liberal agenda. There were those who, in their political maturation from midcentury through the 1870s, steadfastly believed in the universal promises of that democratic-national initiative. They were characterized as *puros* (radical purists) by the far more numerous moderate adherents of liberalism, especially among the *gente alta*. Experience led some to pull back from such a full extension of liberal ideals or compromise them out of necessity. Others' moderation arose from selective adherence, most notably in economic policy and state activism.

An ongoing tension underlay the divisions among these two proponents of liberalism over the degree of limitations on the universal promises of their democratic-national project. For radicals, full expression of those promises meant the diffusion of power and opportunity and corresponding regional articulation of interests from the community and locality upward. Those less pure in their adherence felt a compelling need to reaffirm in varying degrees the canon of hierarchical authority, especially across the social line of respectability. In addition, they pragmatically inferred the necessity of power to realize the economic and sociocultural improvements envisioned by the liberal agenda. The majority of *gente alta* liberals believed the need for limitations was social more than spatial. From this perspective, connection to a national liberal agenda facilitated expanded investments within their districts and regions while assisting in consolidating their political and economic power within their localities and possibly broadening it within their region.[15]

But other *gente alta* liberals (most motivated by economic interests) increasingly saw their interests as much more directly tied to the power and activism of the national state. Members of Mexico's money lending clique (*agiotista*), having reinvested their profits into increasingly varied enterprises, were attracted to the liberal tenets of privatization and legal codes to facilitate new investment and of the need for a large-scale program of public improvements. Even more, their interests had moved beyond what a political framework based on regional autonomy could provide. They needed a state national in scope that could ensure public security, eliminate internal tariffs and barriers, support industrialization, underwrite public improvements, and be able to collect revenues to finance them.[16]

The large majority of *gente alta* in Argentina's interior and littoral provinces had long resisted any effort by Buenos Aires to impose its will on the rest of the country. But most chose to make their peace with the national liberal coalition based in Buenos Aires that had taken power during the War of the Triple Alliance. Through the 1870s, they steadily expanded their influence and turned the national government's increasing power to their advantage. The most connected and perceptive intermarried with a powerful network of *porteno* (inhabitants of Buenos Aries) families. The rest settled for the largesse deriving from the expansion of public offices, federal subsidies to provincial governments and enterprises, and public improvements that enhanced or opened up economic opportunities.[17]

One of the subsidies that proved alluring to the provincial powers-that-be was that for building new primary schools. Though the Constitution of 1853 had left control over primary education to the provinces, few provinces could afford to finance its expansion. The national government employed temporary subsidies as a wedge to loosen the constitutional restrictions. Within a couple of years, it created an inspector general's office to oversee federal funds and coordinate school statistics on a national basis. With a constitutional mandate over "general and university learning," Presidents Bartolomé Mitre (1862–1868) and Domingo Sarmiento (1868–1874) instituted a nationally controlled secondary school system, focusing on the first normal schools to train a new generation of teachers in a uniform curriculum. Sarmiento also secured passage of legislation (1871) providing the constitutional basis for permanent national underwriting of the country's primary schools. Not only did provincial bureaucrats have a stake in a strong national government; so, too, did the newly trained native professoriat.[18]

Through their democratic-national initiative, by 1880 liberals in most countries of Latin America had succeeded in fundamentally changing the discourse and significantly altering the practice of politics in Middle Period society. A now proliferating foreign presence in many countries reinforced the liberal agenda's rise to prominence.

Foreign Presence beyond the First Dimension

Up to midcentury, the foreign presence had remained within a single dimension: resident merchants in principal commercial centers serving as intermediaries with external markets, pressuring state and national governments to protect their interests (or often eluding restrictions), and sometimes intermarrying with prominent local families. Some government leaders had lauded the prospect of immigrants from the North Atlantic, even formulating some proposals. But only Mexico and Nicaragua had succeeded in attracting significant numbers of settlers. Their experience hardly suggested imitation. The immigrants' demographic dominance in sparsely settled territories, combined with the Mexican government's instability, precluded both assimilation and effective enforcement of colonization laws. The entire far north of Mexico was lost in the war with the United States. Nicaragua's unstable, weak government was forced to negotiate autonomy for both the Mosquito Indians and foreign settlers drawn to the Mosquito Coast after 1840 by growing interoceanic trade opportunities and interest in a waterway, leaving the coast virtually independent until the 1890s.[19]

The maxim of Argentine liberal ideologue Juan Alberdi was turned on its head: to populate was not to govern. Indeed, the lesson regarding immigration seemed clear: be able to govern before populating. As the onset of a new multidimensional wave of immigration began at midcentury, the growth in effective national government developed a symbiotic relationship with the growing presence of foreign residents. Liberal tenets of the free flow of capital and human resources in the economy and of the promotion of rapid economic expansion along the lines of the North Atlantic nations offered a strong magnet. Moreover, liberal practice relied increasingly on an activist national state. Its expanded responsibilities and capabilities—including reform of legal codes, expansion of education, promotion and sponsorship of public improvements, and reduction of commercial restrictions and duties—

enhanced opportunities for the ambitious from abroad (as well as for nationals). Some national governments even began instituting programs to promote and facilitate immigration.

Large numbers of humble immigrants brought another dimension to the foreign presence in Latin America, an influence not seen since the surge of *peninsulares* in the preceding century. Most were initially drawn to the countryside by the prospect of landownership, which was increasingly difficult in Europe. In regions where vacant lands were abundant and still unclaimed, they realized their dream of making it in America. Germans in the southern region of Brazil and Chile did so. In the former, they became leading players in a dynamic market economy, diversifying into commerce and then industry and becoming a "modernizing" segment of the *gente decente*; some achieved notability.[20]

By contrast, in regions where landownership was well-established and concentrated, immigrants labored for others. Argentina's large *estancieros* (owners of estancias) recruited Irish, Scottish, English, and Basque shepherds to convert refined grasslands for sheep raising as the North Atlantic's industrialized market for wool soared by midcentury. They were joined by Italian and Spanish sharecroppers and tenant farmers on the long-grazed lands nearer the coast, beginning in the 1870s. The most skilled and ambitious of such rural workers (and not infrequently those with some luck as well) were able to accumulate enough capital to become independent producers; a few even became large estate owners themselves. Such a prospect was far less likely for the thousands of contract laborers from China working first the guano beds and then the hacienda fields of coastal Peru, nor for those from South Asia laboring on the sugar plantations in Trinidad and British Guiana.[21]

Lack of opportunity and mobility in the countryside in most regions where large numbers of immigrants first settled sent many to urban centers, especially cities. There, they became part of a poor, laboring immigrant population that would grow rapidly after 1880. Buenos Aires is most noteworthy in this regard, but so are cities such as Córdoba and Rosario in Argentina and Lima, Peru. Those with ambition, and often with client connections, joined those from abroad who had immigrated straight to the city to establish themselves in commerce as petty traders, shopkeepers, and clerks in large mercantile establishments. Some accumulated enough capital to become independent businesspeople and join the ranks of the *gente decente*.

Far less numerous, but far more influential and present in far more regions in Latin America, were entrepreneurs and professionals arriving from Europe and North America. With their acquired training, education, experience, and often capital, they were generally well received (when not sought after) and accepted among the respectable. They took advantage of the less restricted business climate, frequently working directly with the liberal state in its reform programs. As contractors or engineers, they began to supervise the construction of a range of public improvements. As educators, they helped establish and initially staff nationwide and provincial systems of education. As professionals in varied fields, they filled positions in a number of sectors of the bureaucracy. Some of these immigrants of means became notables by developing substantial business interests, providing exemplary service, or marrying into prominent families.[22]

Whether they made a fortune, established themselves among the respectable, found skilled jobs, or had to settle for the lot of poor laborers, the presence of growing numbers of immigrants from Europe and North America generally reinforced the liberal national project. In some regions, those of humble origins provided the large-scale supply of labor for expanded export production. In Brazil and Peru, they provided an alternative to continued slavery, replacing or displacing the freed slaves. They had little if any identity with a *patria chica* in their new homeland, or attachment to long-standing institutional structures and cultural mores to which most native *gente baja* anchored themselves. Rather, they were adrift in the emerging, expanding liberal economic order. The large majority found only minimal success at best, but a significant minority prospered, validating liberal promises. Those from abroad who came with education and capital most clearly linked their fortunes with the liberal national project. They thrived in the more privatized, secularized, and dynamic economy while often benefiting directly from the state's expanded role. They also served as a generally well received cultural bridge to the North Atlantic world among the *gente alta*.

In one area, however, immigrants (whether of high or low station) undermined the liberal agenda. Because they retained strong ties to their nationality, they proved to be obstacles to the development of cultural uniformity within the nation. Ethnic endogamy predominated among most immigrant groups, who held on to their language and many of their customs. Voluntary associations arose to fill in gaps in social services and to serve as mechanisms to provide greater structure to the immigrant community and to mediate immigrant-national relations. Immigrants of means benefited most from such formal associations, constituting their leadership and often their core members.[23]

Yet even in this manifestation of cultural separation, immigrants were anticipating an important new force beginning to emerge in the liberals' national project. Notables were the first nationals to begin making use of voluntary associations to protect and enhance their interests.

The *Gente Baja* Alternative: Pluralistic Federation

Across Latin America's diverse regions the *gente baja* were no mere bystanders to the portents of destabilization arising around and among them from midcentury to 1880. Following independence, with varying degrees of initiative, they had seized upon the enhanced space and leverage resulting from the new equilibrium in Middle Period society and even expanded them. Now after midcentury, that space and leverage were in question. The immigrants' accelerating presence was beginning to disrupt measurably their economic and cultural lives. The *gente alta*'s national ideological initiatives were projecting new economic, political, and cultural patterns into their daily lives. When these projects came into open conflict or when foreign threats materialized, *gente baja* were caught up in them as victims (as neutrals or partisans) but also sometimes as protagonists.

Most *gente baja* (especially among the popular classes) employed whatever leverage they possessed to counter these destabilizing forces. However, some (particularly among *gente de profesiones*) envisioned or saw the necessity of articulating existing popular belief and worldview with the new ideological currents penetrating their barrios and communities. In some localities and districts they had already begun to do so before midcentury.[24] Now there was a greater and more widespread urgency. Translating *gente baja* aspirations and institutional patterns into the emerging national discourses was possible, thereby giving them sanction and protection. But there was also the less likely but more secure prospect of constructing an alternative national discourse centered in the commoner's own worldview. Projecting out upon the whole of the nation, it would institutionalize the uneasy equilibrium sustaining Middle Period society since independence.

The construction of such a popularly based alternative, however, met with the stark reality of the *gente baja*'s lack of commonality. They were divided by work rhythms, ethnicity, community status, and urban or rural settings. Still, among them was one group that could serve as a catalyst in such an endeavor. The *gente de profesiones* had found a measure of opportunity and social mobility but still possessed a continuing solidarity with the various segments of the popular classes with whom they generally shared their lives. They frequently served as both leaders among commoners and as intermediaries with those on the other side of the line of respectability. That is why so many of them found the construction of a popularly based alternative discourse so appealing: a bridge that offered both a means for ambitious *gente baja* to cross that line, as well as a binding connection that kept *gente alta* and commoners accountable to one another.

Components of a Gente Baja Discourse

Despite differences among *gente baja*, after midcentury some prevailing ideological tenets and notions emerged among them. Some were long-standing; others metamorphosed into republican form; a few were newly born of republican or liberal discourse. An increasing number of *gente baja* began to perceive after midcentury that in the increasingly liberal world around them, they might not only negotiate the degree of autonomy for their own small worlds but also participate in the construction of that larger world beyond—dare, in a few cases, to even propose an ideological edifice largely conforming to their own design.

Social justice was the cornerstone of this popularly based discourse. In the countryside, that meant a just allocation of resources (principally land) that made subsistence sustainable while offering the prospect of greater prosperity for those with the ambition and acumen to pursue it, though not at the undue expense of others' subsistence. For those without land who were laboring for others, acquiring land was a long-term goal. A more immediate sense of social justice could be found in the concept of a living wage and the freedom to pursue it. This goal was of paramount importance to urban *gente baja* as well. For some *gente de profesiones*—principally independent rancheros, itinerant peddlers and tradespeople, teamsters, and small shopkeepers—the forces of market competition muddied this principle of social justice. Some among them called for protection of their livelihoods; others based their claims on fair competition. For all commoners, upon whom the burden of raising public revenues fell heaviest, tax equity was an important part of their notion of social justice, for its inequity threatened their subsistence.

Closely linked to social justice was the tenet of the community's political autonomy (separate from, or as a part of, the locality). From long experience and more immediate post-independence reality, *gente baja* knew full well that social justice was often fragile and fleeting when it depended on the control and goodwill of others nearby. It also left them with scant leverage in negotiating their well-being with those beyond their locality. Republican ideology and institutions enhanced the possibility of political autonomy by expanding the number of *municipios* and elected local officials. That was especially true in the countryside, where communities struggled to end their legal and political dependence on large estates or other communities. In urban areas, *gente baja* neighborhoods were part of larger local polities and subject to the influence of political bosses and the manipulation of electoral politics. Still, they sought greater leverage in negotiating more control within their barrios.

A corollary of political autonomy was the accountability of officials. The more autonomous commoners were in their neighborhoods and communities, the more able they were to hold officials to their responsibilities of service and equity. Even when local authorities were considered outsiders, the degree of community autonomy was critical in determining the leverage *gente baja* could exert to make those officials respond to their needs and promote the general welfare of all citizens.

Gente baja notions of citizenship were even more consequential in forging stable, equitable links with the larger polities being constructed in the world beyond. For now, after three decades or more of civil war and foreign conflicts, their claims to citizenship went beyond the constitutional theories and abstractions that accompanied independence. They had fought, served, struggled, and sacrificed for the nation-state, for which they sought recognition and reward: full citizenship and a just stake in the newly formed national polity. Their claim, however, was not only one of outcome but also of process. Such a national polity must be constructed from the bottom up, including the important right to elect state and national representatives. Without such guarantees, they understood that their subordination to the world beyond their locality and district would be reinstituted and their local autonomy in time eroded.

With a few exceptions (notably Ecuador), liberalism emerged as the dominant political force and discourse out of the struggles with conservatism after midcentury. Thus, in both a cause and effect relationship, the nascent *gente baja* republican discourse became increasingly articulated with the liberal ideology espoused by growing elements among the *gente alta*. On the whole, liberalism (in theory at least) seemed to offer a greater likelihood of meeting more of the commoners' interests and concerns: a more open, egalitarian, participatory societal framework. Yet left unbridled, that liberal framework in the end might threaten values that most *gente baja* held dear.

Inviolable private property rights and absolute freedom in the marketplace could lead (and had led) to the loss of commoners' access to resources and sustainable livelihoods. Such liberal economic tenets needed to be tempered by a commitment to the viability of a community's holding of land and to the need for protection in securing a living wage or an independent livelihood in the face of undue or unfair competition in the marketplace. Reciprocity—long held by *gente baja* as the lubrication that overcame friction and promoted the smooth workings of community institutions—was seen as the guarantee of solidarity and accountability among the disparate elements of the new liberal republican society. Moreover, membership in such a society should be based on honorable actions, such as service for the general welfare and especially sacrifices in times of armed conflict, not determined only by the level of one's education and social status. This was an egalitarianism born of deeds rather than of presumption.

Finally, for commoners, construction of a national polity did not translate into uniformity across the nation's boundaries. Rather, they thought in confederative terms, elaborating on that old notion from the imperial era of two distinct operative political worlds. Over time, as Middle Period society developed, *gente baja* notions of the familiar world had expanded more firmly from locality to district and region. Their sense of autonomy did center itself generally in their community and locality. Yet since 1750, expanding economic and political connections and social and cultural ties had created a consciousness of the regional basis for ordering their lives. That scale was the one on which they could comfortably and effectively act, directly or through intermediaries, in which reciprocity and accountability would more likely function.

What would best serve the *gente baja*, then, was a federation of extralocal (but nonnational) entities. These might range from a collection of compatible districts through a state or province to a region— whichever possessed the necessary societal cohesion to accommodate the commoners' political and cultural sensitivities. The nation-state, in turn, provided a larger framework for their common defense, for working out disputes among the federated entities, and for creation of common guarantees and promotion of the general welfare. A national polity deferring to the prerogatives and peculiarities of its distinct regional components, an open marketplace for individual pursuits tempered by community solidarity, social justice, and reciprocity—these were the fundamental principles that *gente baja* (as articulated by their local intellectuals and leaders) wished to graft onto the liberal ideology that was becoming firmly entrenched in most of Latin America by 1880.[25]

Ideological Fissures

How pervasive this popularly based republican discourse was among *gente baja* is limited by the scope of historical research to date, as is the extent to which the complexity of its articulation extended beyond their leaders, intellectuals, and intermediaries. That large numbers of commoners supported its fundamental tenets through direct action seems evident in a growing number of sources. Also apparent is the fact that economic, political, and cultural realities so compromised and refracted the understanding and translation of that discourse in its application to daily life that *gente baja* were often in conflict with one another because of it.

In the countryside, land tenure and community autonomy cut several different ways, fragmenting the *gente baja*. For those already in autonomous corporate communities, the necessity of tempering liberal sanctification of private property ownership was clear, as was maintaining municipal autonomy. But how far did that principle extend? To that village's *sujetos* (subordinate communities)? The latter, as well as those subject to a hacienda, saw in such principles of political decentralization the right to their own municipal autonomy. If lands of large estates became vacant through bankruptcy or confiscation, should they benefit resident workers or those who could buy them in the competitive marketplace? Likewise, what should be the fate of public lands divested by the government? Landless peasants, tenant farmers, communal landholders, and independent small farmers often had different interests in the resolution of such questions. They found in popularly based republican-liberal discourse divergent emphases and meanings in justifying those interests.[26]

Another source of divergence was cultural. Some communities and neighborhoods accepted the addition of the civic religion of the liberal nation-state to the customary focus of ritual and discourse centered on Roman Catholicism. National celebrations, along with liberal-affiliated institutions such as lay public schools or national guard units (and in Mexico, philharmonic bands) vied for preeminence in local cultural life with religious rituals and lay brotherhoods.[27] But others saw this as an unwanted intrusion on their traditional culture and sought to limit, if not reject it. The latter stance led many communities and barrios to affiliate with conservative movements.

Divisions among *gente baja* also arose from their loyalty to (and the accountability of) intermediaries operating at two levels. Those coming from among commoners themselves were generally *gente de profesiones*, who had gained respect and influence through service to the community or their acquired experience and contacts in the larger society. They conveyed the commoners' interests and discourse to those socially above and beyond them while translating and accommodating liberal ideology to popular republican-liberal ideas. Depending on the extent to which they had come to internalize the tenets of liberalism espoused by the *gente alta*—and the degree of their community's leverage and their own autonomy vis-à-vis the *gente alta*—such intermediaries could be simply the latter's agents, the community's willing and faithful representatives, or somewhere in between. Another group of intermediaries came from above the line of respectability. Through client relations, or ideologically perceived mutual interests, they, too, mediated between *gente baja* communities and neighborhoods in their localities and the emerging national-liberal state. Sometimes, especially as large estate owners with resident *peones*, they did so directly. Usually, they did so through the commoners' own intermediaries. At this level, the intermediary's leverage could be more decisive, their accountability less tangible.

As the *gente baja* calculated the degree to which they could accept the *gente alta*'s liberal ideology and graft their own popular tenets to it, the intermediaries' influence led to varying degrees of negotiated (and sometimes imposed) articulations between the two emerging variants of liberal discourse.[28] The result was that no broad consensus emerged among *gente baja* in any Latin American country around a popular liberalism that espoused a pluralist-federative framework as the basis for a national polity. Moreover, some segments ended up following conservative movements or shifted back and forth across the political spectrum in their political-ideological affiliations.

Nevertheless, the failure of popular liberalism to take hold in Latin America—and thereby institutionalize the uneasy equilibrium into which Middle Period society had settled—was not the *gente baja*'s alone. A fundamental contradiction existed between their liberal discourse and that of the *gente alta*. Segments among the latter might find mutual interest in the preeminence of regional societies in the ordering of people's lives. They might agree with or at least acquiesce in the need for a more just allocation of resources. They might endorse the commoners' claims to citizenship and the desirability of official accountability. But few among the *gente alta* would give themselves over to the notion that those below the line of respectability should have a credible stake in determining and implementing political discourse and practice. *Gente alta* liberals might differ over whether and how many individual commoners could rise to respectability in the new order of things, but very few contested the assumption that society's direction, at all levels, should remain in the hands of those whose very respectability entitled them to it. Deference, they held, was the only proper response for the great majority of commoners.

The *gente baja* were unable to forge solidarity among themselves in support of an alternative pluralist-federalist framework to institutionalize the uneasy equilibrium of Middle Period society. The *gente alta* had been unable to find their own consensus on a political framework that would preserve the line of respectability and ensure their social and economic hegemony. After 1880, the convergence of accelerating foreign penetration, the liberal-national initiative, and the expanding power of notable family networks would combine with the emergence of new circumstances and a new discourse to shatter that equilibrium. In so doing, it would usher in Latin America's passage to the modern world.

Notes

1. Nicos Poulantzas, *State, Power, Socialism* (London: New Left Books, 1978), 128.

2. Mark Wasserman, *Capitalists, Caciques, and Revolution: The Native Elite and Foreign Enterprise in Chihuahua, Mexico, 1854–1911* (Chapel Hill: University of North Carolina Press, 1984), 15–36, 167–70.

3. Florencia E. Mallon, *Peasant and Nation: The Making of Post-Colonial Mexico and Peru* (Berkeley: University of California Press, 1995), chap. 1.

4. Bushnell and MaCauley, *Emergence of Latin America*, 190–92, 287–89.

5. Langer, "Abolición de la comunidad indígena," 64–82.

6. Bushnell and MaCauley, *Emergence of Latin America*, 190–92, 287–89; David A. Brading, "Liberal Patriotism and the Mexican Reform," *JLAS* 20 (May 1988): 30.

7. Brading, "Liberal Patriotism," 27–30, 34–41.

8. Ibid., 33–34; Szuchman, *Order, Family, and Community*, 170–75, 229; Mallon, *Peasant and Nation*, 36–42, 94.

9. José Resendiz Balderas, "El agua y la propiedad agraria en Nueva León: De la independencia a las reformas liberales (1821–1870)," in *Monterrey, Nueva León, el Noreste: Siete estudios históricos*, ed. Mario Cerruti (Monterrey, Mexico: Facultad de Filosofia y Letras de la Universidad Autonoma de Nueva León, 1987), 31–35; Brading, "Liberal Patriotism," 27.

10. Szuchman, *Order, Family, and Community*, 170–74.

11. Brading, "Liberal Patriotism," 38–40; Mallon, *Peasant and Nation*, 17, 43–44, 52–53, 185–86.

12. Thomson, "Bulwarks of Patriotic Liberalism," 31–40; Mallon, *Peasant and Nation*, 23–25, 74–77, 84, 148–51, 161, 185–97, 207–16.

13. Blinn Reber, "Demographics of Paraguay," 315–19; Burns, *Brazil*, 231, 236–37, 259; Emilia Viotti da Costa, *The Brazilian Empire: Myths and Histories* (Chicago: University of Chicago Press, 1985), 73–74, 169, 212–14; David Rock, *Argentina, 1516–1987: From Spanish Colonization to Alfonsín* (Berkeley: University of California Press, 1985), 128–31.

14. Marichal, *Century of Debt Crisis*, 90–95; Rock, *Argentina*, 125, 129–30; John E. Hodge, "The Formation of the Argentine Public Primary and Secondary School System," *The Americas* 44 (July 1987): 45–48.

15. Mallon, *Peasant and Nation*, 33, 132–33, 160–61, 166.

16. Tenenbaum, *Politics of Penury*, xiv–xv, 116–20, 130–37, 141–66.

17. Rock, *Argentina*, 125, 129–31; Balmori, Voss, and Wortman, *Notable Family Networks*, 134, 217, 225.

18. Hodge, "Argentine School System," 47–59, 65.

19. Weber, *American Southwest under Mexico*, 156–78, 190–206; Olien, "Mosquito Coast," 262–80.

20. Marian Katheryn Pinsdorf, "German-Speaking Immigrants: Builders of Business in Brazil's South" (Ph.D. diss., New York University, New York, 1976).

21. James B. Scobie, *Argentina: A City and a Nation* (New York: Oxford University Press, 1971), 83–87, 119; Julia Alfaro Vallejos and Susana Chueca Posadas, "El proceso de hacer la América: Una familia italiana en el Perú" (M.A. thesis, Pontificia Universidad Católica del Perú, 1975), 37–38, 48–55; Watt Stewart, *Chinese Bondage in Peru* (Durham, NC: Duke University Press, 1951); William Claypole and John Robottom, *Caribbean Story*, vol. 2 (London: Longman, 1993), 12–40.

22. Szuchman, *Mobility and Integration in Urban Argentina*, 40–46, 124–29; Scobie, *Buenos Aires*, 92–95, 166–67; Janet E. Worrall, "Italian Immigration to Peru, 1860–1914" (Ph.D. diss., University of Indiana, Bloomington, 1977), 237–38; Hodge, "Argentine School System," 51–60; Vallejos and Posadas, "Una familia italiana en el Perú," 48–67, 73.

23. Worrall, "Italian Immigration to Peru," 58–59; Szuchman, *Mobility and Integration in Urban Argentina*, chaps. 4–6, 8–9; Deborah Jakubs, "The Anglo-Argentines: Work, Family, and Identity, 1860–1914," in *English-Speaking Communities in Latin America*, ed. Oliver Marshall (London: Macmillan, 2000), 150–56.

24. Guardino, "Republican Law"; Mallon, *Peasant and Nation*, 141–48.

25. This composite of *gente baja* republican-liberal discourse draws upon the detailed work of a number of sources, principally Mallon, *Peasant and Nation*; Szuchman, *Order, Family, and Community*; Klein, *Haciendas and Ayllus*; Langer, "Abolición de la comunidad indígena"; and Daniel Nugent, *Spent Cartridges of Revolution: An Anthropological History of Namiquipa, Chihuahua* (Chicago: University of Chicago Press, 1993).

26. Mallon, *Peasant and Nation*, chaps. 2–4; Klein, *Haciendas and Ayllus*, chaps. 3–5.

27. Guy P. C. Thomson, "The Ceremonial and Political Roles of Village Bands, 1846–1974," in *Rituals of Rule, Rituals of Resistance: Public Celebrations and Popular Culture in Mexico*, ed. William H. Beezley, Cheryl English Martin, and William E. French (Wilmington, DE: Scholarly Resources, 1994), 310–22.

28. Mallon, *Peasant and Nation*, chaps. 6–7.

7

The Notables' Consensus

A century before, a conjuncture of historical forces had metamorphosed the Iberian colonial order into a new society and a new
era. Now, in the 1880s, after six decades of relative equilibrium, that
historical process began to accelerate. No political framework had been
successfully negotiated to institutionalize and stabilize that equilibrium in the face of such a quickened pace of change. Moreover, the
historical forces themselves had become altered markedly in both scope
and character.

Demographic growth was once again on a noticeable upswing,
though it varied considerably by region and was less dramatic in terms
of natural increase. *Mestisaje*, a significant part of eighteenth-century
population growth that had continued apace following independence,
now became the dominant force in most regions. In time, those of mixed
race would become the social and cultural emblem of society. More
immediate and acknowledged was the change in immigration, which
expanded on an unprecedented scale in most regions. In some, its impact was monumental. Moreover, its character was profoundly different, no longer overwhelmingly Iberian. Immigrants were now coming
in large numbers from all over Europe (especially the Mediterranean),
as well as western, southern, and eastern Asia. The exception was Africa because of the closing of the slave trade.

The presence of extralocal government—at the state and provincial level but especially at the national level—began to increase noticeably. Unlike its imperial predecessor, the nation-state had little patience
with pluralism and saw its function as that of setting a firm course in
policy, unhindered by serving as arbiter for competing claims of
subsocieties. Guided by republican principles of legal equality, indi-
viduality of citizenship, and electoral representation (albeit generally
manipulated), state and national authorities expanded their scope of

initiative, their capability greatly enhanced by growing fiscal resources, trained expertise, and technological support. They could increasingly manage on a larger scale, communicate more readily, and move more rapidly and extensively.

Technological proliferation was also a principal agent in the resurgence of commercialized economic activity. In the accelerating pace and expanding scale of market production, innovation foreshortened time and space and made exploitable on a seemingly exponential scale a wider range of primary products that the rest of the world desired. The mode of commercialization was also being altered. Commercial capitalism, which had driven the economic changes after 1750, was yielding to the industrial capitalism that had been transforming the economies of the North Atlantic world. Moreover, merchant-entrepreneurs, long operating individually or in partnership, increasingly became directors and managers of corporate business structures. New districts and regions were becoming converted from isolated environmental (or autonomous Amerindian) frontiers into integral parts of an increasingly interconnected national space. In other areas, the intrusion of immigrants and migrants, the international market, new technology, and extralocal government began to change the patterns of life upon which long-time residents had come to depend.

Notables moved into the center of this multifaceted historical process, with added leverage bordering on hegemony. In part, it was their own doing. For three generations they had expanded and developed their networks into private, familial forms of organization reaching into almost every facet of Middle Period life. Flexible, adaptable, and cohesive, they were in an organizational class by themselves by the late nineteenth century. They had transformed their family portfolios into quasi-public enterprises, closely articulated with municipal, state, and even national governments. What they lacked was a workable consensus around a political framework and worldview that would maintain and advance their place in Middle Period society.

The veritable technological revolution, combined with foreigners' markedly increased presence (whether in the form of international markets, capital, enterprise, or labor), presented notables with a momentous opportunity. In seizing upon it, they found it necessary to reach and maintain a requisite consensus among themselves. With the resulting increased leverage, they destroyed the post-independence equilibrium upon which Middle Period society rested and established their own hegemony over that society. They became even more notable in their wealth and refinement, more socially and politically dominant in a more secure hierarchy. They felt compelled to cut most of their ties with those beneath them socially, while linking their fortunes to a North Atlantic world in which corporate structure spread on an ever grander scale and their dependence on primary exports and international markets expanded unceasingly in scope. That world also brought modernizing change in economic and social relations over which they would increasingly lose control.

The destruction of the post-independence equilibrium would set in motion a popular reaction. *Gente baja*, joined at times by segments of the *gente decente* (cooperatively or separately), sought to restore the old equilibrium or adopted novel ways to find a new one. In the process, they found new sources of leverage. They formed voluntary associations that had come to embody the modern formal institutions that had spread through the North Atlantic world. They lent their electoral (and sometimes armed) support to strong national governments that attended to their demands. They accepted—and sometimes enthusiastically celebrated—nationalizing cultures that affirmed their heritage while calling upon their participation in far more encompassing, uniform patterns of daily life.

With the coming of worldwide economic depression, these twin forces of a strong national government and a nationalizing culture would become the dominant force in everyone's life. In the process, both the notables' hegemony and the regional ordering of life would be supplanted.

The Modernizing Triad

Since the emergence of the Middle Period society in the late eighteenth century, the *gente baja* had largely continued to rely on the relations of family, parish, and community as the pillars upon which rested the security and shared meaning in their lives. The *gente alta* (especially the notables among them) had found otherwise. Their world, their horizons had been inflating.

Increasingly, two components of this traditional triad, when not a burden or hindrance, had become irrelevant. Most *gente alta* remained believers and articulated important occasions in their private lives with church rituals. But especially for men of prominent families, secularization was pulling their interests, responsibilities, and preoccupations in a different direction. The church by 1880 had little utilitarian purpose in terms of occupation, capital source, or political influence. Its public message for a society confronting forces of change at odds with Iberian tradition seemed less and less germane. For a growing majority of notables a sense of shared heritage and space had moved beyond their locality. Their diversifying political and economic interests had branched into other districts and regions, into the national capital, and even across national borders and overseas. Socially and culturally, their identities were moving beyond their regions to encompass the national territory and beyond. On the family, however, notables knew only too well how much their success depended. Three generations of expanding and interconnected kin relations had enabled them to prosper economically, aggrandize their influence politically, and enhance their position socially.

Yet it was not only the family in the traditional triad that remained of great magnitude in notable minds. There was also the principal end to which, for them, that triad had served—hierarchy. After 1880 the rush of modernizing currents emanating from North Atlantic nations began to overflow into Latin America (along with many other parts of the world). The challenge was to find a way to infuse hierarchy into a progressive society. In such a society, individuals were autonomous, defined by the merit and accomplishment of their work and guided by the spirit of equal citizenship under the law rather than any collective identity or religious direction. Then, too, there was the need to address the social problems that increasingly manifested themselves in this process of change. From the notables' perspective, these were almost wholly to do with the *gente baja*, the result of an intensification of their proclivities toward negative behavior. That threatened notables at their points of contact with the *gente baja*: in the workplace, the street, and even the home.[1]

By the 1880s, notables had fashioned a societal platform of their own making. They set out to sustain their place in the existing social hierarchy through a "modernizing" triad. The culmination of several specific trends reaching back into the early nineteenth century, this triad was new because of the scale of these trends by the 1880s and the interlinkage resulting from their conjuncture. This was not an overnight conversion by the whole of the notables. Some moved only partially beyond the traditional triad. Many others (especially those middle-aged and beyond) accepted the modernizing triad out of recognized necessity, with varying degrees of enthusiasm. As might be expected, it was among the generation come of age in the late nineteenth century that the vision to which it pointed and the practices it prescribed were most fervently endorsed and fully internalized.

From Merchant Capitalism to Industrial Capitalism

After midcentury, notable families had begun to employ corporate structures to rationalize and formalize the growing diversification and interlocking of their economic interests and establish formal ties of business. Nevertheless, the first generation of banks had essentially just extended mercantile activities, formalizing banking functions performed by merchant-entreprenuers through their commercial houses. These banks provided a secure place for monetary holdings, facilitated the exchange of local and external bills of credit, and guaranteed substantially lower interest rates. They appeared first in those countries already enjoying a high level of exterior commerce and generating sufficient capital (Brazil, Argentina, Chile, Peru, and Cuba most notably). Most did not survive the worldwide market depression that began in 1873.

The 1880s brought a new generation of banking institutions that became the foundation of a new industrial capitalist economy, reflecting a conjunction of several factors. Commercialization of production leapt forward unprecedentedly, supported by and benefiting more stable and empowered state and national governments. Both partly resulted from a veritable revolution in transportation and communications. The flow of foreign capital was also unprecedented. Banks were established in almost all countries (proliferating in many) and founded by regional, public, and foreign capital, both separately and in various combinations. Many continued to focus on supplying short-term credit, principally to commerce. Others specialized in middle-term credit, above all to foster industrial enterprises. Mortgage banks also arose, offering long-term financing and using real estate as collateral for capital devoted not only to agricultural production but also to a variety of other enterprises.[2] Capital was being generated for investment in a wide range of economic sectors whose interconnection and interdependence was the hallmark of the age of industrialization.

Banking's transition after 1880 was also true of corporate structures in general. Through the example of the growing number of foreign companies in their midst and through study or travels abroad, notables were learning a crucial lesson: the advantages of economies of scale through modern corporate organization. Within each family, they employed interlocking directorships to forge a common investment strategy and coordinate intrafirm activities. In the larger network, family entrepreneurial captains acted as brokers. They formally combined their interests to pursue monopolies and cartels that would achieve market control in every promising activity that opened up, to a degree and scale previously unknown.[3]

National and Cosmopolitan Affiliation

The augmented horizons of Latin America's prominent families were spatial as well as economic. The essential spatial linkage until 1880 had been that between rural estate holdings and urban residence within a given locality or district. Notable families had relocated to another district or region when necessity pushed or opportunity pulled with uncustomary force: political persecution, an economic bonanza, a natural calamity. Since independence, educational opportunities and political officeholding had led members of prominent families to state capitals, other regional urban centers, and national capitals for varied lengths of time, some taking up permanent residence.

By 1880 the size of notable families after three generations alone made spatial expansion more feasible. The quickening pace and amplified reach of the commercializing economy made it more opportune to do so. Many sent members to the countryside and lesser municipalities in their district of origin to establish new or associated enterprises or fill political posts that governed small rural communities. Others branched out economically and politically into other districts to diversify or augment the family's portfolio. They set up family operations in extractive centers, ports, regional marketing and manufacturing cities, and capitals. More novel were the networks of notable families whose interests also extended into other states and regions, giving them a portfolio that was seminational in scope. There were a few national notable networks emerging (in Argentina, for example), based in national capitals that were becoming modern metropolitan centers.[4]

Notable families with extralocal interests were most able to take advantage of the transregional forces of change gathering momentum by the 1880s. National (and state) governments were crystallizing into instruments of power, building upon the national-liberal initiatives of the preceding three decades. The smattering of improvements in transportation and communications multiplied. As economic activity accelerated and new managerial procedures and expertise were adopted, rising revenues permitted the creation of full-fledged government bureaucracies. Customs agents, professional technicians, educational supervisors and inspectors, tax assessors and collectors, medical officers, armed forces, and police personnel reached down into the workings of the localities as never before. They were empowered by a plethora of nationally encompassing regulatory laws governing education, water use, mineral rights, land tenure, banking, internal and external trade, and public services. State governments echoed this change.

Accompanying this semitransformation of the public realm was the proliferation of foreign contacts that had begun to make their presence significantly felt in some regions after 1850. In many regions droves of immigrants arrived annually, working in fields and factories, opening stores and professional practices, and lending expertise to large enterprises and governmental institutions. More pervasive spatially were foreign entrepreneurs and companies setting up large operations in agricultural districts, extractive centers, and cities. The spreading print media brought news of foreign happenings that seemed less and less distant from local and regional life. Strange words, different customs, newfangled things, new machines, and unfamiliar designs entered everyday life on an unprecedented scale in most regions of Latin America. Elsewhere, they were only a railroad track, steamboat ship, telegraph line, school, government office, or newspaper edition away. The world was growing smaller, broadening horizons in the process.

The increasing parallel interests between notables with extralocal enterprises and government officials (interrelated by kinship, if not one and the same) initially extended strongly to enterprising foreigners, though after 1900 questions grew about that mutuality. Local notables could look enviously on this sharp turn of events, seeking a connection that might enable them to expand their family portfolios. They could content themselves with reaching a modus vivendi with the new currents penetrating their localities. Or, alarmed at the implications of such changes, they could seek ways to arrest them. Whatever strategy they chose, they were increasingly compelled to factor things national into thought and action. The determination of their status was moving rapidly beyond their control. For the standard Latin America's prominent families used to gauge their notability was now a cosmopolitan one, shaped by the dynamic industrializing, modernizing North Atlantic societies.

Interest in and admiration of things European (and later North American) had manifested itself in varying degrees since independence. Foreign influences, especially French, had affected artistic and literary styles, educational methodology, fashion, political ideology, and commercial practices, among others. But now, among growing numbers of notables, there sprung forth an infatuation with things North Atlantic bordering on worship. Association with that North Atlantic world meant being connected to the most successful of human societies, to a world of seemingly assured progress. To share in that world was surely the height of notability. By that standard, their nations and regional societies had fared at best modestly; their own prominence appeared wanting.

Until the late nineteenth century, manners had pivoted upon the display of the most refined American adaptations of Iberian culture, sprinkled with samples of European material luxuries and latest cultural styles. Accompanied by gracious talk and the showing of proper deference, this accustomed etiquette was most regularly played out at family gatherings at the home of the dominant kinsman. Now, the cultural requirements of proper socialization for those claiming or seeking prominence were becoming more and more complex. The display of acquired North Atlantic tastes—no longer samples but the full menu—and a distinct, recognizable set of manners to codify them increasingly became the signature of notability. A broader range of rituals arose, at once more encompassing in composition and more public in setting. Manners crafted abroad, above all in England and France, were becoming the seal of social success and the guarantee of acquired deference, newly legitimizing social relations and confirming the hierarchical order.[5]

The spatial context for notable women was expanding within these new national and cosmopolitan horizons. Their normal lot had been to learn the required but then limited graces of literate and artistic expression in their late teens and marry. After a decade or more of ensuring the continuance of the family bloodline (and if they had survived childbirth), they settled into their important roles of socialization. Through their comportment and cultivated graces, they helped to signal the family's status in the limited arenas of their social life: extended family gatherings, religious services and rituals, and the occasional public event. They also saw to their daughters' preparation for a similar future. Such a life pattern had required only minimal education and societal experience.

Now, after 1880, their world and the demands it placed upon them were being amplified. New modes of transportation fostered their venturing farther from home, and those of communication widened their familial and social contacts. The array of new technological innovations emanating from Europe and North America added novel experiences, manifold refinements, and greater complexities. In such circumstances, notable women required greater refinement and much broader public experience to maintain their important functions as ornaments, projectors of family social position, and facilitators of family networking. To traditional expectations were added facility in other languages, greater familiarity with the arts, more knowledge of public and external affairs, and greater confidence in the company of men.[6] This expansion of notable women's education and the scope of their public activity was initially driven by their fathers and husbands and subject to male desires and ambitions. But once into this expanding social context for their lives, a growing number of notable women would seize the initiative and work to push its boundaries ever further.

Voluntary Associations

The scale and specialization of industrial capitalism, broadened cultural horizons, and the growing complexity of social life and its adjudged precedent in North Atlantic societies induced notables to utilize a new institutional form to support their status at the top of the social hierarchy. A new set of social organizations appeared in which membership was neither hereditary nor compulsory but voluntary. Lines of social relations were horizontal rather than vertical as within the family, church, and community. Unlike the corporate bodies of the colonial era, voluntary associations were private, not beholden to (or supported by) law in their internal workings.[7]

Notables had long engaged in horizontal relations within their families and increasingly among them. But now, given the increasing scale of economic and bureaucratic activity and the growing social complexity in the towns and cities in which they resided—compounded by the expanding spatial context to their lives—accustomed forms of informal networking were less and less effective. Moreover, though still essential, informal networking was proving no longer sufficient in maintaining the exclusivity that notability necessarily implied. Family rituals had performed this function in the past. Yet the sheer size of notable families by the turn of century and the rising standards of notability more and more required an additional mechanism. So, too, did the expanding scope of their family portfolios and social relations.

Notables turned to voluntary associations to solve the problem of sustaining and demarcating their position in the social hierarchy. They enabled their families to bridge spatially and sectorally the larger and more diverse economic activity in which their members now worked. Notables could spread their influence and contacts by placing family representatives in such formal bodies, without initially having to depend on the more slowly evolving, time-consuming informal networking among family kin. The latter could be selectively employed over time through the widening circle of contacts. Business and professional associations could be more narrowly formed to acquire and maintain control of a market, or they could be vehicles to make family influence felt in more broadly based associations. In the Sociedad de Agricultores de Colombia, coffee producers in the center of the country became the principals, attaining national influence. In countless cities across Latin America, notables formed chambers of commerce.[8]

Voluntary associations were also organized to serve primarily social and political purposes. The social club (first appearing after midcentury) was a locale for after-hours diversions and business contacts. Women of the family joined their husbands, sons, and brothers for balls and other special social activities. The club's very expensive membership fees and lavish decor signaled the inflating level of wealth and education attained by the notables. Voluntary associations took on more public functions as well. Often under government sponsorship (particularly funding) or working closely with public officials, notables associated on a short-term basis to tackle pressing problems and promote public improvements. *Juntas de mejoras* (boards of public improvements) were formed to plan and oversee, for example, paving of sidewalks and streets, renovation of public markets and parks, and illumination of public places. They also drew up health restrictions on food sales, regulations for parking carriages, and systems for numbering streets.[9] Such quasi-public, temporary associations also organized and presided over important public occasions: annual festivities surrounding days of national independence or commemorative battles, inauguration of important public improvements, or visits of distinguished personages.

The modernizing triad of industrial capitalism, national and cosmopolitan horizons, and voluntary associations was neither ingrained nor practiced to the same degree by Latin America's notables. It was internalized most readily in the large, urban centers, where currents of change were moving most swiftly after 1880. Towns and cities ephemerally arising in the midst of extractive centers motivated notable thinking similarly, though in a much-compressed timeframe. Its adoption by prominent families in small district towns was less pervasive. But given the force and logic of historical currents, to ignore the notables' emerging consensus in vision and practice seemed foolish. To resist it appeared disadvantageous, if not risky.

On an Economic Roll

Confirmation of the modernizing triad seemed to come most rapidly and pervasively in the economy. Since independence, market economic activity had advanced very unevenly. Foreign investors' mercurial interest, interruptions of civil and national wars, instability and inconsistencies in governmental policy, and resistance of affected segments of the *gente baja* had all taken their toll. The North Atlantic panic of 1873 and ensuing years of depression had deflated most of whatever economic advances had been made in a number of regions since midcentury. Then in the 1880s, the market economy quite simply began to roll, both figuratively and literally (on rails). The accelerating pace slowed somewhat in the 1890s and then sped ahead until forced into a serious deceleration with the North American–derived panic of 1907. Recovery resumed in most regions within a couple of years. Though World War I led to dislocations in some areas and the brief postwar crisis slowed activity in considerably more, the by-now-industrializing economy steadily picked up steam through the 1920s.

By 1910, however, serious underlying bottlenecks were clearly surfacing. So, too, were social costs. World market conditions and increased government intervention temporarily papered them over, but the economic ride of nearly a half century was on increasingly vulnerable tracks. Still, in those first decades after 1880, the roll of economic growth seemed unstoppable; the verity of the modernizing triad difficult to refute. Nowhere did this appear more evident than in the transformation of communication, transportation, and mechanical devices.

The Technological Revolution

The marked rise in available capital (both foreign and domestically accumulated) greatly enhanced the ability to exploit resources and was accompanied by enlarged markets. More stable and capable government provided important supports. But to profitably extract resources from the ground in large enough quantities and at low enough costs, and to transport them to market cheaply enough (and in some cases fast enough without perishing)—that required a profound change in the existing technology.

The technological revolution, under way in the North Atlantic nations since the late eighteenth century, had been delayed in coming to Latin America. Geography alone was almost always an obstacle rather than a conduit. Long, wide, gently flowing rivers were the exception. Arduous terrain, climate, and vegetation were the rule, not only hampering construction and making it more costly but also making repair and maintenance formidable. These obstacles had put location, large pools of capital, and firm public support at a premium. Thus, internal improvements had been limited. A few generally short railroad lines leading in from the coast, and some steamboats operating along coasts and up several major rivers, pointed the way. But in their meager number, they bespoke the general failing. Still, during this delay, technological innovation emanating from the North Atlantic nations had been accumulating. Thus, when it came, supported by much larger sources of capital and governmental assistance, it had a far greater, more immediate impact.

On land, the iron rail became the driving force of change and an emblem of the new era. Railroads linked export centers to the coast, crossed fertile agricultural zones, and connected a growing number of towns and cities. Tramways and short spur rail lines serviced primary production zones. Streetcars traversed urban space. Telegraph lines became widespread. Telephones were installed within export production zones, between these and urban centers, and within cities themselves among notables and businesses. With few extensive coal deposits, power had been one of Latin America's main economic shortcomings. Modern shipping and rail lines made use of imported coal feasible for coastal regions and interior production centers. Electricity was employed promptly in the 1890s, where financial resources could afford it. Some hydroelectric plants appeared after 1900, as did oil exploration and production, but large-scale development did not really begin until after World War I. Mechanical devices so essential to industrializing production also spread: processing machines; extractive machinery; barbed wire (and agricultural implements to a lesser degree); refrigerated boxcars, ships, and storage containers, along with ice plants.

This package of technological innovation began quickly to dislocate and rearrange economic activity, shifting population to an extent not seen since the European conquest. In the upheavals in economic relations after 1750, technological innovation had played only a minor role. Now it was a large, permeating force, magnifying the impact and speed of the market economy once again surging forward. In a short passage of time (in some cases, almost overnight), communities and districts were transformed. With the railroad's arrival from neighboring Arizona, seemingly overnight the hamlet of Cananea became a copper-mining city of more than 20,000 in the northern state of Sonora. There, as in numerous other previously sparsely settled regions, an integrated hierarchical network of commercial centers arose. In older, more densely settled regions, this process was fortified and intensified and became more complex. The balance and relations among regions was also profoundly altered. As new options for some regions opened, those for others diminished or closed. The dependence and interdependence among regions also changed. The railroad's penetration from the Pacific Coast worked such changes in Bolivia. The recovery of the southern sierra's long-depressed silver mines led to foreign imports displacing textiles and flour from Cochabamba and sugar from Santa Cruz in the eastern mountains and valleys. Meanwhile, agricultural producers in the highland region around La Paz, connected by rail, supplied commodities to the capital and the tin-mining operations opening up in neighboring districts.[10]

The technological revolution also markedly increased the role of export production, becoming the prime motor of market economy expansion in most regions. The existing state of transportation, power, and processing equipment had set limits on the kinds and location of export production since the mid–eighteenth century, principally to regions near a coast with fairly level terrain and accessible water transportation. The difference after 1880 was the scale of export production: its variety of commodities, breadth of coverage, and sheer volume. Minerals with industrial applications, tropical fruits, fibers, and fresh meat joined the burgeoning output of such long-standing commodities as precious metals, sugar, cacao, and coffee.

Reorganization of Production

The technological revolution greatly enhanced opportunities for notables (especially in the countryside). With urban population growth again accelerating, capital more available and in large amounts, new equipment obtainable, and especially transportation costs greatly reduced, large producers by 1880 were moving increasingly to secure more direct control over production. Control over land and other natural resources was crucial to hacendados and those engaged in extractive enterprises alike. In some regions, it was a matter of acquiring public lands, made newly available by government survey and sale. More generally, notables acquired private lands, not infrequently employing forced acquisition. Irrigation water could be withheld, bureaucrats and judges bribed, the breaking up of communal holdings legislated, public or private armed forces used as threats and retribution, mortgages foreclosed, and loans liquidated. On property so acquired or already held, direct control of production could be attained by terminating tenancy leases and using administrators and various forms of paid labor. Where soils were less fertile and terrain difficult, sharecropping was employed. In some regions (such as in the pampas of Argentina and Uruguay and the coffee districts of Brazil and Colombia), tenancy was used as a short-term strategy in developing uncultivated lands. In extractive centers and urban areas, large, capital-intensive, vertically integrated firms producing for transregional markets rapidly began to extend their control over manufacturing.[11]

Labor was another key ingredient in seizing upon the new commercial possibilities. With slavery's abolition in Brazil in 1888, the last vestiges of legal involuntary servitude all but ended. Nevertheless, coercive labor continued or arose in some regions, and free wage labor was often qualified by the actions of employer or laborer, or mutually. Peasants tended to resist pure wage relations, fearing eviction above all. Cash advances tied some free wage laborers to their employers; others voluntarily sought debt as a perquisite. There were also sharecroppers whose family provided unremunerated labor, along with renters covering rent in labor rather than in cash.

The particular or dominant labor arrangement in a given enterprise, community, or district depended upon the mix of several important factors. Foreign firms, with extensive capital resources, were far more likely to rely on wage laborers alone. By contrast, where demand was very strong, voluntary labor scarce, notable leverage potent, and government backing vigorous (through illegal force or legal neglect), highly coercive debt peonage appeared. It constituted an innovative departure from colonial practices, a modern version of chattel slavery. The most notorious area was in southern Mexico. The large majority of notables, however, employed a variety of labor arrangements in between these extremes, generally relying on a mixture to maximize profits and maintain flexibility.

Population growth in many rural areas was an important source for creating labor surpluses, as it had been a century earlier. Although the rate of natural increase generally rose, the influx of immigrant workers was unprecedented; in some regions it was huge. Those from Mediterranean countries were most noticed in Brazil, the La Plata, and Chile. Contract laborers from India and China supplied plantations in the Caribbean, coastal Peru, and several regions in Mexico. A third source of labor surplus was the thousands of rural commoners who were losing their land. Even where labor was scarce, notables had far more leverage than in prior decades because their augmented capital holdings enabled them to provide sufficient incentives (when surplus labor elsewhere did not drive workers to them) and they could call upon supportive government forces or legislation to convert recalcitrant subsistence peasants into workers. Notables without ample working capital turned to sharecropping and labor tenancy.[12]

Unlike in the countryside, wage labor was the overwhelming rule in towns and cities. Long valued among urban commoners and offering the maximum flexibility required in the industrial capitalist economy for their employers, only in domestic employment was this pattern qualified. But as in the countryside, labor surplus or scarcity also critically shaped labor relations. In urban centers that grew up around new extractive centers, initial (and often continuing scarcity) necessitated wage incentives, which could be recouped through company stores and rented housing. But elsewhere, population growth from urban migration and immigration generally gave employers heightened leverage. So, too, did automation and mechanization. The general onset of inflation in the modernizing economies reinforced the employers' leverage even further. When workers did resist the regimen and compensation imposed upon them, government almost always could be counted on to intervene.[13]

Nevertheless, labor was not universally reorganized. In the Cochabamba region of Bolivia, notables no more held the upper hand than they did a century earlier. As large estate owners, they faced the loss of highland markets because of free trade and new property taxes levied by the national government, while peasants were adding to their holdings through petty capital accumulation. In Chile's central valley, notables dislodged from wheat export markets through international competition shifted away from direct agricultural production. They turned over much of the production on their land to tenants; then, taking advantage of rising land values, they used mortgages to raise capital for more lucrative investments in urban and mining sectors.[14]

Activist/Laissez-Faire Government

By 1880, through their family networks, notables had begun to secure control over public affairs at all levels. Thereafter, they moved to consolidate and extend that control, making it hegemonic. In municipal councils, state legislatures, and the national congress, family members filled the large majority of seats, often holding them for decades. They also occupied most judicial and administrative posts. When they did not, non-notables in these positions who failed to become their allies or clients did not prosper for very long. Moreover, notables came to realize that common economic interests required a substantial measure of political stability. Acceptable boundaries in waging and tolerating opposition were increasingly recognized as accommodation's benefits and political defeat's costs rose. Revolts and civil wars did erupt in some countries (most notably in Brazil, Chile, Colombia, Ecuador, and Uruguay), but only in Mexico did they approach the long, destructive conflicts of the mid–nineteenth century. Chronic political instability did continue to plague some nations in the Caribbean Basin (particularly Haiti, the Dominican Republic, and Nicaragua).

With their newly found mastery of and accommodation in politics, notables maintained the liberal laissez-faire state in theory. They generally desired the state's removal from the economy so enterprising individuals could freely pursue their interests. But that did not imply an inactive government. Building upon the preceding generation, a host of laws were passed to facilitate private enterprise and ensure greater business certainty through standard procedures. In specific instances, government intervened directly, principally in the construction of public improvements (as owner or investor) and in operating financial institutions. Above all, notables sought government assistance to foster private enterprise. São Paulo's state government accelerated planter and urban employer efforts to seek out immigrant workers (including a state-funded program of recruitment). In Bolivia, the national government legislated communal village lands out of existence and then began steadily to enforce it, accelerating the advance of large estates across the altiplano (long, broad high plain in central Bolivia). In Mexico, the rurales (a national police force) was employed not only to rid the countryside of banditry but as well to assist hacendados when they encountered resistance to their land claims and labor demands.[15]

Such sectoral government interventions in support of notable interests were surpassed by the countless intercessions on behalf of individual enterprises. At all levels, governments granted concessions to pursue them, subsidies to support them, and, when necessary, armed force and judicial manipulation to protect them. Notable officeholders and bureaucrats (and their clients) did their part in advancing their families' portfolios. In the end, the notable political consensus regarding the economy translated into an activist government on their behalf (and that of their clients and associates) and a laissez-faire government for everyone else.

Concentration of Control over Resources

The combined technological revolution, reorganization of production, and selective government intervention generated an unprecedented concentration of control over resources and of wealth. By comparison, the initial market-driven economic transformation of the last decades before independence seems modest. Most striking was the transfer of rural land, as agricultural holdings reached the tens and hundreds of thousands, even millions of acres. In the west-central Mexican region

surrounding the burgeoning city of Guadalajara, fifty haciendas possessed 60 percent of the land by 1910, while 92 percent of rural commoners had no land. Moreover, there were 25 percent fewer large estates
than thirty years before. Paraguayan laws setting up public land sales
in the mid-1880s resulted in 5 percent of the buyers obtaining 81 percent of the land, with the next 5 percent receiving 12 percent. *Gente baja*
who had occupied those lands for generations, either renting from the
state or settling on them independently, were evicted. Even where this
process was delayed after 1900, land concentration accelerated. In urban centers, control of assets was also being concentrated. Notables
bought up urban real estate for rental income, new businesses, and
speculation. They held the mortgages of small individual homes in
new suburban neighborhoods. Large industrial enterprises displaced
artisans and small cottage-shop owners, the pace varying depending
upon particular crafts and the proximity of railroad lines.[16]

Whether in countryside or city, notables understood that control
of (or at least dominant access to) the critical forces driving the industrial capitalist economy was paramount: investment capital, railroads,
power, and machinery. Control over banking institutions gave notables
access to investment capital while excluding others from it. In Buenos
Aires province, the great bulk of bank loans went to large entrepreneurs, who invested considerable sums in fixed capital improvements.
Small producers (especially tenants), by contrast, paid dearly in interest rates for the short-term funds acquired largely from country store
merchants, almost all of it used for operating expenses. Location of rail
lines was also decisive. Though most notable networks did not build
or own railroads, by providing political, legal, or managerial services
to those who did, they were often able to secure the necessary proximity of the route to their enterprises. Or, possessing the capital resources,
they could move or open family enterprises in new areas being opened
up by rail. The Laguna district in north-central Mexico saw that nation's
most spectacular agricultural growth before the 1910 revolution. Trum-
peted as "the Miracle," the epitome of the Porfirian regime's development strategy, it was even more emblematic of the notables' growing
hegemony as the new century dawned.[17]

By then, that hegemony in regions across Latin America had
brought notable families wealth and economic power on a scale previously unknown. Yet that wealth and power had created its own limitations. For notables were prone to settle for accustomed business
strategies—principally cheap labor and market control rather than
improved productivity and volume expansion—to generate relatively
quick, easy profits in the spreading industrial capitalism. Most invested

in new technology at best modestly, usually to survive competition. Few invested in their workers' capabilities. And rather than trying to overcome the tide of the industrialized countries' technological head start, they decided to run with it.[18] In the short run, it would prove a sensible strategy, and they rode on top of it. In the long run, they would be submerged by it.

Alliance with the North Atlantic

The decision of Latin America's notables to cast their lot with the North Atlantic world was not only economic but social and cultural as well. All but a small minority admired that progressive world's accomplishments. A growing number were becoming infatuated with it and reached out to absorb and imitate it. In doing so, they found it increasingly necessary to open up their own society and share their prosperity, even their hegemony. Notables welcomed as partners those whom they considered the best of that world. They received many others as positive contributors. Some with non–North Atlantic origins they accepted as necessary others. But in time, the problem of selectivity and control in the alliance with the North Atlantic became steadily more apparent.

Sources of Progress

More and more notables became convinced in the late nineteenth century that by means of industrial-technological exploitation they (and the nations they led) could take their place alongside the world's other advanced societies. As they did so, it seemed quite obvious to most that patterning themselves after the North Atlantic nations would ensure such progress. Enterprising European and North American immigrants or representatives in their midst were one source of modeling. They brought knowledge of and expertise in corporate management and finance and technological innovations. They seemed to crop up wherever something economically important was going on. In some locales and regions they led the way.[19] They also served as models in stores, on the streets, at public functions, and in the home. The books on their library shelves, the furniture in their salons, the china and cutlery on their dining room tables, the most modern conveniences in their bathrooms, and the very designs of their residences, all pointed to what was tasteful and fashionable in the North Atlantic world. So, too, were the suits, dresses, hats, and parasols they wore in the parks, at the concert halls, or at grand balls.

Increasingly, however, notables went to the source directly. For decades a small number of adults had returned from Europe with then current political ideas, economic practices, and literary and artistic forms. But in the late nineteenth century, the scope of seeking out North Atlantic ways became magnified, even systematic. By 1900, sons of Mexican notables by the hundreds had studied abroad, growing numbers attending schools and colleges that focused on applied technology and practical methods in agriculture, engineering, metallurgy, and business, as well as learning English and French. The grand tour abroad became not only a fashion among notable families but also an important source for adopting practices, obtaining investment ideas, and acquiring the latest cultural tastes, designs, and objects. Argentinians visiting North Atlantic countries carried home with them images and designs of palatial beaux-arts residences, remodeling Buenos Aires into the Paris of South America.[20]

Once home, notable travelers followed up on contacts they had made. In business they kept abreast of fluctuating international market conditions and new practices by subscribing to magazines and periodicals. As officials they obtained copies of novel legislation and codes governing various business sectors. As art patrons they acquired building designs, arranged for touring companies, and later listened to recorded music on the phonograph. Notables increasingly acquired and surrounded themselves with the material life of Europe and North America. They maintained cleanliness in porcelain bathtubs and washstands, using fine English soap and French fragrances. They donned straw hats, felt bowlers, and canes or the latest dresses and coiffures. They played pianos in salons and rode bicycles on estate grounds and select streets. Inside sumptuous new public buildings they listened to current operas, stepped appropriately to new dances, and practiced fashionable manners and conversation. Salons in private residences provided a more restricted, intimate setting for such displays. For although most notables retained much of their regional culture in the privacy of their family, public evidence of the North Atlantic cultural milieu was becoming a must.[21]

Partners, Leaven, and Others

The alliance with the North Atlantic was more specifically and pragmatically played out in the varied relations (especially economic) in which notables engaged foreigners. The most accomplished from those nations were regarded as partners in pursuit of common interests. The most distant and unfettered were the large entrepreneurs permitted or sanctioned to take the lead role in exploiting an economic opportunity. Sometimes this effort occurred on a regional scale, as large fruit and mining companies moved into the previously sparsely settled areas of Central America's Atlantic coast. Usually, it meant a district or locality. Notables soon moved in as junior partners in ancillary sectors and as suppliers and providers of services. A tighter but still dependent relationship was that between foreign companies that supplied credit, new lines of transportation and power sources, or marketing to notable commodity producers. International Harvester held the latter leveraged relationship with Mexican henequen producers in the Yucatán, as did chewing gum manufacturers with notable contractors controlling those who harvested chicle in the tropical forests of Mexico and Central America. Notables were also literal partners. In some cases, they sold enterprises they had developed, retaining a minority interest. In others, large capital requirements for expansion led to their bringing foreign investors into the firm. Frequently, foreigners joined a group of notables in establishing a corporation, such as a bank or multifaceted manufacturing enterprise.[22]

Then there were dependent relationships that ran both ways. Members of prominent families worked directly for foreign firms as managers or provided services for them, particularly legal assistance in negotiating with government officials. To a greater extent, in turn, notables called upon esteemed foreigners for services as managers of rural estates and manufacturing establishments, architects and engineers, doctors and pharmacists. As (or through) public officials they also contracted professional and technical know-how. The Argentine government brought in engineers from the United States and Belgium to suggest remedies for the struggling port projects in Buenos Aires. Under contract, Germans set up normal schools in several countries and professionalized armed forces. North American engineers were contracted to superintend construction of rail lines in places ranging from Cuba across the Caribbean Basin and down the west coast of South America. Peru contracted with U.S. engineers to direct a nationwide campaign to eradicate yellow fever and to design all public works in the main urban centers, funded largely by the Rockefeller Foundation.[23]

These North Atlantic partners were almost always welcome in the notables' new voluntary associations. As members or guests of chambers of commerce, specialized producers' associations, or social clubs, they increasingly socialized with notables. Most married within their nationality, but not infrequently they deepened their associations with notables by marrying into their families.[24]

There were others from North America and Europe—far, far greater in number—who came in agricultural colonies, as independent small farmers and tenants, and as urban laborers, skilled and unskilled. They were pragmatically sought as the means to ensure an adequate labor force, supplying sometimes scarce skills and serving to keep wages down. Yet they were also welcomed as leaven to raise the *gente baja* to standards acceptable in the North Atlantic world. Notables did not agree on the probability or even possibility of that happening. But given their growing internalization of racial theories emanating from Europe and the United States, the more "white blood" and progressive minds notables could incorporate into their societies, the more likely their nations would be able to join the ranks of the "civilized" world. Italian communities in Peru were among those North Atlantic immigrants most fulfilling these expectations, integrating well and enriching the society.[25]

Of other foreigners, nothing more was expected or wanted than their labor. The vast majority had come as contract laborers. Whether they were Chinese building railroads in Mexico and Cuba or laboring in plantation fields in Panama, Cuba, and Peru, or South Asians tending sugar cane in the Caribbean, they were viewed as racially and culturally inferior by notables (and most other nationals as well). In some countries, large numbers of immigrants came not from overseas but from other Latin American countries (or colonies). Tens of thousands of West Indians of African descent constructed the Panama Canal, cut cane in Cuba, picked bananas in Central America, and built railroads in Ecuador. These immigrants were held in the same regard as those from Asia—a necessary evil.

Growing Concerns

In the first years of the new century, notables were beginning to entertain some nagging doubts, even some serious questions, about the alliance with the North Atlantic. Increasing numbers of the "other" immigrants were proving unwilling to remain docile unskilled laborers. Chinese, in particular, moved into petty commerce, retailing goods and services to the *gente baja*. A few who had accumulated capital were able to establish large commercial firms and manufacturing enterprises. Immigrants from the Middle East in Argentina did so as well, though they had avoided agricultural labor from the beginning whenever they could. Rationalizing the apparent contradictions between these immigrants' achievements and assumed theories of racial inferiority, notables attributed this success to dishonesty born of avarice. More potentially troubling, competition from immigrants in general as laborers and business competitors was provoking rising popular unrest. In southeastern South America, notables were beginning to see the sheer numbers of European immigrants as having a deleterious effect. The teeming masses of urban workers had accumulated alongside rising crime, mendicancy, alcoholism, and labor agitation. To explain this degenerating urban milieu, notables in the La Plata region increasingly settled on immigration's excess. Meanwhile, an excess of successful, socially mobile European immigrants in business and the professions began to threaten the notables' monopoly in political power and social prestige. Selecting just a few of them for inclusion in network families would not keep them at bay.[26]

More direct were the signs of adverse effects coming from the initiatives of North Atlantic immigrants whom Latin America's notables considered close working partners. Most troubling was the emerging sense that they might very well be losing control in that assumed alliance of interests. Growing numbers of Mexico's notables felt this concern perhaps most strongly. Guadalajara's foreign entrepreneurs were coming to dominate the city's commercial spheres. In Cananea's meteoric mining center, William Greene's interconnected companies controlled the water people drank, the gas and firewood with which they cooked, the electricity they used, the meat they ate, the homes in which most of the workers lived, as well as many of the commercial outlets where they purchased consumer goods. To the South, in Sonora's Yaquí Valley, the Richardson Construction Company possessed more than 400,000 acres and a large water-use concession.[27]

Though concerns about such unforeseen consequences of the alliance with the North Atlantic grew after 1900, they did not yet shake most notables' confidence in the validity of this important tenet in their vision of progress. Another tenet's ramifications they understood far more dimly.

Severing Ties with Those Below

Although the notables' vision of a community beyond was expanding—through state and national capitals across the ocean to the North Atlantic's industrializing nations—that of the community in their midst was contracting. As doors opened outward to those with whose progress they wished to identify, other doors closed on their fellow countrypeople. The vast majority were far poorer, far less educated and refined, and almost always less white. Even when not so lacking, notables, with now quite sizable families and success in achieving hegemony, had less need of such notables-in-waiting.

Exclusivity in Voluntary Associations

Severing ties with those deemed socially inferior was not simply the result of a change in worldview. Notables, along with the *gente decente*, had long worried about the problems of social disorder. They had relied on the accustomed vertical means of affirming the hierarchical social order in their localities: from a core of family and ritual kin down through patronal and client relations to the integration of all segments of local society through community rituals and celebrations.[28] But the rising standards of notability and (for many notables) the application of imported racial theories strongly suggested the need for an alternative way of dealing with the rest of society. Visual and personal association with those found wanting in their color and backwardness attenuated the notables' claim to membership in the "civilized" community of nations. Long-held feelings of superiority over the *gente baja* were giving way to those of contempt and a growing sense of vulnerability. Increasing social mobility and accompanying inclusion of those of mixed blood had lowered the *gente decente*'s social credentials. Moreover, the accumulating wealth of some presented a challenge to the clear delineation of notability.

Technology, scale of wealth, and patterns of association after 1880 provided the means for a new strategy for handling the rest of society. Technological innovations allowed notables at once to withdraw from and transcend the traditional boundaries of social and cultural space. Railroads and streetcars allowed them to separate office, recreation, and residence. They could withdraw from the center city to exclusive residential neighborhoods and maintain distant retreats. Their multiplying wealth enabled them to construct palatial urban estates (with elaborate decor, furnishings, and grounds) that set them clearly apart. There they could display their prominence while avoiding contact with all but their equals. Their wealth could convert baptisms, important birthdays, weddings, anniversaries, and even funerals into lavish occasions restricted to fellow notables but witnessed from a distance by others, or conveyed to them in photographs on newspaper society pages. So, too, private celebrations connected with observances of national and religious holidays, which formerly had been largely community occasions.[29]

Voluntary associations increasingly became the mechanism for distinguishing invited guests from distant witnesses on such occasions.

Private schools (often parochial) maintained the exclusivity of young notables in their training and bonding, as public education expanded to meet the growing needs of the industrializing economy and progressing society. Social clubs performed the same function for the whole family. Though less straightforward, voluntary associations also fostered exclusivity in more public settings. Entertainment events were carefully restricted through expense and sometimes invitations. Domination of arrangement committees likewise allowed notables to limit participation at special activities accompanying public commemorations. At such public congregating of notables—for each other inside and for observers of their coming and going outside—financial worth was marked, cultural refinement was displayed, and social position was announced.[30]

Beyond such special public occasions, notables increasingly sought to extend their exclusivity by insulating themselves in public places. These were cleared of *gente baja* practices and coloration and stamped with the imprint of signs of North Atlantic "civilization." Broad, airy boulevards were constructed, along with new public and cultural buildings. Parks were built and plazas remodeled. Enlarged police forces were employed to enforce the new cultural order. Notables were given first priority in extension and improvement of public services in transportation, communications, and utilities.[31]

Discarding Patronal Obligations

The same forces facilitating their social exclusivity were distancing notables from the formerly wide range of personal, informal contacts that had served to reinforce the mutual, though uneven, exchange of obligations that were part of the quid pro quo for their dominant position in local society. More importantly, the worth of those obligations to notables was steadily declining. Given the enlarged profits to be made by more rational decisions dictated by intensifying competition in the marketplace, those patronal obligations were becoming more costly to maintain.

In the countryside, where a labor shortage required labor tenancy, plots of land, or rations as necessary inducements, hacendados modified the strict capitalist regimen of direct production and free wage labor. But elsewhere, traditional obligations that were part of an enduring relationship with peasants were being jettisoned. A graphic though fictional account is seen in Jorge Icaza's novel, *Huasipungo* (The villagers). An Ecuadoran hacendado enters into a business deal with a

North American to exploit several extractive enterprises. Pressed for funds to keep up his end of the deal, he terminates his patronal obligations to his *peones*: small subsistence plots, the right to glean fields, and annual *socorros* (rations). "[Those] barbaric custom[s] are ended," he declares to his *mayordomo* (administrator or steward). "Let them buy. They'll have to pay me. That's why they are working." When the Indians engage in resistance, beset by growing hunger and despair, they are displaced with the help of the federal army.[32]

In towns and cities, such customary patronal obligations were fewer and less well-defined. Mechanization was loosening the ties that had traditionally bound employers to their workers, especially those with skills and crafts. Beset more and more by growing regimentation of work, irregularity of employment, overcrowding in housing, and inflation of basic commodities, urban workers found notable employers little concerned with their mounting frustrations. Some owners did try to secure their workers' loyalty by providing schools, medical assistance, and special entertainment and festivities. But most sought merely to discipline their workers more harshly, regarding their resistant, escapist behavior as uncivilized.[33]

Above the line of respectability, *gente decente* were finding their accustomed relations with notables eroding as well. They had long depended in varying degrees on client relations with them, especially those who were poor relations of prominent families. Increasing commercialization and industrialization in the economy, along with the public bureaucracy's expansion, was enlarging opportunities but heightening insecurities as well. Foreigners undermined *gente decente* retail trade or took business away from their professions. Inflation ate away at their accustomed lifestyle, which accorded them the respectability distancing them from the *gente baja* and the credentials for eventual ascent to notability. Recurring business downturns emanating from abroad made them even more vulnerable. Meanwhile, notables were cornering resources, lucrative professional opportunities, and high-paying administrative positions for their multitude of family members.[34]

Securing client ties was thus becoming more important for the *gente decente*, yet notables were increasingly less willing to extend them. The declining minority who succeeded in doing so shared in the notables' prosperity, though with greater dependence and vulnerability. The rest, especially poor relations of prominent families, faced growing frustration that engendered bitterness. Novels and short stories of the period vividly depict the *gente decente*'s plight. Ramón Beteta, in his semifictional "memories," records the social and economic slide of his father as he becomes progressively disconnected from his wife's notable relatives.[35]

The Public Sector as Agent of Control

Physical distance, social separation, and discarding patronal obligations did not fully alleviate notable concerns about their place atop the social hierarchy. For industrial capitalism was proving to be a two-edged sword. It was bringing them a prodigious prosperity and enhanced refinement, a connection they saw most clearly. At the same time, it was fomenting growing social problems (especially in urban areas), a linkage most failed to discern. Instead, they increasingly coupled these social problems with the vices they had traditionally ascribed to the *gente baja*.

The old fears of a century before of growing social disorder were revived. Notables now saw unwanted vicissitudes that were seemingly growing out of control. Crime, alcoholism, homelessness, and even disease—these were the result of *gente baja* proclivities toward depraved behavior. For many notables, racial and Darwinist theories gave added verification to their long-held assumptions. Mere observation seemed to confirm it for many more. The *gente baja* appeared ill equipped for the era of progress and order that was dawning. Moreover, notables increasingly sensed an inadequacy of their own. The North Atlantic world, in calling them toward more impersonal relations in the economy and more exclusivity in social interactions, made paternalism appear increasingly impractical, even obsolete. Consequently, they turned to the public sector as the principal agent of social control. Notable reliance on private prerogative gave way to the joining of their private purpose to public power.[36]

The notables' near dominant hold on political power after 1880 facilitated this transfer of power and initiative from private to public. For example, a representative of the hacienda of Hueyapan (east-central Mexico) sat on the ayuntamiento, and the estate owner had close business relations with its president. In time, an estate employee was appointed local judge. In serious cases of unrest, the national rural police could be called upon. State penitentiaries were built to confine troublemakers more securely. Urban officials employed municipal ordinances and enlarged police forces to clear desired streets of *gente baja* concessionaires, amusements, and spontaneous processions. Public health was also an arena for action. Although public services were extended to Rio de Janeiro's *gente alta*, the solution for deteriorating living conditions among commoners, which bred infectious disease, was a wholesale campaign of forced smallpox vaccination (1904).[37]

In his novel *The Bosses*, Mariano Azuela illustrates most tellingly the notables' growing reliance on the public sector to deal with social problems more customarily addressed by patronal means—and not infrequently to turn a profit from it. After the family patriarch's death, the lone daughter urged compliance with his last wishes that the family distribute alms among the poor. A recent drought had driven up the price of necessities. Her three brothers had other ideas. With a subordinate sitting on the municipal council to shepherd the proposal through, they concocted a deal that credited their benevolence without spending a penny. The *ayuntamiento* accepted their donation of corn for public distribution, in return for instituting a four-month ceiling of half the market price for all sales. The brothers bought up additional corn at that low price and then turned around and sold it for twice the price when the ceiling was lifted.[38]

Frequently, notables employed voluntary associations to supplement the growing efforts of government officials to "improve" the *gente baja*. Charitable endeavors continued to address the consequences of calamitous events such as famines, floods, and epidemics. But they were more and more likely to be focused on self-help programs and services for the poor to instruct and conform them in the ways of the new, progessing order of things. Women often took the lead in these charitable committees, usually working closely with (or under the authorization of) local officials.[39]

There was, however, no common agreement among notables on whether, how many, or to what extent *gente baja* could be uplifted. Some, taking the most extreme racial-Darwinist position, pessimistically gave up on the nonwhite masses, looked to white immigration to ameliorate the problem, and advocated direct governmental control. Others pointed to centuries of servitude and ignorance rather than innate inferiority in arguing that *gente baja* were capable of sharing in progress. Still, their attention was on individuals who, through education and personal drive, were joining society's successful. Even here, the few's success seemed to demonstrate the selectivity of the fit. Far more notables concluded that through active intervention (increasingly public), most *gente baja* could be "cultivated" to a level that allowed their useful integration into the progressive industrializing society then forming. As a by-product, social control would be strengthened.[40]

One means of "civilizing" the *gente baja* was through educating them technically and formally. A second-tier, "practical" education focused on teaching necessary basic skills for functioning in the changing society and instilling an ethic of discipline in work and citizenship. Guatemalan authorities enlisted the services of Protestant missionaries to assist in the masses' conversion (especially Indians in the countryside) into docile, industrious workers loyal to the secular state. They made little headway, except in the capital. In Mexico after 1905, Protestant missionaries became too successful, adding lessons in democracy and civil rights to instruction in private virtues and basic skills.[41] Working through government at all levels, notables also strove to modify traditional *gente baja* behavior by legislatively defining acceptable amusements. Popular festivities and street entertainment were suppressed to curb their associated vices and replaced with civic celebrations to inculcate "progressive" virtues among the nonwhite masses.[42]

Women were an important focus in the *gente baja*'s remaking. Notables (and *gente decente* as well) saw women's public work as a major cause of the social problems confronting them. For them, females' crucial function in the progressive societies they were leading was in the home as nurturer, stressing life-long habits of industry and morality. And although married women were paragons of *gente alta* virtue, the standards were applied differently across the line of respectability.

Gente alta women had always been involved in the economy, though more generally in a temporary or indirect capacity. Now, the accelerating market economy infused with industrial capitalism and the public sector's expansion provided new opportunities, especially for widows and the unmarried. With their families' accumulating wealth, it was largely a matter of choice resulting from the woman's ambition and the patriarch's accommodation. Depending upon the region, census records reveal a rise in the number of notable women engaged in agricultural production, landholding for rent, and university and secondary school teaching. By 1900, they were even beginning to enter some of the prestigious professions, especially in medicine. For *gente decente* women, necessity increasingly accompanied individual ambition. Rising standards of respectability combined with greater economic vulnerabilities to direct more and more into the workforce, especially those without a husband. Some continued as store managers or proprietors (most commonly in the apparel trade). But by far the greatest opportunities emerged in the expansion of education (and less so of public health), above all in primary school teaching (and midwifery).[43]

These growing dimensions of *gente alta* women's public work were not, however, linked to the social problems their male relatives increasingly decried. That was reserved for women below the line of respectability. *Gente baja* women's extensive role in the market economy had been going on for more than a century. What had changed was *gente alta* consciousness of the extent of these women's public labor roles, either by the scale of their economic activity passing some threshold of cognizance or by its measurement in the systematic census records being instituted by government.

The proportion and scope of *gente baja* women's occupations varied widely, depending upon land tenure patterns, demographic variations, degree of industrial capitalism, a given commodity being produced or manufactured, family size and life cycle, and social organization. In the district of Córdoba (eastern Mexico), where a coffee boom was re-shaping the countryside, women comprised one-seventh of the cultivators, one-sixth of the permanent day workers, as many as half the temporary laborers, and four-fifths of the processing workers. To the south, by 1907 women comprised 15 percent of wage laborers in Oaxaca state, and in some villages one-fifth to one-third of the smallholders (largely from privatizing communal lands). In urban areas throughout Latin America, the numbers of the traditionally largest female occupations among the popular classes—domestic service and laundering—expanded as the wealth and numbers of the *gente alta* families who hired them grew. But their numbers as factory workers were rising proportionately more rapidly. *Gente de profesiones* women remained largely in their existing roles as small landowners, petty traders, and shopkeepers, and in craft activities and service tasks. With increasing frequency, they brought in outside income when their husbands were unemployed, or when they were permanently left the sole breadwinner.[44]

A common thread running through the rising numbers of *gente baja* women engaged in the public realm of work was their households' growing dislocation and impoverishment, especially if they headed them. The spread of the market economy had had the same effect a century before. Following independence, these pressures had generally stabilized. Now, market economy penetration was again accelerating, greatly intensified in its impact by the industrial capitalist mode increasingly driving it. When competitive production techniques, breakdown of market barriers, loss of access to land, or overabundance of labor depressed the family's income-earning capacity, women went to work in fields, processing plants, and factories. A two-tiered wage scale, paying them generally only half of what their male counterparts earned, made them increasingly valuable to employers seeking profits in the increasingly competitive marketplace. They were cheap, passive, generally supplementary. Or, *gente baja* women could always turn to domestic service and laundering. One brought more security, the other more independence, but both offered little remuneration. In

Guadalajara (Mexico) nearly half of all women were engaged in some gainful employment by 1900. In Rio de Janeiro, a similar proportion was counted in 1906.[45]

Nevertheless, in their growing preoccupation with social ills the *gente alta* rarely appraised *gente baja* women as such important contributors to the economy. They marked them as prostitutes, beggars, petty thieves, derelict mothers, abandoners of children, even killers of infants. Though they received some attention in protective labor legislation after the turn of the century, notable public discourse and initiatives focused on disciplining them. Notables enlisted state-licensed midwives to police pregnant women to track down abandonment and infanticide. They tried state-regulated brothels to reduce the number of individual prostitutes out on the streets and sanitize the remainder for their health and that of their customers—frequently the *gente alta* themselves. Still, notable civic leaders also took more positive steps. They began to establish clinics and maternity wards and sought to recenter these women in the home through a school curriculum that stressed domesticity and morality.[46] Such disciplining and "civilizing" of *gente baja* was an important component in the notables' vision of order and progress. In its goal and methods, it also reflected the new ideology that interpreted and guided their vision.

The Positivist Prescription

The watchwords of order and progress were deeply embedded in the positivist ideology (and philosophy) that spread through the ranks of notables (and many *gente decente*) in the late nineteenth century. It was at once to them an answer to past failures, a prescription for progress, and a guarantee of the future. Liberals and conservatives had been coming toward that ideology from different directions since the 1870s. Liberals had found their national project frustrated and compromised. Federalism had resulted in neither stability nor a more open politics. They were coming around to the view that progress (particularly the economic progress then taking hold) required order above all. Conservatives were also beginning to give primary focus to the new economic opportunities opening up. No longer considering order primarily a mechanism to maintain the status quo, they were willing to accept more evolutionary changes to realize those economic ambitions.

The new ideological currents embodying positivism seemed to both liberals and conservatives to mirror the pragmatic progressivism they were coming to hold in common. According to positivist doctrine, economic progress would gradually bring political changes in the long duration, as it raised per capita income, facilitated illiteracy's elimination, expanded higher education, absorbed and applied technology, and led inevitably to the forging of modernizing societies. A strong government (especially at the national level) would maintain order and pursue progress.

To liberals, positivism offered a rationalization for their failures. They could retain greater individual freedom and participation as long-term goals, safe in positivist assurances that these would be fulfilled in time through economic progress, while discarding such already compromised goals in the short run in favor of economic opportunities now foremost in their priorities. They could rationalize troubled consciences, compromise purist liberal principles. Positivism preached evolutionary change, and time appeared to be on the side of the liberals, whether notables for generations or newcomers. Conservatives focused on the short run. Positivism appeared to offer them a means to pursue economic goals and enhance their cultural refinement with the security that society would change only gradually and that their social inferiors would be kept under control through a limitation on their political participation. Certainly, the political structures that solidified after 1880 met their concerns. Notables consorted with (and usually absorbed) the military caudillos who were soon replaced by authoritarian civilian presidents (as in Mexico, Venezuela, and Central America). Or they chose one from competitors among themselves (Argentina, Uruguay, and Ecuador). Elsewhere, they settled on a closed oligarchic politics, competing in political parties with one another.

To say that liberals and conservatives had arrived at a political and ideological understanding is not to say that their movements dissolved into one or that there was no longer any conflict. Some revolts and coups did occur. The clerical issue remained a sticking point, as did the extent of political reform. But the mid–nineteenth century's politics to the death had ended. Politics was to be solely the province of notables themselves and was not to lead to a situation in which order would break down into a state of continuing disorder.

In accepting positivism, liberals and conservatives in middle or old age were altering their goals to reach a compromise based upon a new political arrangement. Positivism was their children's first ideological love affair. They accepted the economic opportunities it promised as they started out in life. The lessons of their parents were clear to them as they internalized positivist discourse. For they were also being increasingly schooled in the new scientific education and the new technology, as doctors, engineers, agronomists, accountants, and businesspeople. Their education, they assumed, would not lead them into internecine preoccupation with politics at the cost of economic progress. Rather, by applying positivism's scientific tenets in the economy and public sector, they would be able to foster progress for their families and in the nation as a whole. The new era that was dawning was theirs. They set out to make the most of it in building on what their parents had begun.

In the first years of the new century, however, as these notables bequeathed this era of positivist progress to the next generation, the certainties with which their lives had seemingly unfolded, were coming into question. The dynamic economy was becoming less manageable, the alliance with the North Atlantic world more costly. More ominous, the rest of society, from whom they had steadily disassociated themselves, was beginning to seriously challenge their hegemony.

Notes

1. Vaughn, "Primary Education," 31–33; Jeffrey D. Needell, *A Tropical Belle Epoque: Elite Culture and Society in Turn-of-the-Century Rio de Janeiro* (New York: Cambridge University Press, 1987), 1–4, 19–21; Sandra Lauderdale Graham, *House and Street: The Domestic World of Servants and Masters in Nineteenth Century Rio de Janeiro* (New York: Cambridge University Press, 1988), 24–27; William E. French, "Prostitutes and Guardian Angels: Women, Work, and the Family in Porfirian Mexico," *HAHR* 72 (November 1992): 529–34.

2. Francisco Nuñez de la Pena, "Un banco que vino del centro: Una crónica," 209–10, Carlos Marichal, "El nacimiento de la banca mexicana en contexto latinoamericano: Problemas de periodisación," 234–50, 263–64, and José Antonio Batíz V., "Trayectoria de la banca en Mexico, hasta 1910," in *Banca y poder en México*, ed. Leonor Ludlow and Carlos Marichal (Mexico: Editorial Grijalbo, 1986), 279, 284–87.

3. Alfonso W. Quiroz, "Financial Leadership and the Formation of Peruvian Elite Groups, 1884–1930," *JLAS* 20 (May 1988): 55–61; Larissa Adler Lomnitz and Marisol Pérez-Lizaur, *A Mexican Elite Family, 1820–1980* (Princeton, NJ: Princeton University Press, 1987), 116–18; Ellen McAuliffe Brennan, "Demographic and Social Patterns in Urban Mexico: Guadalajara, 1876–1910" (Ph.D. diss., Columbia University, 1978), 161–72.

4. Balmori, Voss, and Wortman, *Notable Family Networks*, 43–47, 117–23, 218–27, and chap. 4; Quiroz, "Peruvian Elite Groups," 61–73; Needell, *Tropical Belle Epoque*, 57–58, 63–71.

5. Needell, *Tropical Belle Epoque*, 116–31, 154–55; Balmori, Voss, and Wortman, *Notable Family Networks*, 49–50.

6. Needell, *Tropical Belle Epoque*, 131–37.

7. James A. Henretta, *The Evolution of American Society, 1700–1815: An Interdisciplinary Analysis* (Lexington, MA: D. C. Heath, 1973), 206–14.

8. Michael F. Jimenez, "Traveling Far in Grandfather's Car: The Life Cycle of Central Colombian Coffee Estates: The Case of Viota, Cundinamarca (1900–1930)," *HAHR* 69 (May 1989): 193–94; Needell, *Tropical Belle Epoque*, 89.

9. Needell, *Tropical Belle Epoque*, 63–71; Balmori, Voss, and Wortman, *Notable Family Networks*, 21–23; Adler Lomnitz and Pérez-Lizaur, *Mexican Elite Family*, 119–20; Miguel Tinker-Salas, *In the Shadow of the Eagles: Sonora and the Transformation of the Border during the Porfiriato* (Berkeley: University of California Press, 1997), 217–18.

10. Ibid., chaps. 6–8; Stuart F. Voss, "Towns and Enterprise in Northwestern Mexico: A History of Urban Elites in Sonora and Sinaloa, 1830–1910" (Ph.D. diss., Harvard University, 1972), 467–75, 485–91, 508–10, 522–36; Larson, *Agrarian Transformation*, 309–12; Klein, *Haciendas and Ayllus*, chap. 6.

11. Simon Miller, "The Mexican Hacienda between the Insurgency and the Revolution: Maize Production and Commercial Triumph on the Temporal," *JLAS* 16 (November 1984): 309–36; Stephen H. Haber, "Assessing the Obstacles to Industrialization: The Mexican Economy, 1830–1980," *JLAS* 24 (February 1992): 13–17; Berry, "Rural Small-Scale Manufacturing," 300–2, 309–16; Michael J. Gonzales, "Chinese Plantation Workers and Social Conflicts in Peru in the Late Nineteenth Century," *JLAS* 21 (October 1989): 403–5; David McCreery, "Land, Labor, and Violence in Highland Guatemala: San Juan Ixcoy (Huehuetenango), 1893–1945," *The Americas* 45 (October 1988): 237–47.

12. Alan Knight, "Mexican Peonage: What Was It and Why Was It?" *JLAS* 18 (May 1986): 41–74; Gonzales, "Chinese Plantation Workers," 392–99, 423–24; William K. Meyers, *Forge of Progress, Crucible of Revolt: Origins of the Mexican Revolution in La Comarca Lagunera* (Albuquerque: University of New Mexico Press, 1994), chaps. 2–3.

13. George Reid Andrews, "Black and White Workers: São Paulo, Brazil, 1888–1928," *HAHR* 68 (August 1988): 493–97, 519–20; Tony Morgan, "Proletarians, Políticos, and Patriarchs: The Use and Abuse of Cultural Customs in the Early Industrialization of Mexico City, 1880–1910," in *Rituals of Rule, Rituals of Resistance: Public Celebrations and Popular Culture in Mexico*, ed. William H. Beezley, Cheryl English Martin, William E. French (Wilmington, DE: Scholarly Resources, 1994), 152–54.

14. Larson, *Agrarian Transformation*, 312–16; Bauer, "Chilean Rural Society," 197–214.

15. Haber, "Industrialization," 10–12; Marichal, *Century of Debt Crisis*, 131–44; Andrews, "Black and White Workers," 493–97, 523–24; Langer, "Abolición de la comunidad indígena," 83–88; Paul Vanderwood, *Disorder and Progress: Bandits, Police and Mexican Development* (Wilmington, DE: Scholarly Resources, 1992).

16. Brennan, "Social Patterns," 10–23, 222–28; Diego Abente, "Foreign Capital, Economic Elites and the State in Paraguay during the Liberal Republic (1870–1936)," *JLAS* 21 (February 1989): 65–68; Wasserman, *Capitalists, Caciques, and Revolution*, 100–1; Scobie, *Buenos Aires*, chap. 4, 177–86; Berry, "Rural Small-Scale Manufacturing," 300–2.

17. Jeremy Adelman, "Agricultural Credit in the Province of Buenos Aires, Argentina, 1890–1914," *JLAS* 22 (February 1990): 72–86; Frederick Vincent Gifun, "Ribeirao Preto, 1880–1914: The Rise of a Coffee County or the Transition to Coffee in São Paulo as Seen Through the Development of Its Leading Producer" (Ph.D. diss., University of Florida, Gainesville, 1972), 41–45, 85–100, 135–36; Meyers, *La Comarca Lagunera*, 28–43, 87–98.

18. Haber, "Industrialization," 17–26.

19. Brennan, "Social Patterns," 161–72; Quiroz, "Peruvian Elite Groups," 60–61, 71–73, 77–81; Worrall, "Italian Immigration to Peru," 184–85.

20. Hodge, "Argentine School System," 47–54; Needell, *Tropical Belle Epoque*, 54–63, 104–6; Matilda Bazant, "Estudianos mexicanos en el extranjero: El caso de los hermanos Urquidi," *HM* 36 (April–June 1987): 739–42; Voss, "Towns and Enterprise," 445–46, 452–53; Scobie, *Buenos Aires*, 129–32.

21. Tinker-Salas, *Transformation of the Border*, 205, 221; Needell, *Tropical Belle Epoque*, 109–15, 163–81.

22. Abente, "Foreign Capital in Paraguay," 62–80; Peter Sollis, "The Atlantic Coast of Nicaragua: Development and Autonomy," *JLAS* 21 (October 1989): 486–90; Gilbert Joseph and Alan Wells, "Summer of Discontent: Economic Rivalry among Elite Factions during the Porfiriato in Yucatán," *JLAS* 18 (November 1986): 258–61; Herman W. Conrad, "Capitalismo y trabajo en las bosques de las tierras bajas tropicales mexicanas: El caso de la industria del chicle," *HM* 36 (January–March 1987): 465–78; Paul J. Dosal, "The Political Economy of Guatemalan Industrialization, 1871–1948: The Career of Carlos P. Novella," *HAHR* 68 (May 1988): 325, 330, 337–40.

23. Meyers, *La Comarca Lagunera*, 96–97; Scobie, *Buenos Aires*, 86–88; Marcos Cueto, "Sanitation from Above: Yellow Fever and Foreign Intervention in Peru, 1919–1932," *HAHR* 72 (February 1992): 6–12.

24. Tinker-Salas, *Transformation of the Border*, 155–60.

25. Andrews, "Black and White Workers," 493–506; Eduardo A. Zimmerman, "Racial Ideas and Social Reform: Argentina, 1890–1916," *HAHR* 72 (February 1992): 223–32; Worrall, "Italian Immigration of Peru," chaps. 3 and 7, 237–38; Darien Davis, "British Football with a Brazilian Beat: The Early History of a National Pastime (1894–1933)," in *English-Speaking Communities in Latin America*, ed. Oliver Marshall (London: Macmillan, 2000), 267–80.

26. Tinker-Salas, *Transformation of the Border*, 224–29; Gonzales, "Chinese Plantation Workers," 406–13, 422–23; Carl Solberg, *Immigration and Nationalism: Argentina and Chile, 1890–1914* (Austin: University of Texas Press, 1970), 40, 66–89, chap. 4; Andrews, "Black and White Workers," 520–23.

27. Brennan, "Social Patterns," 143–60; Voss, "Towns and Enterprise," 526–35.

28. William H. Beezley, "The Porfirian Smart Set Anticipates Thorstein Veblen in Guadalajara," in *Rituals of Rule, Rituals of Resistance: Public Celebrations and Popular Culture in Mexico*, ed. William H. Beezley, Cheryl English Martin, William E. French (Wilmington, DE: Scholarly Resources, 1994), 178–79.

29. Scobie, *Buenos Aires*, 232; Meyers, *La Comarca Lagunera*, 90–91; Beezley, "Porfirian Smart Set," 178–81, 184.

30. Beezley, "Porfirian Smart Set," 184–86; Vaughn, "Primary Education," 43–45; Solberg, *Immigration and Nationalism*, 81–82; Needell, *Tropical Belle Epoque*, 61–81.

31. Lauderdale Graham, *House and Street*, 132–35.

32. Jorge Icaza, *The Villagers (Huasipungo)*, trans. Bernard Dulsey (Carbondale: Southern Illinois University Press, 1964), 135–51, 198–201; Edith B. Couterier, "Hacienda of Hueyapán: The History of a Mexican Social and Economic Institution, 1550–1940" (Ph.D. diss., Columbia University, 1965), chap. 7.

33. Morgan, "Proletarians and Patriarchs," 154, 157–61; Brennan, "Social Patterns," 222–24.

34. Brennan, "Social Patterns," chap. 7; Meyers, *La Comarca Lagunera*, 140–43; David S. Parker, "White-Collar Lima, 1910–1929: Commercial Employees and the Rise of the Peruvian Middle Class," *HAHR* 72 (February 1992): 56–57.

35. Adler Lomnitz and Pérez-Lizaur, *Mexican Elite Family*, 53–103; Ramón Beteta, *Jarano*, trans. John Upton (Austin: University of Texas Press, 1970), 5–66.

36. Lauderdale Graham, *House and Street*, 65, 108–27; David Sowell, "The 1893 'bogotazo': Artisans and Public Violence in Late Nineteenth Century Bogotá," *JLAS* 21 (May 1989): 272–73.

37. Couterier, "Hacienda of Hueyapán," 188–92, 197–216; William E. French, "Progreso Forzado: Workers and the Inculcation of the Capitalist Work Ethic in the Parral Mining District," in *Rituals of Rule, Rituals of Resistance: Public Celebrations and Popular Culture in Mexico*, ed. William H. Beezley, Cheryl English Martin, William E. French (Wilmington, DE: Scholarly Resources, 1994), 192; Beezley, "Porfirian Smart Set," 177, 184; Teresa Meade, "Living Worse and Costing More: Resistance and Riot in Rio de Janeiro, 1890–1917," *JLAS* 21 (May 1989): 243–51.

38. Mariano Azuela, *Two Novels of Mexico*, trans. Lesley Byrd Simpson (Berkeley: University of California Press, 1956), 125–33.

39. Beezley, "Porfirian Smart Set," 184; Lauderdale Graham, *House and Street*, 97–98.

40. Zimmerman, "Racial Ideas," 25–32, 38–41; Voss, "Towns and Enterprise," 312–14, 456–57.

41. Tinker-Salas, *Transformation of the Border*, 217; Vaughn, "Primary Education," 45–49; Virginia Garrand Burnett, "Protestantism in Rural Guatemala," *LARR* 20:2 (1989): 127–31; Deborah Baldwin, "Diplomacía cultural: Escuelas missionales protestantes en México," *HM* 36 (October–December 1986): 287–310.

42. Beezley, "Porfirian Smart Set," 175–77, 185; French, "Capitalist Work Ethic," 192; French, "Prostitutes and Guardian Angels," 535–36, 540–41.

43. Scobie, *Buenos Aires*, 216; Lauderdale Graham, *House and Street*, 5–6; Brennan, "Social Patterns," 201–5; Francie R. Chassen-Lopez, " 'Cheaper than Machines': Women in Agriculture in Porfirian Oaxaca, 1880–1911," in *Women of the Mexican Countryside, 1850–1990*, ed. Heather Fowler-Salamini and Mary Kay Vaughn (Tucson: University of Arizona Press, 1994), 29–31, 36–37, 42.

44. Heather Fowler-Salamini, "Gender, Work, and Coffee in Cordoba, Veracruz, 1850–1910," in *Women of the Mexican Countryside, 1850–1990*, ed. Fowler-Salamini and Mary Kay Vaughn (Tucson: University of Arizona Press, 1994), 52, 58; Chassen-Lopez, "Women in Agriculture," 34–35, 39–43; Lauderdale Graham, *House and Street*, 5–6; Scobie, *Buenos Aires*, 143, 152–53, 216; Brennan, "Social Patterns," 218–21, 233–34.

45. Fowler-Salamini, "Gender, Work, and Coffee," 59–68; Chassen-Lopez, "Women in Agriculture," 39; Scobie, *Buenos Aires*, 143; Andrews, "Black and White Workers," 513–20.

46. Kristan Ruggiero, "Honor, Maternity, and the Disciplining of Women: Infanticide in Late-Nineteenth Century Buenos Aires," *HAHR* 72 (August 1992): 353–57, 365–70; French, "Prostitutes and Guardian Angels," 542–51; David McCreery, " 'This Life of Misery and Shame': Female Prostitution in Guatemala City, 1880–1920," *JLAS* 18 (November 1986): 333–34, 336–39; Lauderdale Graham, *House and Street*, 82–86; Donna Guy, "White Slavery, Public Health, and the Socialist Position on Legalized Prostitution in Argentina, 1913–1936," *LARR* 23:3 (1988): 60–80.

8

The Popular Reaction

In the twentieth century's first years, Brazil's capital underwent a wholesale remaking of its center city. As a rapidly growing population had put increasing stress on housing, sanitation, public health, and open public space, notables had steadily withdrawn to new suburban neighborhoods. However, their work and public affairs remained behind. Innovations in transportation and communication provided a secure link between the two spheres. Still, notables had a firm control only over their private sphere. The conjuncture of political stability, secure financing, their alarm at accumulating social problems, and their fetish with things foreign combined to propel the undertaking of a wholesale urban renewal. In their intent to "reimpose" order on downtown space, reclaiming it for "respectable" people's near exclusive use, they had the federal government's firm support.

The inspiration and model was the transformation of Paris a half century earlier, beset with the bloated population and congestion born of industrialization. For Rio de Janeiro's notables, France and its national capital were the epitome of North Atlantic progress and "civilization." The heart of Rio's urban renewal was the Avenida Central, a spacious boulevard extending nearly a mile and one-quarter in length (and 40 yards wide). In lesser degrees the transformation rippled out along neighboring streets: they were given more uniformity, widened, and paved; and were accompanied by sidewalks, public gardens, and modern services of sanitation, lighting, and transportation. Along the grand boulevard, new public and cultural edifices arose in the Beaux Arts style, including a version of Paris's grand opera house. Most other new construction was similarly styled but in façade only; grafted onto a plain functional building, these ornate fronts created an unintended symbolism of the depth of notable reimaging of the city center.

But from the notables' immediate point of view, it was a vital urban space transformed. Supported by a raft of municipal ordinances, a more effective police force, and the spreading transportation and communications network, Rio's notables rushed to fill this companion sphere to their private estates (joined by *gente decente* to the extent their incomes could afford it). The men managed the family portfolios and public business from commodious offices. Their nearby clubs offered a more relaxed setting for these endeavors, as well as for recreation. The women came in to shop at the trend-setting stores and boutiques or converse with friends and family in choice restaurants, sidewalk cafés, or lovely parks. Children sometimes came along to play and take in the sights or on special occasions joined the rest of the family for dinner out. In the evening, elegant dining might be followed by a bejeweled appearance at the opera, the theater, or a gala.

To make way for the notables' reclamation of the center city, much of the *gente baja*'s world in the old Rio was demolished or circumscribed. Nearly one-half lost their place of dwelling; 590 buildings were demolished in one year alone. In surrounding barrios, overcrowding worsened, as did associated problems of sanitation, public health, and crime. Many were pushed to the city's outskirts, to the emerging hillside *favelas* (slums), or to the industrial zone to the north, where they became dependent on Rio's most outdated and inefficient modes of transportation and struggled to pay the rising fares. Socially and culturally, the center city had been a hodgepodge of different social strata and ethnic groups. Now it was being made singularly the domain of the respectable. Though not wholly successful, municipal ordinances prohibited the petty business around which much of *gente baja* interchange centered, the street-corner gathering places, and various customs and amusements labeled "uncivilized."

In short, the heart of the nation's capital was declared off-limits to *gente baja*, except as workers. Notables judged their general lifestyle unhealthy and inefficient, their consumption patterns semirural, the facades of their dwellings and shops unbecoming, their entertainment vulgar. Few *gente baja* would deny the growing squalor in which so many lived, the deteriorating diet with which they tried to sustain themselves, and the consequences of both that more and more beset their lives—disease, high infant mortality, mental and physical disabilities, and diversionary habits gone destructive. Nevertheless, in their eyes the problem lay not in their own customs and mores. It derived from the new economic forces and political realities over which their leverage was eroding. They did try to negotiate (and resist when they felt necessary), as they had done for decades. But their petitions were dismissed, their grievances left unresolved, their protesting crowds dispersed, their acts of violent resistance crushed.[1]

Through their urban renewal project, Rio's notables were declaring their intention to rid the city of its social ills and impediments to progress. The bane and affront of this to the *gente baja* was twofold. Notables showed little inclination to address those same social ills in spaces to which *gente baja* could still lay claim or were consigned. At the same time, notables were now increasingly bent on rooting out the very customs and mores by which *gente baja* had long sought to order their lives, even in those urban spaces left to them.

The ominous, shifting reality confronting Rio's *gente baja* was engulfing their counterparts throughout Latin America by 1900, in countryside, town, and city. The dynamic commercial, industrial economy was increasingly uprooting their lives and stripping away their leverage in the allocation and remuneration of resources. The notables' growing political hegemony left commoners less and less able to negotiate their grievances. The notables' gospel of North Atlantic civilization and progress threatened to deprive them of any measure of cultural autonomy, any self-determined place in the region and nation of which they were a part. So the *gente baja* reacted, fragmented at first, in disparate places, and employing tested modes of protest and resistance. But then, as they had in the independence struggle, as they had in coming to terms with republican discourse and institutions thereafter, they began adapting to the new realities. They turned to new modes of interpreting their situation, organizing their efforts, and accommodating their interests (especially *gente de profesiones*).

At the same time, growing numbers of *gente decente* were making similar adjustments and in so doing discovering a new identity. In the process they were coming to see their fate more associated with that of those socially beneath them. The line of respectability, although still of import, was becoming overshadowed by a line of exclusiveness and hegemony that notables were drawing above them. Below that line, challenges to the notables' consensus among *gente baja* and *gente decente* became more and more articulated, such that the reaction became a "popular" one. Its commonality was born of situation rather than status.

The Violation of Customary and Negotiated Understandings

The three strands of the notables' consensus forged in the late nineteenth century—a spreading industrial capitalist economy, a growing North Atlantic connection, and a reduction in obligations to and interchange with those below—undermined the negotiated hierarchy that had been the essential foundation of Middle Period society. The rights and obligations of the various social strata, the networks of personal relations, and the shared rituals that had maintained that hierarchy were being discarded. Indeed, from the *gente baja*'s view, they were increasingly violated in the fullest sense of the word. Notables were imposing the new "progressive" hierarchy, not negotiating it. Being steadily uprooted from the security of their accustomed collectivities, increasingly devoid of any political power or economic autonomy, the *gente baja* found themselves little able to hold their own, much less advance.[2] Their customs and mores were scorned, their racial coloration disdained. They might find a legitimate, respected place in the notables' hierarchy, but not as they were, only as the notables said they should become. Even then, many of those same notables were declaring or questioning whether they would ever be fit to make their way in the new era.

Eroding Autonomy

What (in the light of industrial capitalism) notables judged as unproductive, non-rational economic arrangements, *gente baja* saw otherwise. These arrangements meant access and security in terms of the means of production, whether in land, working capital, or labor. They had negotiated or fought to secure and then defend them since independence, generally with success. Rural commoners knew only too well that in access to land lay their greatest economic autonomy and security. Now the most vital of the established arrangements ensuring that access was breaking down around them.

The most secure and autonomous form of land tenure for rural commoners had always been that held by villagers communally. Until 1880 they had been comparatively strong enough to negotiate (or resist when necessary) their way around liberal legislation intended to privatize such landholding. But thereafter in country after country, market incentives combined with the notables' growing political domination and the state's enhanced resources first to carry out privatization and then relentlessly alienate village lands. Laws generally claimed unused or rented communal lands for resale. Government surveyors peeled away undocumented holdings. Lawyers and the courts stripped away a significant portion of the land villagers defended with documents. Debts from court or title fees, from loans for operating expenses, from payment of taxes, and from subsistence and ritual purposes forced the sale of much of the remainder. Though the extent and timing of this land grab varied by region and district, the historical momentum was firmly established.[3]

The same fate was befalling tens of thousands of independent smallholders, whether owners or cash renters (or occupiers) of land. Most had obtained possession or access after independence, either on public lands or lands large estate owners put up for sale or tenancy. But by 1900 more entrepreneurial hacendados—employing mortgaged debt, jacked-up rents, terminated contracts, litigation, and force—were stripping them of much of their autonomy as independent producers.[4]

The lot of many former communal villagers, independent smallholders, and cash-rent tenants was to fall into dependent arrangements. Increasingly, as large estate owners moved to gain greater control over and expand commercial production, they settled on sharecropping as an essential strategy. It added unremunerated laborers (family members), cut substantially the need for cash wages, and offered the recovery of invested capital through extension of credit, sale of supplies, and a monopoly over marketing of the crop. By increasing indebtedness and lowering the committed crop's sale price, hacendados could squeeze out much of the limited autonomy sharecroppers possessed. The latter only had leverage when their numbers were scarce. The subsistence security of resident *peones* and service tenants was confined to the plots of estate land—and often food rations and the use of wood, pastures, and other resources—granted in return for their labor. Large estates, increasingly viewing them as unproductive and costly, retained them only when their need for a permanent labor component and market forces dictated it. Usage grants, when not ended, were made subject to fees. Though not to the same degree, *gente de profesiones* who performed skilled and lower supervisory tasks began to suffer the withdrawal of these perquisites as well.[5]

Even as market opportunities led more and more hacendados to abandon old paternalistic obligations, they produced countervailing pressures that undercut what economic leverage rural workers possessed. The distending labor surplus in most regions (from natural increase, immigration, loss of access to land, and rising impoverishment) left rural workers with declining options. Informal nonhiring agreements among employers (especially for those skilled or indebted) eroded mobility even further. Population growth and the conversion of more and more land to nonfood production (or food for export) drove the cost of living steadily upward, especially after the turn of the century.

In such conditions, rural workers looked for employment that offered continuing access to credit and the protective security of noncapitalist labor practices like food rations and corn plots in return for days of free labor. But through the coercive threat of eviction—and when necessary, the use of spies, armed guards, flogging, and jail— large estate owners steadily moved to restrict their workers' mobility, lengthen their workday, impose far more discipline, and equalize their remuneration and former degrees of hierarchical status. *Gente de profesiones* suffered from these restrictions too, along with the loss of initiative and authority and the imposition of tighter supervision from their superiors.[6]

Unlike their rural counterparts, urban *gente baja* were already immersed fully in the commercial marketplace. And except for the minority (mostly in small towns) who had backyards for gardens and a few animals, they lacked the subsistence cushions possessed by many in the countryside. Only self-employed artisans, shopkeepers, and petty traders among them possessed any other means of production except labor with which to assert some economic autonomy. Even these *gente de profesiones* were finding their position ever more tenuous.

Industrial capitalism (whether by plant or product) was beginning to penetrate even the smallest of towns. Some artisans were able to survive, even to grow in numbers, as they served such buoyant sectors of the economy as transportation, public utilities, construction, printing, and some personal services. Still, few could avoid becoming someone else's employee. Petty traders, cantina operators, and other shopkeepers faced immigrant competition in many regions, unreasonable taxes, and growing public restrictions on the breadth and scope of their operations (in some cases, prohibition). Some prostitutes, in terms of economics and craft (though not in terms of social acceptance), could have been considered a cut above the popular classes who also plied the trade. But as their mobility and independence were proscribed, they joined the much larger number of popular class women confined to regulated brothels, under the tight control of madams and managers who skimmed off most of their income. The great majority were reduced to being "piece" workers in degrading and often brutal conditions.[7]

Even when they could retain a competitive niche or avoid government restrictions, the urban *gente de profesiones'* position was being undermined by the general decline in living standards among both urban and rural commoners (the latter were important consumers in small towns). Basic commodity prices were rising, and real wages were failing to keep pace or falling. Taxes of various sorts were increasing. Notable-dominated governments limited the availability of one potential cushion (improved public services) or provided it at too great a cost. The latter led the popular classes to avoid the services—that is, children were kept from school to provide additional income. Mandated purchases, such as the installation of sanitary plumbing, ate even further into popular class incomes.[8]

Faced with diminishing living standards and a growing labor surplus in all but the highly skilled jobs, the urban popular classes lost most of what little leverage they possessed. The spatial reconfiguration of neighborhood and work only added to this problem, as did the augmented power of government, over which they had less and less influence. As a result, employers could curtail their mobility, subjecting them to the longer hours and stricter, nonreciprocal regimen of industrial work. Their time and subsistence security were being squeezed just like that of rural commoners.

The loss of self-determination in the *gente baja*'s lives, whether urban or rural, was not only economic. Though often less realized than threatened, it was also social and cultural. Protestant missionaries sent out to the Indian villagers in Guatemala were intent on ridding them of their folk Catholic rituals and superstition. Growing numbers of large estate owners began failing to extend ritual kinship ties and to circumscribe or replace customary celebrations. Factory employers, in their zeal to regiment their workforce, also sought to limit such traditional diversions, replacing them with festivities that served the purposes of greater worker loyalty and acquiescence. Most tellingly in urban areas, *gente baja* were losing the battle for control of the streets. The regulation (sometimes the banning) of gambling, fairs, circuses, bullfights, dances, spontaneous parades, and other diversions pushed them out of more and more public spaces, while threatening to deprive them of their accustomed social and cultural ambience in much of the space left to them. If the notables had their way, they alone would determine commoners' social and cultural practices.[9]

A poignant example of the extent to which *gente baja* felt the growing loss of control over their lives can be seen in the sacrifices made by many female servants in Rio de Janeiro at the turn of the century. They were among the majority of servants without sufficient resources to work only days and live on their own. As their notable employers strove to narrow their social world and extend greater supervision over them, they struggled to maintain at least a measure of independence, as tenuous and meager as it might be. They expended up to half their monthly wage just to maintain a separate place clandestinely, even if they could spend only as little as one night a week there.[10]

Disarranged and Uprooted

That the *gente baja*'s mobility in the labor market was deteriorating is not to say that they were not increasingly on the move. A century earlier, their movement had generally been within their region or to neighboring ones, to large estates and provincial cities. Now, with the technological revolution and a much enlarged scale of operations (especially in centers of extractive and monocrop production), the numbers and distances of *gente baja* on the move were on a much larger scale. The large majority moved because they had no other choice. Their eroding economic autonomy—and the growing gap between the cost of living and their income—left them with little bargaining power in whatever commercial agricultural district, extractive center, town, or city they went to look for work. In the process their lives were becoming increasingly disarranged. Rural families in particular were separated, and when they were not, the rhythms of their lives were changed.

New primary production centers in previously underpopulated areas uprooted rural commoners' lives the most. The *chicleros*, who tapped the chewing gum resin in remote tropical forests of southeastern Mexico and were mostly underemployed workers from towns and villages, led an isolated, rudimentary life based in camps. Growing numbers of impoverished Bolivian peasants in the eastern mountain valleys crossed the Andes to work in the nitrate mines of northern Chile. When opportunities began to dry up there after 1910, they moved on to the new tin mines being opened in highland districts in their native country. To escape forced work on nearby haciendas, Chiriguano Indians on Bolivia's eastern frontier migrated to northwestern Argentina to find subsistence-wage work.[11]

A growing number of rural workers were on the move more continually. The vast majority of large employers had long used a mixed labor system, combining resident workers and part-time labor (often a majority); the latter's numbers expanded after 1880. Large numbers were recruited from beyond the immediate area, especially the migrant workers performing seasonal work and then moving on, which had not been the case before the 1880s. In the cotton and guayule (a shrub cultivated as a source of rubber) fields of the Laguna district in northern Mexico, part-time workers, living in small, impoverished communities on the outskirts of towns and railheads, constituted one-third of the rural population by 1910. Migrant workers numbered close to 40,000. Much of the huge demographic increase in the booming coffee district of Córdoba in east-central Mexico (soaring from 26,000 in 1877 to 91,000 in 1910) was made up of impoverished rural families migrating from the central highlands. At the same time, the growing poverty of peasants native to the district led more and more males in those families to migrate out, particularly to work on the sugar plantations of Morelos. The women remained at home, comprising nearly one-third of the farmers in the district. Many more were forced to find work outside the confines of the rural household.[12]

Despairing rural commoners in the *sertão* (backlands) of northeastern Brazil in the 1890s found an island refuge of hope in a sea of upheaval. Severe drought and government's inexorable penetration from the coast in the form of higher taxes, adverse regulation of fairs, secularization laws, and increased threat of the military draft were disassembling their world. In 1893, a failed *gente decente* admiringly called Conselheiro began a small, egalitarian community striving for economic and cultural autonomy, rooted in the region's folk culture, and infused later with a messianic vision. Canudos, as the town came to be called, tripled in population in the mid-1890s, reaching 15,000.[13]

Nevertheless, throughout Latin America there were few such rural havens (and that at Canudos was short-lived). Finding the alternatives unavailable, unsustainable, or unbearable, ever larger numbers of rural *gente baja* headed to the towns and cities. Some moved as parts of families; others left families. Singleness was increasing. The large majority of migrants, like most of those already rooted in urban life, found little employment security in the fluctuating, labor-saturated economies prevalent in most urban areas. Their existence remained precarious, generating a rise in mortality (especially among males and infants), mental illness, trauma, and abuse. Many found they had to keep moving to another neighborhood, another town, or another city.[14]

There was a counterpoint to this amplifying theme of disarrangement in the lives of the *gente baja*. Districts and regions where Indian community solidarity held firm, as among the villages of Chayanta province in Bolivia's southern highlands, largely kept their existing way of life intact. But there, defiant resistance faced only lukewarm market incentives, unlike in Guatemala's highlands. The most remote villages were spared, but the remainder at best were able to compromise only their time, performing seasonal labor in return for being left alone. Some sought to adjust by engaging in small-scale coffee production on their own plots, or they withdrew to more remote areas to begin again. But non-Indians soon followed, steadily acquiring their land and labor. Mestizo squatter settlements in Venezuela's western Andes held on a bit longer, largely thanks to that country's political instability until the 1910s. Then, a strong national government (through privatization and an alliance with local notables) reduced the vast majority of independent smallholders to cash-rent tenancy.[15]

Faring far better were areas where a protagonistic peasantry had taken hold. Economic constraints on notable entrepreneurs in central Colombia (primarily limited transportation and credit sources and scarce labor) benefited service tenants on coffee estates. By the 1910s, a peasant household economy was becoming embedded in the region. It had been so in the Cochabamba region of Bolivia's eastern mountain valleys for more than a century. Privatization of communal lands only added to the numbers of small-scale cultivators, whose blend of subsistence and commercial activities shielded them from the impact of free trade and railroads on highland grain markets. These petty producers' increased leverage over hacendados continued through the early twentieth century. Still, there was a long-term problem for such peasant producers: population was outrunning available land. Those unable to maintain the upper hand in the resulting growing social differentiation would slip into the ranks of landless laborers and tenants or be forced to migrate.[16]

In many of Latin America's urban barrios, though under growing pressures, the accustomed continuity and stability in *gente baja* lives endured. More commonly, these were the neighborhoods where artisans and shopkeepers survived in significant numbers. Their craft shops, corner stores, cantinas, and billiard halls (and, one might add, brothels) continued to serve as important places of social interchange and expressions of popular culture. For rural migrants, especially, these areas had some of the feel of the village life in which they felt most comfortable.[17] But here, too, the intruding forces of industrial capitalism, an ever more vigorous state, and a modernizing cosmopolitan culture seemed to press relentlessly. Their effects were far from uniform, as were the *gente baja*'s responses to them.

Fragmentation and Commonality amid a Broadening Sense of *lo Popular*

Divisions among the *gente baja* were long-standing and many. Race and ethnicity, the urban-rural dichotomy, the basis of access to land, the degree of freedom in rendering labor, and to a lesser extent gender had all shaped the formation of subgroupings. A fundamental split was between the *gente de profesiones* and the popular classes. Now, these century-old divisions were again being altered. In some cases, the historical forces propelled by the notables' consensus intensified them.

Of greater import, those forces metamorphosed other divisions such that the very lines of social stratification that had characterized Middle Period society began to be reconfigured. That reconfiguration was also owing to the emergence of new sources of common ground among various segments of the *gente baja* and even the *gente decente*.

Changing Divisions among the Gente Baja

The surge of large-scale immigration after 1880, accompanied by racial determinist theories from the North Atlantic, elaborated and aggravated racial-ethnic divisions. Economic competition for land and jobs heightened the sense of separateness. As much lifestyle as purely biological, the dissonance between Indians and mestizos appears to have somewhat deepened, especially where Indian communities strove to hang on to communal solidarity and traditional syncretic culture and in urban areas, where Indians became seen as wholly rural by definition.[18]

The division between white and nonwhite commoners (which had largely dissipated except where slavery continued) reappeared in some regions as large-scale European immigration arrived. Professing the doctrines of scientific racism, Brazilian notables created a surplus of labor and drove a wedge between those of African descent (especially ex-slaves) and European immigrants. In general, they marginalized blacks economically and socially, but they were quick to hire them as strikebreakers, aggravating this racial division. Elsewhere in eastern and southern South America, the distinction was drawn between European immigrants and the *gente baja* more generally, who were perceived by the respectable as being of mixed blood. Gauchos and urban migrants vied with immigrants for jobs in factories and fields and sparred culturally with one another on streets and in cantinas. Even among immigrants, ethnic loyalties fostered separate communities. Though small in number, immigrants from the United States—by disseminating that nation's accentuated racial attitudes and patterns of segregation after 1880—divided commoners with Indian or white ancestry from those of African descent and blacks from mulattoes.[19]

South and East Asian contract laborers in various regions of the Caribbean Basin and much of the west coast of South America also established communities that were economically and culturally at odds with native-born *gente baja*. In addition, immigrants were moving from one part of Latin America to another. Thousands of West Indian laborers, recruited to work on banana plantations in eastern coastal areas of Central America and on the Panama Canal, encountered considerable racial discrimination. In return, the black immigrants formed a rather closed community, condescendingly insisting that their offspring were British subjects. In Honduras, the government fostered a strong anti–West Indian workers policy, and labor-organizing strategies relied on racial discrimination. Black immigrants were singled out as a main cause of Honduran workers' plight. Hostility was directed also at the influx of over 12,000 Salvadorans in the 1920s, reinforcing the repatriation campaign.[20]

Divisions along gender lines rarely became so divisive among commoners. After 1880, on a scale in aggregate numbers and a proportion of the work force much greater than a century earlier, rural *gente baja* women were being drawn in rapidly growing numbers to work for others outside the confines of the rural household. Their labor was seen as supplemental and temporary, and their wages were usually half that of their male counterparts. The stated employer rationale was the general belief that women could do only 50–60 percent as much work as men; the underlying calculation was that they had hardly any leverage (except in times of labor scarcity) to demand anything greater. The end result was increased gender differentiation in the division of labor.[21]

Gente baja women's impact in the urban labor force was less marked. A high proportion had worked as domestics and laundresses since the rise in urban growth in the late eighteenth century. As urbanization accelerated after 1880 (and *gente alta* families multiplied generationally and in correlation with the expanding commercial-industrial economy), the numbers of domestics and laundresses rose dramatically. In Buenos Aires, they jumped from nearly 30,000 in 1887 to nearly 93,000 in 1914. Though smaller in number, far greater in impact for gender divisions in the labor force were the growing numbers of women leaving preindustrial, household-integrated activities to work in factories, where they received only one-half of men's wages.[22] They joined the significant number of women who had been recruited to work in the first modern factories after 1850.

Most profound and consequential were those divisions among the *gente baja* resulting from their changing relation to the means of production. In rural areas, the fundamental split emerging was between those whose labor was still linked to access to resources and the rising numbers of those whose labor was not. The situation in the production process of resident *peones*, service tenants, or sharecroppers bespoke the past, when a large ongoing workforce was required. The proliferating numbers of temporary and migrant workers, in contrast, pointed to the future. Though independent wage laborers, they were hired on the cheap, insecurely tenured, and subject to harsher working conditions than resident laborers. Many commuted from within their own locality. More and more left their homes seasonally (or for longer periods of time) or moved periodically in and out of the impoverished communities springing up on the outskirts of towns, extraction centers, and railheads. They constituted a rural proletariat in formation upon whom employers relied more and more.[23]

In Latin America's towns and especially its cities, labor's separation from the other means of production had occurred a century earlier (a process completed in the years after independence in areas where slavery was retained). Now, the industrialization of the economy was undermining the position and status of the *gente de profesiones* that had set them apart from other urban commoners. At the same time, it was augmenting the status of some segments of those popular classes.

The technological revolution and the notables' commitment to ending internal commercial barriers left growing numbers of artisans (in an expanding number of crafts) in a losing battle with industrial manufacturing. Tailors, weavers, shoemakers, blacksmiths, coopers, and food preparers in particular were vulnerable. Even where they did manage to hang on, it was with shrinking incomes from price competition and the general decline in popular class living standards. By contrast, those whose trades were needed by the more dynamic sectors (especially construction and the new, modern utilities and transport services) grew in numbers and even generally prospered. The fortunes of those with a marked stake in the industrialization process and its support systems improved as well. The range of their skills and training varied, their jobs required few of their own tools, and their tenure was highly subject to the fluctuations of the markets and business cycles, but when employed they had leverage and received the highest wages. When transport workers, dockworkers, miners, utility workers, and factory machine operators disrupted the flow of business activity, employers and government officials took notice.[24] It was from these two segments of the *gente baja*—prospering craft artisans and industrial-related workers—that a new social strata was beginning to form.

Artisans and shopkeepers had long played a pivotal role in Middle Period society as economic, political, and cultural mediators between the popular classes and the *gente alta*. That continued to be the case in varied conflicts across Latin America generated by the imposition of the notables' consensus. In contrast, the newly emerging social stratum among the urban *gente baja* was steadily distancing itself from its fellow urban commoners. These workers more readily adapted to the modern industrial norms of employment and advancement within large production units and of an advanced division of labor. Increasingly, they sought to reform those norms, focusing grievances on working conditions and wages rather than on consumption and popular class concerns about the general deterioration in the quality of life. They relied more and more on formal organizations to press their interests. They also organized for cultural purposes; craft artisans generally provided the backbone for such endeavors. In sponsoring and attending night school and more "cultivated" entertainment, they revealed their proclivity toward disproving the *gente alta*'s disparaging view of them and gaining respect and acceptance as members of progressive society in good standing. At the same time, they sought to modify and refashion positivism's moralizing discourse in accordance with some experiences and notions shared with other *gente baja*.[25] Still, in economic and cultural orientation, these craft and industrial-related workers had begun to form a modern working class.

Emerging Common Ground

In both city and countryside, the ultimate consequence of the spreading industrial capitalist economy—a declining standard of living leading to impoverishment for many—provided a basis for solidarity in some situations. So, too, did the *gente baja*'s own perceptions of individual rights and of public authorities' accountability. Workers shared common experiences: a regimented workweek; abusive managers and unjust practices at the company store; and the need to focus tactically and collectively on demanding improvements when conditions were favorable rather than when desperate living conditions provoked protests. Such common experiences fostered solidarity among previously hostile racial-ethnic groups, at least in the workplace and sometimes beyond it. In Costa Rica, common workplace grievances among West Indian immigrants and native *gente baja* replaced racial-cultural differences after 1920. Native Costa Ricans included West Indians in their labor movement, and the latter assumed a broader vision of their place in the nation's economy and society.[26]

In the countryside there was an emerging broadened consciousness within the various sectors of the *gente baja*, but little solidarity among them to bridge their racial and economic differences. Tenants and sharecroppers engaged in strikes. Village farmers and migrant workers staged on-going resistance and sometimes violent protests and uprisings. But rarely were these interconnected. Even in the Mexican Revolution of 1910, where movements national in scope vied with one another, rural divisions were very much in evidence. The huge egalitarian community of Canudos did bring together a cross-section of commoners in Brazil's northeastern backlands. But perhaps because it did so, notable-led authorities moved quickly to brutally eliminate it.[27]

A more important, continuing source of common ground derived from *gente baja* subsistence strategies, more so in regions where their occupational and geographic mobility was less constricted. By deriving incomes from varied economic activities, they were trying to turn to their advantage the very accelerating technological innovation, scale of production, and specialization of labor that was uprooting and fragmenting their lives. Many individuals and families combined a subsistence plot of land with seasonal or part-time work on a large estate, in a mining center, on the railroads, or in craft workshops or factories in towns or even cities. In other cases, individual *gente baja* (either for their families or themselves alone) moved from job to job sequentially over the course of several years. This trend not only broadened the consciousness of rural and urban commoners alike; it also forged the basis for potential alliances when circumstances propelled them toward collective action.[28]

The notables' alliance with the North Atlantic world—economic, demographic, and cultural—spawned another source of common ground among the *gente baja*. The breadth and longevity with which this alliance now affected their lives defined more clearly and comprehensively the nationalism awakened previously in conflicts with armed foreign forces and spread it more widely. Commoners were compelled to delineate what it meant to be a citizen or inhabitant of a nation, if they wished it not to become foreign. In doing so, they sorted through and elevated their own regional and racial traditions for articulation with the accumulating rituals and customs arising from the experiences of the nation since independence. The resulting deepened, more pervasive sense and spirit of nationalism increasingly infused their worldview and public actions after 1900.[29]

Gente Decente: *No Longer in Waiting*

Gente baja were not alone in their resentment animated by heightened nationalist feelings. From independence, *gente decente* had possessed a well-defined sense of the nation beyond their region, frequently acting to help shape its development. Now they felt their nation falling more and more under the grip of foreigners, and with it the denial of their own personal prospects. It was bad enough that North Atlantic immigrants were assuming increasing control over the principal business enterprises, deepening the nation's dependency, weakening its citizens'

self-confidence, and in some countries quite possibly leading to territorial loss or even political dependence. But on a personal level, they
felt cheated. Escalating foreign penetration threatened to limit the
chances of attaining their ultimate goal: becoming notables. More immediately and acutely, they felt their respectable livelihood endangered.
Foreigners were opening up modest commercial establishments that
were grabbing off the trade of commoners in particular, though regionally this trend varied considerably in scope. They were also setting up local manufacturing establishments and were often first chosen
to fill managerial, technical, and clerical positions. Their professional
practices were proliferating.

Very few *gente decente* entertained the notion that this success resulted from foreigners' superior ability or character. Many conceded
that such a rationale applied to the nonrespectable, but not to them.
Moreover, many of those foreigners getting ahead at their expense were
not even from the North Atlantic. They were Chinese, Syrians, Leba-
nese, and Jews. No, the foreigners' success, they said and wrote with
increasing frequency, was the product of notable and foreigner favoritism in hiring, contracting, and funding. *Gente decente* claimed that it
stemmed from unfair and unseemly practices: overstocking and un-
derselling, often with shoddy goods; gouging terms of credit; and cheat-
ing on weights and measures. Most grating, perhaps, was the fact that
foreign employees were often paid higher salaries for the same work
or in gold or silver instead of in depreciating paper money.[30]

The impact of proliferating foreign presence was part of a larger,
more pressing *gente decente* preoccupation: how to maintain their respectability in the face of the squeeze created by incomes not keeping
pace with rising expenses. Income's importance was steadily mounting because the norms of respectability that signaled and confirmed
their status were not only cultural but very much material. Those standards, which reflected the idealized notable lifestyle they hoped one
day to achieve, were rising along with their cost: imported clothing,
the cultivation of certain interests (such as sports), housing befitting
their station in space and decor, non-working wife, privately schooled
children, and domestic servants. Rising inflation, an increased tax burden that they widely held to be discriminatory, and growing indebtedness were leaving many *gente decente* surviving from paycheck to
paycheck. For the better paid, prolonged illness or loss of employment
portended a precarious, perhaps untenable hold on respectability.
Notable-dominated governments often did not provide the public services (especially in health and sanitation) that might have alleviated
some of their worries.[31]

Ironically, the very forces that in both perception and actuality endangered *gente decente* status were also enlarging their numbers. The expanding corporate organization of business required augmented numbers of *empleados* (salaried white-collar workers). As managers, bookkeepers, sales personnel, and retail clerks, their requisite skills in mathematics, writing, and handling specialized knowledge bespoke their advanced education. Personal recommendations (based to a great extent on family ties), client connections with notables, and common formative experiences marked other aspects of their claim to respectability. Expanding government bureaucracies also offered growing opportunities, especially in office personnel, education, and lower-level administrative positions. The economy's general growth necessitated more retail stores and professional services.[32]

The *gente decente*'s growing numbers reduced the odds of their individual advancement to the ranks of the notables. The latter's own expanding families and their hold on government lowered the odds even further. Waiting to become a notable, as had been their custom, seemed less and less plausible. The *gente decente* were more and more frustrated with that reality (added to that of a more tenuous hold on respectability), which fueled their resentment against those they held responsible for it—foreigners and especially notables. This notable action and *gente decente* reaction amplified the social distance and hardened the prior, relatively pliant line separating them as *gente alta*.

At the same time, the line between *gente decente* and *gente baja* was softening, not because the former had any diminished sense of respectability, but because their composition was changing. The proportion of *gente decente* offspring and fallen prominent families was decreasing markedly. In their place, depending upon regional demographics, were foreigners (especially their children) and those of mixed blood who were rising from the ranks of the *gente de profesiones* through education, economic acumen, or good fortune.[33] The newcomers were less determined to seek notability and more focused on securing their respectability.

Gente decente (whether newcomers or of families with established credentials) increasingly realized that many long-standing assumptions about the workings of Middle Period society no longer appeared valid. By the early twentieth century, race and family had declined in importance. Client connections with notables were proving less and less reliable and harder to clinch. Instead, increasingly it was income that enabled them to keep up respectable appearances, especially for the majority who were salaried or remunerated for contracted services. In turn, occupations and posts providing that income were becoming more and more based on advanced education and training.

As a consequence of these altering perceptions about their place in Middle Period society, the *gente decente* began to discern distinct interests that distinguished them from both commoners below and notables above. In the spreading industrial capitalist economy, the power to market their goods and skills for sufficient income—along with greater regularity and prestige of occupation—set them above the *gente baja*. Diminishing ability to increase that economic power distanced them more and more from the notables. In this awareness of essentially class-based social distinctions lies the emergence of ever-increasing numbers of the *gente decente* as a middle class. This process began in such countries as Argentina, Brazil, and Chile at the end of the nineteenth century and continued into the mid–twentieth century, when it took hold among the smaller, less industrialized countries and peoples of the Caribbean Basin.

This emerging middle class assumed an increasingly more activist role in public affairs. Working collectively, their efforts were directed toward clearly delineating and securing their interests and distinct place in society. As they did so, their discourse changed. They began to speak of class-based social divisions and refer to themselves as "middle class." They censured notables for allowing foreigners so much influence, for using government almost exclusively for their own private gain and to the neglect of badly needed services for others. They called for reforms to break up monopolistic practices, open up politics, and address mounting social and economic grievances—but not only their own.[34]

In the *gente decente*'s new frame of mind and through the industrializing economy's very workings, their lives were becoming more intertwined with those of commoners (though not out of their desire for it). With greater frequency, they shared *gente baja* concerns about better remuneration, reduced and more controlled times of work, and lower consumer prices while insisting their material needs were different. From often close contact in their lines of work, *gente decente* came to know them more and more as mineworkers, millhands, farm laborers, transport workers, village farmers, and sharecroppers, each with their specific list of grievances against the notables' hegemony. They saw commoners' lives being uprooted as the dynamic industrial capitalist economy sorted them out into economic interest groups. They knew firsthand in fields, factory floors, stores, and offices (far more than the notables) the growing ferment building up from below. It alarmed them and yet attracted them.[35] For though the *gente baja*'s perceived needs were judged distinct, the causes for their grievances were seen as related and sometimes even similar. This broadened sense of mutual interests at odds with the notables' hegemony expanded the notion of *lo popular* (that which was of the people) to include the *gente decente*, especially as they became a middle class. From their perspective, the political and economic structures (along with the cultural discourse) that had evolved under the notables' consensus had to be reformed for the welfare of "the people." Nevertheless, the reform's extent and its allocation of benefits were not so clear.

In matters of behavior, *gente decente* were appalled by what they perceived as causing the mounting transience in commoners' lives: the increasing breakdown in *gente baja* morality (or, more subjectively, an intensification of their proclivity toward improper behavior). Still, along with their condemnation, they strove to reverse this trend and transform *gente baja* behavior. Concrete expressions of receptivity to this moralizing discourse and signs of self-improvement among many of the *gente de profesiones* and embryonic working class spurred the reformers on. That gave *gente decente* hope of a common cultural ground among "the people," even as they stressed their own superior practice of that morality and greater sophistication in expressing that progressive culture.[36]

In this emerging association of interests, both *gente decente* and *gente baja* faced a common choice in the manner in which they would react to the notables' positivist vision for their society. In the resolution of this choice, the emerging working and middle classes within this popular reaction would find the most success and the most common ground.

The Crucial Dilemma

As the notables' determination to impose their will steadily unraveled the uneasy equilibrium that had given balance and stability to Middle Period society, those below in the social hierarchy increasingly faced a crucial dilemma. Of course, for those enthusiastically endorsing the notables' new vision, for those acquiescing to it, or for those too afraid or feeling powerless to challenge it, there was no choice to make. But for mounting numbers of *gente baja* (and of *gente decente*, though delayed somewhat), the choice was a very real and fateful one. Should they rely on traditional means of resistance, which had served them well in the past? Or should they commit themselves to creating new forms of resistance by adapting the very formal associated structures that notables were employing so successfully in forging their hegemony? Those in the countryside were prone to choose the former, only adopting new forms to any significant degree after 1920. Among urban segments, their use became widely adopted only after the turn of the century, and then they were concentrated among the emerging working and middle classes. Whichever means of resistance they chose—traditional or modern—the outcome often did not follow from their initial intention. And in the process, they themselves were transformed.

Traditional Resistance

From the late imperial period, *gente baja* had taken action (especially in times of economic crisis) when their subsistence was threatened by what they perceived as avarice in pursuit of private gain pushed beyond acceptable limits, or when their social betters tried to intrude unjustly on mores and practices they held dear. When rural and urban commoners moved to reverse the material and cultural aggrandizement, they generally first employed formal petitions or peaceful protests to call attention to their grievances. The focus was usually on a single issue in a particular neighborhood or community. When ignored by the private parties or officials involved, they turned to the threat of force. If their demands still went unmet, they resorted to purposeful and selective violence. Not infrequently, other social strata supported them until the eruption of violence and government repression unraveled it.[37] After independence, *gente de profesiones*, when not initiating the resistance themselves, continued playing a pivotal role as leaders and intermediaries of the popular classes. The necessity of multistrata coalitions grew, and their scope spatially and programmatically was enlarged.

Not surprisingly, then, most *gente baja* turned to this tried and tested response to challenge the imposition of the notables' consensus. Small farmers, especially communal villagers in regions heavily populated by Indians, readily employed the full range of traditional strategies and tactics in the face of proliferating land seizures. They petitioned state and national government to reverse prejudicial legislation or unfavorable court rulings, often hiring lawyers. They also called on government to intervene when local notables and officials went outside the law to take their land or deprive them of access to other resources they had long used. In doing so, they frequently received support from local artisans, shopkeepers, and modest farmers with whom they did business or who also felt the threat of losing access to resources. When pressed, smallholders took matters into their own hands. They suspended any labor obligations, attacked the property and agents of large estate owners or the government, and took up armed defense of their own communities. Ultimately, they resorted to rural uprisings, broadening to the district and even regional level. For some, armed resistance proved a successful long-term holding action. For most, it only delayed land alienation into the near future. For others, it resulted in immediate repression.[38]

The landless also engaged in militant protests and selective violence, especially after 1900. The swelling groups of dispossessed were joined by *peones* whose usufruct plots had been converted to commercial production and by rural laborers. They massed together to demand higher wages, lower rents, lower company-store prices, and restoration of noncash benefits. When they felt desperate or sensed government authority weakening, they occupied estate and public lands. In small bands, not a few turned to banditry. Nonwhite veterans of Cuba's independence war rustled estate livestock and attacked country stores. They combined forces to mount major operations against foreign-owned infrastructure, large sugar and tropical fruit plantations, and refineries, receiving considerable support from the local population. In Mexico, bandits became legitimate revolutionaries, joining millions of rural commoners (with only partial, spotty success) to restore lost lands and to break the haciendas' power in by far the greatest expression of rural resistance.[39]

In Latin America's urban centers, *gente baja* resistance was somewhat more uniform. The growing threat to subsistence maintenance centered on the cost of basic necessities in food, housing, and transportation. The notables' stepped-up efforts to impose changes in their lifestyle (aided by a far more concentrated population and a government more present than in the countryside) added to their frustration. Urban commoners initially sought relief in customary ways. They took to the streets, mocking and hurling insults at targets of their frustration: suppliers of basic necessities deemed unjustly priced and, even more, agents of authority failing to uphold *gente baja* interests in the matter or trying to force *gente alta* behavioral sensibilities on their lifestyle. When pressed, they formed large crowds to parade through the streets to make their demands more visible. Sometimes they submitted petitions, often penned and presented by members of the *gente de profesiones*. When increasingly after 1880, officials dismissed their petitions, police dispersed crowds, and grievances were left unresolved, the popular classes (sometimes joined by segments of the *gente de profesiones*) then turned to selective violence. Rio de Janeiro's *gente baja* targeted streetcars, whose erratic service and escalating fares epitomized the inflation and neglect eating away at their already meager living standard. A law requiring smallpox vaccination triggered a general urban riot there in 1904.[40]

The riot in Rio also embodied another characteristic of traditional *gente baja* resistance. A multistrata coalition formed around the general protest. However, when urban renewal of the center city provided *gente decente* with improved services, the alliance of grievances largely disintegrated. Indian villagers in Bolivia's central highlands incurred a worse fate in supporting a liberal-federalist revolt in the hope of arresting the alienation of their lands. Their *gente alta* allies, once triumphant, betrayed them; suppression of Indian military forces in bringing the war to a close dealt their resistance a mortal blow. The same outcome befell the autonomous utopian community of Canudos in Bahia, Brazil.[41]

Associative Action

Alongside these traditional forms of *gente baja* resistance, new patterns were beginning to appear, though irregularly and haltingly at first. In the 1880s and 1890s, agrarian radicals in Mexico—of *gente decente* and *gente de profesiones* origins and drawing heavily on libertarian socialist ideology emanating from Europe—strove with very gradual success to build a system of agrarian cooperatives linked together through village congresses in the states. In Buenos Aires, a general lack of unity doomed both efforts in the 1890s to organize tenant committees and a spontaneous citywide tenant strike in 1907.[42] *Gente baja* generally were slow to adopt such new means of resistance, being unaccustomed to any formal, impersonal, ongoing voluntary association. The communal village was the only cooperative body among them that resembled it, and its binding force was neither impersonal nor voluntary. The new, modern forms of organization began to be taken up by two particular segments, one long-standing and the other newly emerging.

The foundation for organization among artisans stretched back to the guilds of the colonial order. However, their modern roots lay in the mutual aid societies that began to appear in the mid–nineteenth century (most notably in Mexico and Colombia). As growing industrialized competition undermined their livelihoods, all these organizations provided personal assistance to members, many came to undertake educational endeavors, and some established savings banks. They also entered the political arena from time to time, writing articles for newspapers and pamphlets and practicing direct political action. But by 1880, mutual aid societies had begun increasingly to center their concerns on labor issues, extolling the worth and societal contribution of those engaged in manual labor and stressing reform of or even resistance to the spreading industrial capitalist order to defend their collective interests. In some regions, students (some of artisan origin) imbued with various socialist and anarchist ideas played a role in this ideological and strategic transition. In others, the infusion came from immigrant workers and intellectuals. Yet efforts to construct permanent labor organizations spanning cities, districts, and regions met with little success before 1900. More moderate artisans (generally in the most prestigious crafts and especially proprietors) did at times support surprisingly militant action. But they remained cautious about entrusting their fortunes to then radical forms of labor organizations.[43]

Not so were the growing numbers of craft artisans employed by or directly serving the dynamic industrial-driven sectors of the economy and even less so the multiplying numbers of skilled and semiskilled workers who came to those sectors outside the craft tradition. The income of this emerging working class was almost wholly tied to their wages, and in work stoppages they found they had some leverage, especially when the economy was on an upswing. In some regions and countries, notable employers and government officials fostered the organization of workers (primarily mutual aid societies), trying to stem their independent mobilization.[44]

The initial expressions of this new labor movement were in often poorly organized, almost spontaneous work stoppages that grew in number and sophistication through the late nineteenth century. This militant form of action broadened into the general strike in the first decade of the twentieth century. Guided by the radical, heavily politicized discourse of anarchist supporters, the largely autonomous local labor organizations were brought together in massive confrontations with authorities to force wholesale changes in economic relations. Systematic state repression was the primary outcome, though some labor legislation was introduced (but often left without enforcement). To counter that scale of force, labor leaders moved to tighten their organizational control of members and weld existing disparate groups into mass district, regional, or even national federations. Notable unity and government use of co-optation strategies also put a premium on coordination, cohesive organization and planning, and flexible tactics stressing negotiated improvements in wages and working conditions. This favored the syndicalist branch of the growing labor movement, which rose to dominance in the 1910s and 1920s as a rising proportion of craft and industrial workers became firmly rooted in trade union membership. By then, the transition to industrial manufacturing in the formal economy had been completed and working-class consciousness raised (above all, by the anarchists).[45] This process was delayed in most smaller and less industrialized countries.

The emerging middle class could not help but take serious stock of the rising organization and radicalization of the new working class. On the one hand, they were frightened by it. From a traditional *gente alta* perspective, they feared its potential for degenerating into social chaos. Of more immediate concern was the growing possibility that the line of respectability that separated them from these organized workers might become blurred beyond distinction. Strikes and collective bargaining were beginning to win shorter hours and somewhat higher wages, with which workers donned clothing of a *gente decente* cut and sought more schooling and refined entertainment. On the other hand, the trade union movement demonstrated how, through voluntary associations, those beset by inflation-eroding living standards and depersonalized work relations could defend their interests.[46]

Still, the *gente alta* ideal of personal ties, mutual loyalty in economic relations, and a shared lifestyle of respectability was not easily reconciled with the trade union's organizational strategy and strike tactic. Thus, initially the *gente decente* followed the lead of the artisans' mutual aid societies, some having participated individually, often serving in the leadership. By 1900, they had begun to form their own mutual aid societies based on their particular common economic interest. Self-employed *gente decente*—a segment coming more slowly to a middle-class identity—began to follow the notables' lead in forming voluntary associations. Organizations formed by physicians, middling merchants, and modest farmers petitioned and lobbied government to protect their interests.[47]

It was among *gente decente* who were employees that middle-class identity first crystallized and voluntary associations took on a more militant character. A mutual aid society organized by Peruvian commercial *empleados* in 1903 became a vehicle for defending and promoting the economic interests of white-collar workers in general within a few years. When a workers-led general strike in January 1919 secured an eight-hour day, *empleados* began to hold meetings and demonstrations to protest their unequal treatment, spurred on by a group of young employees who spoke in a new class-based discourse. That September they organized a strike of their own, winning a pay raise and shorter hours and inspiring continued organizing to secure pensions and other protective legislation. Yet in doing so, they pulled back from trade union organization and collective bargaining, instead lobbying for moderate reform. The Empleado Law of 1924 secured several important benefits, legally defined the customary distinction between white-collar employees and *obreros* (workers), and universalized benefits previously reserved for only the most senior employees, thereby achieving a degree of job security and class identity never before envisioned.[48]

Reconciling Means to Ends

The experience of Lima's white collar workers reveals that ends and means were frequently at cross-purposes as growing segments of the *gente baja* and *gente decente* turned to voluntary associations to counter notable hegemony. Even when they relied on traditional forms of resistance, the experience itself often (whether soon or eventually) took them in directions not previously intended or imagined. Brazil's ex-slaves, determined to avoid slavish work in a free wage system, demanded conditions as far from slavery as possible, especially an end to women and children working. By contrast, immigrants saw that working in family units was the only path to building a nest egg for future mobility. With a growing labor surplus, Afro-Brazilians bargained themselves into economic marginalization in the new industrial capitalist economy. Those who did turn to associative action compounded that marginalization politically. The Black Guard spawned a number of informally affiliated groups in several states in response to the efforts of many notables to institute new systems of forced labor, harsh vagrancy laws, and forced military recruitment to control former slaves. But their alliance with monarchists and their increasing turn to violent resistance deepened *gente alta* notions of black inability to act responsibly. In the voluntary associations that emerged in succeeding decades to challenge the notables, Afro-Brazilians were all but excluded.[49]

Villagers in central and southern Mexico, who formed the core of Emiliano Zapata's revolutionary movement in the 1910s, hoped to restore the significant degree of autonomy they had struggled to attain after independence, culminating in the War of the Reform (1858–1860). They envisioned a nation rooted in local autonomy centered in the free *municipio* and cemented by truly federative and democratically representative relations. But with Zapata's treacherous assassination and his *gente decente* "secretaries" soon assuming direction of the movement, the villagers were steadily integrated into agrarian political parties dependently allied with a new centralizing government in Mexico City.[50]

The labor movement in Latin America was also initially rooted in local, independent action and inspired by anarchist discourse that denounced industrial capitalism's centralizing corporate patterns. Yet in challenging that system, the emerging working class increasingly found that rather than being able to overthrow it or transform it, organized workers were more and more having to come to terms with it. General strikes (in most countries) or even armed revolution (as in Mexico) won only limited concessions. An increasingly pragmatic trade unionism (syndicalism) came to dominate the labor movement. Concerns became more parochial. Labor organization became more centralized and its leadership more hierarchical and more distant from its members. Politically, no independent labor organization could sustain itself. The working class was forced steadily into the role of client ally of those who controlled (or aspired to control) the state.[51]

As they evolved after 1900, Latin American labor movements found their social goals confined as well. The emerging working class (especially its leaders in varying degrees) initially envisioned itself as a vanguard among the *gente baja*. In published and spoken discourse, it claimed to speak for a much broader spectrum of the society. In militant action, principally the organization of general strikes, it incorporated popular class grievances. Yet such militant associative action produced unintended outcomes, as in Ecuador's first general strike in Guayaquil in 1922. The first independent, radical labor organization—constituting itself as a regional federation early that year in the port city amid a growing economic crisis—sought to broaden the workers' movement by incorporating general reforms for the popular classes, including an end to the sugar monopoly and to certain taxes, distribution of unused land to peasants, and repeal of a hike in trolley car fares. Masses of unorganized laborers responded, but in the traditional mode of a spontaneous *gente baja* uprising, provoking a brutal military repression. Trolley car workers held out, negotiating shorter hours and pay raises. But popular class grievances and those of other sectors of organized workers (who had returned to work discouraged) went unmet. Although it had been tactically sympathetic to workers' efforts to organize, the government now labeled them "bolshevik." Major labor leaders were forced into exile, the federation broke up, and what organized movement remained became intimidated and cautious.[52]

Gente decente were also encountering difficulty in reconciling means and ends as they turned to voluntary associations and sought allies across the line of respectability. Argentina's Socialist Party (founded in the mid-1890s) proposed a popular challenge to notable hegemony based on middle-class leadership in an alliance with workers. A modern political party highly centralized in organization, much of its program addressed *gente baja* grievances. The socialists' fundamental assumption was that the spread of industrial capitalism would necessarily disseminate and raise worker consciousness, leading them to vote in support of the party's program. Party members concentrated on assisting this process through literacy and voter registration campaigns and immigrant naturalization drives. By the 1920s it was clear (to all but perhaps the socialists themselves) that they had badly misjudged existing political and social realities. Most immigrants preferred to retain their original citizenship. Working-class consciousness did indeed spread among Argentina's urban commoners. But they first rallied around the anarchists' militancy and then turned to participation in trade unionism, all the while voting for the Radical Party, whose movement (the Radical Civic Union founded in 1891) rested on the panacea of democracy and popular solidarity to break the notables' hegemony. The socialists concluded that their electoral failure was the result of the false consciousness of the workers, who were still unable to move beyond their traditional *gente baja* worldview.[53]

Growing segments of the *gente decente*, as an emerging middle class, were coming to see themselves as a progressive force for change. More and more conscious of their own interests in the spreading industrial capitalist society, they were willing to join with *gente baja* to challenge notable dominance, whether as moderate reformers or even radical militants—but on their own terms. These *gente decente* becoming middle class assumed that the two social strata would be drawn together as commoners conformed to their worldview. They translated *gente baja* grievances into their own plans for the society; when these ideas did not fit, they neglected the *gente baja* or cast them off. When commoners (particularly the new working class) sought to give their own cast to the use of voluntary associations or asserted an agenda beyond the scope of middle-class intentions, the latter recoiled in mistrust and apprehension.[54]

It was then that *gente decente* presuppositions resurfaced to deflect blame for failures of popular collective action while allaying fears of social leveling. The emerging middle class desired to maintain a clearly distinct and superior place among "the people." The popular alliance did not seem to guarantee that important end. But neither, increasingly, could notable patronage and favor be counted on to do so. By their dominance and exclusivity, notables were closing off accepted channels of mobility and discarding the common social bond and identity of respectability. Remaining *gente decente* led to entrapment in a social position more and more untenable. Becoming middle class left one in a bind, with no sure nexus between means and ends.

Biding Their Time

The popular reaction to notable hegemony—spotty and fragmented in the late nineteenth century—became a mounting challenge after 1900. Strikes became widespread and generalized, moving out from urban centers into those rural areas where commercialization and industrialization of primary production had taken hold. Rural uprisings, though not so prevalent, broadened in scope and began to take on a more associated character. Mass political parties arose. This gave formal, continuing structure to the coalescence of growing segments of the *gente decente* into a middle class and to their alliance with groups from the *gente baja*, the new working class in particular.

Then, in the 1920s, overt militant resistance receded in most regions of Latin America. Cleavages within the popular reaction—between rural and urban, working class and popular classes, and middle class and commoners—weakened and dissipated the challenge, as did governments' frequent resort to brutal repression. Yet repression had limits, for growing elements of the police and military who enforced it and for the sensitivities (and often calculations) of reform-minded notables who had come of age. Under their leadership, notables turned increasingly to token reforms to fragment and quiet the opposition, co-opting its discourse and forms of organization. For a decade, they seemed to have succeeded, even in places like revolutionary Mexico and political reform–minded Argentina.

Looking past the general failures of mass strikes, rural revolts, and electoral struggles to break the notables' dominance, the popular reaction was most successful in its refusal to submit to an imposed new order. The uneasy equilibrium of Middle Period society may have been destabilized beyond recovery, but the *gente baja* were unwilling to abandon their lifestyle (and the economic and cultural autonomy that sustained it) without a fight or at least without negotiation. Few surrendered unconditionally. Some came to see a new order in which they would be equal, if not dominant.

Thus, one must look more with a microscope than a telescope to see the popular reaction in its most enduring profile. Though harried by government control and sanitation policies, many prostitutes operated clandestinely, changing name and residence, frustrating official efforts to eliminate them. In the face of public health campaigns that totally ignored *gente baja* opinions and perceptions, commoners continued to rely on *curanderos* (folk healers) and self-medication based on traditional remedies. In Rio de Janeiro's carnival (and its celebration in many Latin American towns and cities), *gente baja* annually bestowed on their common lifestyle a legitimacy that notables increasingly strove to deny them. The popular reaction achieved successes on a larger, though more limited scale. The Indian villagers of Chayanta district in the Bolivian Sierra, in great part through their fiercely violent resistance, staved off government efforts to fragment their *ayllus*. Some villagers in Mexico recovered lost lands by revolutionary force of arms or through government-directed agrarian reform. In numerous Latin American urban centers, strikes (but increasingly legislation) secured limited gains for workers.[55]

Through collective action, the emerging middle class began to secure similar reforms for white-collar workers. Perhaps their broadest success came in university reform, for which the movement in Argentina (1918–19) served as a culmination of initial efforts and catalyst for the universalization of that reform in succeeding decades. The reforms not only secured governing (though not financial) autonomy of the university but also the expansion of higher education, which had become a principal demand of the swelling middle class. The movement also advocated a social mission and a national popular consciousness.[56]

Yet despite their defiant resistance and the limited satisfaction of their grievances, the fact was that the strata of Middle Period society who came together in this popular reaction were being unalterably transformed. This change resulted less and less from resisting the new economic and political structures and more and more from struggling to control them and negotiating an acceptable place in them. It was reflected in the generic populist political program that became generalized over most of Latin America by the 1920s, which advocated inclusive and democratic representative government through wide suffrage, fair elections, and mass-based parties. It looked to, or was increasingly forced to rely on, a strong government role in correcting the inequities and erosion of economic opportunity and in improving the common welfare in such areas as education and modern services. It espoused nationalism to reduce (if not eliminate) economic and cultural dependency. In doing so, intellectuals (especially those considering themselves middle class) inquired into various facets of *gente baja* cultural traditions and held them up as an integral part of the nation's identity and ritual.

The limited achievement of some goals of this popular political program was in considerable part the result of efforts by reform-minded notables. Discerning that their strata's hegemony could no longer be maintained alone by official repression, unconditional imposition, or exclusion of other strata from public affairs, they moved in to inspire popular movements or dominate their leadership. As officials they legislated or negotiated the limited concessions made to the demands of the other social strata, now aligned against the notables. Many reformist notables were guided by more than empathy or notable self-interest. In fact, the notables' consensus was finding increasing difficulty in holding together. The centralization of economic and political control had not stopped at the boundary that separated notables from everyone else in Middle Period society. By 1900, it had begun to leave growing numbers of notables behind, threatening to elevate small cliques to unprecedented levels of power and influence.[57] Networks whose interests remained centered at district and regional levels were especially becoming restive. The alliance of state and national notable cliques with foreign interests was undermining their prerogatives and circumscribing their future opportunities.

Mexico's notables generally lost control politically as a new generation of politicians of largely *gente decente* origins and military chiefs of plebian background came to dominate postrevolutionary governments. But elsewhere, token reformism (along with official repression when necessary) quieted the popular challenge to notable hegemony. Generally favorable international markets, an acceleration of factory production, and generous foreign loans (increasingly by United States banks) made the token reforms less burdensome for the government and more tolerable for notables.[58] An air of normalcy had seemingly returned by the 1920s.

It would be short-lived. External circumstances would change, accelerating the spread of industrial capitalism in sometimes unforeseen ways. But that economic force had not been the sole agent transforming Middle Period society under the notables' dominance. The nation-state, which notables had enlarged to serve their own purposes, had also been altering fundamental relations and structures of Middle Period society. By the 1920s it had acquired such importance that it was becoming more than simply an instrument of notable hegemony.

Notes

1. Meade, "Riot in Rio," 243–48; Lauderdale Graham, *House and Street*, 132–35; Needell, *Tropical Belle Epoque*, 28–45.
2. Vaughn, "Primary Education," 31–32.
3. Klein, *Haciendas and Ayllus*, 148–56; Michaela Schmolz-Haberlein, "Continuity and Change in a Guatemalan Highland Community: San Cristobal-Vera Paz, 1870–1940," *HAHR* 76 (May 1996): 230–42; Erick O. Langer, "Franciscan Missions and Chiriguano Workers: Colonization, Acculturation

and Indian Labor in Southeastern Bolivia," *The Americas* 43 (January 1987): 307–10, 315–20.

4. David W. Walker, "Homegrown Revolution: The Hacienda Santa Catalina del Alamo y Anexas and Agrarian Protest in Eastern Durango, 1897–1913," *HAHR* 72 (May 1992): 251–53; LeGrand, "Colombian Frontiers," 33–35; Couterier, "Hacienda of Hueyapán," 222–30.

5. Walker, "Agrarian Protest," 241–50; Bauer, "Chilean Rural Society," 218–20; Knight, "Mexican Peonage," 48–49, 60–64; Piedad Peniche Rivero, "Gender, Bridewealth, and Marriage: Social Reproduction of Peons on Henequen Haciendas in Yucatán, 1870–1901," in *Women of the Mexican Countryside, 1850–1990*, ed. Heather Fowler-Salamini and Heather Kay Vaughn (Tucson: University of Arizona Press, 1994), 74–89.

6. Couterier, "Hacienda of Hueyapán," chap. 7; Meyers, *La Comarca Lagunera*, 116–34; Walker, "Agrarian Protest," 245; Knight, "Mexican Peonage," 48–49, 60–68; Fowler-Salamini, "Gender, Work, and Coffee," 59, 61.

7. Alan Knight, "The Working Class and the Mexican Revolution, c. 1900–1920," *JLAS* 16 (May 1984): 52–65; Sowell, "Artisans and Public Violence," 268–69, 278–80; Brennan, "Social Patterns," 222–32; McCreery, "Female Prostitution," 335–42, 347–51.

8. Scobie, *Buenos Aires*, 143, 188–89, 196–97; Knight, "Working Class and the Mexican Revolution," 61–65; Meade, "Riot in Rio," 243–45; French, "Capitalist Work Ethic," 203; Brennan, "Social Patterns," 234–44.

9. Burnett, "Protestantism in Guatemala," 132–33; Walker, "Agrarian Protest," 245; Morgan, "Proletarians and Patriarchs," 158–62; French, "Capitalist Work Ethic," 192, 196; Beezley, "Porfirian Smart Set," 177.

10. Lauderdale Graham, *House and Street*, 55–58, 60–62.

11. Conrad, "La industria de chicle," 480–85; Larson, *Agrarian Transformation*, 316–18; Langer, "Chiriguano Workers," 318–21.

12. Meyers, *La Comarca Lagunera*, 116–34; Fowler-Salamini, "Gender, Work, and Coffee," 63.

13. Robert M. Levine, " 'Mud-Hut Jerusalem': Canudos Revisited," *HAHR* 68 (August 1988): 529–35, 540–43, 548–56, 562–66.

14. McCreery, "Female Prostitution," 336–37, 342–45; Brennan, "Social Patterns," 97–115; Szuchman, *Mobility and Integration in Argentina*, 31–46.

15. Larson, *Agrarian Transformation*, 311, 317; Schmolz-Haberlein, "Guatemalan Highland Community," 242–46; Yarrington, "Public Land Settlement," 36–52.

16. Jimenez, "Coffee Estates," 202–17; Larson, *Agrarian Transformation*, 310–19.

17. Scobie, *Buenos Aires*, 196–97, 201–6; French, "Capitalist Work Ethic," 197; Knight, "Working Class and the Mexican Revolution," 61–65.

18. Schmolz-Haberlein, "Guatemalan Highland Community," 236–37, 243, 246; Icaza, *The Villagers*, 96–103.

19. George Reid Andrews, "Black Political Protest in São Paulo, 1888–1988," *JLAS* 24 (February 1992): 154–56; Andrews, "Black and White Workers," 497–506; Ronaldo Munck, "Cycles of Class Struggle and the Making of the Working Class in Argentina, 1890–1920," *JLAS* 19 (1987): 20–21; Scobie, *Buenos Aires*, 214–15, 230–32; Samuel L. Bailey, "Marriage Patterns and Immigrant Assimilation in Buenos Aires, 1882–1923," *HAHR* 60 (February 1980): 32–48; Leslie B. Rout, *The African Experience in Spanish America, 1502 to the Present Day* (New York: Cambridge University Press, 1976), 275, 302; Michael L. Conniff, *Black*

Labor on a White Canal: Panama, 1904–1981 (Pittsburgh: University of Pittsburgh Press, 1985), 22–44.

20. Claypole and Robottom, *Caribbean Story*, vol. 2, 29–35; Gonzales, "Chinese Plantation Workers," 408–13, 422–24; Elisavinda Echeverri-Gent, "Forgotten Workers: British West Indians and the Early Days of the Banana Industry in Costa Rica and Honduras," *JLAS* 24 (May 1992): 272–84, 297–305.

21. Fowler-Salamini, "Gender, Work, and Coffee," 62–68; Chassen-Lopez, "Women in Agriculture," 38–40, 52.

22. Brennan, "Social Patterns," 228–34; Scobie, *Buenos Aires*, 152–53, 216; Graham, *House and Street*, 73–74, 77–80.

23. Meyers, *La Comarca Lagunera*, 115–34; Knight, "Mexican Peonage," 41–74; McCreery, "Land and Labor in Guatemala," 239–44, 247–49.

24. Knight, "Working Class and Mexican Revolution," 61–71; Brennan, "Social Patterns," 218–44; Scobie, *Buenos Aires*, 196–97, 210–12.

25. Sowell, "Artisans and Public Violence," 272–79, 282; Thomas Benjamin and Mark Wasserman, eds., *Provinces of the Revolution: Essays on Regional Mexican History* (Albuquerque: University of New Mexico Press, 1990), chaps. 5–10; Knight, "Working Class and Mexican Revolution," 63–65, 68–71; Meade, "Riot in Rio," 259–66; French, "Capitalist Work Ethic," 193, 205–7; Munck, "Working Class in Argentina," 21–25.

26. Munck, "Working Class in Argentina," 21–29; Echeverri-Gent, "West Indian Workers," 294–97, 300–305.

27. Walker, "Agrarian Protests," 258–59; Moises González Navarro, "El maderismo y la revolución agraria," *HM* 37 (July–September 1987): 14–16; Benjamin and Wasserman, *Provinces of the Revolution*, chaps. 3, 5–10; Levine, "Canudos Revisited," 548–61, 566–72.

28. Juan Felipe Leal and Margarita Menegus Bornemann, "La violencia armada y su impacto en la economía agrícola del Estado de Tlaxcala," *HM* 36 (April–June 1987): 604–11; Knight, "Working Class and Mexican Revolution," 61–63, 65–68; French, "Capitalist Work Ethic," 192–93.

29. Scobie, *Buenos Aires*, 240; Ramón Eduardo Ruiz, *Cuba: The Making of a Revolution* (New York: Norton, 1970), chaps. 2–4.

30. Solberg, *Immigration and Nationalism*, 72–80.

31. Parker, "White-Collar Lima," 52–56; Meade, "Riot in Rio," 243–45; Brennan, "Social Patterns," 97–98, 117, 120, 268–70; Scobie, *Buenos Aires*, 139, 141–42.

32. Parker, "White-Collar Lima," 48–52; Munck, "Working Class in Argentina," 29–30.

33. Brennan, "Social Patterns," 262–69; Meyers, *La Comarca Lagunera*, 140–43; Parker, "White-Collar Lima," 52, 55, 61–64.

34. Parker, "White-Collar Lima," 56–63; Brennan, "Social Patterns," 262–69; Meyers, *La Comarca Lagunera*, 140–43.

35. Parker, "White-Collar Lima," 63, 71–72; Voss, "Towns and Enterprise," 575–89.

36. French, "Prostitutes and Guardian Angels," 532–37, 545–53.

37. Sowell, "Artisans and Public Violence," 280–81; Meade, "Riot in Rio," 241–42.

38. LeGrand, "Colombian Frontiers," 37–40; Larson, *Agrarian Transformation*, 311; John M. Hart, *Anarchism and the Mexican Working Class, 1860–1931* (Austin: University of Texas Press, 1987), 68–69.

39. Louis A. Perez, Jr., "The Pursuit of Pacification: Banditry and the U.S. Occupation of Cuba," *JLAS* 18 (November 1986): 313–32; Leal and Bornemann, "La violencia armada," 611–40.

40. Meade, "Riot in Rio," 244–57; Sowell, "Artisans and Public Violence," 272–80; French, "Capitalist Work Ethic," 196.

41. Meade, "Riot in Rio," 248–53; Langer, "Abolición de la comunidad indígena," 85–86; Andrews, "Black Political Protest," 152–56; Levine, "Canudos Revisited," 537–46.

42. Hart, *Mexican Working Class*, 66–73; Scobie, *Buenos Aires*, 156–57.

43. Sowell, *Artisans and Politics*, chap. 3, 86–93, 102–8; Hart, *Mexican Working Class*, 17, 27–30, chap. 4.

44. Morgan, "Proletarians and Patriarchs," 164–69; Ron F. Pineo, "Reinterpreting Labor Militancy: The Collapse of the Cacao Economy and the General Strike of 1922 in Guayaquil, Ecuador," *HAHR* 68 (November 1988): 717–18.

45. Echeverri-Gent, "West Indian Workers," 289–97; Munck, "Working Class in Argentina," 20–39; Ruth Thompson, "The Limitations of Ideology in the Early Argentine Labor Movement: Anarchism in the Trade Unions, 1890–1920," *JLAS* 16 (May 1984): 81–99; Hart, *Mexican Working Class*, chaps. 7–10.

46. French, "Capitalist Work Ethic," 199–200, 205–6; Parker, "White-Collar Lima," 59–70.

47. Meyers, *La Comarca Lagunera*, 143.

48. Parker, "White-Collar Lima," 57–61, 63–67.

49. Andrews, "Black and White Workers," 513–520; Andrews, "Black Political Protest," 152–56; Michael Trochim, "The Brazilian Black Guard: Racial Conflict in Post-Abolition Brazil," *The Americas* 44 (January 1988): 285–300.

50. John Womack, *Zapata and the Mexican Revolution* (New York: Alfred A. Knopf, 1968).

51. Munck, "Working Class in Argentina," 21–38; Thompson, "Early Argentine Labor Movement," 83–99; Knight, "Working Class and Mexican Revolution," 72–79.

52. Pineo, "General Strike," 714–32.

53. Rock, *Argentina*, 185–88; Jeremy Adelman, "Socialism and Democracy in Argentina in the Age of the Second International," *HAHR* 72 (May 1992): 211–38.

54. French, "Prostitutes and Guardian Angels," 551–53; Parker, "White-Collar Lima," 71–72.

55. McCreery, "Female Prostitution," 342–43; Guy, "White Slavery," 60–63; Cueto, "Yellow Fever in Peru," 20–21; French, "Capitalist Work Ethic," 196; Graham, *House and Street*, 66–71; Larson, *Agrarian Transformation*, 311, 317; Victoria Lerner, "Las zozobras de los hacendados de algunos municipios del oriente de San Luis Potosí (1910–1920)," *HM* 36 (October–December 1986): 347–59.

56. Parker, "White-Collar Lima," 47, 59, 64–67; Rock, *Argentina*, 200–201.

57. Noteworthy examples of these reform-minded notable politicos are Francisco Madero (Meyers, *La Comarca Lagunera*, chaps. 6, 8–9); Roque Sáenz Peña (Rock, *Argentina*, 189–90), and Augusto B. Leguía y Salcedo (Howard Karno, "Augusto B. Leguía: The Oligarchy and the Modernization of Peru, 1870–1930" [Ph.D. diss., University of Southern California at Los Angeles, 1970], chaps. 3–6).

58. Marichal, *Century of Debt Crisis*, 189–90.

9

Triumph of the Modernizing Nation-State

Independence had proclaimed the nation-state throughout most of Latin America. But its potential in scope and purpose had remained largely unfulfilled as Middle Period society settled into an uneasy equilibrium centered in a regional ordering of life. It was the liberal-national initiative (prevailing in all but a few countries by 1880) that had laid the foundations for the nation-state: setting forth a national religion of civic virtue; breaking the corporatist and spatial fetters constricting individual initiative; setting in motion economic forces whose interests increasingly took on a national orientation; and relying more and more on the operative logic of an enlarged and invigorated national government. In line with positivist discourse, late-nineteenth-century notables began erecting a modernizing nation-state on these liberal foundations, largely to serve their own purposes. By the 1920s they were becoming heavily dependent upon it to contain popular reaction to their hegemony. The paramount issue now was whether they could continue to control that state.

The scale and scope of national institutions were reaching levels outpacing the ability of notable family networks to master them. The military had become professionalized and its leadership more socially diverse. The civil bureaucracy had been growing exponentially, its middle and lower ranks filled by increasingly restive members of the emerging middle and working classes. Outside the government, these two new social strata led a growing trend among nonnotables to engage in an ever-widening and interconnected scope of associated action, with the growing assistance of (and dependence on) a new breed of political intermediaries whose opportunities and influence expanded in tandem with the distending reach of the nation-state.

Culture was also taking on a more national orientation but not because notables were succeeding in imposing North Atlantic values and practices. The emerging middle class, in general, did readily adopt most of them. The new working class (and, more slowly, the popular classes) selectively incorporated some practices (less so the values) into their lifestyle. Yet none ceded to the notables exclusive control over the discourse that interpreted the meaning of those imported practices and values for their lives. They rejected the dependency and subordination that notable infatuation with things foreign implied while elevating various strands of popular culture as embodiments of the nation. For the emerging middle class these choices were confirmation of a distinct cultural commonality clearly demarcating the nation within and the world without. For the working and popular classes, it was an affirmation of their rightful participation in the nation. Still, though generally refusing to conform to the North Atlantic ways unilaterally thrust upon them, commoners were becoming engaged in a process of cultural conformity all the same—on a scale not seen since the Conquest.

Positing a national popular culture and mobilizing nonnotables in associated action did more than guide the strategies of opposition movement leaders. A growing number of notables themselves were turning to stratagems of token inclusion and accommodation to shore up their besieged hegemony. In doing so, increasingly both notables and their opponents found in the nation-state a useful and necessary agent. No more was this so than with the onslaught of worldwide depression that rushed into Latin America following the stock market crash on Wall Street in late 1929. Few, if any, were prepared for the magnitude of this downturn in the industrial capitalist business cycle. Opportunity and necessity of response on a national scale approached equivalency. The modernizing nation-state—along with the nationalizing institutions and strands of culture that had fallen within its orb—became the primary force at work in people's lives. With this a watershed was reached beyond which Middle Period society could not longer sustain itself.

Creation of National Institutions

Middle Period society had been spatially rooted in regional identities and orbits of interaction. Institutionally, extraregional contacts, interests, and experiences had failed to crystallize throughout most of the century. Those who controlled the apparatus of government, with few exceptions, had placed it at the service of their regional or personal interests. In the 1860s and 1870s, the first veritable national institutions had begun to coalesce in a significant range of nations. As they became entrenched in power after 1880, they built upon this foundation in a virtuous cycle of expanding economic activity, foreign capital, public revenues, and governmental involvement in fomenting private enterprise and public improvements. After the turn of the century, their numbers and influence accelerated.

Forerunners: The Military and the Bureaucracy

Until the 1880s, in all but a few countries military forces had been highly personalist or regional in their organization and functioning and generally quite fragmented. The foreign and civil wars of the 1860s and 1870s did strengthen the cohesion of existing armies and forge the unity of those newly created. However, the fiscal resources and political stability born of the notables' consensus thereafter led to the first widespread institutionalization of national armed forces in Latin America. Notable family members, in-laws, and clients formed the core of the officer corps. As politicians, others directed an ample share of rising revenues to professionalize and modernize the military. Pay was standardized and regularized. National war colleges were established (or expanded) to ensure uniform training of an integrated officer corps. Foreign arms were purchased to upgrade weapons. European military missions (most prominently from Germany) were brought in to modernize organization and tactics in South America. U.S. military personnel created national armies or constabulary forces in Panama, Nicaragua, Cuba, Haiti, and the Dominican Republic.[1] In part, notables were projecting a rather poor imitation of North Atlantic power politics onto Latin America. But the professionalized force played an essential role in enforcing their hegemony when resistance presented a formidable challenge.

The bureaucracy's expansion also strengthened national government. For a half century, municipal and state and provincial governments had enjoyed considerable leeway in devising and carrying out public policy, whether the national constitutional framework was federalist or centralist in design. However, beginning in the 1870s in some countries and spreading to practically all the rest thereafter, the centralization of governmental power accelerated. Paradoxically, subnational governments' resources and ability to control the public were growing as well. Municipal and state governments were playing an ever-greater role in people's lives. Nevertheless, they were doing so increasingly in the service of those levels of government above them. In great part, this trend was owing to the notables' consensus about the nation's general direction. As their family networks secured control of government and steadily intertwined their interests, as they increasingly discerned the utility of government in serving those interests (including jobs for their expanding families), they were willing, if not eager, to see the scope of governmental activity enlarged.

Especially in the district seats, municipal governments expanded their functions, focusing on public works, education, public health, and law enforcement. But in doing so they were increasingly dependent upon state subsidies and under the oversight of state government. Notable cliques at the state level employed economic enticements, electoral manipulation, and force when necessary to forge deals with pliant notable networks at the local and district levels. Much of the newly found muscle of the state regimes lay, in turn, in the support they received from those controlling national government. Increasingly, if they resisted or tried to cross the latter's policies, their power was soon undercut and pacts were made with their rivals, as local and district notables went around state officials, appealing directly to the national capital. Even if such end runs were unsuccessful, they tempered thoughts of attempting to exercise state prerogative. So, too, did the enhanced military capability of the armed forces and the communications and transportation revolution that markedly shrank time and distance.[2]

Thus, national governments faced waning resistance as they extended their functions and presence after 1880, in large part by expanding bureaucracies. The initial impact was felt in matters of public security, taxation, and control of customs duties, but it soon spread to other functions as well. All across Latin America, national governments were making constitutional and enforceable their claims of control over coastlines, major rivers, mineral deposits, and nonlocal lines of communication and transportation. Initial efforts to finance, build, and operate improvements in infrastructure in the late nineteenth century gave way generally to subsidizing private enterprise. But after 1900 in a number of countries, national governments began purchasing services or instituting infrastructure itself. The reformist government of José Batlle y Ordóñez in Uruguay carried this de-privatization of infrastructure far beyond the norm. He gradually brought under public ownership railroads, electric systems, telephone and telegraph companies, and street railways, foreshadowing the role of national government that was soon to come.[3]

The Batlle government was also the most radical in extending its economic role, securing public ownership of banks, meatpacking plants, and some other enterprises to serve as standards for regulating private firms in those sectors. Elsewhere, national governments generally employed more indirect means. Some national and state banks were established, but the legislative institution and regulation of national banking systems were far more common. Subsidies were granted to encourage the initiation or expansion of manufacturing and primary production in numerous sectors.[4]

Education was a particular focal point for the enlargement of governmental power. After 1880, there was a general movement toward creating comprehensive national educational systems, with direct control through legislated authority and a division of bureaucrats. Argentina moved rapidly in this direction. A nationwide educational system was instituted in 1884, providing uniform guidelines to establish, fund, and operate local schools and a national board of education to inspect, supervise, and administer the entire system. The board's powers to inspect schools and to set curricular standards extended to private schools. Provisions were made for adult education, mobile schools, and public libraries.[5] Growing centralized control over public instruction yielded mixed results. Expansion of schooling and literacy varied widely: generally, it was minimal in the countryside, limited in small towns, and substantial in large cities. Overall, these changes failed to meet expectations. But by the early twentieth century, in few other functions had the national government become so fully dominant.

National government involvement in public health, as in education, varied greatly from rural communities to large urban centers. But it had not yet become as systematized or comprehensive in its reach into local life. Legislation was formulated (and, with some frequency, passed after 1900) to improve hygienic conditions, especially as they pertained to the workplace. Bureaucratic entities were created (like Argentina's Department of Hygiene) with considerable powers of inspection and control. In 1920 Peruvian president Augusto Leguía y Salcedo used a national sanitary campaign to eradicate yellow fever to expand governmental authority in the country's urban centers. He put the North American professionals contracted to run the yellow fever campaign in charge of all public works in thirty-three cities to improve sanitation, usurping the prerogatives of regional and local officials in health matters. In doing so, he laid the foundations for a national public health system that would emerge in the 1930s.[6]

To contend with rising labor militancy and organization, national governments expanded their functions and bureaucracy in still another direction. After 1900, through legislation, they strove to curb labor militancy and intervene as a pacifying agent in employer-worker relations, thus bringing a vital sphere of the economy far more directly under their supervision. In Argentina, the radical government used the National Labor Department as a vehicle for mediation and arbitration and to oversee the implementation of labor legislation. In Mexico, President Plutarco Elías Calles converted the Confederación Regional Obrera Mexicana (CROM—Mexican Regional Worker Confederation) into a virtual public instrument for regulating labor-management disputes in the mid-1920s. He also pushed through the creation of a Federal Board of Conciliation and Arbitration, which was armed with the power to authorize and arbitrate all strikes. It constituted the first stage in the nationalization of labor affairs in Mexico.[7]

Brazil, constitutionally and politically, should have run against the grain of growing national government activity and presence. The imperial regime's demise (1889) had given rise to perhaps Latin America's most decentralized federalist regime at the end of the nineteenth century. State governments were given exclusive authority over state matters plus powers usually reserved for national governments: to borrow abroad without federal approval; to levy export duties (even on goods destined for other states); and to control subsoil rights, rivers for power-generating purposes, and all public lands not deemed necessary for national defense. They also maintained militias. Still, the general forces of industrial capitalism and export-led growth at work across Latin America made Brazil's national government the principal economic player by the 1920s. From the international market, it secured expanding financial resources (both loans and revenues) to provide the capital and bureaucracy to intervene increasingly in the economy. Recurring economic crises, largely induced from abroad, made public involvement increasingly necessary and acceptable.

Large-scale involvement began with the maintenance of the state-owned railroads inherited from the imperial era. After 1900, Brazil nationalized twelve private companies, having previously guaranteed their profits and then rescued those that were failing. The crisis of overproduction of coffee (Brazil's main export) resulted in government-guaranteed loans used by the states to buy up coffee surpluses to maintain prior profitable price levels. World War I gave the greatest impetus to government intervention. Disruptions in foreign markets and capital flow and a heightened nationalist sentiment fomented a growing sense of the need for self-sufficiency and for the national government to foster it far more actively. Over the next fifteen years, it took control of the Banco de Brasil, giving it a monopoly over the issue of currency. Through large foreign loans, the government financed infrastructure to aid the depressed northeast and improve transportation generally, as well as to finance the purchase of coffee surpluses.

By 1930 the national government owned 59 percent of the nation's railroads, whose low fares, free services, and maintenance of unprofitable routes had made them central to economic growth and territorial integration. In a far more limited way the national government also assisted industrial manufacturing, planting the seed of state intervention to promote strategic industrial sectors that would soon bear fruit.[8]

Nationalization of Interest Groups

The Brazilian government's increasing economic intervention was to a significant degree the result of growing pressure by organizations operating on an ever larger spatial scale. Producers of other major export commodities soon joined coffee growers in seeking (unsuccessfully) federal aid to support their sectors' prices. In the 1910s and 1920s, several organizations called on the government to increase national self-sufficiency and security through greater involvement in the economy. The largest, Acão Social Nacionalista (National Social Association, or ASN), was a notable-oriented confederation of civic organizations with more than 180 affiliates and 250,000 members at its height in 1921. The ASN lobbied the national government to intervene in finance, infrastructure, and industry. Railroad workers numbering in the tens of thousands were another powerful national force by the 1920s.[9]

Across Latin America, especially in countries where industrial capitalism had made the greatest inroads into the economy, collective action became increasingly national in scope. Business organizations emerged to further the interests of large-scale entrepreneurs. Agricultural producers came together in national organizations, as did chambers of commerce and even the fledgling sectors of manufacturing. More fragile were the national labor confederations (and, in some countries, agrarian leagues) that began to weld regional movements together, though loosely and often ephemerally. Still, CROM's symbiotic relationship with Mexico's official revolutionary party, and the latter's growing intervention in labor relations in the 1920s, led to the formation of a nationwide confederation of employers to counter the intrusion.[10]

Collective action among religious bodies was also assuming a national scale. In Argentina, the Catholic Education League was formed to promote state support of parochial schools after legislation made public schools nonsectarian. The league also pressed affiliated lay committees to demand that public schools provide the religious instruction still allowed by law. In Mexico, Protestant churches organized a lobbying committee (and significant numbers of their members entered the bureaucracy) to represent their interests in the new revolutionary regime, especially in education.[11]

Many of these nongovernmental organizations worked jointly with the mass-based national political parties that arose after 1900. Most influential were those parties in which the emerging middle class (and remaining *gente decente*) predominated in membership. In varying degrees, they sought to reform the political and economic systems that had arisen under the notables. Noteworthy among them were the Radical Party in Argentina (begun in the early 1890s), and the Democratic Party in Brazil. In a few cases, as in Colombia, independent workers' parties were formed but endured only a few years. Liberal and conservative parties, which in the nineteenth century had been only loosely affiliated coalitions of notables and their clients, remained notable-dominated but saw the need to broaden their membership base. Some, like the Radical Party in Chile, became predominantly middle class. Uruguay's Colorado Party, the most radical in its reform program, incorporated important segments of the working class as well.[12]

Increasingly appearing at the points where the national government, nongovernmental organizations, and now mass-based national political parties intersected was a new breed of political intermediary. These new politicos prospered as they embodied and served the new mode of modern republican political organization, their power resting neither on private economic leverage, nor kinship ties, nor personal loyalty. Rather, their authority and muscle derived from their mastery of successfully brokering the interests of the associated groups they represented. The political stock they marketed was the electoral force of their clients. The return they secured for their clients was the fulfillment of the latter's demands (or at least promises to do so). Their commission was the enhanced political power that delivery of such services earned for them. Most new political brokers were middle class (or *gente decente*) in origins and outlook. Some were disgruntled notables. In countries where popular resistance to notable dominance was most militant and violent (most notably in the Mexican Revolution), military chiefs, peasant leaders, and labor organizers sometimes became such brokers.

Whatever their origins, the new politicos took advantage of the growing social discontent and political instability as the popular reaction challenged the notables' hegemony. First representing popular associated groups, then holding positions in mass-based political parties, and eventually serving in elected governmental offices and bureaucratic posts, they built their clientele and increased their leverage over them. The extent of the brokers' autonomy depended upon their clients' political or economic resources and cohesiveness. Success was increasingly a function of their ability to provide the linkage between the collective associations that formed their clientele (at whatever spatial level they operated) and the national political arena.[13]

Chilean lawyer Arturo Alessandri Palma was one of the most successful new politicos in grasping the possibilities of brokering for new political constituencies. Entering politics through the Liberal Party, he went to the northern mining districts to win over notable elements in the party. But he found a better base for power in the labor unions then forming among nitrate workers in the region, in part serving as a lawyer for the more important labor leaders. By 1920, he had moved on to bring the urban *gente baja* (elements of which were also becoming unionized) into national politics, forging a national liberal alliance that triumphed in the closely contested elections that year. In 1924, he secured a congressional majority that enabled him to enact a broad social welfare program, including labor union recognition. However, notable politicians frustrated the implementation of most of his program, leading to his resignation as president and military intervention.[14]

Nationalizing Culture

A growing number of this new breed of politicians embraced and exploited the nationalist currents of culture then emanating from a variety of sources. They astutely perceived that such expressions of identity could be a valuable ally in cementing the linkages that were the source of their power and influence. Still, they were not the first to seize upon the uses of a nationalizing culture. Notables of the preceding generation had begun employing the nation-state's growing resources and presence to foster a common culture as part of their political agenda. Yet there was nothing in their minds to broker. It was a simple question of imposition. The popular reaction to that imposition did intensify the nationalization of culture, but the outcome was contrary to what notables had intended.

The Notables' Paradox

The consensus emerging among notables by the 1880s fostered an increasingly national view of cultural life. Mutual economic goals, growing business and marital interconnections, recognition (or at least acceptance) of the advantages of an activist national government, and modern forms of transportation and communication had all facilitated this notion. They had internalized a common culture, one that crisscrossed the national territory. Also, the more notables abandoned their patronal relations with the other social strata, the more they needed government at all levels as an instrument of social control. They had come to view promotion of a culture that permeated the nation—one whose definition was solely in their hands—as essential to that control.[15]

The attempt to monopolize public celebrations (at the expense of religious, popular, and regional expression) had been integral to the notables' imposition of a nationwide culture. Through national holidays, the disparate events and celebrated historical figures of the nation's past had been amalgamated into a history that testified to its unity and glory. Creating and placing statuary in traditional and new arenas of civic renown had similar ends. In each municipal and district seat, each state and national capital, acting as public officials and in *juntas patrioticas* (patriotic commissions or committees), notables organized and oversaw the celebration of similar civic rituals, renaming of public places, and inauguration of an integrated pantheon of nationalized symbols. These civic lessons were designed to inculcate among "lesser" social strata acceptance of a common, notable-interpreted past and notable-directed future.[16]

The classroom taught such lessons more formally. The great majority of children in the steadily expanding number of schools only attended for a year or two. But from the notable/official point of view, that was sufficient to begin their training as docile, more productive workers and to instill in them a sense and spirit of the nation as the notables perceived it. Ministries of education, assisted by subordinate agents down through the state governments into the local classrooms, focused on instruction in Spanish (or Portuguese), uniform textbooks, detailed observances of national holidays, and ceremonies of allegiance.[17]

In Porfirian Mexico (1876–1910), the Paseo de la Reforma had become the showpiece of the national capital. However, it contained mixed messages. On the broad thoroughfare connecting the old central city with the official residence of the president (Chapultepec Castle), Mexican history had been rewritten. A statue honoring the Aztec resistance leader was co-opted to serve Porfirian purposes. Racially, Cuauhtemoc's features were whitened, acceptably reconfiguring him as the ancestor of the independence hero, Miguel Hidalgo y Costilla. Geopolitically, the subordination of other pre-Columbian state societies on the base and pedestal of the column on which the statue was mounted connoted the supremacy of the Valley of Mexico in the evolution of the nation. Making this lesson more emphatic, the government of Porfirio

Díaz lined the boulevard with statues of heroes donated by each state in a symbolic rendering of tribute. Though nationalist in purpose, the statues were foreign-inspired, most the work of a Mexican sculptor just returned from five years in Paris. Therein lay the paradox of the Paseo de la Reforma and of the nationalist culture of Latin America's notables at the turn of the century.

Although Mexico City's modern thoroughfare possessed a nationalizing intent, it bespoke even more a culture procreated outside the nation's boundaries. Foreigners soon owned the development rights of most lots along the Reforma, which had been built primarily to impress and attract them. Foreigners and notables erected a new series of mansions in the current European styles, linked to nearby shops, parks, and offices in new suburban subdivisions. One of them, the Zona Rosa, was unabashedly imitative, with street names such as Dinamarca, Londres, Roma, Liverpool, Genova, and Florencia, among others. In the heart of the Reforma was the monument to independence, the Porfirian regime's final statement. Unveiled in 1910, the names and statuary depictions of independence heroes were cast in a generically European setting.[18]

Whether centered in national capitals like Mexico City, Bogotá, Buenos Aires, and Santiago or followed in provincial cities and towns, the culture Latin America's notables proclaimed and practiced was nationwide but not of the nation. Increasingly borrowing cultural resources from abroad, they discounted to the point of worthlessness the cultural discourses long practiced within their nations, those emanating from the *gente baja*. That left them, in their prejudices, little choice but to strive to inculcate the culture of progress from abroad and disseminate it as widely throughout their nations as possible. In some cases, they even handed over the transmission of the imported culture to outsiders. In a number of countries, the latter were recruited to establish normal schools and military academies to impart cultural norms as well as technical training. The notables' working assumption had been that as transmitters of the imported culture of progress disseminated across the nation, they would find that it furthered their hegemony over Middle Period society. In the twentieth century's first decade, a significant minority of them began to question that assumption.

Popular Culture Made National

By 1910 there was a growing sense among many notables in southern South America (especially in Argentina) that the process of cultural transmission was slipping out of control. Not withstanding concerns about the extent of foreign influence in the economy and of immigrant masses straying from the model of pliant, productive workers (transmitting militant unionism or, worse, anarchism), notables were becoming anxious about the immigrants' cultural exclusiveness. They were prone to marry within their own nationality, banded together in fraternal and mutual aid societies, and celebrated the patriotic holidays of their native lands. They retained their language or spoke "contaminated" Spanish. The issue was cultural assimilation.[19]

Immigrants did not bring with them a universalized, homogenized version of North Atlantic culture, particularly one filtered and amalgamated by the notables. (Immigrants from South and East Asia, of course, brought no version of Western culture.) Moreover, the ethnic exclusiveness of the various immigrant groups threatened the nation's cultural unity. Notables discounted the popular cultural expression of the native citizenry. Still, they nonetheless assumed that a common cultural framework existed (or could be constructed) from which they could expunge *gente baja* traditions and to which they could liberally add North Atlantic traits and practices. There was a common historical experience and a common religious tradition. Language and citizenship were perhaps the most fundamental of starting points. The unwillingness of so many immigrants to fit into such a basic cultural framework (particularly the large groups from humble origins) more and more concerned notables. This paralleled the resistance of native commoners to the cultural mold that notables sought to impose on them, though notables did not discern the similarity.

Indeed, notable intellectuals in Argentina who had used the European immigrant as model for the *gente baja*'s cultural transformation ironically began proposing a rehabilitated image of the native-born commoner as a model for immigrant nationalization after 1900. The once-scorned mestizo commoner (symbolized above all in the gaucho) was idealized into a symbol and representative of the true national culture and character. What these intellectuals meant by this was that the gaucho, in a subordinate role, shared with the notables a common historical experience in defense of the nation, a common language and faith, and certain other (acceptable) cultural traditions.[20]

In Guatemala, *gente alta* intellectuals emerging in the more open political climate of the 1920s were more tentative in their embrace of *lo popular*, for the impetus to discovering the national culture's popular roots was the demographic predominance of indigenous peoples who had resisted (with considerable success) the centuries-long attempts to Hispanicize them. The preceding positivist generation had proclaimed the Maya primitive remnants of a civilization decadent well before the Conquest, if not dead. But the new generation of *gente alta* activists opposed both the nation's past cultural and political structures as they searched for an encompassing definition of natives of the land and of being Guatemalan. Rather than dismiss indigenous peoples as outside that definition, they increasingly began to delve into Mayan history, lore, and culture. How much that was a reaction to foreign influence in the country—or the desire to follow the then fashionable interest in "primitive" origins among intellectuals in Mexico, the United States, and Europe—is not altogether certain.[21]

Intellectuals and politicians from among the emerging middle class felt far less need to be tentative in discovering popular cultural symbols and traditions. Indeed, increasingly they urged and worked for the latter's inclusion in the national consciousness and culture because these traditions were a prime adhesive joining them to the *gente baja* in a popular alignment against foreign domination and notable hegemony. Writers and artists made the case rationally and emotionally. Political brokers pursued it rhetorically and pragmatically. In not a few cases, intellectual and politician were the same.

Nowhere was this cultural agenda more pursued than in Mexico in the wake of the revolution of 1910. Muralists such as Diego Rivera, José Orozco, and David Siqueiros decried foreign and notable oppression while they celebrated the *gente baja*'s traditions and struggle on the walls of countless public buildings. In particular, they lifted up indigenous villagers and the urban working class. Writers such as Mariano Azuela penned the same themes in *indigenista* and revolutionary novels and short stories. The high-water mark of this popular-centered cultural campaign came with the virtual crusade of José Vasconcelos, minister of education in the early 1920s. Commissioning artistic and literary works, supporting folk art, and staging public festivals, he strove to promote cultural pride through weaving together various cultural strands that had developed within the nation into a nationalizing culture. Central to his program was a national educational campaign that reached out to rural and urban commoners alike. Normal school graduates and young practitioners of the arts were sent out as missionaries to combat illiteracy, spread the knowledge of practical skills and crafts, encourage local artistic traditions, and arouse people to cooperative action on behalf of their communities and the nation.[22]

Likewise in Brazil, intellectual and political ferment intertwined in promoting a national, popular-infused culture. A few scholars at the turn of the century had begun raising the question of African and

Amerindian contributions to the nation. But a new generation of intellectuals bursting on the scene in the 1920s—in what became known as the "modernist movement"—resoundingly called for a cultural independence that would "brazilianize Brazil." By defining and fostering a national culture, they intended to reduce the grip of foreign culture on the nation and challenge the established order on a variety of fronts at the same time. Musicians such as Heitor Villa-Lobos and writers such as Mario de Andrade creatively drew from the multitude of folkloric studies that were pursued by a wide range of scholars. Most prominent was the young sociologist Gilberto Freyre, who introduced and popularized the theme of Brazil's uniqueness lying in the contributions of three races.[23]

Alongside this national cultural initiative of the emerging middle class (joined by some disgruntled notables and *gente decente*) was the spatial undermining of the cultural foundations of *gente baja* life, especially in urban barrios. New forms of transport and communication, the spread of education, and the increasing necessity of associated action were drawing them out of their neighborhoods and communities, away from the local and regional cultural habits that had so long governed their lives.[24] The new national cultural discourse respected their cultural roots and bespoke a vision of inclusiveness. This served as a pull reinforcing the push then nudging (if not propelling) them away from their customary patterns.

The Strategic Issue

In the years following World War I, popular reaction to notable hegemony steadily mounted. It was given form in associated action ever greater in diversity and scope and given voice in a rising sentiment and rhetoric of cultural nationalism at once exclusive (antiforeign) and inclusive (popular). Its intensity and cohesion ebbed and flowed, according to the receptivity of political regimes, the fortunes of the economy, and the degree to which economic forces of change had unsettled the social order of Middle Period society.

The strategic issue facing the respective social strata (old and new) centered on their judgments about the extent of change wrought in Middle Period society since the 1870s and how best to respond to that change. First, how viable were the conventions underlying Middle Period society for the past century: social deference; negotiated rights, prerogatives, and obligations; and personal/client relations? Most notables still expected deference but had ceased honoring reciprocal obligations, retaining them only when pragmatically necessary. The more successful among the *gente decente* stayed the increasingly less certain course as notables still in waiting. *Gente baja* had begun to lose faith in the validity of these conventions as guarantees of subsistence security and cultural space. The emerging working and middle classes rejected deference and personalism altogether, as they struggled to secure rights and opportunities in the new economic realities they faced.

Second, how could the growing imbalance in the uneasy equilibrium in Middle Period society be corrected, or should a new equilibrium be sought? Notables debated the extent to which governmental attention to popular grievances was now necessary to control the rising restiveness of those beneath them and thereby maintain the social hierarchy. Where the threat to subsistence maintenance was most severe and where notable hegemony seemed more vulnerable, the *gente baja* became most emboldened and militant. But in general, they sought to restore the old equilibrium, recovering the access to resources, benefits of reciprocal relations, and cultural space they had lost. The respectable who remained *gente decente* continued to place their fortunes in notable hands. They surely wished to restore more fluidity of access to the ranks of notability, but they were not prepared to challenge notables to obtain it. In contrast, the new working and middle classes were moving beyond restoration, a position very much shaped by their own experiences in voluntary associations and growing class identity. The former equilibrium had become so skewed that a new one needed to be negotiated, far more formally and impersonally determined and more egalitarian in character. Differences among and between these two new social strata were arising over the extent of that egalitarianism and of the public participation that determined it.

The Continuum of Incorporation and Control

The strategic issue increasingly confronting Middle Period society in the post–World War I years spanned a continuum. At one end was the prospect of full incorporation of those below the notables as formal, active participants in the public decisionmaking of an increasingly egalitarian society. At the other, the continuation of a hierarchical society in which public participation was strictly limited. Cultural and political discourse were important in defining one's position on the continuum: the nationalizing popular culture by then gaining momentum versus the positivist vision that underlay notable hegemony.

Increasingly marginalized from this continuum—whether in political structure or discourse—was the regional, pluralistic basis for such a society. Large segments of the *gente baja* and some notables still trusted in the efficacy of vertical collaboration centered at the local and regional levels to preserve their way of life and hierarchical position respectively. In the Mexican Revolution, a number of regional movements were based on this premise, some enjoying brief success. Yet the growing size and scope of the national state was proving to be a powerful magnet for everyone else, as that revolution in time also made clear.[25]

Most notable-dominated regimes in the years after World War I failed to see the need to move beyond the narrow, strict control of the strata below them, especially the popular classes and the new working class. Even in discourse, they thought it unnecessary to hold out a limited vision of incorporation. The two notable-dominated political movements emerging after Paraguay's defeat in the War of the Triple Alliance remained unresponsive to either *gente baja* needs, the rise of a radicalized (if not large) middle class in the late 1920s, or the growing mobilization of a small but active working class. In 1927, the Liberal and Colorado Parties agreed in an accommodation pact to exclude any third force. One group in Paraguay, however, did become responsive to these new political forces: young officers (many of middle-class orientation) recruited as part of a new and vigorous attempt in the 1920s to professionalize and revitalize the military. In the following decade, that affinity would grow into a powerful opposition alliance.[26] This pattern was developing generally in Latin American countries during the 1920s; in several its political impact was felt before 1930.

As the military became professionalized, civilian politicians acquired increasing control over the institution, steadily injecting notable family ties as the basis for promotion. Those of humble or modest origins (now comprising a large and growing percentage of the junior officer corps) more and more felt passed over. Moreover, they were coming to see notable hegemony as aggravating, not solving, the growing social unrest that they were obliged to quell. Above all, they feared anarchic violence and Marxist revolution. They began to offer themselves as brokers, not through electoral politics but as caretakers of constitutional government. They would intervene to solve the nation's immediate problems through institution of reform programs and strong, centralized government and then turn the government back over to constitutional rule.

Thus, the new generation of officers (often with senior officers as patrons or titular leaders) became more and more involved in politics, hatching plots, coups, and barracks revolts. A few were successful, like that which brought Col. Carlos Ibáñez to power in Chile in the late 1920s. Though politically repressive and paternalistic in his reform of labor relations, he undertook a large-scale expansion of public works and education that provided jobs for the working and middle classes while encouraging the growth of industrial activity. But most military interventions, such as the *tenentes* (junior officers) revolts of 1922 and 1924 in Brazil, failed.[27] Still, by 1930, junior officers there and in most other Latin American countries—ranging from moderates to reformers, some even flirting with socialist ideas—had come to oppose continued notable hegemony. They commonly agreed on the need for the military's intervention in politics as a highly organized, disciplined force.

University students, too, were responding to popular grievances and the call for reform. In many ways, their experience paralleled that of the junior military officers. Educational expansion since 1880 had resulted in a growing proportion of students from modest backgrounds. They had begun speaking out against the closed nature of notable rule as they found it in the universities: a narrow, expensive, authoritarian educational system run by and for the notables. More and more, they came to see their problems as part of the whole society's ills. By 1910 they were employing strikes to demand a radical reform of the university, including a call for university extension services to address working- and popular-class problems. The strike at the University of Córdoba (Argentina) in 1918 spread the principle of university autonomy throughout the greater part of Latin America. The social mission of the university and of student organizations also became firmly rooted, taking on an almost exclusively antiforeign discourse with ever more radical notions of reform.[28]

Many university alumni in the 1920s joined the new breed of politicians from the middle class and the ranks of alienated notables who were seeking to enlarge the electorate and mobilize opposition forces. Some were wholly crusaders for reform. Most were political brokers who realized that securing popular support required a new discourse, one that fused together nationalism, symbols of *gente baja* culture, articulation of working- and popular-class grievances, and proposals for their solution. The latter included trade union recognition, improved working conditions, agrarian reform and communal ownership of land, expansion of education, and extension of public services.

Such a popular reformist discourse offered new possibilities, in many cases a new vision. But more fundamentally, how far could these new politicos go—how far should they go—in delivering on such promises? Argentina's Radical Party, through its refusal to participate in manipulated elections, forced genuine electoral reform in 1912 that enabled it to come to power in 1916. But the radicals led by Hipólito Yrigoyen proved timid in their reforms, relying on token changes and populist discourse in the brokering of support. They backed away from support of labor and small producers as they became ever more emboldened and militant and instead focused on expanding the bureaucracy to enlarge middle-class support. In this, they differed only somewhat from regimes dominated by "progressive" notables, who saw that mere reliance on political exclusion and repressive control would not longer suffice.[29] At the other extreme was José Batlle's Colorado Party, which pushed through far-reaching reforms in neighboring Uruguay, including enactment of a broad range of social welfare reforms aimed at workers. In contrast to Argentina's radicals, the Colorado Party had a far more dominant middle-class base and working-class support, centered in the capital of Montevideo, which by then comprised half the nation's population.[30]

Most reform movements and parties in the years after World War I responded to the strategic issue somewhere between Argentina's radicals and Uruguay's Colorado Party. Only on the far left, in the fledgling socialist and communist parties then beginning to organize, did the rhetoric and platform call for truly far-reaching transformation of Middle Period society. But even there, shifting political and economic circumstances, along with long-standing realities, forced them to move back from the continuum's end. It was true even more of those closer to the center. In Brazil, the legacy of scientific racial doctrine and economic marginalization left blacks out of all opposition movements.[31]

The Brokers' Foresight

Among opposition movement leaders, political brokers discerned more clearly and correctly the limits such circumstances and realities imposed on mobilizing (and controlling) constituencies and on negotiating reforms. By the end of the 1920s there seems to have been a fairly common pair of working axioms among these new politicos on the strategic issue of incorporation and control. First, Middle Period society had become so unsettled that exclusion and mere repressive control could no longer sustain it. Nor could nineteenth-century patterns of personal, informal negotiation set it right again. To challenge notable hegemony successfully, nonnotables had to be mobilized and organized formally into mass-based constituencies through a new political discourse that integrated their grievances and demands but that was popular (of and about "the people"), incorporating them as integral to the nation's life and direction. However much one had to tailor and compromise reforms to existing circumstances, such an inclusive, popular-based discourse was now mandatory in political mobilization.

Second, political mobilization and organization had become national in scale. Loosely confederated alliances and vertical collaboration were no longer practical. The economy had become too reorganized, communication and transport technology too transformed, and voluntary association too advanced for that. However much the new politicos organized constituencies at local and district levels, their brokering was premised on these groups' integration into nongovernmental bodies that would become (if not already were) national in scope.

Little did these political brokers know that the most serious threat to notable hegemony—at least in the short run—would not come from this formally organized, popular-based challenge within their nations. It would come from the outside in the form of worldwide depression. Such a profound economic crisis would shake the notables' imposed consensus to its foundations and in its wake prove the political brokers more than correct in their assumptions.

The Watershed of the Great Depression

Though notables were beginning to lose their political grip by the end of the 1920s (in Mexico, their hold on politics was rapidly slipping), the rest of the system was still intact—or so it seemed. They continued to wield their economic and social dominance as they tried to weather the political storm. Few realized that by the 1920s the economic foundations of their whole system were in trouble. That threat was obscured by an illusory prosperity that pervaded most countries in the 1920s, helping to moderate the previously rising social tensions and political conflicts. In some countries, notably Argentina, prosperity in the late 1920s even exceeded that of prewar years. Yet an illusion is finely wrought, delicately built, and easily breakable. The Great Depression, which came quickly to Latin America in 1930 with an unprecedented scale and impact, did more than simply confirm the call for reforming the notables' hegemonic system. It brought into fullness economic and social conditions that had only recently appeared and generated new ones. This process, in turn, created new economic problems and possibilities and new political repercussions that the political brokers and their constituencies had not even foreseen. In the process, the fabric of Middle Period society, already stretched and frayed, did not hold.

Shaking the Foundations

World War I had brought an initial warning signal to Latin American economies, which had expanded and prospered since 1880 as they had become adjuncts of the international market, increasingly dependent on the smooth functioning of that world economy. The flow of most commodities was disrupted, shipping was dislocated, imports were curtailed, and government revenues were impaired. Despite a brief boom at the war's end, by the early 1920s difficulties had reappeared. European consumption of Latin American foodstuffs and raw materials was now decelerating, especially as other areas of the world (Asia and Africa in particular) expanded their output of primary products. In some countries like Cuba, where the price of sugar dropped dramatically, there was an immediate economic crisis. Elsewhere, prices of exported commodities declined gradually, and the impact appeared only cumulatively in the last years of the decade.

Foreign capital, the other pillar supporting the export-oriented economies, experienced a largely different pattern. North American capital rushed in to fill the growing vacuum created by Europe's need to finance recovery from the war's destruction. As important, a tide of foreign capital entered in the form of loans to governments, which employed them to maintain the expansion of public works, education, and the bureaucracy to create jobs in the face of mounting political pressure from below while supporting notable economic enterprises. A cut was also set aside for corruption. Across the political continuum, dependence on foreign loans grew steadily. Then, at the decade's end, as the need for foreign capital became even more pressing, its supply began to wane. The foreign loan boom abated as declining commodity prices affected foreign trade earnings and revenues. Direct foreign investment also began to taper off as U.S. capital was diverted into speculation on the New York Stock Exchange.

When Wall Street's crash in the fall of 1929 dried up the flow of capital, triggering a worldwide depression, debtors everywhere were caught out on a speculative limb, and the branch broke. With creditors calling in debts and economic retrenchment setting in, international export markets contracted precipitously. The slide in foreign earnings meant fewer and fewer imports could be purchased, which in turn drastically curtailed government revenues. Simultaneously, foreign creditors were calling in the loans of recent years. Only a few governments avoided suspension of debt payments; all cut back heavily on expenditures. Public servants were dismissed. Soldiers suffered a drop in pay; in some cases, they even went unpaid. Large numbers of laborers, workers, and employees were thrown out of work as businesses folded.[32]

The political response to this unprecedented economic crisis was the alteration or overthrow of national regimes almost everywhere in

Latin America. Only in Venezuela, Guatemala, Honduras, and Argentina were notables spared, largely because of military intervention to preserve the notables' economic and social hegemony. Elsewhere, the forces of reform—ranging from disgruntled notables to moderate reformers to new Marxist movements—challenged that hegemony with varying degrees of success. Getúlio Vargas's multiclass political movement in Brazil proved the most enduring. Radical reform movements came to power only briefly or sporadically in Chile, Peru, Paraguay, and Bolivia (in the latter two cases, pushed to the threshold by the Chaco War between them in 1932–1935). But the exclusive hold of the former notable-dominated parties was never restored. Political power changed hands among various parties and coalitions. Armed radical revolutions broke out in El Salvador, Nicaragua, and Cuba. In Mexico, the one Latin American country to break the notables' hegemony before 1930, a reenergized revolutionary movement fully integrated labor and peasant organizations into a new corporately structured official revolutionary party.

The closed politics forged by the notables' consensus after 1880 had ended. In some countries (and for some brief periods), personal or military dictatorships might still impose the notables' economic and social hegemony. But politics was now once again an open process. The foundations of the notables' hegemony had been irrevocably shaken. The Depression had ushered in this new political reality, but its continuance rested on a mix of recent and new circumstances.

Conjuncture of Accumulating Forces

The Depression engendered the culmination of certain forces that had been building for three decades, thereby strengthening and confirming the need for reform or even radical change that various elements of the middle, working, and popular classes had been demanding. At the same time, the Depression brought about the conjuncture of other forces that would launch a new society, a new era in Latin America.

Since the turn of the century a rising tide of antiforeign sentiment had been spreading over Latin America. The Depression brought it to an apogee. Notables, it was argued, had led their countries down the road to dependence ending in a disaster. Latin American nations should become independent of fluctuations in foreign markets and capital, but they could never do so simply as exporters of primary products. Economic independence also came to be seen as a function of economic diversification. Notables had left their nations' economic fortunes very vulnerable in skewing the economy toward the primary export sector (and a few principal commodities within that). The Depression, for most, made the lesson abundantly clear. The expansion of national industry to substitute for imports rapidly became the generally accepted policy alternative, along with a complementary agricultural diversification that would supply raw materials to factories and foodstuffs to workers.

The Depression's economic consequences also undermined the whole premise upon which notable political hegemony rested: that politics was their exclusive province. It was no longer a question of making the notables' politics of order and progress more individually free, competitively open, and socially just. The imperative was to find a new ideology, one that would chart a radically new direction. Now political brokers were increasingly offering comprehensive ideologies to reorganize society and the nation, and interest groups were buying into them. The ensuing years saw a politics of ideological fluidity and experimentation. Electoral and military majorities, along with some modern-day caudillos, shifted from one grand solution to another.

To confront economic crisis and implement sweeping ideological programs for change, more and more groups now looked to government. Increasingly, national governments were being seen as the prime agent to bring about economic recovery, diversification, and independence. In external trade, that meant regulating exports, assisting in marketing or disposing of surpluses, supervising import volume and composition, and controlling foreign exchange rates. To promote industry, national governments were expected to provide protection, help finance new industries, and secure national control over key industries through nationalization when necessary. National governments were also looked to as the prime agent to promote social change and cultural unity. In the wake of the Depression, popular demands for social change—on nonnotable terms and through the national government—expanded markedly. To be sure, there was still considerable disagreement among the middle, working, and popular classes about the scope and character of such change. Nevertheless, the promotion of a national culture fostered more harmony among these social strata as it integrated and affirmed the various traditions among them.[33]

The Depression was thus consequential enough to transform minor but growing political tendencies into widely supported political tenets and to alter public policy debates and initiatives dramatically in the years that followed. But in and of themselves these political tenets were not sufficient to consolidate and solidify a new, popularly based, nationalizing political framework. Rather, it was the conjuncture of several forces (most with origins in the preceding decades) that verified and rooted these tenets in the body politic of Latin America.

The Depression set in motion a prolonged virtuous circle that promoted industrialization, assisted heavily by government subsidies, tariff manipulation, and credit facilities. Preparations for another war in Europe and then the worldwide conflict itself extended this new economic force. Not only large industrial concerns but also numerous modestly sized firms arose to provide substitutes for formerly imported goods. Industry's growth had social repercussions as well, augmenting significantly the numbers of those with a stake in industrialization. Middle-class ranks were enlarged with owners, managers, and employees. New working-class components were created, which diminished the importance of this group's original craft-oriented base. Those of modest or humble beginnings who became owners of large successful enterprises soon constituted a new, industrial-based element among the wealthy, joining the notables in what was becoming a less familial, more generalized upper class.

The mushrooming of industrial activity was fortuitous, for a demographic revolution was just beginning. The cumulative effect of efforts since 1900 to improve public health in general, combined with the use of modern medicine to combat epidemic diseases by the 1920s, cut death rates (especially for infants and young children), while birth rates continued to be very high. The population explosion that began to gather momentum by 1930 was more rapid (and perhaps more profound) than previous ones in Europe and North America. As in the late imperial period, the countryside could no longer hold its population. Only now, the scale of urban migration was far greater, especially to metropolitan centers, given the labor demands created by rapid industrial growth and the rise of mass communications. Those finding jobs in manufacturing and the expanding service sector comprised a new, in time dominant, component of the urban working class (the first in some smaller and less developed countries). Yet as urbanization soon began to outpace economic development, not all could be absorbed, resulting in an accelerating expansion of urban marginals. Such an oversupply of urban labor kept wages low, fostering inefficient industrial establishments and growing worker dependence on government intervention to maintain living standards.

The nation-state was much more integral to the accelerating participation of its citizens in the life of the nation. The Depression's impact magnified the previous rise of political brokers, spread of voluntary association, and affirmation of popular culture symbols that had fostered the receptivity of the popular and working classes to a more national orientation in their lives. A truly national society in the making was rapidly penetrating isolated areas and previously marginalized groups. Along a proliferation of roads financed largely by national governments moved new modes of transportation—the automobile, truck, and bus. Politicians and political parties quickly availed themselves of new mass media—radio, movies, and comic books. Through a multiplying number of schools and cultural programs, national governments (much more than previously) sought to nationalize culture, instilling loyalty and refocusing identity. There were still those who sought hierarchy's preservation or sought to control and restrict popular political participation in the national society being forged. But their attempts to do so were in a new context. Universal participation in the nation had become legitimized in public discourse and increasingly pursued by leaders and followers alike.

Notes

1. Balmori, Voss, and Wortman, *Notable Family Networks*, 154–61, 183; Frederick M. Nunn, "Emil Körner and the Prussianization of the Chilean Army: Origins and Consequences, 1885–1920," *HAHR* 50 (May 1970): 300–22.

2. Chandler, *The Feitosas*, chap. 5; Yarrington, "Public Land Settlement," 42–51; and Meyers, *La Comarca Lagunera*, chaps. 3, 6, and 8.

3. Tulio Halperín Donghi, *The Contemporary History of Latin America*, ed. and trans. John Charles Chasteen (Durham, NC: Duke University, 1993), 186–88.

4. Marichal, "La banca mexicana," 250–257; Batiz V., "Trayectoria," 284–95; Steven Topik, *The Political Economy of the Brazilian State, 1889–1930* (Austin: University of Texas Press, 1987), chap. 5.

5. Hodge, "Argentine School System," 47–54, 60–65.

6. Zimmerman, "Racial Ideas," 38–39; Cueto, "Yellow Fever in Peru," 6–12, 18.

7. Munck, "Working Class in Argentina," 33–34; Viviane Brachet-Marquez, *The Dynamics of Domination: State, Class, and Social Reform in Mexico, 1910–1990* (Pittsburgh: University of Pittsburgh Press, 1994), 65–68.

8. Topik, *Brazilian State*, 15–16, 43, 47, chaps. 3–6, 161; Burns, *Brazil*, 290; Marichal, *Century of Debt Crisis*, 197.

9. Topik, *Brazilian State*, 69, 110, 147–48.

10. Ibid., 47; Sowell, *Artisans and Politics*, 137–46, 150–53; Brachet-Marquez, *Dynamics of Domination*, 66–68; Moisés Poblete Troncoso and Ben G. Barnett, *The Rise of the Latin American Labor Movement* (New Haven, CT: College and University Press, 1960), chaps. 3–5.

11. Arthur F. Liebescher, S.J., "Institutionalization and Evangelization in the Argentine Church: Cordoba under Zenon Bustos, 1906–1919," *The Americas* 45 (January 1989): 373–75; Baldwin, "Escuelas misionales protestantes," 310–16.

12. Sowell, *Artisans and Politics*, 138, 146–49.

13. Stuart F. Voss, "Nationalizing the Revolution: Culmination and Circumstance," in *Provinces of the Revolution: Essays on Regional Mexican History*, ed. Thomas Benjamin and Mark Wasserman (Albuquerque: University of New Mexico Press, 1990), 281–84; Karno, "Augusto B. Leguía," 184–87, 227–28, 255.

14. Halperín Donghi, *Contemporary History of Latin America*, 193.

15. Needell, *Tropical Belle Epoque*, 57–58, 63–71, 89, 102–10.

16. Beezley, "Porfirian Smart Set," 175–78, 186; Mary Kay Vaughn, "The Construction of the Patriotic Festival in Tecamachalco, Puebla, 1900–1946," in *Rituals of Rule, Rituals of Resistance: Public Celebrations and Popular Culture in Mexico*, ed. William H. Beezley, Cheryl English Martin, and William E. French (Wilmington, DE: Scholarly Resources, 1994), 216–19.

17. Scobie, *Buenos Aires*, 240–44; Hodge, "Argentine School System," 60–65.

18. Barbara A. Tenenbaum, "Streetwise History: The Paseo de la Reforma and the Porfirian State, 1876–1910," in *Rituals of Rule, Rituals of Resistance: Public Celebrations and Popular Culture in Mexico*, ed. William H. Beezley, Cheryl English Martin, and William E. French (Wilmington, DE: Scholarly Resources, 1994), 130–47; Beezley, "Porfirian Smart Set," 176.

19. Solberg, *Immigration and Nationalism*, 132–40.

20. Ibid., 152–60.

21. Carol Hendrickson, "The Idea of 'Civilización' in Guatemala's IV Centenario Celebration" (paper, annual meeting of the New England Council of Latin American Studies, Mount Holyoke College, October 18, 1997), 1–6.

22. José Vasconcelos, *A Mexican Ulysses: An Autobiography*, trans. W. Rex Crawford (Bloomington: University of Indiana Press, 1963), 167–73; Donald H. Frischmann, "Misiones Culturales, Teatro Consupo, and Teatro Comunidad: The Evolution of Rural Theater," in *Rituals of Rule, Rituals of Resistance: Public Celebrations and Popular Culture in Mexico*, ed. William H. Beezley, Cheryl English Martin, and William E. French (Wilmington, DE: Scholarly Resources, 1994), 287.

23. Burns, *Brazil*, 367–70, 375–83.

24. Scobie, *Buenos Aires*, 207.

25. Benjamin and Wasserman, *Provinces of the Revolution*, see especially chaps. 6–7.

26. Diego Abente, "The Liberal Republic and the Failure of Democracy in Paraguay," *The Americas* 45 (April 1989): 532–39, 540–46.

27. Brian Loveman, *Chile: The Legacy of Spanish Capitalism* (New York: Oxford University Press, 1979), 241–53; Burns, *Brazil*, 391–92; Nunn, "Chilean Army," 315–20.

28. Jesús Chavarría, "The Intellectuals and the Crisis of Modern Peruvian Nationalism," *HAHR* 50 (May 1970): 268–78; Mark J. Van Aken, "University Reform before Cordoba," *HAHR* 51 (August 1971): 447–62.

29. Rock, *Argentina*, 185–86, 189–90, 199–213; Diana Juanicó, "Partidos, facciones políticas y elecciones: Tlaxcala en 1924," *HM* 37 (July–September 1987): 82–97.

30. E. Bradford Burns, *Latin America: A Concise Interpretative History* (Englewood Cliffs, NJ: Prentice-Hall, 6th ed., 1994), 190–93; Milton I. Vanger, "Politics and Class in Twentieth Century Latin America," *HAHR* 49 (February 1969): 84–89.

31. Andrews, "Black Political Protest," 154–56.

32. Luis E. Aguilar, *Cuba, 1933: Prologue to Revolution* (New York: Norton, 1972), 40–49, 55–60, 95; Marichal, *Century of Debt Crisis*, 201–11; Quiroz, "Peruvian Elite Groups," 73–76.

33. Conrad, "La industria de chicle," 479–80; Abente, "Foreign Capital in Paraguay," 85–87; Angus Lindsay Wright, "Market, Land, and Class: Southern Bahia, Brazil, 1890–1942" (Ph.D. diss., University of Michigan, 1976), chap. 4; Victoria Lerner, "Historia de la reforma educativa, 1933–1945," *HM* 29 (July–September 1979): 94–104, 116–17; Jorge Mora Forero, "Los maestros y la práctica de la educación socialista," *HM* 29 (July–September 1979): 142–60; Vaughn, "Patriotic Festival," 222–29.

Epilogue

By 1940, Latin America was a very different place than it had been before the outbreak of worldwide depression. The notables' hegemony was broken beyond repair. Even more, Middle Period society itself had become part of Latin America's past. The regional orientation of life spatially governing that society had been supplanted. In its stead was a national ordering of life that at once embraced the disparate regional cultural strands, even as it sought to meld them into more encompassing and more uniform patterns of daily and public life. At the center of this emerging national society was the nation-state, committed to the modernization of that common life.

The issue of hierarchy, however, had not been resolved. Though egalitarianism had become fully legitimated in discourse—and widely accepted in practice as an alternative in socially restructuring the emerging national society—it did not yet rule the day. Nevertheless, the issue would no longer be settled by the social system that had embodied Middle Period society. Deference had first lost its practicality, then its credibility. Personal and client relations had increasingly given way to formal voluntary association as the principal nexus in public social relations. Only remnants of the formative social strata of Middle Period society could still be found. The *gente de profesiones* persisted only where economic marginalization and lack of voluntary association had allowed them to survive. The *gente decente* had become an anachronism; one could no longer wait to become a notable. For the notables themselves were being subsumed in a larger upper class in which wealth (inherited or self-made) was becoming the principal credential for entrance. Indeed, respectability had yielded to class as the fundamental basis for social stratification. The middle and working classes had become major components of society. Only the popular classes retained a significantly visible presence. Still, their numbers were eroding as they became part of the working class (sometimes, even the middle class). In the indigenous communities and unorganized laborers of the countryside and among urban marginals, their essence could still be observed.

The new class-based, nationally oriented society had moved beyond the bounds of Latin America's Middle Period. It was the social and spatial expression of a new era, a modern age that was now dawning. Still, the shades of night into which Latin America's Middle Period had passed still lingered. Like the morning star and the moon not yet overshadowed by the rising sun, remnants of that era and its society were yet visible after 1940. In certain circumstances, practices that underlay the working of Middle Period society were still useful, sometimes even indispensable.

Personalism and Petty Production

The rise of modern Latin America entailed a commitment to a more formal, impersonal organization of society, yet many still relied on personalism. Family networking continued to play an important role in business and political organization and conduct. Names of officeholders at various levels of government and of private and public boards of directors reveal that notable family names still carried weight. Though businesses increasingly modernized in organization and management, many firms still relied on familial trust. Among the lower strata, family and community ties remained strategic in struggling to meet life's necessities, especially in the countryside. Many of those migrating to cities in ever-rising numbers sought to adapt those ties in the process of urban relocation.

The popular and working classes also found that universal participation and egalitarianism—declaimed integral to the modern era—were not always operative. They often fell back upon informal ties between patron and client. Politically, they linked themselves to modern-day caudillos and local bosses, who displayed evidence of respect for their station and could deliver on some of their rising expectations. Economically, they relied on personalized credit arrangements of kin, employer, and corner-store owner. Unions often negotiated (or settled for) patron-client relations with government officials. The middle and sometimes upper classes had not entirely weaned themselves from such informal dependent ties to protect or advance their social position. Political cliques and business relations frequently rested on such linkages, especially in an authoritarian climate.

Though detested by most, dependent patron-client relations had been a necessity for the large majority of *gente baja* in Middle Period society as a way of coping when alternative strategies proved too risky or unfeasible. Some, especially communal villagers, valued autonomous self-subsistence most highly. Others, particularly *gente de profesiones*, trusted more in the opportunities of the marketplace, if it was just. But growing numbers had found that engaging in marketable petty production was perhaps the most effective way to respond to the inroads of commercial and then industrial capitalism. They had sought to carve out as large a portion of autonomy in the market economy as their degree of leverage at a given time permitted. Communal village farmers, independent rancheros and *minifundistas* (small farmers), tenants and sharecroppers, artisans, and even slaves with garden plots or artisanal skills—the measure of autonomy of all depended upon the degree to which they controlled access to resources and labor skills, since they possessed little capital.

Also decisive to petty producers' success was the extent of reciprocity and solidarity among the *gente baja*, even that based solely on mutual self-interest. Within specific segments, it was manifested in communal decisionmaking of villages, cooperative efforts of independent farmers in sharing access to water and other natural resources, and mutual aid societies among artisans. But it was also the case in relations among many of these segments. They were suppliers and consumers for one another. This microstrategy served as a counterpoint in the macroworld of first merchant and then industrial capitalism, ebbing and flowing in the competition of the marketplace and as historical circumstances changed.

After 1940 the reach and scope of Latin America's industrializing, nationalizing economies seemed to expand without impediment. Ever more efficient modes of communication and transport accelerated the process, from which petty production retreated steadily. Since 1970 the tide seems to have turned a bit. Economic crises triggered by escalating oil prices and then by staggering sums of unpaid debt resulting from a U.S.-induced worldwide recession have left vast numbers of Latin America's poor struggling to stay afloat. Whether by preference or more likely now by necessity, they have fallen back on a tried and tested strategy for survival. Its nomenclature has changed; ironically becoming much more contrapuntal in terminology: the "informal" economy. The poor's renewed reliance on petty production in the late twentieth century suggests that modern Latin America is part of a larger historical process, the first phases of which occurred during Latin America's Middle Period.

Cycles of Market Penetration

Certainly for those situated comfortably in Latin America's history since the 1750s, there have been periods of political turmoil or economic crisis followed by ones of prosperity and relatively stable politics. But from their perspective, Latin America's evolving history over the past 200 or more years has been linear. Progressively, their world has become more prosperous, more sophisticated, more cosmopolitan, more modern. Yet for a much, much larger proportion of Latin Americans those same centuries have brought only fleeting comfort and nearly continuous struggle to maintain a minimally secure way of life. Their experience of that history has been far more cyclical. They have found themselves beset by historical waves of commercialization and international marketplace penetration, increasing in scope and impact, that have churned up their lives.

The first wave undermined the colonial order. Compensatory securities in corporatism and imperial protection eroded. Large numbers of *gente baja* lost access to resources and to leverage in their labor. Many were spatially dislocated and their families fragmented, leaving more and more women as heads of households. But in the weakening of racial caste stratification, they found an avenue for some social mobility and revised self-identity. In the competitive marketplace, petty production created possibilities for new strategies for subsistence survival and expanded space for economic autonomy. In erosion of imperial authority, avenues were opened for the assertion of greater cultural autonomy and for the negotiation of political rights and obligations.

With independence, penetration of the international market slowed. The new nation-states were weak. The world beyond grew hesitant, even apathetic, as it became preoccupied elsewhere. Its presence was limited or at most localized. In such a relative vacuum, the *gente baja* found historical space to consolidate their social position and to foster the economic possibilities that Middle Period society had opened to them. Though no one could fully realize it then, these were the years when Latin America's commoners enjoyed the greatest control over their way of life.

By the 1880s, however, a second, greater wave of commercialization and international market penetration was upon them. Unlike a century before, the *gente baja* had considerably less historical room in which to maneuver. Once again, they lost access to resources (catastrophically in some regions); the leverage of their labor dropped markedly. Once again, spatially dislodged, they were forced in growing numbers to leave their families and communities to survive. Social cohesion eroded as crime, alcoholism, and infant mortality rose. Culturally, commoners were under siege as notables moved to impose foreign and subordinated ways of life. The notables' new imitative world view and political power rendered negotiations with those below unnecessary and disdainful. Only a small segment of the *gente baja*—those with skills vital to the emerging industrializing sectors—made any headway. But in that segment's use of modern, formal modes of organization (unions, especially), an avenue of effective resistance opened up for Latin America's struggling masses. Through voluntary associations, whether economic or political, they increasingly learned that they could challenge the notables' hegemony. And they encountered allies among the new middle class.

With the onslaught of worldwide depression in 1930, followed by the preoccupations of World War II, international market penetration ebbed for a second time. Once again, commoners enjoyed a relative respite in which to regain greater ability to meet life's necessities. Yet unlike the post-independence years a century before, there was no political vacuum. Indeed, it was the very strength of the modern nation-state now emerging that served as a mediating force on their behalf. But there was a price. In the increasingly national ordering of life, cultural autonomy had to be abandoned in favor of incorporation of popular and regional legacies into a national culture and identity. The popular classes and new working classes were also expected to conform to the mandates of a modern, industrial economy. Their formal participation in public life—rather than the more autonomous post-independence mechanism of informal negotiation—was to be the mechanism through which their grievances were to be aired and addressed. In the process, though differences among them narrowed and they came together in ever larger numbers, those who had political power (now much more centralized and encompassing) were more difficult to challenge and influence.

A third wave of international market penetration began to sweep over Latin America after 1960, leading national governments first to take on escalating debt to keep development in pace with an exploding population and rising expectations, and then to head off the consequences of escalating world oil prices. That left them ever more vulnerable to the worldwide recession of the early 1980s and the accompanying tidal surge of globalization that broke over Latin America. Faced with the import substitution model's growing inability to cope with this new international reality, governments have yielded to the apparent "immovable force" of globalization. In the process, they have steadily abandoned their mediating role on behalf of Latin America's poor and working classes.

The population explosion since midcentury has meant that accelerating spatial dislocation has become an ever-growing fact in the lives of Latin America's poor. The effects of increased stress on family life have been manifested in a rising rate of crime, substance abuse, and households headed by single females. Latin America's poor and laboring masses have turned to petty production out of necessity. In the process, they have more economic autonomy, even as they have less economic security. Through a return to constitutional, representative government, they have greater potential for political influence. But so far, this potential has seemed only to make governments more cautious. The use of nongovernmental organizations by growing numbers of Latin America's popular and working classes seems to have been more effective in solving their pressing problems. In this, ironically, they have found growing external support.

Perhaps nowhere is this larger cyclical perspective on Latin America's historical evolution more suggestive than in the conflict that emerged in the Mexican state of Chiapas in the mid-1990s. Over the past decade, Mexico's ruling Institutional Revolutionary Party has committed the nation to the North American Free Trade Agreement and a reorientation of Mexico's overall place in the "new world" of globalization, profoundly impacting the nation. In challenging this new tidal wave of globalization, the Zapatista National Liberation Front, centered in the Indian villagers of Chiapas, has spread its message through mass global media and through the Internet. But its content seems to recall a past in which rights and obligations were negotiated and villagers sought economic autonomy and cultural space within a federated national framework. That so many Mexicans have expressed solidarity with the Zapatista movement raises even more the question of how much the legacy of Latin America's Middle Period is still present.

Suggestions for Further Reading

The fundamental premise of this volume has been that a local/regional orientation underlay Middle Period society. As such the vast majority of sources consulted were more spatially limited studies such as monographs and especially journal articles. What follows is a selective list of titles—principally books—that provide a representative sample of the diverse research carried on at the local and regional level by historians of Latin America over the past three decades. In many cases, they are expanded monographs drawn from the journal articles and dissertations cited in the text. Readers who wish to explore more broadly the vast array of such studies in the periodical literature should consult journals such as *Hispanic American Historical Review, Journal of Latin American Studies, Latin American Research Review, The Americas, Comparative Studies of Society and History, Luso-Brazilian Review, Journal of Inter-American Studies and World Affairs, Latin American Perspectives, Journal of Latin American Cultural Studies, Colonial Latin American Review,* and *Journal of Caribbean History.* Historical periodicals are found in each Latin American country, such as *Historia Mexicana, Boletín de la Academia Nacional de la Historia* (Venezuela), and *Revista do Instituto Histórico e Geográfico Brasileiro.*

General

There are no existing general texts on Latin American history that fit within the bounds of the Middle Period (1750–1930). A few regional studies come fairly close: John Tutino, *Insurrection to Revolution in Mexico, 1750–1940* (Princeton, NJ, 1986); David McCreery, *Rural Guatemala, 1760–1940* (Stanford, CA, 1994); and Lawrence J. Nielsen, "Rural Society in Sabará and Its Hinterland, 1780–1930" (Ph.D. diss., 1975). Diana Balmori, Stuart F. Voss, and Miles Wortman provide a general synthesis and three case studies in *Notable Family Networks* (Chicago, 1984). In Hilary Beckles and Verene Shepherd's anthologies for the supraregion of the Caribbean, *Caribbean Slavery in the Atlantic World* (Kingston, Jamaica, and Princeton, NJ, 2000) and *Economy and Society from Emancipation to the Present* (Princeton, NJ, 1996), there are an abundance of studies about the various islands. Gabriel García Márquez's celebrated novel, *One Hundred Years of Solitude* (New York, 1970), provides an allegory for the Middle Period, centered on the fictional Colombian town of Macondo.

Many other local and regional studies span much of the period or overlap with the colonial and modern periods on either side. Some of these works consider the locality or region more generally: Jane Rausch, *The Llanos of Colombia, 1531–1831* (Albuquerque, NM, 1984); Stuart F. Voss, *On the Periphery of Nineteenth Century Mexico* (Tucson, AZ, 1982); Mario Cerruti, ed., *Monterrey, Nueva León, el Noreste* (Monterrey, Mexico, 1987); Stanley J. Stein, *Vassouras* (New York, 1970); and Daniel Nugent, *Namiquipa, Chihuahua* (Chicago, 1993).

Most are more narrowly topical. Those with a socioeconomic focus include David A. Brading, *Haciendas and Ranchos in the Mexican Bajío* (Cambridge, England, 1978); Herbert S. Klein, *Rural Society in the Bolivian Andes* (Stanford, CA, 1993); Brooke Larson, *Colonialism and Agrarian Transformation in Bolivia: Cochabamba* (Princeton, NJ, 1988); Mark D. Szuchman, *Mobility and and Integration in Urban Argentina: Cordoba* (Austin, TX, 1980); Arnold J. Bauer, *Chilean Rural Society* (Cambridge, England, 1975); Catherine LeGrand, *Frontier Expansion and Peasant Protest in Colombia* (Albuquerque, NM, 1986); and Cynthia Radding, *Colonialism, Ethnic Spaces, and Ecological Frontiers in Northwestern Mexico* (Durham, NC, 1997).

Many temporally broad local and regional studies focus on ethnic and other social groups: Evelyn Hu-DeHart, *Spanish Contact with the Yaqui Nation* (Tucson, AZ, 1982) and *Yaqui Resistance and Survival* (Madison, WI, 1984); David Sowell, *Artisans and Politics in Bogotá* (Philadelphia, 1992); Sylvia M. Arrom, *Women of Mexico City* (Stanford, CA, 1985); Heather Fowler-Salamini and Mary Kay Vaughn, eds., *Women of the Mexican Countryside* (Tucson, AZ, 1994); John M. Hart, *The Mexican Working Class* (Austin, TX, 1987); Silvia Arrom and Servando Ortoll, eds., *Riots in the Cities, Popular Politics, and the Urban Poor in Latin America* (Wilmington, DE, 1996); Mark Wasserman, *Native Elite and Foreign Enterprise in Chihuahua* (Chapel Hill, NC, 1984); Hendrik Kraay, ed., *Afro-Brazilan Culture and Politics: Bahia* (London, 1998); Florencia E. Mallon, *Peasant and Nation: The Making of Post-Colonial Mexico and Peru* (Berkeley, CA, 1995); and Oliver Marshall, *English-Speaking Communities in Latin America* (London, 2000). Larissa Adler-Lomnitz and Marisol Pérez-Lizaur, *Mexican Elite Family* (Princeton, NJ, 1987), Billy Jaynes Chandler, *The Feitosas and the Sertão Inhamuns* (Gainesville, FL, 1972); and Darrell Levi, *The Prados of São Paulo* (Athens, GA, 1987) are three of numerous individual family studies. Friedrich Katz's anthology, *Riots, Rebellions, and Insurrections: Rural Social Conflict in Mexico* (Princeton, NJ, 1986), covers diverse sociopolitical conflicts in a wide array of Mexican regions. William H. Beezley, Cheryl English Martin, and William E. French, eds., *Rituals of Rule, Rituals of Resistance* (Wilmington, DE, 1994) focuses on Mexican popular culture in parallel fashion.

The Emergence of a New Society, 1750–1820

The dynamics of economic and demographic growth is a major theme in local and regional studies during the last decades before independence. Collective works under the editorship of Ida Altman and James Lockhart, *Early Provinces of Mexico* (Los Angeles, 1976), and of David Robinson, *Social Fabric and Spatial Structure in Colonial Latin America* (Ann Arbor, MI, 1979) portray diverse regions caught up in socioeconomic change. Among such works by individuals are Michael Swann, *Settlement and Society in Colonial Durango* (Boulder, CO, 1982); Eric Van Young, *Rural Economy of the Guadalajara Region* (Berkeley, CA, 1981); Cheryl English Martin, *Rural Society in Morelos* (Albuquerque, NM, 1985) and *Chihuahua in the Eighteenth Century* (Stanford, CA, 1996); Carlos A. Mayo, *Estancia y sociedad en la pampa* (Buenos Aires, 1995); Sonya Lipsett-Rivera, *Struggle for Water Resources in Puebla* (Albuquerque, NM, 1999); Arij Ouweneel, *Crisis and Development in Central Mexico* (Albuquerque, NM, 1996); Enrique Tandeter, *Silver Mining in Potosí* (Albuquerque, NM, 1993) and *The Market of Potosí* (London, 1987); Juan Carlos Garavaglia and Juan Carlos Grosso, *Puebla desde una perspectiva microhistoria* (Mexico, DF, 1994); Michael P. McKinley, *Pre-Revolutionary Caracas* (Cambridge, England, 1985); and Linda Greenow, *Credit and Socioeconomic Change in Guadalajara* (Boulder, CO, 1983).

Works more narrowly focused on social groups are David A. Brading, *Diocese of Michoacán* (Cambridge, England, 1994); John K. Chance, *Spaniards and Indians in Oaxaca* (Norman, OK, 1989); John E. Kizca, *Colonial Entrepreneurs in Bourbon Mexico City* (Albuquerque, NM, 1983); Adriaan C. Van Oss, *Parish History of Guatemala* (Cambridge, England, 1986); Robert J. Ferry, *Colonial Elite of Early Caracas* (Berkeley, CA, 1989); Jackie Booker, *Veracruz Merchants* (Boulder, CO, 1993); and Jonathan C. Brown, *Decline and Fall of Spanish Merchants in Buenos Aires* (Austin, TX, 1987). Specific analyses of changes in social stratification can be found in Rodney D. Anderson, *Guadalajara a la consumación de la independencia* (Guadalajara, 1983); and in Elizabeth A. Kuznesof, *Household Economy and Urban Development: São Paulo* (Boulder, CO, 1986).

Various facets of the Bourbon reforms are covered in Linda Arnold, *Bureaucrats in Mexico City* (Tucson, AZ, 1988); John D. Fisher, *Era of Free Trade* (Liverpool, 1985) and *Intendant System in Peru* (London, 1970); Susan M. Socolow, *Bureaucrats of Buenos Aires* (Durham, NC, 1988); Susan Deans-Smith, *Tobacco Monopoly in Bourbon Mexico* (Austin, TX, 1992); Allan J. Keuthe, *Crown, Military, and Society: Cuba* (Knoxville, TN, 1986); Kendall Brown, *Imperial Reform in Eighteenth Century Arequipa* (Albuquerque, NM, 1986); and D. S. Chandler, *Social Assistance and Bureaucratic Politics: Mexico* (Albuquerque, NM, 1991).

Imperial reform, combined with the transforming socioeconomic changes, ignited various revolts across the Ibero-American empires. Some involved Indian communities and tribes: Ward Stavig, *World of*

Túpac Amaru (Lincoln, NE, 1999); John R. Fisher, Allan J. Keuthe, and Anthony MacFarlane, eds., *Reform and Insurrection in Bourbon New Granada and Peru* (Baton Rouge, LA, 1990); and Roberto Salmon, *Indian Revolts in Northern New Spain* (Lanham, MD, 1991). Others were more general in social composition: Martin Minchom, *Change and Unrest in the Underclass: Quito* (Boulder, CO, 1994); John L. Phelan, *Comunero Revolt in Colombia* (Madison, WI, 1978); Eric Van Young, *Estructura agraria y rebelliones populares de la Nueva España* (n.p., 1992); and Kenneth Maxwell, *Conflicts and Conspiracies: Brazil* (Cambridge, England, 1973).

Various general works cover the independence wars. See John Lynch, *Spanish-American Revolutions* (New York, 1986); Timothy Anna, *Spain and the Loss of America* (Lincoln, NE, 1983); Richard Graham, *Independence in Latin America* (New York, 1994); Jaime E. Rodríguez O., *Independence of Spanish America* (Cambridge, England, 1998); and François-Xavier Guerra, *Independencias americanas y liberalismo español* (Madrid, 1995). Others treat what would become individual new nations, including: T. O. Ott, *The Haitian Revolution* (Knoxville, TN, 1973); A. J. R. Russell-Wood, ed., *Essays on the Independence of Brazil* (Baltimore, 1975); Brian R. Hamnett, *Roots of Insurgency: Mexican Regions* (Cambridge, England, 1986); and Eric Van Young, *Popular Violence, Ideology, and the Mexican Struggle for Independence* (Stanford, CA, 2001).

The Uneasy Equilibrium, 1820–1880

Still the least researched period in Latin American history, the post-independence years remain largely seen from a national perspective. Within such works, one can find local and regional examples and case studies: Lowell Gudmunson, *Costa Rica before Coffee* (Baton Rouge, LA, 1986); Peter Blanchard, *Slavery and Abolition in Early Peru* (Wilmington, DE, 1992); Paul Gootenberg, *Peru's "Fictitious Prosperity" of Guano* (Berkeley, CA, 1993) and *Between Silver and Guano* (Princeton, NJ, 1989); Stanley C. Green, *Mexican Republic: First Decade* (Pittsburgh, 1987); Barbara A. Tenenbaum, *Debts and Taxes in Mexico* (Albuquerque, NM, 1986); Donald F. Stevens, *Origins of Instability in Early Republican Mexico* (Durham, NC, 1991); Pedro Santoni, *Mexico at Arms* (Fort Worth, TX, 1996); John Hoyt Williams, *Rise and Fall of the Paraguayan Republic* (Austin, TX, 1979); and Richard Graham, *Patronage and Politics in Nineteenth Century Brazil* (Stanford, CA, 1990).

There are a few monographs focused on specific regions: David J. Weber, *The American Southwest under Mexico* (Albuquerque, NM, 1982); Margaret Chowning, *Wealth and Power in Provincial Mexico: Michoacán* (Stanford, CA, 1999); David Walker, *Martínez del Rio Family* (Austin, TX, 1986); Moisés González Navarro, *Guerra de castas y el Yucatán* (Mexico, DF, 1970); José Deustua, *Social Economy of Mining: Peru* (Athens, OH, 2000); Juan Rolf Englesen, "Social Aspects of Agricultural Expansion in Coastal Peru" (Ph.D. diss., 1977); Mark D. Szuchman,

Order, Family, and Community in Buenos Aires (Stanford, CA, 1988); Peter Guardino, *Peasants, Politics, and Formation of the Mexican State: Guerrero* (Stanford, CA, 1996); Felix V. Matos Rodríguez, *Women and Urban Change in San Juan, Puerto Rico* (Gainesville, FL, 1999); and Mary C. Karasch, *Slave Life in Rio de Janeiro* (Princeton, NJ, 1987). Most local and regional studies for this period can be found as parts of works beginning in the late imperial period or overlapping with the late nineteenth and early twentieth centuries or in scholarly journals.

Passage to the Modern World, 1880–1929

In contrast to the pre-1880 period, the half century following is rich in local and regional studies from quite varied topical perspectives. The economic interests of notable families are explored in numerous monographs and dissertations across Latin America, including Paul J. Dosal, *Rise of Guatemala's Industrial Oligarchy* (Westport, CT, 1995); Allen Wells, *Yucatan's Gilded Age* (Albuquerque, NM, 1985); Michael F. Jimenez, *Life Cycle of Central Colombian Coffee Estates* (Princeton, NJ, 1988); Frederick V. Gifun, "Ribeirão Prêto: Transition to Coffee in São Paulo" (Ph.D. diss., 1972); Alex M. Saragoza, *Monterrey Elite* (Austin, TX, 1988); Angus Lindsay Wright, "Market, Land, and Class: Southern Bahia" (Ph.D. diss., 1976); Warren Dean, *Industrialization of São Paulo* (Austin, TX, 1969); and Alfonso W. Quiroz, *Estructura financiera y economía peruana* (Lima, 1987). Discussions of political networking by notables can be found in such works as Mark Wasserman, *Persistant Oligarchs: Chihuahua, Mexico* (Durham, NC, 1993); Linda Lewin, *Politics and Parentela in Paraiba* (Princeton, NJ, 1987); and William S. Langston, "Coahuila in the Porfiriato" (Ph.D. diss., New Orleans, 1980). Cultural studies manifesting the notables' worldview include Jeffrey Needell, *Tropical Belle Epoque: Rio de Janeiro* (Cambridge, England, 1987); William E. French, *Manners, Morals, and Class Formation in Northern Mexico* (Albuquerque, NM, 1996); and Donna Guy, *Sex and Gender in Buenos Aires* (Lincoln, NE, 1995).

A number of local and regional studies examine the socioeconomic changes in the lives of various social groups resulting from the notables' economic, political, and cultural hegemony: Michael Conniff, *Black Labor on a White Canal: Panama* (Pittsburgh, 1985); James R. Scobie, *Buenos Aires: From Plaza to Suburb* (New York, 1974); Miguel Tinker Salas, *Sonora and the Transformation of the Border* (Berkeley, CA, 1997); Reid Andrews, *Blacks and Whites in São Paulo* (Madison, WI, 1991); Doug Yarrington, *Land, Society, and Politics in Duaca, Venezuela* (Pittsburgh, 1997); William K. Meyers, *Forge of Progress, Crucible of Revolt: La Comarca Lagunera* (Albuquerque, NM, 1994); June Hahner, *Poverty and Politics* (Albuquerque, NM, 1986); Dain Borges, *The Family in Bahia, Brazil* (Stanford, CA, 1992); Thomas Holloway, *Immigrants on the Land* (Chapel Hill, NC, 1980), and *Policing Rio de Janeiro* (Stanford, CA, 1993); Janet E. Worrall, *La inmigración italiana en el Perú* (Lima, 1990); and Sandra

Lauderdale Graham, *House and Street: Rio de Janeiro* (Cambridge, England, 1988).

Of growing note are the monographs examining the popular resistance to notable hegemony: Robert M. Levine, *Revisiting the Canudos Massacre in Northeastern Brazil* (Berkeley, CA, 1992); Teresa Meade, *"Civilizing" Rio: Reform and Resistance* (University Park, PA, 1997); David S. Parker, *Idea of the Middle Class* (University Park, PA, 1998); Louis A. Pérez, Jr., *Social Banditry and Peasant Protest in Cuba* (Pittsburgh, 1989); Ronn F. Pineo, *Life and Work in Guayaquil* (Gainesville, FL, 1996); Erick D. Langer, *Economic Change and Rural Resistance in Southern Bolivia* (Stanford, CA, 1989); Allen Wells and Gilbert Joseph, *Summer of Discontent, Seasons of Upheaval: Yucatán* (Stanford, CA, 1996); John Womack, *Zapata and the Mexican Revolution* (New York, 1969). Collective works providing local and regional case studies within countries and across Latin America include Thomas Benjamin and Mark Wasserman, eds., *Provinces of the Revolution* (Albuquerque, NM, 1990); Jeremy Adelman, *Essays in Argentine Labor History* (Basingstoke, England, 1992); Ronaldo Munck, ed., *Argentina: Workers, Unions, and Politics* (London, 1987); and Ronn F. Pineo and James A. Baer, eds., *People, Protests, and Progress in Urbanizing Latin America* (Boulder, CO, 1998).

Varied novels, short stories, and plays from this period illustrate well the above historical themes: Mariano Azuela, *The Underdogs* (New York, 1962) and *The Flies* and *The Bosses* in *Two Novels of Mexico* (Berkeley, CA, 1956); Jorge Icaza, *The Villagers (Huasipungo)* (Carbondale, IL, 1964); Florencio Sánchez, *Representative Plays* (Washington, DC, 1961); Joaquín María Machado de Assis, *Dom Casmurro* (New York, 1997); Aluiso Azevedo, *Mulatto* (Austin, TX, 1993); Heriberto Frías, *Tomochic* (Mexico, DF, 1968); Eugenio Cambaceres, *Sin Rumbo (Aimless)* (Buenos Aires, 1983); and Rómulo Gallegos, *Doña Bárbara* (New York, 1970).

Index

Latin American Silhouettes
Studies in History and Culture

William H. Beezley and
Judith Ewell
Editors

Volumes Published

Brian Loveman and Thomas M. Davies, Jr., eds., *The Politics of Antipolitics: The Military in Latin America*, 3d ed., revised and updated (1996). Cloth ISBN 0-8420-2609-6 Paper ISBN 0-8420-2611-8

Dianne Walta Hart, *Undocumented in L.A.: An Immigrant's Story* (1997). Cloth ISBN 0-8420-2648-7 Paper ISBN 0-8420-2649-5

William H. Beezley and Judith Ewell, eds., *The Human Tradition in Modern Latin America* (1997). Cloth ISBN 0-8420-2612-6   Paper ISBN 0-8420-2613-4

Donald F. Stevens, ed., *Based on a True Story: Latin American History at the Movies* (1997). Cloth ISBN 0-8420-2582-0 Paper ISBN 0-8420-2781-5

Jaime E. Rodríguez O., ed., *The Origins of Mexican National Politics, 1808–1847* (1997). Paper ISBN 0-8420-2723-8

Che Guevara, *Guerrilla Warfare*, with revised and updated introduction and case studies by Brian Loveman and Thomas M. Davies, Jr., 3d ed. (1997). Cloth ISBN 0-8420-2677-0   Paper ISBN 0-8420-2678-9

Adrian A. Bantjes, *As If Jesus Walked on Earth: Cardenismo, Sonora, and the Mexican Revolution* (1998; rev. ed., 2000). Cloth ISBN 0-8420-2653-3 Paper ISBN 0-8420-2751-3

A. Kim Clark, *The Redemptive Work: Railway and Nation in Ecuador, 1895–1930* (1998). Cloth ISBN 0-8420-2674-6 Paper ISBN 0-8420-5013-2

Louis A. Pérez, Jr., ed., *Impressions of Cuba in the Nineteenth Century: The Travel Diary of Joseph J. Dimock* (1998). Cloth ISBN 0-8420-2657-6 Paper ISBN 0-8420-2658-4

June E. Hahner, ed., *Women through Women's Eyes: Latin American Women in Nineteenth-Century Travel Accounts* (1998). Cloth ISBN 0-8420-2633-9 Paper ISBN 0-8420-2634-7

James P. Brennan, ed., *Peronism and Argentina* (1998). ISBN 0-8420-2706-8

John Mason Hart, ed., *Border Crossings: Mexican and Mexican-American Workers* (1998). Cloth ISBN 0-8420-2716-5 Paper ISBN 0-8420-2717-3

Brian Loveman, *For* la Patria: *Politics and the Armed Forces in Latin America* (1999). Cloth ISBN 0-8420-2772-6 Paper ISBN 0-8420-2773-4

Guy P. C. Thomson, with David G. LaFrance, *Patriotism, Politics, and Popular Liberalism in Nineteenth-Century Mexico: Juan Francisco Lucas and the Puebla Sierra* (1999). ISBN 0-8420-2683-5

Robert Woodmansee Herr, in collaboration with Richard Herr, *An American Family in the Mexican Revolution* (1999). ISBN 0-8420-2724-6

Juan Pedro Viqueira Albán, trans. Sonya Lipsett-Rivera and Sergio Rivera Ayala, *Propriety and Permissiveness in Bourbon Mexico* (1999). Cloth ISBN 0-8420-2466-2 Paper ISBN 0-8420-2467-0

Stephen R. Niblo, *Mexico in the 1940s: Modernity, Politics, and Corruption* (1999). Cloth ISBN 0-8420-2794-7 Paper (2001) ISBN 0-8420-2795-5

David E. Lorey, *The U.S.-Mexican Border in the Twentieth Century* (1999). Cloth ISBN 0-8420-2755-6 Paper ISBN 0-8420-2756-4

Joanne Hershfield and David R. Maciel, eds., *Mexico's Cinema: A Century of Films and Filmmakers* (2000). Cloth ISBN 0-8420-2681-9 Paper ISBN 0-8420-2682-7

Peter V. N. Henderson, *In the Absence of Don Porfirio: Francisco León de la Barra*

and the Mexican Revolution (2000).
ISBN 0-8420-2774-2

Mark T. Gilderhus, The Second Century: U.S.-Latin American Relations since 1889 (2000). Cloth ISBN 0-8420-2413-1 Paper ISBN 0-8420-2414-X

Catherine Moses, Real Life in Castro's Cuba (2000). Cloth ISBN 0-8420-2836-6 Paper ISBN 0-8420-2837-4

K. Lynn Stoner, ed./comp., with Luis Hipólito Serrano Pérez, Cuban and Cuban-American Women: An Annotated Bibliography (2000). ISBN 0-8420-2643-6

Thomas D. Schoonover, The French in Central America: Culture and Commerce, 1820–1930 (2000). ISBN 0-8420-2792-0

Enrique C. Ochoa, Feeding Mexico: The Political Uses of Food since 1910 (2000). ISBN 0-8420-2812-9

Thomas W. Walker and Ariel C. Armony, eds., Repression, Resistance, and Democratic Transition in Central America (2000). Cloth ISBN 0-8420-2766-1   Paper ISBN 0-8420-2768-8

William H. Beezley and David E. Lorey, eds., ¡Viva México! ¡Viva la Independencia! Celebrations of September 16 (2001). Cloth ISBN 0-8420-2914-1 Paper ISBN 0-8420-2915-X

Jeffrey M. Pilcher, Cantinflas and the Chaos of Mexican Modernity (2001). Cloth ISBN 0-8420-2769-6 Paper ISBN 0-8420-2771-8

Victor M. Uribe-Uran, ed., State and Society in Spanish America during the Age of Revolution (2001). Cloth ISBN 0-8420-2873-0   Paper ISBN 0-8420-2874-9

Andrew Grant Wood, Revolution in the Street: Women, Workers, and Urban Protest in Veracruz, 1870–1927 (2001). ISBN 0-8420-2879-X

Charles Bergquist, Ricardo Peñaranda, and Gonzalo Sánchez G., eds., Violence in Colombia, 1990–2000: Waging War and Negotiating Peace (2001). Cloth ISBN 0-8420-2869-2 Paper ISBN 0-8420-2870-6

William Schell, Jr., Integral Outsiders: The American Colony in Mexico City, 1876–1911 (2001). ISBN 0-8420-2838-2

John Lynch, Argentine Caudillo: Juan Manuel de Rosas (2001). Cloth ISBN 0-8420-2897-8 Paper ISBN 0-8420-2898-6

Samuel Basch, M.D., ed. and trans. Fred D. Ullman, Recollections of Mexico: The Last Ten Months of Maximilian's Empire (2001). ISBN 0-8420-2962-1

David Sowell, The Tale of Healer Miguel Perdomo Neira: Medicine, Ideologies, and Power in the Nineteenth-Century Andes (2001). Cloth ISBN 0-8420-2826-9 Paper ISBN 0-8420-2827-7

June E. Hahner, ed., A Parisian in Brazil: The Travel Account of a Frenchwoman in Nineteenth-Century Rio de Janeiro (2001). Cloth ISBN 0-8420-2854-4 Paper ISBN 0-8420-2855-2

Richard A. Warren, Vagrants and Citizens: Politics and the Masses in Mexico City from Colony to Republic (2001). ISBN 0-8420-2964-8

Roderick J. Barman, Princess Isabel of Brazil: Gender and Power in the Nineteenth Century (2002). Cloth ISBN 0-8420-2845-5 Paper ISBN 0-8420-2846-3

Stuart F. Voss, Latin America in the Middle Period, 1750–1929 (2002). Cloth ISBN 0-8420-5024-8 Paper ISBN 0-8420-5025-6

Lester D. Langley, The Banana Wars: United States Intervention in the Caribbean, 1898–1934, revised and updated (2002). Cloth ISBN 0-8420-5046-9   Paper ISBN 0-8420-5047-7

ISBN 0-8420-5024-8